3-87

P9-DTS-584

Roadside Silhouettes

1 BEE-EATER
2 HOUSE SPARROW
3 STARLING
4 CHAFFINCH
5 HOUSE MARTIN
6 SWALLOW
7 WOOD PIGEON
8 JACKDAW
9 LITTLE OWL
10 WHINCHAT
11 KESTREL
12 RED-BACKED SHRIKE
13 MAGPIE
14 WAGTAIL
15 SKY LARK
16 LAPWING
17 PHEASANT
18 BLACKBIRD
19 PARTRIDGE
20 ROOK

A FIELD GUIDE TO THE
BIRDS OF BRITAIN
AND EUROPE

A FIELD GUIDE TO THE

BIRDS OF BRITAIN
AND EUROPE

ROGER TORY PETERSON
GUY MOUNTFORT
P. A. D. HOLLOM

Fourth Edition
Revised and Enlarged

Introduction by
SIR JULIAN HUXLEY

HOUGHTON MIFFLIN COMPANY
Boston 1983

TO OUR
LONG-SUFFERING WIVES

She laments, sir, . . . her husband
goes this morning a-birding.
SHAKESPEARE – *Merry Wives of Windsor*

Library of Congress Cataloging in Publication Data

Peterson, Roger Tory, date
    A field guide to the birds of Britain and Europe.

    Includes index
    1. Birds – Europe – Identification.   2, Birds – Great
Britain – Identification.   I. Mountfort, Guy.   II. Hollom,
P. A. D. (Philip Arthur Dominic)   III. Title.
QL690.A1P4 1983   598.294   83–10807
ISBN 0–395–34416–6

Printed in Great Britain by Jolly & Barber Ltd, Rugby

Contents

CONTENTS

Line Illustrations

Colour Plates

Introduction to the First Edition
by Sir Julian Huxley

In common with every British ornithologist who has ever travelled (or ever intends to travel) on the Continent, I have often longed for a good handy book on the birds of Europe. Without such a guide, how could I be sure that the woodpecker I saw near Paris was a Middle Spotted Woodpecker? How could I find out the name of a strange warbler I heard in the woods of North Italy? How could I distinguish the two species of treecreepers on the Continent? How should I learn all the exciting new species of birds to be seen, or expected, in Switzerland or in Portugal? And I am sure that Continental ornithologists must share that longing, for the boundaries between their countries are, biologically speaking, even more artificial than that between our islands and the rest of Europe. The only handy works on the subject are half a century old, and have no pictures. One cannot carry around large systematic works like Dresser's *Birds of Europe*, and anyhow they are not designed to help the observer in the field.

What are the criteria for a good book on European birds, which will meet the needs of the field naturalist? In the first place it must be in one volume, and not too bulky to travel with, or for actual use in the field. Secondly, it must be fully illustrated, and must concentrate first and foremost on helping the naturalist to identify the new species with which he is confronted on his travels. Thirdly, it should help the naturalist to understand something of the distribution of the birds he sees. Finally, it should be scientific, based on the latest facts and the best theoretical interpretations.

This new Field Guide to the Birds of Britain and Europe seems to me to meet these requirements admirably. All three of its authors have special qualifications for the task. Guy Mountfort had for long planned to write a handbook of Continental birds. He has travelled and observed birds in more than a hundred different countries. For ten years he lived on the Continent, where he made an intensive study of West European birds.

Roger Peterson is a passionate lover and student of birds. He has the distinction of having produced a bird book whose sales far exceed those of any other ever written. His success has been due to the combination of high artistic skill with personal knowledge of birds in the field. This led to the designing of his particular method of illustration for identification, in which the bird is portrayed with pointers indicating the special features by which it can be distinguished. His systematic working out of this method, first for birds, then for mammals, then for other organisms, has met with an overwhelming response from amateur naturalists in America. Though an American, he has a wide knowledge of Europe, and has spent much of the last three years travelling there to familiarize himself with European birds.

Finally P. A. D. Hollom, widely travelled and known to British ornithologists as the editor of *The Popular Handbook of British Birds* and an editor of the magazine *British Birds*, has made a specialist study of the geographical distribution of the birds of the Old World.

Guy Mountfort met Roger Peterson in 1949 on Hawk Mountain in Pennsylvania, where ornithologists gather annually to watch the spectacular migration of birds of prey – buzzards, eagles, hawks and falcons – riding the thermal currents above the range of the Kittatinny Mountains. Within a few minutes of their meeting, they had en- thusiastically decided to go into partnership in the publication of a Field Guide to European birds, on the same general pattern as that of Peterson's Field Guides to American birds, which had been so successful in the New World, and which had already made their influence felt in the bird literature of Europe. And when it was later discovered that Hollom too had been planning a book on European birds, they decided to collaborate.

During the next three years, the authors travelled all over Europe, from Arctic Lapland to Southern Spain, from Britain to Turkey, putting the final touches to their field notes and contacts with foreign ornithologists, and combing through all the relevant literature. Between the three of them they have seen and watched in their natural habitats all but an insignificant fraction of the 602 species described in this book. Peterson has been primarily responsible for the illustrations and the accompanying caption pages, Mountfort for the main descriptive text, and Hollom for the maps and notes on distribution; however, the book is not just the sum of three separate contributors, but in all respects a product of close and critical teamwork.

The result seems to me extremely satisfactory. The book is of manageable size, a field guide to be consulted on the spot. Peterson's system facilitates quick and accurate identification of birds of either sex and every age. Hollom has provided maps of the breeding and winter distributions of all the species in Europe. It is remarkable that we have had to wait so long for this visual aid to the study of ornithology, and I am sure that this feature will be of the greatest value to all serious students. Finally, Mountfort's text conveys the maximum of necessary information in the minimum of space. The common names of the birds are given for the most ornithologically important European languages, and facts are included on voice, behaviour, habitats and nest-sites, which may help identification and pave the way for further study, though obviously a pocket-size field guide cannot be expected to cover all aspects of ornithology.

The birds are arranged according to the latest scientific classification, thus indicating their true relationship. And, while due recognition has been given to the facts of subspecific differentiation, emphasis is laid throughout on the species as the primary unit of study; subspecies which are recognizable in the field are briefly listed and described at the end of the account of each species.

The publication of this Field Guide seems to me an event of considerable importance to science as well as to natural history. It will certainly extend the range of interest of ornithologists in this country; it will promote international liaison between the naturalists of Western Europe; it will help to convince them that the study of the natural history of single countries is insufficient and that European ornithology deserves to be pursued in its entirety. It will, I hope, pave the way for a comprehensive handbook of the European birds, which will perform the same sort of service to European ornithology as *The Handbook of British Birds* has done for ornithology in these islands. I congratulate authors and publisher alike on their enterprise.

JULIAN HUXLEY

Preface to the First Edition

*'Though it must not be said that every species of birds has a manner
peculiar to itself, yet there is somewhat in most genera at least that
at first sight discriminates them, and enables a judicious observer to
pronounce upon them with some certainty.'*

GILBERT WHITE, 1778

No branch of natural history has been endowed with a richer literature
than ornithology. New books about birds, good, bad, and indifferent,
pour forth upon a seemingly insatiable public at an average of one for
every two weeks of the year, in Great Britain alone. To produce yet
another, requires a word of explanation.

People whose vocation in life is to sell books, affirm that a major part
of today's demand for those about birds takes two forms and stems
from two sources. Knowledgeable ornithologists who already possess
one or several of the encyclopædic works, such as Witherby's five
volume *Handbook of British Birds*, ask for a similarly authoritative and
complete reference book 'small enough to carry in the pocket'. A far
more clamorous demand is for a 'really simple' book, which will enable
the general public to identify birds 'at a glance' and without expert
knowledge. Both demands, for quite different reasons, are *cris du
coeur*. The experienced ornithologist is understandably loath to carry
several heavy and costly volumes with him on his expeditions, and the
existing single volume works omit, for reasons of space, the very
rarities which he is ever seeking. Beginners, and the vast numbers of
people whose interest is often more sentimental than scientific, long for
a book which will enable them to identify the birds they see around the
garden, without having to disentangle the wealth of detail and
technicalities which confuses them in much of the existing literature.

There is, we are told, also a third demand, from the growing
numbers of bird watchers who travel each year to new ornithological
territories, where unfamiliar birds occur. Because of linguistic dif-
ficulties, the local handbooks, which are available in some countries,
are often debarred to them. Hence the call for a book which includes
illustrations of *all* European species. In this category nothing has been
produced since Dresser's monumental nine-volume masterpiece of
1871–80, which today costs a fortune.

A Field Guide to the Birds of Britain and Europe attempts to fulfil all
three of these seemingly conflicting requirements. Absolute simplicity
is its keynote. It is non-technical. It embraces all the birds of Europe,
including rare vagrants, from the tundra of northern Finland to the
Mediterranean islands, westwards to Iceland, and eastwards to the
Black Sea.

Vernacular names are given in English, Dutch, French, German and Swedish, and, because many European species are conspecific with those in the United States and Canada, the North American equivalents are also shown, where they differ from the British. The English vernacular names are those in popular usage, for this, as Dr David Lack pointed out, must always be the ultimate criterion.

The illustrations are primarily paternistic and functional, rather than 'portraits'. All are drawn strictly to scale. Similar species are shown adjacent to each other and in identical positions, occasionally regardless of systematic relationship, in order to assist comparison. Arrows indicate clearly the significant 'field marks' not shared by related species. Further comparisons are given in the accompanying text. Descriptive detail of only general (i.e. non-specific) interest has been ruthlessly expunged; notes on behaviour are included only where they aid identification. Maps show the summer and winter ranges of the species, excepting those of only accidental occurrence, or where a written description can give the information more clearly. Finally, the dimensions of the Field Guide fulfil the requirement that it should literally 'fit in the pocket'. Those who prefer their bird books to be specialized, narrative, or even anthropomorphic in form, will find a wide choice in every bookshop: in this respect the Field Guide is non-competitive and supplementary to existing literature on the subject.

The information on which this book is based has been compiled from various sources. First, the authors' own field notes, made during many years of travel and study. Second, from intimate collaboration with leading ornithologists throughout Europe, who have generously made available their own records on such subjects as local distribution of species. Third, from a continuing study of all available ornithological literature and periodicals – not excepting the Russian. Fourth, from critical examination of skins and living birds in various museums and private collections, notably those of the British Museum of Natural History, the Zoological Society of London, the Wildfowl Trust, the Smithsonian Institution of Washington, D.C., and the American Museum of New York. To the painstaking staffs of these institutions is due the warmest gratitude of the authors. Special mention must also be made of the invaluable advice and facilities provided by Sir Peter Scott in the final preparation of the texts and illustrations concerning ducks, geese, and swans, all of which have had the benefit of his expert scrutiny.

Space unfortunately does not permit the authors to acknowledge individually in print all the help so freely given by ornithologists in many countries. If the Field Guide has merit, it must stem from the fact that it reflects the collaboration of so wide, so distinguished, and so truly international a board of advisers.

R.T.P., G.R.M., P.A.D.H. 1953

Preface to the Fourth Revised Edition

Since this book first appeared in 1954 nearly one million copies have been sold in 12 different languages. With the single exception of its earlier companion volume *A Field Guide to the Birds* (of North America), which Roger Peterson produced in 1934, it has now sold more copies than any other book on birds yet published. The subsequent appearance of several well-produced competitive books on European birds, with titles closely similar to ours, has had surprisingly little effect on its success. Interest in ornithology is obviously still expanding rapidly.

The English edition of *A Field Guide to the Birds of Britain and Europe* was extensively revised in 1966 and again in 1974 with the collaboration of Mr I. J. Ferguson-Lees and Mr D. I. M. Wallace. These editions were reprinted 17 times. In order to keep pace with the constantly increasing knowledge of European species, another revised edition has now become necessary. The text relating to 'difficult' species has been enlarged in order to include more comparisons with similar birds, as have the descriptions of call-notes and songs. The opportunity has been taken to use greatly improved colour reproduction and to rearrange the layout and contents. Twenty-six rare species which since the last edition have now occurred in Europe more than 20 times have been added to the main text and are illustrated, while 27 additional vagrants have been included in the section entitled 'Accidentals'. A few previously accepted vagrants whose records have since been invalidated have been deleted from this section, bringing the total number of species described in the book to 635.

In previous editions the illustrations were spread evenly through the book, an arrangement which proved to be not entirely satisfactory. In a volume intended for the pocket it is impossible to position them so that they are opposite the related descriptions of the species without reducing the text to worthless brevity. The colour plates have therefore now been grouped in a single section of their own. Opposite each plate is a brief descriptive caption, cross-referred to the main text pages. It is hoped that readers will find this arrangement more convenient. All the plates previously treated only in black and white (such as some of the grebes, sea-birds, ducks and birds of prey) are now shown in full colour. With the exception of two plates of miscellaneous rarities and one of introduced species, the illustrations are, of course, as far as possible in the same order of species as the text matter.

Once again the sequence of species and a few of the scientific or vernacular names of species have had to be altered. These problems, which have bedevilled ornithology for many decades, still cause confusion. The order in which birds are classified and the names given to them are at best man-made conveniences and it is a sad reflection on scientific ornithology that universal agreement has yet to be achieved. Nevertheless, in Europe at least, there is now a general movement towards the adoption of the sequence and nomenclature proposed by Professor K. H. Voous in his *List of Recent Holarctic Bird Species*, published in 1977. As this has been adopted by the British Ornithologists' Union and by the Editors of the authoritative *Birds of the Western Palearctic*, we feel we shall serve the majority interest by following suit, instead of retaining the sequence of Peters and Vaurie as used in the Third Edition of the Field Guide.

The geographical ranges of birds are constantly changing in minor degree. All the distribution maps in the Field Guide have therefore again been reviewed in the light of the latest information. They are now grouped, together with their short descriptive captions, in a single section at the back of the book. A welcome improvement is the use of a second colour to denote breeding ranges.

We are indebted to ornithologists throughout Europe who have again collaborated with us in preparing the new edition and only regret that their numbers are too great to mention them all by name. Particular acknowledgement must, however, be given to the Editors of *Birds of the Western Palearctic* for their co-operation and for giving us access to their vast collection of unpublished material. Also to the Editors of the magazine *British Birds* and especially to Mr M. J. Rogers, Secretary of the Rarities Committee. Their illustrated articles on rare or 'difficult' species have been invaluable in refining the details of identification. We thank Mr Ian Dawson, Mr C. Harbard and Dr H. E. Wolters for helping to revise the distribution maps. As Sir Julian Huxley once said, the science of ornithology is deeply indebted not only to professionals but also to the dedication and accurate observation of thousands of amateurs. It is with this still growing number of enthusiasts in mind that the revised Field Guide has been produced.

Our late friend and colleague James Fisher, Natural History Editor of William Collins, fathered the production of the original Field Guide in 1954. It is therefore with particular pleasure that, thirty years later, we acknowledge the enthusiastic encouragement and technical skill of his son Crispin Fisher in the production of this Revised Edition.

R.T.P., G.R.M., P.A.D.H. 1983

A Note to British Readers

This Field Guide covers all the birds of Britain. It also includes all European birds found this side of Russia, the majority of which are on the British list. For the convenience of users in Britain who will turn to the colour plates first when they see a new bird, the following symbols are employed on the caption pages, opposite the illustrations:

● **RESIDENT, REGULAR, OR FREQUENT ANNUAL** occurrence in the British Isles. ('British Isles' is here used to include Eire.)

○ **OCCASIONAL, OR VERY RARE** in the British Isles. Twenty occurrences or more; may occur in numbers during occasional 'invasions'.

△ **ACCIDENTAL** in the British Isles. Fewer than 20 occurrences in total, or very rare in recent years. No symbol means that the bird is not on the British list.

The following sex symbols are used on the illustrations:

♂ means **male**   ♀ means **female**

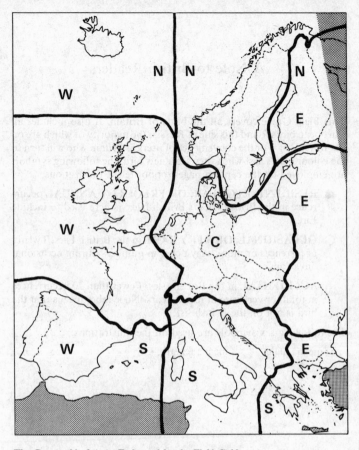

The Geographical Area Embraced by the Field Guide

The birds described are those resident or occurring within the unshaded portion of the map, that is to say in the British Isles and Eire, Iceland and continental Europe, eastwards to the 30° line of longitude. The islands of the Mediterranean basin are included, but Turkey and North Africa are excluded. Species are stated in the text as occurring in N., S., E., W. and C. (central) Europe (but some regions overlap – see map). The regions concerned are:

NORTH	Iceland, Faeroes, Norway, Sweden, Finland.
SOUTH	Portugal, Spain, Mediterranean France, Italy, Yugoslavia, Albania, Greece, Bulgaria.
EAST	Finland, Baltic States, Romania, Bulgaria, Greece.
WEST	Iceland, Faeroes, Britain, Ireland, France, Spain, Portugal.
CENTRAL	Belgium, Holland, Denmark, West and East Germany, Poland, Czechoslovakia, Hungary, Austria, Switzerland.

How to Identify Birds

Many people who are already mildly interested in birds are afraid to pursue the subject because, as they sometimes express it, they 'cannot tell a robin from a sparrow'. Others, perhaps, have shied away from an unfamiliar terminology. Such people do themselves needless injustice. The enjoyment of birds, whether casual or absorbing, which man has developed during centuries of sentimental attachment, depends neither upon intensive study nor academic qualifications. Those who claim to be unable to distinguish a robin from a sparrow certainly recognize an eagle, a gull, a duck, an owl, and many others of the various bird families. They are, in fact, already quite a long way on the road to 'knowing the birds'.

But the terms 'eagle', 'gull', or 'duck', are very broad. There are about 50 different species of eagles in various parts of the world, and many more species of gulls and ducks. The purpose of this book is to show, without recourse to complicated symbols, how to distinguish, at reasonable distance, all the species inhabiting or visiting Great Britain and the European continent.

There are about 8,600 different kinds of birds in the world. We are concerned in Europe with only 504 basic species. All these are given full treatment in this book. An additional 131 species have occurred in Europe fewer than 20 times: these are described briefly in the appendix of 'Accidentals'. Those subspecies which are recognizable in the field are also briefly described in the main text.

What to Look For
The identification of birds is largely a matter of knowing what to look for – the 'field marks'. Exact diagnosis then depends upon a process of elimination, by comparison with other species which the bird may resemble. The arrows on the illustrations facilitate this process. But appearance is only one factor. Call-notes, song, attitudes, behaviour, habitat and range are also important.

What is its Size?
First acquire the habit of comparing strange birds with some familiar 'yardstick' – a House Sparrow, a Blackbird, a Pigeon, etc., so that you can say to yourself 'smaller than a Blackbird, a little larger than a Sparrow', etc. The measurements quoted in this book indicate the *average* length of the bird from bill-tip to tail-tip.

What is its Shape?
Is it plump, like a Robin (left); or slender, like a Wagtail (right)?

What shape are its wings? Are they sharply pointed, like a Swallow's (left); or short and rounded, like a Warbler's (right)?

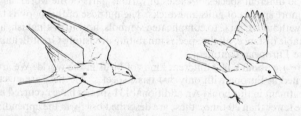

What shape is its bill? Is it small and fine, like a Warbler's (1); stout and short, like a seed-cracking Sparrow's (2); dagger-shaped, like a Tern's (3); or hook-tipped, like a Kestrel's (4)?

Is its tail deeply forked, like a Swallow's (*a*); short and square-ended, like a Starling's (*b*); deeply notched, like a Linnet's (*c*); rounded, like a Cuckoo's (*d*); or wedge-shaped, like a Raven's (*e*)?

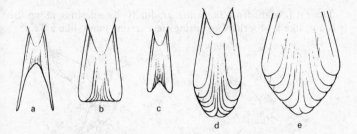

How does it Behave?

Some birds have very characteristic habits. Does it constantly wag its tail, like a Wagtail; quiver its tail, like a Redstart; cock its tail vertically, like a Wren; or sit bolt upright, with its tail downwards, like a Spotted Flycatcher?

Does it climb trees? If so, does it climb upwards in spirals, like a Treecreeper (1); in short jerks, braced on its stiff tail, like a Woodpecker (2); or does it climb, without using its tail as a prop, as readily downwards as upwards, like a Nuthatch (3)?

If it feeds on the ground, does it walk, like a Jackdaw; hop, like a House Sparrow; run spasmodically, like a Wagtail; or shuffle along, close to the ground, like a Dunnock?

If it swims, does it sit high in the water, like a Moorhen (*a*); or low, with its back almost awash, like a Diver (*b*)? Does it dive, like a Coot (*c*); or merely 'up-end', like a Mallard (*d*)?

Does it take off from the water gradually, by splashing along the surface, like a Moorhen; or spring clear in one jump, like a Teal?

Does it hover over the water and dive headlong, like a Tern, or a Kingfisher; or plunge after fish feet-first, like an Osprey; or walk deliberately beneath the water, like a Dipper?

Does it wade? If so, does it stand motionless in the shallows for long periods, like a Heron; or run quickly along the margins, like a Sandpiper; or chase the receding waves, like a Sanderling?

How does it Fly?
Is its flight deeply undulating, like a Woodpecker's (1); or straight and fast, like a Starling's (2)?

Does it beat its wings slowly, like a Heron; or rapidly, like a Mallard; or with alternate periods of wing-beats and 'shooting', like a Fieldfare; or does it soar on motionless wings, like a Buzzard?

What are its Field Marks?
A few birds can be instantly identified by colour alone. There is no mistaking the brilliant yellow and black of a male Golden Oriole, for example. But we need also to look for certain field marks to distinguish most species. These take various forms. They are indicated by pointers

on the illustrations in the Field Guide, and correspond to the italicized portions of the accompanying descriptive texts. Obscure field marks are included only when the problem of identification demands completeness.

Many birds are more or less spotted or streaked below. Are these marks over nearly all the under-parts, as in the Song Thrush (*a*); only on the upper breast, as in the Skylark (*b*); or only on the flanks, as in the Redpoll (*c*)?

a   b   c

Does the tail have a distinctive pattern? Has it a white tip, as in the Hawfinch (1); white outer feathers, as in the Chaffinch (2); or white side patches, as in the Whinchat (3)?

1   2   3

Some birds show a conspicuous white rump in flight – Jay, House Martin, Bullfinch, the wheatears, many waders, and the Hen Harrier, to mention a selection. Where so many species share such a prominent feature, it is necessary to look for additional field marks.

Wheatear   House Martin

Wing-bars are very important in such families as the warblers; some are conspicuous, some obscure, some single, some double.

Eye-stripes are equally important in many small passerines (perching birds). Does the bird have a stripe above, through, or below the eye – or a combination of two, or three, of these stripes? Some warblers have distinctively coloured eyes, or eye-rims, or 'moustachial' stripes. These details are useful only when the bird permits close examination, of course.

Wing patterns should always be noted, particularly with ducks and waders. Wings may be all-dark, or all-white, or half-and-half, or show conspicuous patches of white, or colour. The exact location of such marks on the wings, above or below, is important.

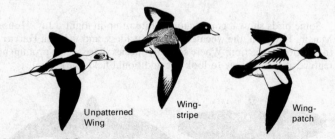

Unpatterned Wing

Wing-stripe

Wing-patch

Call-notes and Song

Expert ornithologists often rely on their ears as much as on their eyes, to identify birds. It is difficult to portray bird voices in writing, because birds rarely make 'human' sounds, and our interpretations vary: one person hears a call-note as '*teu*', another as '*chew*' or '*sioo*'. It must be remembered, also, that birds, like humans, often develop dialectic variations in their 'speech'. In the Field Guide an attempt has been made to portray the chief call-notes and song phrases by simplified phonetics and similes; but the best way to learn voice identification is to go out with someone who knows the birds. Or get the fine set of recordings called *A Field Guide to the Bird Songs of Britain and Europe* by Sturé Palmer and Jeffery Boswall, which are produced in collaboration with the authors of this book. The 15 LPs (or 16 tape cassettes) produced by the Swedish Broadcasting Corporation include the voices of nearly 600 bird species. They are available from record shops or from Sveriges Riksradio A. B., Stockholm 105 10, Sweden.

Where is it Found?
Birds which beginners may have difficulty in identifying by appearance alone, can often be placed by knowledge of the typical habitats. The Long-tailed Duck is likely to be seen only on salt water, but the Pintail, a duck which also has a longish, pointed tail, frequents fresh water. Wood Warblers are birds of the upper leaf canopy of the beech and oak woods, and do not occur out on the low, bushy scrub where one would seek the Grasshopper Warbler. Birds have quite strict limits of geography, habitat, and vegetation. Outside these they are seldom found, except during migration, when they may occur in very unlikely places. The range maps and notes on habitat and distribution, which are included in the Field Guide, should always be consulted in cases of doubtful identification.

When it is Found?
It is always interesting to learn the seasons during which different migratory species may occur in one's area. In a few years it becomes possible to forecast with some accuracy when the first Chiffchaff, or Swift, or Redwing, should appear. These dates may be pencilled in the margins of the Field Guide – for it is intended, not as an ornament to the bookshelf, but as a working companion.

Caution!
Where rarities are concerned, great caution should always be exercised. Detailed written notes and sketches should be made of any suspected rarity *on the spot*. If possible, an experienced member of the local ornithological society should be invited by telephone to corroborate the discovery. Before unusual 'sight records' can be accepted, at least two independent sets of field notes are usually required for critical examination by the ornithological authorities.

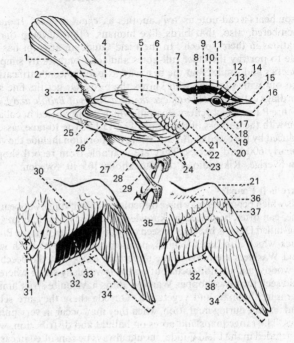

Topography of a Bird

Key showing terms used in this volume

1 Outer
  tail-feathers
2 Upper
  tail-coverts
3 Under
  tail-coverts
4 Rump
5 Scapulars
6 Back
7 Nape
8 Eye-stripe
9 Crown
10 Head-stripe
11 Crown-stripe
12 Supercilium
  (eyebrow)

13 Eye-ring
14 Lores
15 Upper mandible
16 Lower mandible
17 Chin
18 Moustachial-
  stripe
19 Ear-coverts
  (cheek)
20 Throat
21 Bend of wing
22 Carpal (wrist)
23 Breast
24 Wing-bars
25 Primaries
26 Secondaries

27 Flanks
28 Belly
29 Tarsus
30 Wing-coverts
31 Scapulars
32 Secondaries
33 Speculum (duck)
34 Primaries
35 Axillaries
36 Wing-linings
37 Fore-edge of
  wing
38 Rear-edge of
  wing

European Check-List

The sequence and nomenclature in this list conform generally to those employed by Prof. K. H. Voous in his *List of Recent Holarctic Bird Species* and by the Editors of *Birds of the Western Palearctic*. Accidental species (A) are included. Use it to record the species you have seen.

.... Red-throated Diver
.... Black-throated Diver
.... Great Northern Diver
.... White-billed Diver
.... Pied-billed Grebe (A)
.... Little Grebe
.... Great Crested Grebe
.... Red-necked Grebe
.... Slavonian Grebe
.... Black-necked Grebe
.... Black-browed Albatross
.... Wandering Albatross (A)
.... Southern Giant Petrel (A)
.... Fulmar
.... Capped Petrel (A)
.... Bulwer's Petrel (A)
.... Cory's Shearwater
.... Great Shearwater
.... Sooty Shearwater
.... Manx Shearwater
.... Little Shearwater
.... Wilson's Petrel
.... White-faced Petrel (A)
.... Storm Petrel
.... Leach's Petrel
.... Madeiran Petrel (A)
.... Gannet
.... Cormorant
.... Shag
.... Pygmy Cormorant
.... White Pelican
.... Dalmatian Pelican
.... Magnificent Frigatebird (A)
.... Bittern
.... American Bittern
.... Least Bittern (A)
.... Little Bittern

.... Schrenck's Little Bittern (A)
.... Night Heron
.... Green Heron (A)
.... Squacco Heron
.... Cattle Egret
.... Western Reef Heron (A)
.... Little Egret
.... Great White Egret
.... Grey Heron
.... Purple Heron
.... Black Stork
.... White Stork
.... Glossy Ibis
.... Bald Ibis (A)
.... Spoonbill
.... Greater Flamingo
.... Lesser Flamingo (A)
.... White-faced Tree Duck (A)
.... Mute Swan
.... Bewick's Swan
.... Whooper Swan
.... Bean Goose
.... Pink-footed Goose
.... White-fronted Goose
.... Lesser White-fronted Goose
.... Greylag Goose
.... Snow Goose
.... Canada Goose
.... Barnacle Goose
.... Brent Goose
.... Red-breasted Goose
.... Egyptian Goose
.... Ruddy Shelduck
.... Shelduck
.... Mandarin
.... Wigeon
.... American Wigeon

....Gadwall
....Baikal Teal
....Teal
....Mallard
....Black Duck (A)
....Pintail
....Garganey
....Blue-winged Teal
....Shoveler
....Marbled Duck
....Red-crested Pochard
....Pochard
....Ring-necked Duck
....Ferruginous Duck
....Tufted Duck
....Scaup
....Eider
....King Eider
....Spectacled Eider (A)
....Steller's Eider
....Harlequin Duck
....Long-tailed Duck
....Common Scoter
....Surf Scoter
....Velvet Scoter
....Bufflehead (A)
....Barrow's Goldeneye
....Goldeneye
....Hooded Merganser (A)
....Smew
....Red-breasted Merganser
....Goosander
....Ruddy Duck
....White-headed Duck
....Honey Buzzard
....Black-shouldered Kite
....Black Kite
....Red Kite
....Pallas's Fish Eagle (A)
....White-tailed Eagle
....Lammergeier
....Egyptian Vulture
....Griffon Vulture
....Lappet-faced Vulture (A)
....Black Vulture
....Short-toed Eagle
....Marsh Harrier
....Hen Harrier
....Pallid Harrier
....Montagu's Harrier

....Dark Chanting Goshawk (
....Goshawk
....Sparrowhawk
....Levant Sparrowhawk
....Buzzard
....Long-legged Buzzard
....Rough-legged Buzzard
....Lesser Spotted Eagle
....Spotted Eagle
....Tawny/Steppe Eagle
....Imperial Eagle
....Golden Eagle
....Booted Eagle
....Bonelli's Eagle
....Osprey
....Lesser Kestrel
....Kestrel
....American Kestrel (A)
....Red-footed Falcon
....Merlin
....Hobby
....Eleonora's Falcon
....Sooty Falcon (A)
....Lanner
....Saker
....Gyrfalcon
....Peregrine
....Hazel Grouse
....Willow/Red Grouse
....Ptarmigan
....Black Grouse
....Capercaillie
....Chukar
....Rock Partridge
....Red-legged Partridge
....Barbary Partridge
....Grey Partridge
....Quail
....Pheasant
....Golden Pheasant
....Lady Amherst's Pheasant
....Andalusian Hemipode
....Water Rail
....Spotted Crake
....Sora Rail (A)
....Little Crake
....Baillon's Crake
....Corncrake
....Moorhen
....Allen's Gallinule (A)

.... American Purple Gallinule (A)
.... Purple Gallinule
.... Coot
.... American Coot (A)
.... Crested Coot
.... Crane
.... Sandhill Crane (A)
.... Demoiselle Crane
.... Little Bustard
.... Houbara Bustard
.... Great Bustard
.... Oystercatcher
.... Black-winged Stilt
.... Avocet
.... Stone Curlew
.... Cream-coloured Courser
.... Collared Pratincole
.... Black-winged Pratincole
.... Little Ringed Plover
.... Ringed Plover
.... Semipalmated Plover (A)
.... Killdeer
.... Kentish Plover
.... Lesser Sand Plover (A)
.... Greater Sand Plover
.... Caspian Plover (A)
.... Dotterel
.... Lesser Golden Plover
.... Golden Plover
.... Grey Plover
.... Spur-winged Plover
.... Sociable Plover
.... White-tailed Plover
.... Lapwing
.... Knot
.... Sanderling
.... Semipalmated Sandpiper
.... Western Sandpiper (A)
.... Red-necked Stint (A)
.... Little Stint
.... Temminck's Stint
.... Long-toed Stint (A)
.... Least Sandpiper
.... White-rumped Sandpiper
.... Baird's Sandpiper
.... Pectoral Sandpiper
.... Sharp-tailed Sandpiper
.... Curlew Sandpiper
.... Purple Sandpiper
.... Dunlin

.... Broad-billed Sandpiper
.... Stilt Sandpiper (A)
.... Buff-breasted Sandpiper
.... Ruff
.... Jack Snipe
.... Snipe
.... Great Snipe
.... Short-billed Dowitcher (A)
.... Long-billed Dowitcher
.... Woodcock
.... Black-tailed Godwit
.... Hudsonian Godwit (A)
.... Bar-tailed Godwit
.... Little Whimbrel (A)
.... Eskimo Curlew (A)
.... Whimbrel
.... Slender-billed Curlew
.... Curlew
.... Upland Sandpiper
.... Spotted Redshank
.... Redshank
.... Marsh Sandpiper
.... Greenshank
.... Greater Yellowlegs
.... Lesser Yellowlegs
.... Solitary Sandpiper
.... Green Sandpiper
.... Wood Sandpiper
.... Terek Sandpiper
.... Common Sandpiper
.... Spotted Sandpiper
.... Wandering Tattler (A)
.... Willet (A)
.... Turnstone
.... Wilson's Phalarope
.... Red-necked Phalarope
.... Grey Phalarope
.... Pomarine Skua
.... Arctic Skua
.... Long-tailed Skua
.... Great Skua
.... White-eyed Gull (A)
.... Great Black-headed Gull
.... Mediterranean Gull
.... Laughing Gull
.... Franklin's Gull (A)
.... Little Gull
.... Sabine's Gull
.... Bonaparte's Gull
.... Black-headed Gull

....Grey-headed Gull (A)
....Slender-billed Gull
....Audouin's Gull
....Ring-billed Gull
....Common Gull
....Lesser Black-backed Gull
....Herring Gull
....Iceland Gull
....Glaucous Gull
....Great Black-backed Gull
....Ross's Gull
....Kittiwake
....Ivory Gull
....Gull-billed Tern
....Caspian Tern
....Royal Tern (A)
....Lesser Crested Tern (A)
....Sandwich Tern
....Roseate Tern
....Common Tern
....Arctic Tern
....Aleutian Tern (A)
....Forster's Tern (A)
....Bridled Tern (A)
....Sooty Tern
....Little Tern
....Whiskered Tern
....Black Tern
....White-winged Black Tern
....Brown Noddy (A)
....Guillemot
....Brünnich's Guillemot
....Razorbill
....Black Guillemot
....Little Auk
....Crested Auklet (A)
....Parakeet Auklet (A)
....Puffin
....Spotted Sandgrouse (A)
....Chestnut-bellied Sandgrouse
      (A)
....Black-bellied Sandgrouse
....Pin-tailed Sandgrouse
....Pallas's Sandgrouse
....Rock Dove
....Stock Dove
....Woodpigeon
....Collared Dove
....Turtle Dove
....Rufous Turtle Dove (A)

....Laughing Dove
....Ring-necked Parakeet
....Great Spotted Cuckoo
....Cuckoo
....Black-billed Cuckoo (A)
....Yellow-billed Cuckoo
....Barn Owl
....Scops Owl
....Eagle Owl
....Snowy Owl
....Hawk Owl
....Pygmy Owl
....Little Owl
....Tawny Owl
....Ural Owl
....Great Grey Owl
....Long-eared Owl
....Short-eared Owl
....African Marsh Owl (A)
....Tengmalm's Owl
....Nightjar
....Red-necked Nightjar
....Egyptian Nightjar
....Common Nighthawk (A)
....Needle-tailed Swift (A)
....Swift
....Pallid Swift
....Alpine Swift
....White-rumped Swift
....Pacific Swift (A)
....Little Swift (A)
....White-breasted Kingfisher (A)
....Kingfisher
....Pied Kingfisher (A)
....Belted Kingfisher (A)
....Blue-cheeked Bee-eater
....Bee-eater
....Roller
....Hoopoe
....Wryneck
....Grey-headed Woodpecker
....Green Woodpecker
....Black Woodpecker
....Yellow-bellied Sapsucker (A)
....Great Spotted Woodpecker
....Syrian Woodpecker
....Middle Spotted Woodpecker
....White-backed Woodpecker
....Lesser Spotted Woodpecker
....Three-toed Woodpecker

....Acadian Flycatcher (A)
....Bar-tailed Desert Lark (A)
....Desert Lark (A)
....Hoopoe Lark (A)
....Dupont's Lark
....Calandra Lark
....Bimaculated Lark (A)
....White-winged Lark
....Black Lark
....Short-toed Lark
....Lesser Short-toed Lark
....Indian Sand Lark (A)
....Crested Lark
....Thekla Lark
....Woodlark
....Skylark
....Shore Lark
....Sand Martin
....Crag Martin
....Swallow
....Red-rumped Swallow
....House Martin
....Richard's Pipit
....Blyth's Pipit (A)
....Tawny Pipit
....Olive-backed Pipit
....Tree Pipit
....Pechora Pipit
....Meadow Pipit
....Red-throated Pipit
....Rock/Water Pipit
....Yellow/Blue-headed Wagtail
....Citrine Wagtail
....Grey Wagtail
....Pied/White Wagtail
....Common Bulbul (A)
....Waxwing
....Dipper
....Wren
....Brown Thrasher (A)
....Catbird (A)
....Dunnock
....Siberian Accentor (A)
....Alpine Accentor
....Rufous Bush Robin
....Robin
....Thrush Nightingale
....Nightingale
....Siberian Rubythroat (A)
....Bluethroat

....Siberian Blue Robin (A)
....Red-flanked Bluetail
....White-throated Robin (A)
....Black Redstart
....Redstart
....Moussier's Redstart (A)
....Whinchat
....Stonechat
....Isabelline Wheatear
....Wheatear
....Pied Wheatear
....Black-eared Wheatear
....Desert Wheatear
....White-crowned Black
    Wheatear (A)
....Black Wheatear
....Rock Thrush
....Blue Rock Thrush
....White's Thrush
....Siberian Thrush
....Wood Thrush (A)
....Hermit Thrush (A)
....Swainson's Thrush
....Grey-cheeked Thrush (A)
....Veery (A)
....Tickell's Thrush (A)
....Ring Ouzel
....Blackbird
....Eyebrowed Thrush
....Dusky/Naumann's Thrush
....Black/Red-throated Thrush
....Fieldfare
....Song Thrush
....Redwing
....Mistle Thrush
....American Robin
....Cetti's Warbler
....Fan-tailed Warbler
....Pallas's Grasshopper Warbler
....Lanceolated Warbler
....Grasshopper Warbler
....River Warbler
....Savi's Warbler
....Gray's Grasshopper Warbler
    (A)
....Moustached Warbler
....Aquatic Warbler
....Sedge Warbler
....Paddyfield Warbler (A)
....Blyth's Reed Warbler

....Marsh Warbler
....Reed Warbler
....Great Reed Warbler
....Thick-billed Warbler (A)
....Olivaceous Warbler
....Booted Warbler
....Olive-tree Warbler
....Icterine Warbler
....Melodious Warbler
....Marmora's Warbler
....Dartford Warbler
....Tristram's Warbler (A)
....Spectacled Warbler
....Subalpine Warbler
....Ménétries's Warbler (A)
....Sardinian Warbler
....Rüppell's Warbler
....Desert Warbler (A)
....Orphean Warbler
....Barred Warbler
....Lesser Whitethroat
....Whitethroat
....Garden Warbler
....Blackcap
....Greenish Warbler
....Arctic Warbler
....Pallas's Warbler
....Yellow-browed Warbler
....Radde's Warbler
....Dusky Warbler
....Bonelli's Warbler
....Wood Warbler
....Chiffchaff
....Willow Warbler
....Goldcrest
....Firecrest
....Brown Flycatcher (A)
....Spotted Flycatcher
....Red-breasted Flycatcher
....Semi-collared Flycatcher
....Collared Flycatcher
....Pied Flycatcher
....Bearded Tit
....Long-tailed Tit
....Marsh Tit
....Sombre Tit
....Willow Tit
....Siberian Tit
....Crested Tit
....Coal Tit

....Blue Tit
....Azure Tit
....Great Tit
....Krüper's Nuthatch
....Corsican Nuthatch
....Red-breasted Nuthatch (A)
....Nuthatch
....Rock Nuthatch
....Wallcreeper
....Treecreeper
....Short-toed Treecreeper
....Penduline Tit
....Golden Oriole
....Isabelline Shrike
....Red-backed Shrike
....Lesser Grey Shrike
....Great Grey Shrike
....Woodchat Shrike
....Masked Shrike
....Jay
....Siberian Jay
....Azure-winged Magpie
....Magpie
....Nutcracker
....Alpine Chough
....Chough
....Jackdaw
....Daurian Jackdaw (A)
....Rook
....Carrion/Hooded Crow
....Raven
....Starling
....Spotless Starling
....Rose-coloured Starling
....House Sparrow
....Spanish Sparrow
....Tree Sparrow
....Rock Sparrow
....Snowfinch
....Common Waxbill
....Black-rumped Waxbill (A)
....Red-eyed Vireo (A)
....Chaffinch
....Brambling
....Serin
....Citril Finch
....Greenfinch
....Goldfinch
....Siskin
....Linnet

....Twite
....Redpoll
....Arctic Redpoll
....Two-barred Crossbill
....Crossbill
....Scottish Crossbill
....Parrot Crossbill
....Trumpeter Finch
....Scarlet Rosefinch
....Pallas's Rosefinch (A)
....Pine Grosbeak
....Bullfinch
....Hawfinch
....Evening Grosbeak (A)
....Black-and-white Warbler (A)
....Tennessee Warbler (A)
....Parula Warbler (A)
....Yellow Warbler (A)
....Black-throated Green Warbler (A)
....Cape May Warbler (A)
....Magnolia Warbler (A)
....Yellow-rumped Warbler (A)
....Blackpoll Warbler
....American Redstart (A)
....Ovenbird (A)
....Northern Waterthrush (A)
....Yellowthroat (A)
....Hooded Warbler (A)
....Summer Tanager (A)
....Scarlet Tanager (A)
....Rufous-sided Towhee (A)

....Savannah Sparrow (A)
....Fox Sparrow (A)
....Song Sparrow (A)
....White-crowned Sparrow (A)
....White-throated Sparrow
....Slate-coloured Junco (A)
....Lapland Bunting
....Snow Bunting
....Black-faced Bunting (A)
....Pine Bunting
....Siberian Meadow Bunting (A)
....Yellowhammer
....Cirl Bunting
....Rock Bunting
....Cinereous Bunting
....Ortolan Bunting
....Cretzschmar's Bunting
....Yellow-browed Bunting (A)
....Rustic Bunting
....Little Bunting
....Chestnut Bunting (A)
....Yellow-breasted Bunting
....Reed Bunting
....Pallas's Reed Bunting (A)
....Red-headed Bunting (A)
....Black-headed Bunting
....Corn Bunting
....Rose-breasted Grosbeak (A)
....Indigo Bunting (A)
....Bobolink (A)
....Yellow-headed Blackbird (A)
....Northern Oriole (A)

Additional New Accidentals

....
....
....
....
....

The Ornithological Societies

The principal British societies are listed below. They do not compete but, between them, cater for most ornithological interests.

The senior society is the **British Ornithologists' Union**, founded in 1859, for the advancement of the science of ornithology. Its interests are not restricted to Britain, but are world-wide. The BOU issues an important quarterly journal, *The Ibis*, in which authoritative papers are published on such subjects as ecology, behaviour, taxonomy and reviews of British and foreign ornithological literature. Scientific meetings are arranged and in all international ornithological affairs the BOU takes a leading part. Address: *c/o The Zoological Society of London, Regent's Park, London, NW1 4RY*.

The **British Ornithologists' Club** recruits its members from the BOU. The club meets in London periodically at a dinner, which is followed by short communications, films and lectures. The Club *Bulletin* contains articles relating to the subjects discussed, and descriptions of new species and races. Address: *c/o The Zoological Society of London, Regent's Park, London, NW1 4RY*.

The **British Trust for Ornithology** is the focal point for organized field work. Its aim is the encouragement of individual and group research. Members take part in bird-ringing and nest-recording schemes and population studies. Many meetings are held with local societies. Bulletins, reports, the quarterly *Bird Study* and field guides are published. Address: *Beech Grove, Tring, Herts HP23 5NR*.

The **Royal Society for the Protection of Birds** is concerned with the scientific application of conservation and strives to improve and enforce the Protection of Birds Acts. It educates the public and finances and manages a large number of bird sanctuaries. The Society produces an illustrated magazine, *Birds*, and many other publications. It also has a junior section, the Young Ornithologists' Club. Address: *The Lodge, Sandy, Beds SG19 2DL*.

The **Wildfowl Trust** has a unique collection of ducks, geese and swans from all parts of the world. It offers ideal conditions for studying every species occurring in Britain. A large decoy is maintained for catching and ringing ducks, and it is possible to watch flocks of wild geese feeding in the adjoining fields at appropriate seasons. The Trust publishes annually a lavishly illustrated journal, *Wildfowl*, and periodical bulletins. Address: *Slimbridge, Glos GL2 7BT*.

The **Irish Wildbird Conservancy** deals with all aspects of ornithology and bird conservation in Ireland. Address: *South View, Church Road, Greystones, Co. Wicklow, Eire*.

DIVERS: Gaviidae

Large swimming birds of open waters, with sharp-pointed bills. Longer-bodied and thicker-necked than grebes. Dive and swim expertly under water. Submerge quickly when alarmed, or swim with only head above water. Outline in flight is hunchbacked, with slight downward sweep to extended neck. Wings rather small and pointed. In flight, feet project behind rudimentary tail. Voices wailing. Sexes similar. Ground nesting.

RED-THROATED DIVER   *Gavia stellata*   **Pl. 1**
  Du – Roodkeelduiker   Fr – Plongeon catmarin
  Ge – Sterntaucher   Sw – Smålom
  N. Am – Red-throated Loon

Identification: 21–23″. Smaller than Great Northern; about size of Black-throated, but with smaller head. Slender *uptilted* bill affords quick identification even at distance. In breeding plumage has grey head, *red throat-patch* (looks black at distance) and grey-brown *unpatterned* upper-parts. Winter plumage paler than Black-throated, being finely speckled with white; under-parts white; extensive white from sides of head to forehead gives white-faced appearance. Bills of Black-throated and Great Northern are straight, not uptilted; latter's is also much stouter. (But see also rare White-billed Diver.) Occasionally seen in flocks along coast in winter. Looks whiter than other divers in winter.

Voice: Flight-call a repeated guttural, quacking '*kwuck*', sometimes more cackling; on water a high wailing and goose-like clamour. Hoarse growling in display.

Habitat: Mainly coastal waters in winter. Nests on margins of quite small lochs and northern coastal lagoons. Map 1.

BLACK-THROATED DIVER   *Gavia arctica*   **Pl. 1**
  Du – Parelduiker   Fr – Plongeon arctique
  Ge – Prachttaucher   Sw – Storlom
  N. Am – Pacific Loon

Identification: 23–27″. Smaller than Great Northern; near size of Red-throated. Distinguished in breeding plumage by grey crown and hind neck and *straight*, slender, black bill; throat *black*, narrowly striped with white on sides of neck and breast; squarish white spots on upper-parts are arranged in *two distinct patches either side*. In winter looks like small Great Northern, but forehead is blacker than crown and hind neck, both of which are often greyer than back; Great Northern looks obscurely barred above, whereas Black-throated looks uniform blackish and immature is 'scaly'; is best distinguished by *distinctive white thigh-patch* (visible even in flight), less heavy bill, smaller size and less angular contour of head. Distinguished from winter Red-throated by darker appearance and black forehead instead of white face; bill is often as slender, but is *straight*, not uptilted, and is bluish with black tip.

Voice: A barking '*kwow*', deeper than similar flight-call of Red-throated; also a shrill, rising wail.

Habitat: Winters mainly along sea coasts. In breeding season frequents lakes

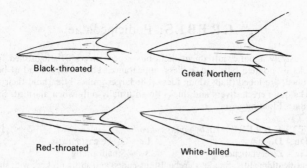

Bills of Divers

with or without trees, among inland hills or coastal lowlands. Nests on islets or verges of deeper and usually larger lakes than Red-throated. Map 2.

GREAT NORTHERN DIVER *Gavia immer* Pl. 1
Du – IJsduiker Fr – Plongeon imbrin
Ge – Eistaucher Sw – Islom
N. Am – Common Loon

Identification: 27–32″. Size of goose. Distinguished in breeding plumage by *chequered black and white upper-parts*, glossy black head and neck, *striped black and white collar and massive dagger-shaped bill*. In winter, upper-parts are dark grey-brown; crown blacker; cheeks, throat and under-parts white, with suggestion of dark collar at base of neck; pattern of breeding plumage often retained into early winter. Bill can be pale in winter (like White-billed) but is always *dark along the ridge of the culmen*. Flight with slightly drooping neck, and feet projecting behind. Thrashes along surface before taking off; alights breast-first with great splash. Seldom on land. Distinguished from Cormorant when swimming by *horizontal* (not raised) bill; in flight by much shorter neck and tail, and more white on under-parts. See other divers.

Voice: Flight-call a short, barking 'kwuk'; on breeding grounds has long wailing cries and weird quavering 'laughter'.

Habitat: Frequents northern lakes, nesting on islets and on grassy promontories. Winters along sea coasts, occasionally inland. Map 3.

WHITE-BILLED DIVER *Gavia adamsii* Pl. 1
Du – Geelsnavelduiker Fr – Plongeon à bec blanc
Ge – Gelbschnäbliger Eistaucher Sw – Vitnäbbad islom
N. Am – Yellow-billed Loon

Identification: 33–34″. Similar to Great Northern, but slightly larger, the head often showing swollen forehead. *Bill yellowish or ivory-white*, straight above, angled below, giving marked *upturned effect* (see diagram). Great Northern's bill can be pale in winter and appear upturned, but always has a dark upper edge. The White-billed's eye appears smaller than Great Northern's and sometimes has a dark ocular spot. Behaviour, voice and habitat similar. Reaches coasts of Norway, Sweden, Finland in winter from eastern Arctic. Vagrant to W. (including Britain), C. and S. Europe.

GREBES: Podicipedidae

Exclusively aquatic; infrequent fliers but expert divers. Distinguished from ducks by pointed bills and 'tailless' appearance. Their feet, instead of being webbed, are lobed (flaps along toes). The larger grebes often hold their thin necks quite erect; divers and ducks do so usually only when alarmed. Sexes similar. Floating nests.

LITTLE GREBE   *Tachybaptus ruficollis*   **Pl. 1**
Du – Dodaars   Fr – Grèbe castagneux
Ge – Zwergtaucher   Sw – Smådopping
Identification: $10\frac{1}{2}''$. Smallest grebe. Blunt-ended and short-necked, with short, relatively stouter bill than other grebes. In summer, is dark brown above, paler below, with *chestnut cheeks and throat*. Yellowish-green at base of bill makes *distinctive light spot* on dark head. Much paler in winter, with white throat, whitish under tail-coverts and buffish neck. Juvenile has bold white streaks on side of head. Flight low and rapid, showing very little white on secondaries. Behaviour more skulking than other grebes, but flies more readily.
Voice: Call-note a loud, high whinnying trill, often prolonged, sometimes rising and falling; also a short '*whit, whit*'.
Habitat: Frequents and breeds on ponds, lakes, reservoirs, backwaters, etc. Winters in estuaries, also inland. Map 4.

GREAT CRESTED GREBE   *Podiceps cristatus*   **Pl. 1**
Du – Fuut   Fr – Grèbe huppé
Ge – Haubentaucher   Sw – Skäggdopping
Identification: 19″. Largest grebe. Easily identified by *blackish ear-tufts*, and, in breeding season, by *prominent chestnut and black frills* on sides of head. Appearance 'tailless', with slender neck, grey-brown upper-parts and gleaming satiny-white under-parts. In winter, lacks frills and looks white-headed, with dark crown and white stripes over eye; distinguished from Red-necked by larger size, thinner neck, white supercilium, *pink* (not yellow and black) bill. Juvenile has black and white striped head and neck, without tufts or frills. Flight low, showing conspicuous white on secondaries, with head and neck low-hung. Has elaborate display ceremonials.
Voice: A barking '*kar-arr*', a shrill '*er-wick*' and various trumpeting, ticking, moaning and whirring noises.
Habitat: Lakes, gravel-pits, reservoirs; winters also on coast. Breeds where vegetation provides anchorage, usually near water's edge. Map 5.

RED-NECKED GREBE   *Podiceps grisegena*   **Pl. 1**
Du – Roodhalsfuut   Fr – Grèbe jougris
Ge – Rothalstaucher   Sw – Gråhakedopping
Identification: 17″. A thick-set grebe with a large, bulbous head. Identified in summer by *pale grey cheeks* contrasting with black crown (with small black ear-tufts), *rich chestnut neck* and bright yellow base to dark-tipped bill. Upper-parts grey-brown, under-parts silky-white. In winter looks grey and white, somewhat resembling dusky winter Great Crested, but distinguished by smaller size, thicker, greyer neck and cheeks, *lack of white supercilium*, black crown

extending to eye-level and *yellow* (not pink) on dark-tipped bill. See also winter Red-throated Diver.

Voice: A variety of growling, barking, crowing and wailing notes. Call-note an abrupt '*cherk*'.

Habitat: Winters mainly along coasts; breeds in reeds and overgrown pools and quiet waters. Map 6.

SLAVONIAN GREBE   *Podiceps auritus*   Pl. 1

Du – Kuifduiker	Fr – Grèbe esclavon
Ge – Ohrentaucher	Sw – Svarthakedopping
N. Am – Horned Grebe	

Identification: 13″. Larger than Little Grebe; smaller than Great Crested. In breeding plumage has large, glossy black head, with a *broad golden stripe through eye*, forming short 'horns', *dark chestnut* neck and flanks. Upper-parts dark, under-parts silky-white. Broad white wing-bar conspicuous in flight. In winter, looks dark above and white below, like Black-necked, but distinguished by flat black crown ending sharply *at eye-level*, more extensive white on head and neck tending to meet on nape, *straight, stubbier* (not uptilted) bill and *snake-like head and neck*.

Voice: Has wide vocabulary when breeding; chief note a long, squealing trill with descending finish.

Habitat: Ponds and lakes. Nests in inland shallows. Winters chiefly in sheltered bays and estuaries, but also on fresh water. Map 7.

BLACK-NECKED GREBE   *Podiceps nigricollis*   Pl. 1

Du – Geoorde fuut	Fr – Grèbe à cou noir
Ge – Schwarzhalstaucher	Sw – Svårthalsad dopping
N. Am – Eared Grebe	

Identification: 12″. Distinguished from Slavonian Grebe in breeding season by black neck, *high black forehead and crown* and less conspicuous tuft of *fan-shaped golden feathers from behind eye*. In winter looks chiefly dark above and white below, but is duskier than Slavonian (which see for other differences) and has more slender, slightly uptilted bill. Juvenile often has less tip-tilted bill and is doubtfully distinguishable from young Slavonian.

Voice: Call-note a quiet '*poo-eep*', also a variety of harsh, rasping crooning notes.

Habitat: As Slavonian Grebe. Breeds in small scattered groups in reedy shallows of ponds, lakes, lagoons. Winters on open lakes and along coasts. Map 8.

ALBATROSSES: Diomedeidae

BLACK-BROWED ALBATROSS   *Diomedea melanophris*   Pl. 4

Du – Wenlbrauwalbatros	Fr – Albatros à sourcils noire
Ge – Mollymauk	Sw – Svartbrynad albatross

Identification: 7 ft. wing-span. Albatrosses are easily recognized by huge wing-span and gliding flight close to waves. Black-browed can be confused with Yellow-nosed and Grey-headed. All three have white or greyish head and neck and white rump and under-parts, contrasting with dark grey or sooty back, tail and upper wing-surfaces. All have dark mark near the eye, but in Black-browed this extends as a short narrow streak through *and behind the eye*. Adult has *pinkish-yellow bill*; white under-surfaces of wings *broadly* margined with black along leading edge and *narrowly* on rear edge. Immature has grey head and neck like many adult Yellow-nosed and most Grey-headed and dark or horn-coloured bill; under-wings have very broad dark margins with *narrow* white centre. Rare vagrant from southern oceans to W., N. and C. Europe; recent fairly regular sightings in Scotland attributed to single individual summering in gannetries.

PETRELS AND SHEARWATERS:
Procellariidae

Oceanic, visiting land only when breeding; tube-like external nostrils. Shear-waters have slender bills, and are longer-bodied than the smaller petrels; they bank and glide on long, narrow, stiff wings. Fulmars are stouter and more gull-like, but also fly on stiff wings. Sexes similar. Hole or cliff nesting.

FULMAR   *Fulmarus glacialis*   **Pl. 2**
   Du – Noordse stormvogel   Fr – Pétrel fulmar
   Ge – Eissturmvogel   Sw – Stormfågel
Identification: 18½". Gull-like in appearance, but is stubbier, with distinctive flight, gliding and banking on stiff wings, close to waves. Distinguished from gulls by *thick bull-neck, and lack of black tips to narrow wings*. Bill yellow, thick and short, with 'tubed' nostrils. Legs bluish. In light phase head and under-parts are white; back, wings *and tail* grey; wings have pale patch at base of primaries. In dark northern phase (so-called 'Blue Fulmar') plumage is smoky grey, with darker wing-tips; much too pale and too stubby-billed to be mistaken for slender-billed Sooty Shearwater. Follows ships. Swims buoyantly, rising from water with some difficulty. On land shuffles on tarsi, sometimes aided by wings; may rise on feet briefly. Common in all northern waters, often in vast numbers.
Voice: Usual note a hoarse cackling or grunting '*ag-ag-ag-arr*'.
Habitat: Strictly pelagic. Breeds colonially on oceanic cliffs and islands; locally on inland cliffs and grassy hillsides. Map 9.

CORY'S SHEARWATER   *Calonectris diomedea*   **Pl. 2**
   Du – Cory's pijlstormvogel   Fr – Puffin cendré
   Ge – Gelbschnabel-Sturmtaucher   Sw – Gulnäbbad lira
Identification: 18". A large grey-brown shearwater, heavier built and looking broader-winged than Great. Further distinguished by *grey-brown hood* (not black cap) *merging gradually* into white throat. Thick bill is *yellow*. Sometimes has narrow white patch at base of tail, as in Great, but more often this is indistinct or lacking. *Never has white collar*. Under-parts pure white, without dark smudges on flanks and belly which occur in Great, but has greyish mottling on sides of breast. Flight action recalls Fulmar rather than Great Shearwater, typically 5–8 flaps followed by a long glide with slightly depressed wings. Nocturnal at breeding grounds. See also Manx Shearwater.

Voice: On breeding grounds, a long wailing note and a gull-like '*ia-gowa-gow*'.
Habitat: Pelagic, occasionally offshore. Breeds socially in crevices among rocks on islands. Mainly resident in Mediterranean. In autumn occurs off SW England, Ireland. Vagrant Faeroes, North Sea and C. Europe. Map 10.

GREAT SHEARWATER   *Puffinus gravis*   **Pl. 2**
   Du – Grote pijlstormvogel   Fr – Puffin majeur
   Ge – Grosser Sturmtaucher   Sw – Större lira
Identification: 18″. Distinguished by *dark cap*, sharply contrasting with pure white throat (head looks narrow), almost complete *white collar*, and *dark, slender bill. Narrow white patch at base of tail.* Upper-parts dark brown, under-parts white, with indistinctly spotted flanks and dark patch on belly. Whitish under-surfaces of wings have darker margins than Cory's. During moult shows irregular white line along centre of upper surface of wing. Flight as Manx; latter is much smaller, blacker above and lacks white tail-patch. See also Cory's.
Voice: Feeding notes raucous, barking and gull-like.
Habitat and Range: Pelagic, occasionally offshore. Breeds in burrows on Tristan da Cunha islands, in S. Atlantic, visiting eastern N. Atlantic (Iceland to Portugal) in summer and autumn. Vagrant in North Sea, also in Mediterranean east to Sardinia.

SOOTY SHEARWATER   *Puffinus griseus*   **Pl. 2**
   Du – Grauwe pijlstormvogel   Fr – Puffin fuligineux
   Ge – Dunkler Sturmtaucher   Sw – Grå lira
Identification: 16″. Heavy-bodied and narrow-winged. Looks all-black at a distance, gliding close to waves in typical shearwater fashion. Often associates with Great Shearwater and has similar behaviour. Distinguished from all other shearwaters in European and N. African waters (except dark examples of western Mediterranean race of Manx *P. p. mauretanicus*) by *uniform sooty plumage.* Under-surfaces of wings have pale areas, usually in form of indistinct whitish stripe along centre of wing. See also dark form of Fulmar and of western Mediterranean race of Manx; also immature Gannet and dark skuas. Silent at sea.
Habitat and Range: Pelagic, occasionally offshore. Breeds in burrows on islands in southern hemisphere. In autumn visits eastern N. Atlantic north to Iceland. A few enter North Sea and English Channel, rarely Mediterranean east to Malta.

MANX SHEARWATER   *Puffinus puffinus*   **Pl. 2**
   Du – Noorde pijlstormvogel   Fr – Puffin des Anglais
   Ge – Schwarzschnabel-Sturmtaucher Sw – Mindre lira
Identification: 14″. Distinguished from other shearwaters by *sharply contrasting black upper-parts and pure white under-parts.* Bill slender. Usually seen in scattered groups gliding on stiff wings with occasional wing-beats. Veers from side to side to follow wave contours, appearing alternately black and white. Does not follow ships. Swims frequently, flocks congregating on water at evening near breeding grounds. Nocturnal at breeding grounds. Above description refers to Atlantic *P. p. puffinus*; eastern Mediterranean race *P. p. yelkouan* is less sharply contrasted; western Mediterranean (Balearic) race *P. p. mauretanicus* is browner and even less contrasted; individuals with dark under-

parts may be mistaken for Sooty Shearwater, paler individuals for Cory's, but Manx is much smaller and slimmer than either.

Voice: Various wild crowing and crooning notes at breeding grounds.

Habitat: Offshore waters rather than pelagic. Breeds locally in dense colonies in burrows, on islands and cliff-tops. Map 11.

LITTLE SHEARWATER   *Puffinus assimilis*   **Pl. 2**
   Du – Kleine pijlstormvogel   Fr – Petit puffin
   Ge – Kleine Sturmtaucher   Sw – Dvärglira

Identification: 10½". Resembles miniature Manx, but feet very dark bluish (not pink) and *black crown does not extend below eye*. Flight less gliding, more erratic and fluttering than Manx. Two races occur accidentally in Europe – the Madeiran *P. a. baroli* is more frequent, and the Cape Verde *P. a boydi*; latter has *black* under tail-coverts and is indistinguishable at a distance from Audubon's. Occasional off coasts of Britain, Ireland; vagrant elsewhere in W., S. and C. Europe.

STORM PETRELS: Hydrobatidae

Small, blackish oceanic birds with white rumps, flitting erratically over the waves. Sexes similar. Hole nesting.

WILSON'S PETREL   *Oceanites oceanicus*   **Pl. 2**
   Du – Wilson's stormvogeltje   Fr – Pétrel océanite
   Ge – Buntfüssige Sturmschwalbe   Sw – Havslöpare

Identification: 7". Very similar to Storm Petrel, but feet have *yellowish webs* and usually extend *beyond* the short squarish tail. Has less obvious area of grey on wing-coverts than Leach's, but more than Storm Petrel. Follows ships. Distinctive flight, alternately gliding and fluttering with swallow-like wing-beats; often 'walks' along surface of water with outspread wings; leading edge of wing looks more curved even than Leach's, which is more sharply angled at carpal joints. A wanderer from Antarctic and sub-Antarctic breeding grounds, which in summer reaches the seas south-west of Ireland and the Bay of Biscay. Vagrant to W. (including Britain), C. Europe and Mediterranean.

STORM PETREL   *Hydrobates pelagicus*   **Pl. 2**
   Du – Stormvogeltje   Fr – Pétrel tempête
   Ge – Sturmschwalbe   Sw – Stormsvala

Identification: 6". Smallest European sea-bird. A long-winged blackish bird with a *conspicuous white rump* and a squared black tail. Has short, faint wing-bar, but more helpful is the *white patch in the wing-pit*. Follows ships well out from land, with weak flitting flight just above waves, at times 'pattering' on surface with dangling black feet. Nocturnal on land. Distinguished from Leach's Petrel by blacker, more uniform upper-parts, white under-wing patch. Rare Wilson's Petrel (which also follows ships) has longer legs and yellowish webs to feet, which extend beyond tail.

Voice: Makes sustained, rising and falling purring noise in nest burrow, terminating with characteristic 'hiccough'; also squeaks and croons.

Habitat: Strictly pelagic, except in breeding season. Nests colonially under rocks, in stone walls, etc., on islands. Map 12.

LEACH'S PETREL *Oceanodroma leucorhoa*   **Pl. 2**
   Du – Vaal stormvogeltje   Fr – Pétrel culblanc
   Ge – Wellenläufer   Sw – Klykstjärtad stormsvala

Identification: 8″. Distinguished from Storm Petrel by longer, more pointed wings, distinctive *bounding* flight, constantly changing speed and direction; at short range also by browner plumage, grey centre to white rump, *pale diagonal bar* on upper surface of wings but *no white under-wing patches*, and, though difficult to see, by forked tail. Unlike Storm Petrel, *does not follow ships.* Nocturnal at breeding grounds. See also Wilson's Petrel.
Voice: Normally silent, but at night on breeding grounds a rhythmic series of purring '*wirra-wirra*' notes, punctuated by an emphatic '*wicka, wicka*', which is also heard in flight. Long crooning notes heard from nest burrows.
Habitat: As Storm Petrel, but usually excavates nest burrows in peaty ground. Map 13.

GANNETS: Sulidae

GANNET *Sula bassana*   **Pl. 4**
   Du – Jan van Gent   Fr – Fou de Bassan
   Ge – Basstöpel   Sw – Havssula
Identification: 36″. A goose-size white sea-bird, identified by *extensive black tips to long, narrow wings*. Twice the size of Herring Gull, *with much longer neck* and *larger, pointed bill* often pointing downward, and *pointed tail* (not fan-shaped). Immature is dusky, closely speckled with white, or boldly pied blackish-brown and white, according to age, but easily identified by characteristic actions and by 'cigar-shaped' body. Direct flight usually low, with brief periods of gliding, but wheels majestically when feeding. Plunges headlong after fish, sometimes from 100 ft. or more. (Gulls sometimes drop into sea for food, but Gannet's submerging plunge is spectacular.)
Voice: Usual note a barking '*arrah*'.
Habitat: Strictly maritime, often seen far out to sea. Breeds in dense colonies on ledges of steep rocky island cliffs. Map 14.

CORMORANTS: Phalacrocoracidae

Large, long-billed dark water-birds, larger (except Pygmy Cormorant) than any duck. Sometimes confused with divers, but tail and wings longer and bill hook-tipped. In flight, neck held slightly above horizontal (divers' necks droop slightly). Fly in line or V formation, like geese. Often perch with wings half open. When swimming, resemble divers, but with necks more erect, bills raised slightly upward. Rock or tree nesting.

CORMORANT   *Phalacrocorax carbo*   **Pl. 3**
Du – Aalscholver   Fr – Grand cormoran
Ge – Kormoran   Sw – Storskarv

Identification: 36″. A large blackish water-bird, easily confused with Shag, but distinguished by larger size, *white chin and cheeks* and, in breeding birds, by *white patch on thighs*, and lack of crest. Juvenile brownish above, distinguished from young Shag by *whitish under-parts* and heavier bill. Perches *upright* on rocks, often with wings hanging half open. Swims low in water like diver, but with neck more erect, bill slightly raised. Flight fairly rapid and direct, neck extended and slightly above horizontal; parties usually fly in line or V formation. Sociable. In breeding season most Continental and some British birds have almost completely white head and neck.

Voice: Usual note a low, guttural '*r-rah*'.

Habitat: Coasts, estuaries, coastal lakes, also inland waters. Breeds colonially, sometimes near Shags, on rocky ledges, also on inland lake islands and trees. Map 15.

SHAG   *Phalacrocorax aristotelis*   **Pl. 3**
Du – Kuifaalscholver   Fr – Cormoran huppé
Ge – Krähenscharbe   Sw – Toppskarv

Identification: 30″. Smaller than Cormorant, with slightly thinner, shorter neck, slighter head and *smaller bill*. Distinguished by *lack of white on face*; also lacks white thigh-patch of breeding Cormorant; at short range by *green-black* instead of bronze-black plumage; in breeding season has short, upstanding crest. Eyes pale blue-green. Immature distinguished from young Cormorant by dark brown plumage with *little, if any, white on breast* (except young of Mediterranean race, which show some white below); bill is more slender than adult's and much finer than young Cormorant's.

Voice: Usual note a loud, rasping croak. At nest, a deep grunt and loud hissing.

Habitat: Maritime, frequenting rocky coasts and islands with steep cliffs and sea caves; in winter occasionally inland. Breeds colonially (sometimes singly) on rocky ledges and among boulders. Map 16.

PYGMY CORMORANT   *Phalacrocorax pygmeus*   **Pl. 3**
Du – Dwergaalscholver   Fr – Cormoran pygmée
Ge – Zwergscharbe   Sw – Dvärgskarv

Identification: 19″. Very much smaller and more active than Cormorant, recalls Coot in flight, but with long tail and *rather small, round head*. In summer, both sexes have dark red-brown head, glossy greenish-black plumage, spotted with white, except for dark grey 'saddle' across centre of back and wing-coverts. Outside breeding season white spots are absent, throat is white, breast red-brown. Juvenile has white chin, brown throat and breast, brownish-white under-parts and yellowish bill. See also Shag.

Voice: Short, harsh barking notes when breeding.

Habitat: Prefers inland waters, including rivers and marshes, to sea coast. Breeds colonially, building untidy nest on bushes in marsh. Map 17.

PELICANS: Pelecanidae

WHITE PELICAN   *Pelecanus onocrotalus*   **Pl. 4**
   Du – Gewone pelikaan   Fr – Pélican blanc
   Ge – Rosapelikan   Sw – Pelikan
Identification: 55–70″. Huge wing-span. *White, with blackish primaries*, long yellowish bill and throat-pouch and flesh-coloured feet. In breeding plumage both sexes have short, shaggy crest on back of head and rosy tint on plumage. At short range, yellowish tuft of feathers at base of neck, and red eye are visible. Juvenile brown, becoming dingy white irregularly speckled with brown. Flight leisurely, with short periods of gliding, head carried well back on shoulders. Flies in regular lines, often at great height. Shows black wing-tips above, *whole rear-halves of wings dark below*. White Stork and Gannet are also white with black wing-tips, but both fly with extended necks and have different bill shapes; Gannet has narrower, angular, pointed wings and longer, pointed tail; Dalmatian Pelican seen from below shows no prominent black on wings (see Pl. 4).
Voice: Low grunting and growling notes.
Habitat and Range: Large inland waters, marshes and shallow coastal lagoons. Nests colonially among reeds. Breeds Romania, Greece and Albania. Accidental W., C. and N. Europe. Migrant.

DALMATIAN PELICAN   *Pelecanus crispus*   **Pl. 4**
   Du – Kroeskoppelikaan   Fr – Pélican frisé
   Ge – Krauskopfpelikan   Sw – Krushuvad pelikan
Identification: 63–70″. Difficult to distinguish from White Pelican except in flight; ranges overlap. In flight shows dusky secondaries and black wing-tips above, *all dirty white below*. Size usually slightly larger. At short range upper-parts look dirty white (instead of faintly rose-white); under-parts *dull greyish-white* with large yellowish patch (not tufted) on lower throat; primaries dark brown; legs lead grey (not flesh); feathers on back of head only slightly elongated and curly (not shaggy or crested); eye pale yellowish (not red). Has distinctive short rasping bark. Juvenile resembles young White Pelican, distinguishable only at short range by feathers on forehead ending in nearly straight line, instead of in a point above upper mandible (adults have similar distinction). Behaviour, flight and habitat as White Pelican. Map 18.

HERONS AND BITTERNS: Ardeidae

Wading birds with long necks, long legs and longish pointed bills. In sustained flight, heads are tucked back on shoulders. Specialized plumes on head, scapulars and neck. Bare parts change colour when breeding. Sexes similar except Little Bittern. Tree or reed nesting.

BITTERN   *Botaurus stellaris*   **Pl. 5**
   Du – Roerdomp   Fr – Butor étoilé
   Ge – Grosse Rohrdommel   Sw – Rördrom
Identification: 30″. A large, brown, heron-like marsh-bird, *richly mottled and*

barred, with large green legs and feet and *distinctive voice*. When hiding, bill is pointed vertically in characteristic elongated pose; walks with shoulders hunched, head lowered. Flight slow and reluctant, neck retracted when well under way: broad rounded wings *distinctively barred black and brown*. Skulking, solitary and usually crepuscular, hiding in reeds by day. Can be confused with immature Night Heron, which is much smaller and spotted. See also American Bittern.

Voice: A harsh '*aark*'. Song, 2–3 quiet grunting noises, an audible intake of breath followed by a deep, booming '*woomp*', like distant fog-horn, sometimes audible for a mile, though curiously muted.

Habitat: Dense reed-beds in fens, marshes, backwaters, lake shores. Nests among reeds. On Continent sometimes nests around small ponds in cultivated regions. Map 19.

AMERICAN BITTERN   *Botaurus lentiginosus*   **Pl. 5**
   Du – Amerikaanse roerdomp   Fr – Butor d'Amérique
   Ge – Amerikanische Rohrdommel   Sw – Amerikansk rördrom

Identification: 26″. Distinguished from European Bittern by *smaller size*, finely freckled upper-parts (not boldly mottled and streaked), slightly narrower, *black-tipped* wings (not barred black and brown), *chestnut* crown and *long black streak down side of neck*. Behaviour and flight are similar to European. Immature Night Heron is about same size, but is greyer, without the black wing-tips.

Voice: When flushed, a rapid, throaty '*kok-kok-kok*'. Song, a series of deep, pumping '*ka-onk*' notes.

Habitat and Range: More likely to be seen in open meadows than European species. Vagrant to W. (including Britain) and N. Europe.

LITTLE BITTERN   *Ixobrychus minutus*   **Pl. 5**
   Du – Wouwaapje   Fr – Butor blongios
   Ge – Zwergrohrdommel   Sw – Dvärgrördrom

Identification: 14″. Distinguished from other small herons by *very small size*, dark crown and upper-parts, very conspicuous *buffish-white wing-coverts* and under-parts. Male's crown and back are greenish-black. Female is streaky dark brown above, streaky buff below, with less conspicuous buff wing-coverts. Bill yellowish (red at base when breeding). Legs green. Juvenile heavily streaked above and below. Flight usually very low, with rapid wing-beats and long glides. In flight *pale coverts contrast strongly with dark wings and back*. Skulking and chiefly crepuscular except in breeding season.

Voice: A variety of short croaking notes. Song (day or night), a deep bark, repeated at about two seconds' interval, sometimes for hours.

Habitat: Overgrown river banks, backwaters, ponds, wooded swamps, reed-beds. Nests near water, occasionally in small scattered groups. Map 20.

NIGHT HERON   *Nycticorax nycticorax*   **Pl. 5**
   Du – Kwak   Fr – Héron bihoreau
   Ge – Nachtreiher   Sw – Natthäger

Identification: 24″. A stocky, rather short-legged heron. Adult is *black-backed* and pale below, with a *black cap*, long drooping white crest, red eyes, and stout bill. Legs yellowish (dull red in breeding season). Immature dark brown above, boldly spotted with buff; no crest; in bad light may be confused with much larger Bittern, but latter has mottled golden-brown plumage. Has stumpy silhouette in flight. Crepuscular, except in breeding season. Usually spends day hidden and inactive, often in trees, flying to feed at dusk.

Voice: A hoarse '*guark*' or '*guok*', usually at dusk.

Habitat: Dense tangled swamps, overgrown river banks, marshes with trees; feeds at dusk in drains, at edges of pools, or in open marshes. Nests colonially, often with allied species, in thickets, trees, locally also in reed-beds. Map 21.

SQUACCO HERON   *Ardeola ralloides*   **Pl. 6**
Du – Ralreiger   Fr – Héron crabier
Ge – Rallenreiher   Sw – Rallhäger

Identification: 18". Stocky and thick-necked, with *pale buff plumage, white wings*; long drooping crest. Bill black and blue when breeding, dark-tipped greenish in winter. Legs greenish (pink at height of breeding season). On ground looks stocky, thick-necked, dingy yellowish-brown; in flight suddenly reveals conspicuous white wings, rump and tail; can then be confused with Little and Cattle Egrets, but darker back and head are distinctive.

Voice: In breeding season a harsh, crow-like '*karr*', usually at dusk.

Habitat: As Little Egret, though less often in open. Nests singly, or in scattered groups, among allied species, in reed-beds, bushes, trees. Map 22.

CATTLE EGRET   *Bubulcus ibis*   **Pl. 6**
Du – Koereiger   Fr – Héron garde-boeufs
Ge – Kuhreiher   Sw – Kohäger

Identification: 20". Looks white at distance. Slightly smaller, much *stockier and thicker-necked* than Little Egret, with which it often nests. *Heavy jowl is distinctive*. Distinguished at short range by long buff tufts on crown, chest and mantle; in winter, buff is very pale. When breeding the bill is yellow with a red base, legs reddish; in winter the bill is yellowish, legs dusky. Eye reddish. Juvenile lacks buff tufts, has yellow bill, greenish-brown legs. Flight and actions like Little Egret. Sociable. Unlike Little Egret, *usually feeds among grazing cattle*. Can be confused with Squacco Heron in flight (see above).

Voice: A variety of croaking and deep bubbling notes in breeding season.

Habitat and Range: Less aquatic than most herons. Usually among feeding cattle in meadows, marshes, or in dry open country. Nests colonially, often with allied species, in reed-beds, bushes, or trees, over water or on dry land. Breeds Spain, Portugal, S. France; partial migrant. Vagrant elsewhere in W. (including Britain), C., N., E. and S. Europe.

LITTLE EGRET   *Egretta garzetta*   **Pl. 6**
Du – Kleine zilverreiger   Fr – Aigrette garzette
Ge – Seidenreiher   Sw – Silkeshäger

Identification: 22". A small snow-white heron with long, slender, black bill, black legs and *yellow feet*, latter conspicuous in flight. Feet become reddish in spring. (Great White Egret is much larger, and has black feet; Cattle Egret and Squacco Heron in flight both look white in distance, but they are much stockier, thicker-necked birds, with shorter bills). In summer, adults have *very long, drooping crest* and greatly elongated scapulars, forming hazy drooping 'cloak'. Feeds in open shallow water, *not among grazing cattle* like Cattle Egret.

Voice: In breeding season, a croaking '*kark*' and a bubbling '*wulla-wulla-wulla*'.

48   ARDEIDAE

Habitat: Marshes, lagoons, swamps. Nests in colonies, often with other herons, in bushes or trees, in wet marsh, swamps, dry open country, sea cliffs and woods. Map 23.

GREAT WHITE EGRET   *Egretta alba*   Pl. 6
Du – Grote zilverreiger   Fr – Grande aigrette
Ge – Silberreiher   Sw – Ägretthäger
N. Am – American Egret

Identification: 35″. Much larger than Little Egret (which also has dazzling white plumage) and has slimmer shape and no real crest. Neck is *very long, thin and angular*. Bill can be all yellow, or partly black from tip. Readily distinguished at close range from Little and Intermediate Egrets (apart from size) by its gape, which extends *behind the eye*. Legs *and feet* greenish-black (Little Egret's feet are yellow); when breeding, upper parts of legs are pinkish-orange. Scapulars greatly elongated in breeding season to form hazy, drooping 'cloak' extending below tail. Squacco and Cattle Egret, which look white in distant flight, are much smaller and stockier.
Voice: Has occasional croaking note '*kraak*'.
Habitat: Lake and river banks, open swamps, lagoons. Nests in dense reed-beds, usually in scattered groups, rarely in bushes or trees. Map 24.

GREY HERON   *Ardea cinerea*   Pl. 5
Du – Blauwe reiger   Fr – Héron cendré
Ge – Fischreiher   Sw – Grå häger

Identification: 36″. Distinguished from other herons by *large size, grey upper-parts, white head and neck with broad streak from eye to tip of long, graceful crest*. Long, dagger-shaped bill is yellowish, legs brownish, both becoming reddish in early spring. Stands motionless for long periods in or near water, with long neck erect, or head sunk between shoulders; also perches in trees. Flight powerful, with slow, deep wing-beats; flight-silhouette is distinctive, with *head back between shoulders*, bowed wings and legs extended.
Voice: A deep, harsh '*frarnk*'. Numerous croaking and retching notes and bill-snapping in breeding season.
Habitat: Water-meadows, rivers, lakes, sea-shores. Nests in colonies, usually in tall trees. Map 25.

PURPLE HERON   *Ardea purpurea*   Pl. 5
Du – Purperreiger   Fr – Héron pourpré
Ge – Purpurreiher   Sw – Purpurhäger

Identification: 31″. Distinguished from Grey Heron by smaller size, much darker coloration, and, when perched, by much more serpentine appearance. Upper-parts and wings dark grey, with elongated chestnut feathers drooping from mantle; crown and crest black; *very long thin chestnut neck boldly striped black*; centre of breast chestnut, rest of under-parts black. Immature is sandier, with chestnut crown, no black on head or neck, and buffish under-parts. In flight, neck bulge *hangs lower and is more angular* and feet look larger than in Grey Heron; latter shows more contrasted wing-pattern. Seldom in trees.
Voice: Higher-pitched than Grey Heron, '*rrank*'.
Habitat: Swamps, overgrown ditches, dense reed-beds, etc. Breeds in colonies, sometimes with other species, in reed-beds, occasionally in bushes. Map 26.

STORKS: Ciconiidae

Large, with long legs, long necks and long, straight bills. Flight slow and deliberate, with neck extended but slightly drooped. Gait a sedate walk. Sexes similar. Tree or roof nesting.

BLACK STORK   *Ciconia nigra*   Pl. 6
Du – Zwarte ooievaar   Fr – Cigogne noire
Ge – Schwarzstorch   Sw – Svart stork
Identification: 38″. Distinguished from White Stork by glossy *black plumage*, with *white under-parts*. Juvenile has brownish breast. Shy and solitary.
Voice: Has considerable range, varying from hoarse gasping to a noise like sharpening a saw, and several quite musical notes. Bill-clattering less frequent than with White Stork.
Habitat: Wild marshy tracts or meadows among coniferous or mixed forests. Nests at considerable height in forest trees. Map 27.

WHITE STORK   *Ciconia ciconia*   Pl. 6
Du – Ooievaar   Fr – Cigogne blanche
Ge – Weissstorch   Sw – Vit stork
Identification: 40″. Easily identified by large size, white plumage with *jet-black flight-feathers* and long, *bright red bill and legs*. Perches on trees and buildings, often on one leg. Walks deliberately. Often soars or flies at great height. Wing-beats are slow. Flight-silhouette distinguished from heron's, pelican's and Egyptian Vulture's by long, *extended neck*. Migrates in irregular flocks, *not* in regular formations. Sociable. See also immature Spoonbill.
Voice: Occasional hissing and coughing notes during breeding season; loud, rhythmic bill-clattering frequent during display.
Habitat: Marshes, water-meadows and grassy plains; in breeding season usually near houses. Nests on buildings, haystacks, or stork-poles, also in trees. Map 28.

IBISES AND SPOONBILLS: Threskiornithidae

Resemble small herons or storks in general form, but with long and decurved or flattened and spatulate bills. Necks extended in flight. Sexes similar. Reed, bush or tree nesting.

GLOSSY IBIS   *Plegadis falcinellus*   Pl. 6
Du – Ibis   Fr – Ibis falcinelle
Ge – Brauner Sichler   Sw – Svart ibis
Identification: 22″. Bill curlew-shaped, but plumage is *uniform, almost black*. At close range plumage is glossed with purple, bronze and green. Immature is *dull* dark brown. Flight-silhouette is distinctive, with narrow body, long round-tipped wings, extended neck and trailing legs; shallow, rapid wing-beats with

occasional gliding can cause confusion with Pygmy Cormorant. Perches freely on trees. Has infrequent, long croak.

Habitat: Marshes, mud-flats. Breeds in colonies, frequently with herons or egrets, in large reed-beds among shallow water, occasionally in bushes or trees. Map 29.

SPOONBILL *Platalea leucorodia*   **Pl. 6**
    Du – Lepelaar   Fr – Spatule blanche
    Ge – Löffler   Sw – Skedstork

Identification: 34″. Easily identified by *snow-white plumage* and *long, spatulate bill*. Adults have ochre tinge at base of neck and, in summer, a *pendant 'horse-tail' crest*. Legs and bill black, latter with yellow tip. Immature has black tips to wings, no ochre on neck, greyish-pink bill and yellowish to greyish legs. Flight regular and slow, gliding and soaring on extended wings; parties usually in file. Distinguished in flight from all 'white' heron-like birds by *extended*, slightly sagging neck and spatulate bill.

Voice: Occasional grunting noise in breeding season. Bill-clattering occurs when excited.

Habitat: Shallow, open water, reedy marshes, estuaries. Breeds in colonies in large reed-beds, on small bare islands, locally in trees or bushes. Map 30.

FLAMINGOS: Phoenicopteridae

GREATER FLAMINGO *Phoenicopterus ruber*   **Pl. 6**
    Du – Ge – Sw – Flamingo   Fr – Flamant rose

Identification: 50″. Unmistakable. An extremely slender, white and rose-pink wading bird, with *abnormally long legs and neck and grotesque down-curved bill*. In flight, *neck and legs are extended* and slightly drooped, wings show magnificent combination of *crimson and black*. Immature is dingy grey-brown. Walks sedately, dipping bill or head in shallow water to feed. Strictly gregarious. Beware 'escaped' Chilean race (immature has grey legs, pink 'knees'; adult has all-pink plumage). See also Lesser Flamingo (Accidentals).

Voice: A goose-like gabble and many trumpeting cries, '*ar-honk*', etc., particularly in flight.

Habitat and Range: Shallow coastal lagoons, or floodwaters, lakes, mud-flats, etc. Breeds colonially on mud-banks, or in shallow water, building mud-heap nest a few inches above water. Breeds, not always annually, S. France, S. Spain; partial migrant. Irregular visitor to Portugal, Holland. Vagrant elsewhere in Europe.

SWANS, GEESE AND DUCKS:
Anatidae

Swans are large waterfowl, with very long, slender necks; like some geese they migrate in lines or V-shaped flocks. Sexes similar. Ground nesting.

Geese are smaller and noisy, but are heavier and longer-necked than ducks. Chiefly terrestrial feeders. Sexes similar. Ground and cliff nesting.
Shelducks are goose-like ducks. Sexes similar. Hole nesting.
Surface-feeding Ducks feed by dabbling or 'up-ending'; taking flight they spring off the water; usually have brightly coloured speculum (rectangular patch) on secondaries; in eclipse (late summer) plumage, males tend to resemble females. Ground or hole nesting.
Diving Ducks dive for food and patter along surface before flying. Wing-bars and patches are important. Hole or ground nesting.
Saw-bills have slender, toothed bills; most have crests and are slender-bodied, more like divers than ducks; in flight appear long-drawn, with bill, head, neck and body horizontal. Ground or hole nesting.

MUTE SWAN *Cygnus olor*   **Pls. 7, 8**
Du – Knobbelzwaan   Fr – Cygne tuberculé
Ge – Höckerschwan   Sw – Knölsvan
Identification: 60″. Same size as Whooper, larger than Bewick's. Distinguished from both by *orange bill with black knob and base* (knob greatly enlarged in male in spring). Also, when swimming, by *gracefully curved neck, with bill pointing downward*. Immature browner than young Whooper, with knobless, greyish-pink bill and grey legs. *Readily assumes aggressive attitude*, with neck curved and wings arched over back. Is often domesticated. Flight powerful and direct, with neck outstretched; *wing-beats make distinctive loud singing noise*. Sociable (sometimes in very large herds), except in breeding season.
Voice: Is not mute, though less vocal than other swans; makes various explosive and hissing noises.
Habitat: May occur anywhere. In truly wild state frequents remote marshes and lakes; in winter, on sheltered sea coasts. Map 31.

BEWICK'S SWAN *Cygnus columbianus*   **Pl. 7**
Du – Kleine zwaan   Fr – Cygne de Bewick
Ge – Zwergschwan   Sw – Mindre sångsvan
Identification: 48″. *Considerably smaller and shorter in neck* than Mute and Whooper; chiefly resembles latter; distinguished by *shorter bill with smaller, more rounded area of yellow, rounded head* and much quieter voice. Immature resembles young Whooper, except in size. Behaviour and habitat like Whooper, but seldom flies in regular formation. Does not arch wings aggressively. Wing-beats lack characteristic singing note made by Mute.
Voice: Quieter than Whooper. Feeding herds make quiet musical babble. Map 32.

WHOOPER SWAN *Cygnus cygnus*   **Pls. 7, 8**
Du – Wilde zwaan   Fr – Cygne sauvage
Ge – Singschwan   Sw – Sångsvan
Identification: 60″. *Lemon-yellow* base to black bill distinguishes Whooper from Mute, which has orange bill with black knob at base. Further distinguished by *stiffly erect neck* and frequent *bugle-call notes*; from Bewick's by long, flat profile to head, considerably larger size, yellow on bill *tapering forward to a point*, and different voice. Immature marked with ashy-brown, greyer than young Mute; bill pale pinkish with dusky tip. Behaviour and flight

like Mute, but walks more easily, does not arch wings aggressively and wing-beats lack characteristic singing note. Usually in noisy herds, except in breeding season, when solitary. Flies in wavering oblique lines, or chevrons.

Voice: Noisiest of swans. Flight-call of flock a loud trumpeting or whooping chorus '*hoop-hoop-hoop*'.

Habitat: Sea coasts, tidal waters, lakes, large rivers. Nests on islets in swamps or lakes, moorland bogs, arctic tundra. Map 33.

BEAN GOOSE   *Anser fabalis*   **Pls. 9, 10**

Du – Rietgans   Fr – Oie des moissons
Ge – Saatgans   Sw – Sädgås

Identification: 28–35″. Browner and *generally darker* than other 'grey geese', pale feather margins appearing brighter. At a distance *head and rather long neck look dark*. No bars on under-parts. *Bill long and black, marked with orange-yellow*, occasionally with some white at base. Legs of adult *orange-yellow*; immature pale yellowish. Behaviour and flight as Greylag, but has dark fore-wing. Adult Pink-footed is slightly smaller, with smaller *pink and black* bill, *pink* legs and blue-grey upper-parts giving greater contrast to dark head and neck. Greylag is slightly larger and paler, especially on head and neck, with light grey fore-wings, white-tipped orange bill and *pink* legs. Adult White-fronted and Lesser White-fronted are smaller, with prominent white at base of bill and broadly barred bellies.

Voice: Less vocal than other 'grey geese'. A rich '*ung-unk*', lower and more reedy than similar call of Pink-footed.

Habitat: Winters inland, on grasslands near fresh water. Breeds in the Arctic among forest trees near rivers and lakes. Map 34.

PINK-FOOTED GOOSE   *Anser brachyrhynchus*   **Pls. 9, 10**

Du – Kleine rietgans   Fr – Oie à bec court
Ge – Kurzschnabelgans   Sw – Spetsbergsgås

Identification: 24–30″. Distinguished from Bean and other 'grey geese' by *pale blue-grey upper-parts* giving strong contrast with *very dark head and neck, small pink and black bill and pink legs*. During summer moult plumage varies greatly from blue-grey to brown-grey. *Blue-grey fore-wings conspicuous in flight*, though less so than in larger, paler Greylag, which lacks the blueness. Immature sometimes has paler legs, and in winter looks browner and often paler-necked than adult. Behaviour and flight as White-fronted. Distinguished from adult White-fronted and Lesser White-fronted by lack of white at base of bill (though some white occurs occasionally) and by lack of black bars on belly; immature extremely difficult to distinguish from immature White-fronts unless leg colour and rounder head can be clearly seen, as bill patterns are very similar.

Voice: Two- and three-syllable honking notes are high-pitched, lacking cackling quality of White-fronted. A musical '*ung-unk*', and characteristic '*wink-wink-wink*', or '*king-wink*'.

Habitat: As Greylag, but more frequently in arable fields. Breeds colonially among rocky outcrops on hillsides and river gorges, also on open tundra. Map 35.

WHITE-FRONTED GOOSE *Anser albifrons* **Pls. 9, 10**
Du – Kolgans Fr – Oie rieuse
Ge – Blässgans Sw – Bläsgås

Identification: 26–30″. Smaller and darker than Greylag. Adults distinguished from Greylag, Bean and Pink-footed by *bold white patch above the pink bill, orange legs and broad irregular black bars on belly*. Immature lacks dark bars on belly and white forehead, but combination of orange legs and lack of extensive black on bill are distinctive. Behaviour and normal flight like Greylag, though wing-beat is quicker and fore-wing brownish. Greenland race *A. a. flavirostris* winters mainly in Ireland and W. Scotland; distinguishable in the field from typical race *A. a. albifrons* by its darker coloration, particularly on head and neck, and orange-yellow bill; juvenile usually shows little or no white at base of bill and often no bars on breast. See Pl. 9. See also Lesser White-fronted.

Voice: Gabbling notes resemble those of other 'grey geese', but are higher-pitched and quicker. Usual notes a cackling *'kow-lyow'*, or *'lyo-lyok'*, di- and trisyllabic.

Habitat: As Greylag, but seldom in stubble or potato fields. Usually breeds sociably in treeless tundra, open marshes, islets in rivers, etc. Map 36.

LESSER WHITE-FRONTED GOOSE *Anser erythropus* **Pl. 9**
Du – Dwerggans Fr – Oie naine
Ge – Zwerggans Sw – Fjällgås

Identification: 21–26″. General appearance resembles small White-fronted, but is distinguished by *much smaller, pinker bill, white forehead extending much higher on to crown* and tips of closed wings usually *extending beyond tail*. Usually looks darker than European White-fronted. At short range bright, swollen *yellow eye-ring* is sure mark. Immature lacks white base to bill and dark bars on belly, but has the yellow eye-ring. Behaviour and flight as in White-fronted, but wing-beats are faster.

Voice: Much squeakier than White-fronted. Most frequent notes *'kyu-yu'*, or *'kyu-yu-yu'* (gander); *'kow-yow'* (goose).

Habitat: Much as White-fronted, but is a low-Arctic species and breeds at high altitudes only where range extends south, in dwarf birch and willow, around mountain lakes. In extreme north of Norway breeds at sea level. Map 37.

GREYLAG GOOSE *Anser anser* **Pls. 9, 10**
Du – Grauwe gans Fr – Oie cendrée
Ge – Graugans Sw – Grågås

Identification: 30–35″. Two European races recognizable in the field: the British and western European race *A. a. anser* has *thick orange* bill; the eastern European race *A. a. rubrirostris* has *thick pink* bill and looks *paler* due to light feather edges. Both are further distinguished from other 'grey geese' by *lack of black markings on bill, pinkish legs and feet, head and neck no darker than body, very pale grey fore-wings* and unbarred belly (but adults often have some black spots on breast). Immature has greyish-pink legs. In distant flight all 'grey geese' look much alike, usually flying in chevrons or lines; all are gregarious outside breeding season and are normally diurnal, flighting to grazing grounds at dawn. Greylag is distinguished from adult White-fronted and Lesser White-fronted by larger size, pale head and neck, lack of white patch at base of bill and, at all ages, by pink (not orange) legs; from Bean and Pink-footed by head and neck being no darker than body, large orange bill (in W. Europe) without black markings and generally paler appearance.

Voice: Same nasal and reedy gabbling notes as domestic bird, '*aahng ung-ung*', etc. Distant flock sounds rather like baaing of sheep.

Habitat: In winter on grasslands, arable fields near coasts, marshes, estuaries. Breeds sociably on moors, marshes, reed-beds, boggy thickets, islets. Map 38.

SNOW GOOSE   *Anser caerulescens*   Pls. 7, 8

Du – Sneeuwgans	Fr – Oie des neiges
Ge – Schneegans	Sw – Snögås

Identification: 25–30". Adult easily identified by *pure white plumage, with black-tipped wings*. Stout, dark pink bill and legs. Head often stained orange. Immature is brownish-grey above, greyish-white below, with dark grey bill and legs. Behaviour and flight as in 'grey geese'. Feeds freely with other species. 'Blue Goose' of N. America, which has occurred in British Isles, is colour phase of this species; it is dusky blue-grey, with white head, neck and 'stern' (sometimes also breast and belly); immature is all dusky with white chin-spot. Snow Goose is easily distinguished from all swans by *shorter neck and black primaries*; from flying Gannet by much smaller head and bill on longer neck, short rounded tail and broader wings.

Voice: In flight a high-pitched '*kow*' and '*whonk*'; an abrupt, harsh '*kaank*'; also a deep '*zung-ung-ung*' conversational gabble.

Habitat and Range: As in 'grey geese'. Breeds colonially on open tundra and lake islands. Vagrant from N. America to British Isles (almost annual) and elsewhere in N., W. and C. Europe.

CANADA GOOSE   *Branta canadensis*   Pls. 7, 8

Du – Canadese gans	Fr – Bernache du Canada
Ge – Kanadagans	Sw – Kanadagås

Identification: 36–40". Largest goose occurring in Europe. Black head and *long black neck contrast strongly with whitish breast and brown body*. Distinguished from other 'black geese' by large size and *broad white patch from throat on to cheek*. Bill and legs black. Distinguished from much smaller Barnacle by *brown body* (not grey), white patch on cheeks (not including face), black extending only to base of neck (not to breast). Brent is even smaller, without white on head. Gregarious outside breeding season. Normally diurnal, grazing in fields like 'grey geese', but sometimes also 'up-ending' in water. Chiefly a fresh-water species. Flies in regular chevron or line formations.

Voice: Flight-note a resonant, nasal '*aa-honk*', second syllable rising.

Habitat and Range: Fields and open marshes near fresh water; sometimes among trees and along sea-shores. Introduced into Europe and occurs frequently in parks. Breeds singly or in small groups on bushy islets in lakes. Feral breeder in Britain, Ireland, Norway, Sweden, Finland; partial migrant to Germany, Holland. Vagrant elsewhere in Europe.

BARNACLE GOOSE   *Branta leucopsis*   Pls. 7, 8

Du – Brandgans	Fr – Bernache nonnette
Ge – Weisswangengans	Sw – Vitkindad gås

Identification: 23–27". Quickly identified by *black and white plumage, conspicuous white face and forehead; black on neck extending down to breast*; lavender-grey upper-parts with bold white-edged black bars, greyish under-parts, white rump and black tail. Legs and small bill black. Flight in close ragged packs. Feeds nocturnally. Strongly gregarious. Distinguished from Brent by larger size, white face and more terrestrial habits; from Canada Goose by smaller size, white face, black breast and grey (not brown) upper-parts.

Voice: Distant flock sounds like pack of yapping lap-dogs. Usual note a rapidly repeated barking '*gnuk*'.

Habitat: Seldom far inland, preferring salt-marshes, grass fields near estuaries, tidal mud-flats, or small grass-topped islands. Breeds colonially, usually on ledges of steep arctic cliffs, rocky river gorges and hillsides, sometimes open tundra. Map 39.

BRENT GOOSE *Branta bernicla*   Pls. 7, 8

Du – Rotgans   Fr – Bernache cravant
Ge – Ringelgans   Sw – Prutgås

Identification: 22–24″. *Smallest and darkest* of the 'black geese' (near size of Mallard), with *dull black head, neck and breast*, dark grey-brown upper-parts, brilliant white 'stern' and *small white fleck on side of neck* (sometimes looking almost like narrow collar, but absent in immature). Dark-bellied form *B. b. bernicla* has dark grey-brown belly; pale-bellied *B. b. hrota* has much paler under-parts, contrasting strongly with upper-parts (both may occur in same flock). More maritime than other geese. Strongly gregarious, feeding at water's edge along coast by day or night; rests on water at high tide; often 'up-ends'. Flight rapid, seldom in formation, usually in irregularly changing flocks. Distinguished from Barnacle and much larger Canada Geese by *all-black head*.

Voice: A soft, throaty '*rronk*' or '*rruk*', also various lesser conversational notes. Flock makes distinctive growling noise.

Habitat: Maritime outside breeding season, frequenting coasts and estuaries where *Zostera* weed abounds. Breeds sociably on high rocky tundra and islets off arctic coasts. Map 40.

RED-BREASTED GOOSE *Branta ruficollis*   Pls. 7, 10

Du – Roodhalsgans   Fr – Bernache à cou roux
Ge – Rothalsgans   Sw – Rödhalsad gås

Identification: 21–22″. Easily identified by contrasting *combination of black, white and chestnut plumage*. At a distance *white flank-stripe* is most conspicuous feature. Legs and very small bill blackish. Immature is paler, duller and browner, with indistinct white patch between bill and eye. Behaviour and flight similar to 'grey geese', but is extremely quick and agile when feeding and seldom flies in regular chevron or line formation. Often associates with Lesser White-fronts.

Voice: A shrill, staccato, '*kik-wik*', or '*kee-kwa*' and various rather squeaky conversational notes.

Habitat and Range: Normally winters on grassy steppes, roosting along sea coast. Breeds sociably on Siberian coastal tundra. Winters Romania, Bulgaria and Greece. Vagrant elsewhere in S., W. (including Britain), C. and N. Europe.

EGYPTIAN GOOSE *Alopochen aegyptiacus*   Pl. 77

Du – Nilgans   Fr – Oie d'Egypte
Ge – Nilgans   Sw – Nilgås

Identification: 27″. A large, rather long-legged, goose-like duck, with greyish or buffish coloration. Distinguished from more uniformly coloured Ruddy

Shelduck by *chestnut eye-patch and patch on lower breast* and by longer legs. Bill and legs pink (Ruddy Shelduck's are black). In flight shows conspicuous white fore-wings, black primaries and green secondaries, but under-parts are whitish (not chestnut as in Ruddy Shelduck). Sexes similar.

Voice: A low-pitched '*kek, kek*' and various husky, bleating and gabbling calls.
Habitat and Range: Fresh-water swamps and marshes. Introduced birds now feral in Britain (East Anglia); vagrant to S. Europe.

RUDDY SHELDUCK *Tadorna ferruginea*   **Pls. 14, 16, 18**
 Du – Casarca   Fr – Tadorne casarca
 Ge – Rostgans   Sw – Rostand
Identification: 25″. Distinguished by goose-like shape, *uniform orange-chestnut plumage with pale head*, smallish black bill and legs, black tail, black wing-feathers with green speculum. In flight, shows *very conspicuous white wing-coverts.* Male has narrow black collar. Female has almost white head. Usually in pairs. Flight resembles Shelduck's. Locally feral Egyptian Goose has similar conspicuous wing pattern, but is paler and with chestnut eye-patch.
Voice: A loud, nasal '*ah-onk*', and a musical '*roo-roo-roo*' and rattling notes.
Habitat: Much more terrestrial than Shelduck. In winter frequents sandy lake shores, river banks, fields and even arid steppes. Breeds in holes in dunes, cliffs, old trees and walls. Map 41.

SHELDUCK *Tadorna tadorna*   **Pls. 14, 16, 18**
 Du – Bergeend   Fr – Tadorne de Belon
 Ge – Brandente   Sw – Gravand
Identification: 24″. A large, rather goose-like duck, appearing white and black at long range. Distinguished by contrasting greenish-black head and neck, white body with *broad chestnut band around fore-part* and dark stripe down centre of under-parts. Scapulars and primaries black, with green speculum. Legs pink; *bill red*, male's having prominent knob. Juvenile is ashy-brown above, lacks chestnut breast-band and has whitish face and throat, pink bill, grey legs. Flight is goose-like, with slower wing-beats than most ducks. When resting on water may be confused with male Shoveler, which also has white upper-breast and dark head, but latter is smaller, sits lower in water and has dark, spatulate bill.
Voice: Seldom vocal outside breeding season. A quick, nasal '*ak-ak-ak*', and a deeper, louder, '*ark, ark*'. Female with young has soft twanging note.
Habitat: Sandy and muddy coasts, occasionally inland. Breeds in rabbit burrows, etc., and on bushy commons. Map 42.

MANDARIN *Aix galericulata*   **Pl. 11**
 Du – Mandarijneend   Fr – Canard mandarin
 Ge – Mandarinente   Sw – Mandarinand
Identification: 17″. Highly coloured male easily distinguished *by upstanding orange* '*sails*' on wings, ample chestnut 'side-whiskers', and multi-coloured drooping crest. Female drab brownish-grey, with large whitish spots on breast and *fine white mark behind and around eye.* Male in eclipse and when immature resembles female but with dark red, instead of blackish, bill.
Voice: A fairly loud, high '*tweek*' not unlike Coot's call; flight-call '*hwick*'.
Habitat: Usually on wooded inland waters and ornamental ponds. Artificially

introduced and now breeding in feral state (in trees) in some parts of England (mainly in SE) and Scotland. Feral or escaped vagrant to other parts of Europe.

WIGEON   *Anas penelope*   Pls. 11, 16, 18
    Du – Smient   Fr – Canard siffleur
    Ge – Pfeifente   Sw – Bläsand

Identification: 18″. Male distinguished by *chestnut head with yellow forehead*, grey body and pinkish breast; in flight *large white areas towards front of wings* and white belly and black 'stern' are distinctive; in eclipse resembles dark female, but distinguished by white shoulders. Female distinguished from Mallard by smaller size, much smaller bill, more rounded head, pointed tail and more rufous plumage; also by partly obscured green and black speculum and shorter-necked appearance. Feeds in shallows, on mud-flats and grazes around ponds, often resting on sea by day in compact flocks. Young male distinguished from young Gadwall by smaller bill, darker head and blackish speculum. See also American Wigeon.

Voice: Male has high whistling '*whee-oo*'. Female has low purring note.

Habitat: Many maritime in winter, numbers also seen on fresh water. Breeds on moors, lake islands, marshes. Map 43.

AMERICAN WIGEON   *Anas americana*   Pl. 15
    Du – Amerikaanse smient   Fr – Canard siffleur d'Amérique
    Ge – Nordamerikanische Pfiefente Sw – Amerikansk bläsand

Identification: 18–22″. Male, unlike mainly grey Wigeon, is mostly *pinkish-brown*, with *broader creamy-white crown*, wide glossy green band from eye to nape and grey cheeks and upper neck. Female very similar to female Wigeon, but head and neck are *greyer*, contrasting with reddish brown chest; closed wing shows strikingly contrasting white edges of almost black tertials (female Wigeon has indistinct off-white edges to brown tertials). Male shows bold white wing-patches (in flight) as Wigeon, but axillaries in both sexes are *white*, whereas Wigeon's are dusky.

Voice: Male has whistling call '*wee, whee-oo*'.

Habitat and Range: Habitat similar to Wigeon's. Vagrant from N. America to W. (including Britain), N. and C. Europe.

GADWALL   *Anas strepera*   Pls. 11, 16, 18
    Du – Krakeend   Fr – Canard chipeau
    Ge – Schnatterente   Sw – Snatterand

Identification: 20″. Smaller, slighter and with more abrupt forehead than Mallard, with which it often associates. Both sexes have *white patch on rear of wing*, conspicuous chiefly in flight. Male is greyish with chestnut wing-coverts, visible chiefly in flight, when *white belly contrasts with black tail-coverts*; the best mark on the water, at a distance, is the *black 'stern'* contrasting with the grey plumage; bill grey, legs orange-yellow; in eclipse resembles female, but retains chestnut wing-coverts. Female resembles female Mallard and Pintail; distinguished from latter by shorter tail, from both by orange panels on sides of bill and *white wing-patch*. Flight like Mallard's, but wings are more pointed.

Voice: Female quacks loudly in falling diminuendo '*kaaak-kaaak-kak-kak-kak*'. Male has a low single note.

Habitat: Like Mallard, but less cosmopolitan and seldom occurs on sea coast. Map 44.

BAIKAL TEAL *Anas formosa*   Pl. 15

Du – Siberische taling   Fr – Sarcelle élégante
Ge – Gluckente   Sw – Gulkindad kricka

Identification: 16″. Larger than Teal. Male has unmistakable *creamy side of head, crossed by black vertical mark from eye to chin*; crown, hind neck and chin black; bold green crescent edged white curving from eye to nape and round side of neck; long, drooping scapulars rufous, cream and black; pinkish breast, grey flanks, black stern, the three colours separated by *two vertical white stripes*. Female resembles female Teal, but distinguished by *bold whitish spot at base of bill* and broken supercilium above dark eye-stripe. Bill and rather long legs grey. Behaviour resembles Teal's, but flight less swift, less erratic.

Voice: More noisy than Teal. Male has curious deep chuckling notes '*wot-wot*' or '*proop*'. Female quacks like Teal.

Habitat and Range: Mainly a fresh-water duck, though occasionally seen at sea. Vagrant from Asia to N., C., W. (including Britain), and S. Europe.

TEAL *Anas crecca*   Pls. 11, 16, 18

Du – Wintertaling   Fr – Sarcelle d'hiver
Ge – Krickente   Sw – Kricka

Identification: 14″. Smallest European duck. Male has conspicuous *horizontal white stripe* on scapulars, *dark chestnut head with curving green eye-patch* and *creamy-buff patches* either side of black 'stern'. At a distance male looks like a *small grey duck with* a *dark head*. Both sexes have glossy green and black speculum and double wing-bar. Female speckled brown and buff; paler and spotted below; distinguished from similar female Garganey by lack of distinct face pattern and *larger, brighter green speculum*. Flight very rapid, in very compact flocks, usually low, often erratic. Male Green-winged Teal *A. c. carolinensis* (subspecies), accidental in Europe, has *vertical* white mark in front of wing, instead of horizontal bar above wing.

Voice: Very vocal. Male has short, low musical '*krrit*'; female, a high, harsh quack; feeding flock makes pleasant chuckling chorus of short nasal notes, like sound of child's toy squeaker.

Habitat: Reedy pools and streams. In winter, frequents marshes, occasionally estuaries and sea coasts. Breeds on moors, marshes, among bracken in woods, often far from open water. Map 45.

MALLARD *Anas platyrhynchos*   Pls. 11, 16, 18

Du – Wilde eend   Fr – Canard colvert
Ge – Stockente   Sw – Gräsand

Identification: 23″. Male has *glossy green head, narrow white collar, purplish-brown breast*, pale grey under-parts, white tail with curled black centre feathers, yellowish bill. Female is mottled brown, with brownish bill (often mottled orange at sides). Both sexes have broad purple speculum between two white bars (very conspicuous in flight), and orange legs. Male in eclipse resembles dark female, but with brighter speculum, darker crown and ruddier breast. Flight rapid, with shallow wing-beats. Female distinguished from Gadwall by larger size, browner coloration, *purple* speculum, less pointed wings, also sits lower in water; from female Pintail by heavier bill and head, thicker neck, white *both sides* of purple speculum, shorter whitish tail; from female Shoveler by larger size, much smaller bill, longer neck. See also male Red-breasted Merganser.

Voice: Male has quiet '*yeeb*'; female quacks loudly.

Habitat: Almost any water; in winter also on sea coasts and estuaries. Nests beneath undergrowth near water, occasionally in holes. Map 46.

Postures of Ducks on Land

Marsh and Pond ducks (Surface-feeders)	*Estuary and Sea-ducks (Divers)*	*Saw-bills (Divers)*	*Stiff-tails (Divers)*	*Shelducks (Surface-feeders)*

PINTAIL *Anas acuta*   **Pls. 11, 16, 18**
Du – Pijlstaart   Fr – Canard pilet
Ge – Spiessente   Sw – Stjärtand

Identification: 22″. A slender, long-necked, surface-feeding duck with a pointed tail. Male has chocolate-brown head and neck, with *conspicuous white streak* from white breast up each side of neck, and long, *needle-pointed tail*. Upper-parts and flanks grey. Male in eclipse and when young resembles female, but with darker upper-parts. Female distinguished from similar females of Mallard, Gadwall and Wigeon by slim shape, thin neck, more pointed tail, obscure speculum and grey bill; in flight, light border on rear of wing is useful detail. Only other duck with long tail is Long-tailed Duck which is smaller, with largely *white* head and is a maritime *diving* duck.

Voice: Seldom vocal. Male has a low whistle. Female has growling note and a low quack.

Habitat: Chiefly coastal in winter. As Wigeon in breeding season, but also nests in sand-dunes. Map 47.

GARGANEY *Anas querquedula*   **Pls. 11, 16, 18**
Du – Zomertaling   Fr – Sarcelle d'été
Ge – Knäkente   Sw – Årta

Identification: 15″. Only slightly larger than Teal, but with more slender neck, flatter crown and straighter bill. Male distinguished in flight by *pale blue-grey fore-wing*, sharply contrasting brown breast and white belly; easily identified when at rest by *conspicuous curving white streak from eye to nape*, also by long drooping black and white scapulars; in eclipse resembles female, but is always distinguishable by blue-grey shoulders. Female like female Teal, but identified by striped head pattern (particularly whitish supercilium and cheeks), paler shoulders and indistinct speculum. Behaviour and feeding habits more like Shoveler's than Teal's. Flight very rapid and agile.

Voice: Male makes peculiar dry rattling or grating noise. Female's quack is like female Teal's, but shorter.

Habitat: Much as Teal, but seldom on salt water. Breeds in long grass or rank vegetation near water. Map 48.

BLUE-WINGED TEAL   *Anas discors*   Pl. 15

Du – Blauwvleugeltaling   Fr – Sarcelle soucrourou
Ge – Blauflügelente   Sw – Amerikansk årta

Identification: 15″. Size of Garganey. Male distinguished by dark grey-brown head with *large white crescent in front of eye*; under tail-coverts black, bordered in front by *conspicuous white patch*; in flight *pale, chalky-blue fore-wing* is brighter, less grey than Garganey's, similar to Shoveler's, but latter is easily distinguished by huge bill. Female resembles female Garganey, but has darker plumage, brighter blue fore-wing and a longer, rather straight bill; is separable from both Garganey and escaped Cinnamon Teal *A. cyanoptera* by distinctive whitish spot on side of face at base of bill. Male's speculum green with white in front; female's duller. Male's bill black; female's dusky with paler base and edges.

Voice: Male has short squeaking note; female quacks faintly.

Habitat and Range: In winter frequents large marshes, rice fields, small ponds. Breeds around fresh-water ponds. Vagrant from N. America to W. (including Britain), N. and C. Europe.

SHOVELER   *Anas clypeata*   Pls. 11, 16, 18

Du – Slobeend   Fr – Canard souchet
Ge – Löffelente   Sw – Skedand

Identification: 20″. Distinguished from all other ducks by *huge spatulate bill*. Male is largely black and white above, with green-glossed head, *chestnut belly and flanks*, white breast and pale blue patch on fore-wing. At rest or flying overhead male has unique pattern: *dark-white-dark-white-dark*. Female is mottled brownish, like Mallard, but has *blue shoulders* (so has male Garganey). On water sits very low in front, with bill pointing downwards. In flight-silhouette *wings appear set far back*.

Voice: Flight-note a deep '*tuk-tuk*'. Male has low double quack; female's resembles Mallard's, though less loud.

Habitat: Less maritime than other surface-feeders. Usually in marshes and over-grown ponds. Breeds in water-meadows, marshes, bushy commons. Map 49.

MARBLED DUCK   *Marmaronetta angustirostris*   Pl. 11

Du – Marmereend   Fr – Sarcelle marbrée
Ge – Marmelente   Sw – Marmorand

Identification: 16″. Slightly larger than Teal with longer neck and bigger head. Distinguished by light and dark brown 'marbled' or dappled plumage with *dark patch or smudge through eye*. Looks uniform pale grey-brown at a distance, with dark eye-patch. No pattern in flight, except pale secondaries and white-tipped tail. Male has slight crest on nape. Juvenile is yellower below, with dark stripe through eye and two whitish spots on wing. Behaviour sluggish and retiring.

Voice: Male has a low wheezing croak; female a feeble quack.

Habitat and Range: A fresh-water species, preferring overgrown to open water. Nests near water, along stream banks, etc. Summer visitor S. Spain, has occasionally bred elsewhere in S. Europe, otherwise vagrant to S., C. and E. Europe.

RED-CRESTED POCHARD *Netta rufina*   Pls. 12, 17, 19

Du – Krooneend	Fr – Nette rousse
Ge – Kolbenente	Sw – Rödhuvad dykand

Identification: 22″. A plump, large-headed duck, sitting high in the water. Male has *red bill*, *rich chestnut head* with paler erectile crown, dark brown upper-parts, black neck, breast and belly-stripe, with gleaming white flanks. In flight shows broad white band *almost full length of wing*. In eclipse resembles female, except for crest and red bill, which also distinguish it from smaller Pochard. Female is drab brown with *pale greyish cheeks contrasting with dark brown crown*; wing-bar dingy white. Female Common Scoter is only other brown duck with pale cheeks, but has stouter bill and no white on wing.

Voice: A grating *'kurr'*, usually in flight.

Habitat: Large reedy fresh-water lakes, or brackish lagoons, seldom on sea. Breeds among vegetation on islands in lagoons. Map 50.

POCHARD *Aythya ferina*   Pls. 12, 17, 19

Du – Tafeleend	Fr – Fuligule milouin
Ge – Tafelente	Sw – Brunand

Identification: 18″. High crown and long, sloping profile to head. Male easily distinguished by *uniform dark chestnut head and neck*, contrasting with black breast and pale grey body. Black bill with pale blue band, grey wing-band and absence of white on wings separate male from Red-crested Pochard (red bill, white on wing). In eclipse resembles female, but is greyer above. Female has brown head and fore-parts; differs from female Scaup and Tufted by indistinct pale patch around bill and chin, bluish ring around bill, and grey (not white) wing-band. Seldom on land, resting on water by day and feeding at dawn and dusk. Dives freely. See also Wigeon.

Voice: Male has hoarse wheezing note. Female makes harsh growling noise. Usually silent, but displaying groups make quiet whistling chorus.

Habitat: Seldom on sea. Frequents large and small lakes, backwaters, etc. Breeds in dense reeds. Map 51.

RING-NECKED DUCK *Aythya collaris*   Pl. 15

Du – Amerikaanse kuifeend	Fr – Fuligule à bec cerclé
Ge – Halsringente	Sw – Ringand

Identification: 17″. Superficially resembles Tufted, or a *black*-backed Scaup, but distinguished by *short* crest, giving head a peaked appearance and (in male) by pale grey flanks coming to a *sharp white peak* in front of wing. Narrow chestnut collar visible only at close range. Both sexes have *two white rings on bill* (most visible in male). In flight shows broad *grey* rear edges to wings (Scaup shows white). Female is slightly paler and greyer than female Tufted and has conspicuous whitish eye-ring and whitish around base of bill. Dives and swims submerged.

Voice: Male has low, wheezy whistle; female growls.

Habitat and Range: Marshes, estuaries, sheltered bays. Vagrant from N. America to W. (including Britain), N. and C. Europe.

FERRUGINOUS DUCK *Aythya nyroca* **Pls. 12, 17, 19**
   Du – Witoogeend   Fr – Fuligule nyroca
   Ge – Moorente   Sw – Vitögd dykand
Identification: 16″. Smaller and more neatly built than Tufted. Both sexes have *rich, dark mahogany head, neck and breast*. White belly and wing-bar are often hidden when at rest. In distance can be confused (particularly the female) with female Tufted Duck, but is usually distinguishable by *white under tail-coverts* and, in flight, by *large curved white wing-bars*; never has white at base of bill. (Tufted occasionally shows white beneath tail, but when seen together Ferruginous sits higher in water and holds tail higher.) Male has *white eyes*. Female duller, with brown eyes. Juvenile like female, but has mottled under-parts; distinguished from somewhat similar female Pochard by darker, much more rufous appearance, brown flanks and white wing-bar. Behaviour more active than Pochard.
Voice: A quiet '*tuk-tuk-tuk*' and low growling notes.
Habitat: Similar to Pochard. Map 52.

TUFTED DUCK *Aythya fuligula* **Pls. 12, 17, 19**
   Du – Kuifeend   Fr – Fuligule morillon
   Ge – Reiherente   Sw – Vigg
Identification: 17″. Black and white male can be confused with slightly larger Scaup, but is distinguished by *uniform black upper-parts and thin drooping crest*. In eclipse resembles dark female. Female is browner, with a rudimentary crest and sometimes a light patch at base of bill (female Scaup looks similar, but shows more white on face than Tufted, also paler upper-parts and larger bill). In flight Tufted and Scaup adults both show bold white bar almost full length of wing. See also Ferruginous Duck.
Voice: Male has very soft whistling courtship note. Female growls like female Pochard.
Habitat: Seldom on sea. Frequents large and small lakes, often joining tame ducks in parks. Breeds, often sociably, on lakes and ponds. Map 53.

SCAUP *Aythya marila* **Pls. 12, 17, 19**
   Du – Toppereend   Fr – Fuligule milouinan
   Ge – Bergente   Sw – Bergand
Identification: 19″. In distance male looks *black both ends and white in the middle*. Head, fore-parts and 'stern' are black, *back pale grey*, flanks and under-parts white. Bill blue-grey. Distinguished from slightly smaller male Tufted by *grey back*, lack of crest and broader beam. In eclipse resembles female, but with greyish back and little or no white on face. Female distinguished from female Tufted by *bold white patch around base of bill and broader beam*. (Female and young Tufted often have pale patch, but never as large.) Young females of both species are very difficult to separate. Young male Scaup is distinguished by greyish back. In flight both sexes show bold white wing-bar, like Tufted. Flies in close irregular flocks or lines. Expert diver, often in rough sea.
Voice: Seldom vocal. Male has soft crooning courtship notes. Female has low harsh '*karr-karr*'.
Habitat: Maritime except when breeding; usually in bays and estuaries. Breeds sociably on lake islands. Map 54.

EIDER *Somateria mollissima*   **Pls. 13, 17, 19**
  Du – Eidereend   Fr – Eider à duvet
  Ge – Eiderente   Sw – Ejder
Identification: 23″. Distinguished from all other ducks by large size, long heavy body, elongated profile of head and distinctive flight. Male is only duck with *black belly and white back*; breast white, tinged pinkish, whole fore-wing white, head white with black crown and pale green patches on nape; easily distinguished from male King Eider by white back and long profile of head. In protracted eclipse male very variable, patchy blackish with lighter breast and white fore-wings. Female is brown, *closely barred* with black (only eiders are so marked); distinguished from female scoters, with which eiders often associate, by warmer brown *barred* plumage; from female King Eider by flatter profile of head (see diagram, Pl. 13). Young male at first somewhat like female, later developing chocolate head and white areas irregularly. Usually flies low, in single file, with head carried rather low.
Voice: Male has low moaning '*coo-roo-uh*', second syllable rising and emphasized. Female has grating '*cor-r-r*'.
Habitat: Strongly maritime, including rocky coasts. Breeds along coasts; locally inland around lakes, or on river islands. Map 55.

KING EIDER *Somateria spectabilis*   **Pls. 13, 17, 19**
  Du – Koningseidereend   Fr – Eider à tête grise
  Ge – Prachteiderente   Sw – Praktejder
Identification: 22″. At distance male's *fore-parts appear white, rear-parts black* (no other duck gives this effect). Distinguished from Eider by *black back*, very different shape and colours of head. Crown and nape pearl-grey, face tinged green; *short bill has large orange shield*; fore-wing has large white patch. Female distinguished from Eider by *less flat profile from forehead to stubby bill* (see diagram, Pl. 13) and considerably more rufous plumage; some females have unmarked throats giving head contrasting effect not seen in Eider. In breeding plumage female has greyish head and behind neck, throat therefore looks darker; scapulars rusty-brown with dark centres, giving stronger contrast than in female Eider. Young male has pale breast and dark brown head, amount of white varying as it acquires adult plumage. (Female Goldeneye also has dark brown head but is greyer bird, with square white wing-patches.)
Voice: As Eider, but also a rapid gabbling.
Habitat and Range: As Eider but usually breeds fairly sociably by fresh-water ponds on tundra. In summer non-breeding N. Norway, Iceland. Winters on N. Norwegian coast south to Arctic Circle, Faeroes, Iceland. Vagrant elsewhere in N., W. (including Britain), C. and S. Europe.

STELLER'S EIDER *Polysticta stelleri*   **Pl. 13**
  Du – Steller's eidereend   Fr – Eider de Steller
  Ge – Scheckente   Sw – Alförrädare
Identification: 18″. Male unmistakable, a black and white bird with *rufous-buff under-parts, white head* with black eye-patch and throat and emerald-green patch on nape. *Round black spot* on right side of rufous breast is distinctive. *White fore-wing conspicuous in flight*. In eclipse looks like female except for wings. Female is more duck-like, with dark buffish plumage mottled brown; sides of head rufous; white wing-bar and purple speculum visible at short range.

Juvenile and female easily distinguished from other eiders by much smaller size and *very different shape of small head and bill* (see diagram, Pl. 13).

Voice: Male's crooning notes resemble Eider's but also some nasal, gull-like notes. Female has growling note.

Habitat and Range: Winters along rocky northern coasts. Breeds on tundra. In winter N. Norway (may have bred) and Baltic. Vagrant elsewhere in N., C. and W. Europe (including Britain).

HARLEQUIN *Histrionicus histrionicus* Pls. 13, 17, 19

Du – Harlekijneend   Fr – Garrot arlequin
Ge – Kragenente   Sw – Strömand

Identification: 17″. A small, very dark, short-billed duck. Male has dark blue-grey plumage (looks black at distance) with *chestnut flanks and bizarre pattern of white spots and streaks* on head, neck and breast. Has same flight-silhouette as Goldeneye, but is *uniformly dark below*. In eclipse male distinguished from female by dark slate-grey upper-parts and lack of white on breast. Female uniformly dark brown with mottled brown and whitish breast, *two indistinct white spots in front of eye, one bright spot behind eye*; distinguished from female Velvet and Surf Scoters by small size, small bill; easily confused with young Long-tailed which, however, is much whiter on belly. Swims buoyantly, jerking head constantly, often cocking tail. Likes to dive in rough surf.

Voice: Usually silent, but male has short quiet whistle. Female croaks harshly.

Habitat and Range: Winters along steep coasts with plenty of submerged rocks. Breeds socially on islands in swift rivers, usually near rough water or waterfalls. Resident Iceland. Vagrant elsewhere in N., W. (including Britain), C. and S. Europe.

LONG-TAILED DUCK *Clangula hyemalis* Pls, 13, 17, 19

Du – IJseend   Fr – Harelde de Miquelon
Ge – Eisente   Sw – Alfågel
N. Am – Old Squaw

Identification: Male 21″, including *long pointed tail-feathers*; female 16″. The only sea-duck combining *white on body with uniform dark wings*; also distinguished by small round head and short bill. Male in winter boldly patterned with dark brown and white: head, neck, belly and scapulars white; breast, back and wings blackish-brown; large dark patch on side of neck; bill banded pink and black. Male in summer is mostly dark brown, with white belly and white patch around eye. Female in winter is dark above, white below, with brown breast-band; head white with blackish crown, *cheek-spot* and bill; normal length tail; in summer is darker, with head pattern similar to male. Juvenile like female, but greyer, with brownish throat. Swims buoyantly, diving with agility in rough sea. Only other long-tailed duck is the larger, *dark-headed* Pintail, which is a coastal or inland surface-feeder.

Voice: Noisy. Male has lively call of about four loud yodelling notes, giving musical goose-like effect from distant flock. Female has low barking note.

Habitat: Mainly maritime except in breeding season. Nests on lake islands, in tundra, or among arctic scrub. Map 56.

COMMON SCOTER *Melanitta nigra*   **Pls. 13, 17, 19**
   Du – Zwarte zeeëend   Fr – Macreuse noire
   Ge – Trauerente   Sw – Sjöorre
Identification: 19″. Male is *the only entirely black duck*; black bill has bright orange-yellow ridge-patch and large black knob at base. Female and immature are dark brown with *whitish cheeks and throat, contrasting with dark crown* and mottled brownish-white under-parts; distinguished from female Red-crested Pochard (which also has pale cheeks but is not a sea-duck) by darker appearance, squat shape and *lack of wing-bar*; from female Velvet and Surf Scoters by different face pattern and by blackish (not reddish) feet (female Velvet Scoter also has conspicuous white wing-bar in flight). Swims buoyantly, with sharply pointed tail often raised. Flight strong, usually in wavering lines or groups.
Voice: Male has variety of melodious, cooing notes and a rapid tittering cry. Female growls harshly.
Habitat: Chiefly maritime except in breeding season, but prefers quieter water than Velvet Scoter. Breeds around lakes on high moors or tundra. Map 57.

SURF SCOTER *Melanitta perspicillata*   **Pls. 13, 17, 19**
   Du – Brilzeeëend   Fr – Macreuse à lunettes
   Ge – Brillenente   Sw – Vitnackad svärta
Identification: 21″. Male distinguished at reasonable range from other scoters by *white patches on forehead and nape* and more massive *red, white and yellow* bill. Both sexes have reddish legs, like Velvet Scoter. Female and immature usually have two whitish patches on side of head, like female and young Velvet Scoters, but both adults and young are distinguished by *absence of white on wings*; female may have whitish patch on nape. (Female and young Common Scoters have contrasting pale cheeks and dark crowns.)
Voice: Seldom vocal, but has a quavering nasal note.
Habitat and Range: Maritime and offshore outside breeding season. Vagrant from N. America to W. (including Britain), N. and C. Europe.

VELVET SCOTER *Melanitta fusca*   **Pls. 13, 17, 19**
   Du – Grote zeeëend   Fr – Macreuse brune
   Ge – Samtente   Sw – Swärta
   N. Am – White-winged Scoter
Identification: 22″. Heavily built, with swollen bill. Both sexes distinguished from smaller Common Scoter by *white wing-patch*, often hidden at rest, but conspicuous when wings are flapped. When diving, reddish feet are noticeable (Surf Scoter's also red, Common's black). Male has *small white patch below eye* and yellow sides to black bill. Female usually distinguishable from Common Scoter by two whitish patches on side of head (more pronounced in young birds); when these are absent, white on wings makes identification positive. Usually in small parties or singly, often with Eiders near shore.
Voice: Much less vocal than Common Scoter. Male's usual note a whistled '*whur-er*'. Female growls harshly.
Habitat: As Common Scoter, but often seen in rougher water. Breeding places vary from offshore islands and open tundra to undergrowth in northern forests. Map 58.

BARROW'S GOLDENEYE   *Bucephala islandica*   **Pl. 12**
  Du – IJslandse brilduiker   Fr – Garrot d'Islande
  Ge – Spatelente   Sw – Islandsknipa

Identification: 21″. An Iceland species. Easily mistaken for Goldeneye, though larger and heavier. Look for *crescent-shaped* white patch in front of eye (Goldeneye has *round* white spot). Male shows greater amount of black on sides of body, but Goldeneye in eclipse can look similar, though never as jet-black on head and wings. Barrow's head is *glossed purple* instead of green and is of remarkable shape, with more abrupt forehead, low rounded crown, and distinct mane on nape. Scapulars boldly barred black and white. Female very like female Goldeneye, but larger, with shorter, deeper bill, more abrupt forehead and slightly ragged nape. Behaviour, voice and habitat as in Goldeneye. Resident in Iceland. Vagrant elsewhere in N., C. and W. Europe.

GOLDENEYE   *Bucephala clangula*   **Pls. 12, 17, 19**
  Du – Brilduiker   Fr – Garrot à oeil d'or
  Ge – Schellente   Sw – Knipa

Identification: 18″. Male strikingly black and white; neck and under-parts white, back and tail black with *boldly streaked scapulars*; head is black, 'triangular' in shape, with short black bill. Distinguished by *large circular white spot between bill and eye*. Legs orange. In flight looks big-headed, short-necked, with conspicuous *square white wing-patches extending almost to front of wing*. In eclipse resembles female, but retains a blackish head and white chest. Female has mottled grey upper-parts with *chocolate-brown, triangular head, a white collar and large square white wing-patches* (showing on closed wing, unlike Tufted and Scaup). Immature is browner, without collar. Rises from water more rapidly than other diving ducks. Wings make characteristic whistling noise. See also Scaup and Barrow's Goldeneye.
Voice: Usually silent. Male has harsh nasal double note. Female's hoarse notes resemble Scaup's.
Habitat: Coastal waters, often also on inland lakes. Breeds in holes in trees, rabbit burrows, etc., along river banks and around wooded lakes. Map 59.

SMEW   *Mergus albellus*   **Pls. 14, 16, 18**
  Du – Nonnetje   Fr – Harle piette
  Ge – Zwergsäger   Sw – Salskrake

Identification: 16″. Much smaller, more duck-like and shorter-billed than other 'saw-bills'. Male looks *uniformly white with conspicuous black eye-patch*; at short range small drooping black and white crest is visible, also narrow black lines across fore-parts and above scapulars; flanks pale grey, back black; in flight looks darker above, with conspicuous black and white wings; in eclipse white wing-patches are larger than female's. Female is smaller and greyer, with slightly crested *chestnut cap and white cheeks and throat.* Immature has brownish-white wing-patches. See females of Red-crested Pochard and Common Scoter, which also have brown and white heads; see also winter Slavonian and Black-necked Grebes.
Voice: Usually silent, except for a low, grating 'uk-uk-uk'. Male has weak whistling note. Female's notes as female Goosander's.
Habitat: Lakes, reservoirs and rivers, occasionally in estuaries and along coasts. Nests in hollow trees near water. Map 60.

RED-BREASTED MERGANSER *Mergus serrator*   **Pls. 14, 16, 18**
Du – Middelste zaagbek   Fr – Harle huppé
Ge – Mittelsäger   Sw – Småskrake
Identification: 23". Smaller than Mallard, with rakish form, very narrow bill and legs, as in larger Goosander. Distinguished from latter by more conspicuous wispy *double crest*. The greenish-black head is separated from *dark chestnut breast-band by wide white collar*; flanks grey; wing pattern resembles Goosander's, but with two narrow black lines across the white patch. Female distinguished from very similar female Goosander by *brownish*-grey upperparts, diffuse white chin-patch, more conspicuous and ragged crest, duller head *blending* into whitish neck. More maritime than Goosander; both may occur on same lake or river.
Voice: Usually silent; male has rasping disyllabic courtship note. Female as female Goosander.
Habitat: Chiefly maritime outside breeding season. Breeds in heather, vegetation among rocks, etc., by wooded lakes or rivers, on islands in sea lochs and in tundra. Map 61.

GOOSANDER *Mergus merganser*   **Pls. 14, 16, 18**
Du – Grote zaagbek   Fr – Harle bièvre
Ge – Gänsesäger   Sw – Storskrake
N. Am – American Merganser
Identification: 26". Long-bodied and rakish. Larger and longer than Mallard, with very narrow red bill and feet. Male has *pinkish-white breast and underparts*, black back, *glossy greenish-black head*; easily identified in flight by white body and wings, with black head and primaries; distinguished from smaller and darker Red-breasted Merganser by lack of wispy crest and by uniform whitish breast, flanks and under-parts. Female has *crested chestnut head*, blue-grey upper-parts and flanks, white under-parts and a *square white wing-patch* conspicuous in flight; distinguished from very similar female Merganser by *sharp division* of chestnut fore-neck from white chest and blue-grey upper-parts. Flight-silhouette distinctively 'long-drawn'.
Voice: Usually silent. Male has double croaking note; female a guttural '*karr*'.
Habitat: Winters on large rivers, lakes, reservoirs. Breeds in hollow trees, holes in peat banks, etc., usually among trees near water, also beyond tree limit in north. Map 62.

RUDDY DUCK *Oxyura jamaicensis*   **Pl. 15**
Du – Zwartkopeend   Fr – Erismature à tête noire
Ge – Schwarzkopf-Ruderente   Sw – Amerikansk kopparand
Identification: 16". Resembles White-headed, but is smaller, with less white on head and the bill in both sexes *lacks the swollen base*. Male distinguished by *uniform ruddy upper-parts and flanks*, dark cap extending to neck; female by smaller, indistinct cheek-bar and stronger barring on under-parts. Both sexes are greyer in winter. Behaviour like White-headed.
Voice: Usually silent. Displaying male makes low chuckling '*chuck-uck-uck-ur-r-r*'.
Habitat: Fresh-water ponds, marshes. In winter also on large reservoirs. Escaped birds now feral in Britain; almost regular France, vagrant elsewhere in W. and C. Europe. (N. American origin.)

WHITE-HEADED DUCK *Oxyura leucocephala*   **Pl. 14**
   Du – Witkopeend   Fr – Erismature à tête blanche
   Ge – Ruderente   Sw – Kopparand
Identification: 18″. The only 'stiff-tail' duck in Europe apart from regionally feral Ruddy Duck. Identified by large head, plump body and long, stiff, pointed tail which is often cocked *vertically* to show white under tail-coverts. Male's bill, swollen at base, is *brilliant pale blue* in courtship season. Male has conspicuous *white head* with narrow black crown, black neck, brownish body. Female is darker, with dark cap, and pale cheek *crossed by a dark line*; also has swollen base to bill, which helps to distinguish from 'escaped' female Ruddy Duck. Behaviour grebe-like. Flight whirring, usually low over water, with characteristic silhouette of big head, stocky body, small uniform dark wings and long pointed tail (looking like projecting feet). Pintail and Long-tailed Ducks have long but flexible tails, smaller heads and thinner necks. See also Ruddy Duck.
Voice: Has various rapid ticking notes.
Habitat: Reedy inland waters and brackish lagoons. Nests among reeds and aquatic vegetation near water. Map 63.

KITES, VULTURES, HARRIERS, HAWKS, BUZZARDS, EAGLES:
Accipitridae

Kites have long, angular wings, forked tails, buoyant, gliding flight. Sexes similar. Tree nesting.
Vultures are very large, eagle-like, with huge wing-spans, short tails and naked heads (except Lammergeier). Sexes similar. Cliff or tree nesting.
Harriers are slim, with long, slightly angled wings and long tails. Flight usually low and wavering, with wings held in shallow V. Ground or reed nesting.
Hawks are smaller than buzzards, with short, rounded wings and long tails. Cruise swiftly among trees at low altitudes and chase or pounce on prey. Females much larger than males. Tree nesting.
Buzzards have broad wings, broad rounded tails and relatively smaller heads and bills than eagles. Usually seen circling and soaring. Sexes similar. Tree and cliff nesting.
Eagles have prominent, projecting heads, unusually deep bills; long, broadended wings: soaring, majestic flight. Sexes similar. Tree or cliff nesting.
   Exceptions to these groupings are Osprey and Short-toed Eagle.

HONEY BUZZARD *Pernis apivorus*   **Pls. 23, 24**
   Du – Wespendief   Fr – Bondrée apivore
   Ge – Wespenbussard   Sw – Bivråk
Identification: 20–23″. Flight-silhouette very different from Buzzard's and Rough-legged Buzzard's in having *narrow-based* broad wings, *longer* tail and *smaller (pigeon-like) head on longer neck*; tail has *dark terminal band and two narrower bands nearer base*; markings on underparts and beneath dark-edged wings are brighter. Plumage very variable. Upper-parts dark brown, head greyish; under-parts heavily scalloped with dark brown, sometimes completely brown. Immature often has creamy marking on head; under-parts streaked.

Soars and hovers less than Buzzard; when gliding, *wings droop very slightly*, with upturned tips. Feeds on larvae of wasps and bees, sometimes mice, small birds, eggs.

Voice: A high squeaky '*kee-er*', quite unlike Buzzard's mewing; also a rapid '*kikiki*'.

Habitat: Open glades or outskirts of woods. Usually builds on old nest of crow. Map 64.

BLACK-SHOULDERED KITE *Elanus caeruleus*   Pl. 21

Du – Grijze wouw   Fr – Elanion blanc
Ge – Gleitaar   Sw – Svartvingad glada

Identification: 13″. A small, stumpy hawk, with long wings and shortish forked tail, which is sometimes held erect. Head whitish, *upper-parts pale blue-grey*, with *whitish tail and black 'shoulders'*. Primaries grey above, but black underneath, in sharp contrast to pure white under-parts. Eyes dark red. Immature grey-brown above, white below, tinged with rufous and lightly streaked with brown. Behaviour not at all kite-like: hovers slowly on long wings, flies slowly like miniature harrier, or more quickly on sharply angled wings. Feeds on mice, large insects, etc. Often crepuscular.

Voice: A weak, whistling '*gree-er*'.

Habitat and Range: Cultivated areas with scattered trees, or woodland glades, forest edges, etc. Nests fairly low in trees. Resident Portugal and Spain. Vagrant elsewhere in S., W., C. and E. Europe.

BLACK KITE *Milvus migrans*   Pls. 21, 22

Du – Zwarte wouw   Fr – Milan noir
Ge – Schwarzer Milan   Sw – Brun glada

Identification: 22″. Resembles Red Kite, but easily distinguished by *much less forked tail* which can look almost straight-ended in flight, slightly smaller size and *much darker plumage*; upper wing-coverts have paler panel from base of wing to carpal joint; is also more sociable and frequently seen over inland waters. Faint whitish patches beneath wings of immature resemble Red Kite's, but are absent in adults. Flight and feeding habits like Red Kite's but also feeds on dead fish. Where numerous, flocks quickly gather on carrion. When gliding holds wings level, not in shallow V like Marsh Harrier, which see.

Voice: Very noisy in breeding season. A thin, quavering, gull-like squeal, sometimes followed by a chatter.

Habitat: In western range usually near lakes or rivers, in areas with woods or scattered trees. In south and east of range more frequently in drier localities and villages. Nests, often sociably, in trees, occasionally on old nest of crow. Map 65.

RED KITE *Milvus milvus*   Pls. 21, 22

Du – Rode wouw   Fr – Milan royal
Ge – Roter Milan   Sw – Glada

Identification: 24″. Easily distinguished by *long, deeply forked chestnut tail*, narrow, strongly angled wings, with *large whitish patches* on undersides of black primaries, red-brown upper-parts with pale edges to feathers, dark-streaked rufous under-parts and *streaked whitish head*. Immature is paler, with brownish head. Effortless soaring flight resembles Buzzard's, but silhouette is unmistakably different and normal flight much more buoyant. Partial to carrion,

70 ACCIPITRIDAE

but also preys on animals as large as rabbits, and small birds. Distinguished from Black Kite by more deeply forked tail, more rufous plumage and more slender silhouette.

Voice: A high, Buzzard-like mewing '*hi-hi-heea*'.

Habitat: Usually in wooded hills, but also locally in lowlands and open country with scattered trees. Nests in trees, occasionally on old nest of crow. Map 66.

WHITE-TAILED EAGLE *Haliaeetus albicilla*   **Pls. 25, 26**
   Du – Zeearend   Fr – Pygargue à queue blanche
   Ge – Seeadler   Sw – Havsörn
   N. Am – Gray Sea Eagle

Identification: 27–36″. A very bulky eagle with *huge, broad, blunt-ended wings and heavy, projecting head*. Adult distinguished by *short wedge-shaped white tail*, pale brownish head and heavy yellow bill. Immature has blackish-brown head, tail and bill, but is readily distinguishable from Golden Eagle by tail being much shorter and wedge-shaped (not full and squared, nor with largely white base of immature Golden). Tarsi are unfeathered. Soars on straight wings, giving vulture-like silhouette. Catches fish on surface, in low cruising flight, occasionally plunging for them; catches mammals as large as weakling Roe Deer, birds as large as ducks; also eats carrion.

Voice: A creaking '*kri, kri, kri*', and a lower, barking '*kra*'.

Habitat: Rocky coasts, or remote inland waters. Nests on cliff-face, or on top of rocky pinnacle, in large trees, occasionally on ground. Map 67.

LAMMERGEIER (BEARDED VULTURE) *Gypaetus barbatus*
                                              Pl. 20
   Du – Lammergier   Fr – Gypaète barbu
   Ge – Bartgeier   Sw – Gamörn

Identification: 40–45″. Distinguished from other vultures by distinctive flight-silhouette, more like huge falcon than vulture, with *long, narrow, angled wings and long diamond-shaped dark tail*. Adults have greyish-black upper-parts, wings and tail, mainly *buff* head with conspicuous broad black patch slanting forward from eye to prominent bunch of black bristles below bill. Under-parts yellowish-orange, vivid orange on breast, contrasting with dark wings. Immature has dark head and neck. Less sluggish than other vultures. Normally solitary.

Voice: Has a thin, querulous cry '*quee-er*'.

Habitat: Remote mountain ranges. Nests in caves on precipices. Map 68.

EGYPTIAN VULTURE *Neophron percnopterus*   **Pl. 20**
   Du – Aasgier   Fr – Percnoptère d'Egypte
   Ge – Schmutzgeier   Sw – Smutsgam

Identification: 23–26″. Much smaller than other vultures. Has distinctive flight-silhouette, with *long, straight-edged but pointed black and white wings* and wedge-shaped *white* tail. Head and throat of adults have *bare yellow skin*, above a shaggy whitish ruff. Plumage dingy white, with contrasting blackish primaries. Bill is *thinner* than in other vultures. Immature varies according to age from dark brown to dirty whitish, with brownish head and ruff. Although not very sociable, occasionally two or three will join Griffons at carcass to eat

what the much larger birds leave. Scavenges for offal. Usually silent. See White Stork, which has rather similar flight pattern.
Habitat: As Griffon, but also frequents village refuse dumps; nests on cliffs. Map 69.

GRIFFON VULTURE   *Gyps fulvus*   Pl. 20
Du – Vale gier   Fr – Vautour fauve
Ge – Gänsegeier   Sw – Gåsgam
Identification: 38–41″. Distinguished from other vultures by flight-silhouette: very long, broad wings with widely spread primaries forming rounded ends *and very short, dark, squared tail*; undersides of wings have pale bars from axillaries towards carpal joint; small head is sunk well back into ruff. Sandy plumage contrasts with dark wing- and tail-feathers. Head and neck covered with white down. Ruff is *pale buffish* in adult, brown in juvenile. Sociable when roosting and feeding. See also Black Vulture.
Voice: Croaking and whistling notes when breeding, roosting or at carcasses.
Habitat: Ranges over all types of country, but normal habitat is mountainous. Breeds sociably in caves, or on ledges. Map 70.

BLACK VULTURE   *Aegypius monachus*   Pl. 20
Du – Monniksgier   Fr – Vautour moine
Ge – Mönchsgeier   Sw – Grågam
Identification: 39–42″. In size and flight-silhouette very like Griffon, but distinguished by larger head, deeper, more massive bill and *longer, slightly wedge-shaped tail* (which, however, is often worn down and can resemble Griffon's); also by *uniform sooty-brown* plumage (looks black at a distance). Seen from above, *wing-coverts are darker* than flight-feathers; seen from below lack typical barring of Griffon. Neck bare bluish-pink skin, above *brown* ruff. Behaviour and voice like Griffon's. Usually rather solitary.
Habitat: Remote mountains and plains. Nests in trees, very occasionally on ledge on cliff-face. Map 71.

SHORT-TOED EAGLE   *Circaetus gallicus*   Pl. 24
Du – Slangenarend   Fr – Circaète Jean-le-Blanc
Ge – Schlangenadler   Sw – Ormörn
Identification: 25–27″. Larger than Osprey. Under-parts and beneath wings *nearly uniform white except for dark upper-breast and throat* (dark markings occasionally lacking). Seen closely, under-surfaces of wings have lines of small dark spots. Has *round* owl-like head, small bill and large orange eyes. Upperparts grey-brown, with blackish primaries. Rather long tail has 3–4 indistinct dark bars. Juvenile browner below, with dark bars. Flight is powerful, wings level when soaring; hovers frequently, with legs dangling. Feeds on snakes, lizards, frogs, etc. See also Honey Buzzard.
Voice: Rather noisy. A harsh, plaintive '*jee*', a rather weak '*ok, ok, ok*', or '*mew-ok*'.
Habitat: Mountain slopes and gorges, secluded woodlands, plantations, marshy plains, coastal dunes. Nests in tree. Map 72.

MARSH HARRIER   *Circus aeruginosus*   **Pls. 21, 22**
  Du – Bruine kuikendief   Fr – Busard des roseaux
  Ge – Rohrweihe   Sw – Brun kärrhök

Identification: 19–22″. Distinguished from other harriers by larger size, heavier build, *broader wings* and *absence of white on rump*. Has *low, quartering flight*, with occasional wing-beats and long, wavering glides, with wings in shallow V. Plumage variable. Adult male distinguished from other harriers by *dark mantle and secondary wing-coverts*, contrasting with grey tail and secondaries; streaked buffish head, nape and breast and rich brown under-parts. Female and immature male usually lack grey and are fairly uniform dark chocolate-brown with *pale heads and shoulders* (females sometimes are all-dark, suggesting Black Kite). First-winter birds are dark chocolate-brown with *bright creamy* crown and throat. Hunts by pouncing from low altitude into reeds, etc.
Voice: A high, Lapwing-like '*quee-a*' in display and a chattering alarm.
Habitat: Almost invariably fens, swamps and marshes, with large areas of dense reeds. Builds large nest in reed-bed usually surrounded by water. Map 73.

HEN HARRIER   *Circus cyaneus*   **Pls. 21, 22**
  Du – Blauwe kuikendief   Fr – Busard Saint-Martin
  Ge – Kornweihe   Sw – Blå kärrhök
  N. Am – Marsh Hawk

Identification: 17–20″. Distinguished from very similar Montagu's by *more conspicuous white on rump*, also, when seen together, by slightly heavier build (particularly in female), slightly broader wings and tail. Ash-grey male distinguished by *white rump, blackish trailing edge to secondaries* (Montagu's has two black bars in centre of wing) and unstreaked belly and thighs. Female and immature have dark brown upper-parts and broadly streaked buffish under-parts. Juvenile distinguished from young Montagu's by *streaked under-parts*. Flight distinctive, usually very low, gliding buoyantly with wings held in shallow V. See also Pallid Harrier.
Voice: A high chattering '*ke-ke-ke*'; also a long wailing '*pee-e*'.
Habitat: More varied than Montagu's. Nests on ground on moors, in swamps, thickets, or crops. Map 74.

PALLID HARRIER   *Circus macrourus*   **Pl. 21**
  Du – Steppenkuikendief   Fr – Busard pâle
  Ge – Steppenweihe   Sw – Stäpphök

Identification: 17–19″. Male looks strikingly white about head and under-parts, with pale blue-grey tail and wings and contrasting primaries *forming small black wedge on wing-tip*. Distinguished from pale male Hen Harrier by *grey* instead of pure white rump, *white* instead of grey breast and sides of head, less black on wing-tips and *lack of dark trailing edge to secondaries*; from pale male Montagu's by paler grey upper-parts, *lack of black wing-bars and unstreaked white under-parts and thighs*. Female and first-winter birds not distinguishable in the field from those of Montagu's, but juvenile distinguished from young Hen Harrier by unstreaked rufous under-parts. Behaviour as Montagu's. Female's cry '*preee-pri-pri-pri*' is distinctive.
Habitat: As Hen Harrier, but also in dry steppes, open plains and hill country with sparse trees. Map 75.

MONTAGU'S HARRIER   *Circus pygargus*   **Pls. 21, 22**
    Du – Grauwe kuikendief   Fr – Busard cendré
    Ge – Wiesenweihe   Sw – Mindre kärrhök
Identification: 16–18″. Slightly smaller and slimmer than Hen Harrier, *with narrower, more pointed wings and noticeably more buoyant flight.* Female closely resembles Hen Harrier, though usually with less white on rump. Male distinguished from Hen Harrier by *greyish* instead of pure white rump, *narrow black wing-bars in centre of wing and brown streaks on belly and thighs.* Immature like female, but with unstreaked rich rufous under-parts. Behaviour like Hen Harrier's. See also Pallid Harrier.
Voice: Querulous '*kek-kek-kek*', more shrill than Hen Harrier's chatter.
Habitat: Marshes, fens, moors with clumps of trees, or agricultural land. Nests in wet vegetation, or on dry heaths, occasionally in cornfields. Map 76.

GOSHAWK   *Accipiter gentilis*   **Pls. 23, 28**
    Du – Havik   Fr – Autour des palombes
    Ge – Habicht   Sw – Duvhök
Identification: 19–24″. Female much larger than male. Resembles *very large female Sparrowhawk* but with sturdier legs and broad-based wings, which, however, often look pointed except when soaring. Upper-parts dark, with *whitish stripe* above and behind eye; under-parts whitish, closely barred with dark brown and with *conspicuous white under tail-coverts.* Juvenile paler above, with buffish under-parts, boldly marked, with dark-brown, drop-shaped streaks. Dashes after birds, doubling among trees with extreme agility. Hunting flight among trees is fast and low, with a few rapid wing-beats and long glides. See female Sparrowhawk.
Voice: A short mew and a loud chattering '*gek-gek-gek*'.
Habitat: Woods (especially coniferous), often near open country. Builds large nest, or adopts old nests of other birds, in secluded wood. Map 77.

SPARROWHAWK   *Accipiter nisus*   **Pls. 23, 28**
    Du – Sperwer   Fr – Epervier d'Europe
    Ge – Sperber   Sw – Sparvhök
Identification: 11–15″. Female much larger than male. Distinguished from other small birds of prey by combination of *short rounded wings and long tail.* Adults have closely barred under-parts and long yellow legs. Male has dark slate-grey upper-parts with rufous cheeks and whitish spot on nape, under-parts finely barred with red-brown, tail boldly banded with grey and dark brown. Female has blackish-brown upper-parts, with white stripe above and behind eye and whitish under-parts closely barred with grey. Female looks like Goshawk, but latter is larger, with relatively shorter tail and white under-tail coverts. Immature like brown female, but is more boldly and irregularly barred below. Hunts by cruising just above hedges, or through woodlands, and pouncing on small birds and other animals. Normal flight consists of a few rapid wing-beats between long glides. See also Levant Sparrowhawk.
Voice: Has large vocabulary in breeding season: a loud, rapid '*kek-kek-kek*', '*keeow*', '*kew*', etc.
Habitat: Chiefly woodlands and farmlands, with coppices, plantations, etc. Nests in spruce or other conifer in mixed woods, occasionally in tall bushes, thickets, etc. Map 78.

Falcons
Pointed wings, narrow tail

Harriers
Long wings, long tail

Accipiters
(Bird Hawks)

Buzzards
Broad wings,
broad rounded tail

Short rounded wings,
long tail

Basic Flight-silhouettes

LEVANT SPARROWHAWK *Accipiter brevipes*   **Pl. 75**
Du – Balkansperwer   Fr – Epervier à pieds courts
Ge – Kurzfangsperber   Sw – Balkanhök
Identification: 13–15″. Female often difficult to distinguish from female
Sparrowhawk, but male is distinctive. Both sexes have *white under-surfaces to
wings with dark wing-tips* and red-brown (not yellow) eyes; wings more pointed
than Sparrowhawk's. Male larger than male Sparrowhawk (disparity between
sexes is less), has *clear blue-grey on nape, mantle and upper wing-surfaces*; under-
parts can look almost white, but usually have buff towards wing-roots
contrasting with white lower wing-surfaces; cheeks greyish (not rufous), with
buff on sides of neck. Female greyer above than female Sparrowhawk, with
brown spots on throat and *blackish wing-tips*. Immature has large brown spots
on very white under-parts.
Voice: A shrill '*keeveck-veck-veck*' (very unlike Sparrowhawk).
Habitat: Much as Sparrowhawk, though more often in the open and in
deciduous woods. Map 79.

BUZZARD *Buteo buteo*   **Pls. 23, 24**
Du – Buizerd   Fr – Buse variable
Ge – Mäusebussard   Sw – Ormvråk
Identification: 20–22″. Buzzards may be identified by flight-silhouette (*broad
wings, ample rounded tails and very short necks*). Adults very variable, generally
dark brown, mottled with white below. Amount of white on under-parts and
beneath wings varies, but is rarely as pronounced as in Rough-legged.

Distinguished from latter by *narrowly barred* brown and grey tail with broad dark terminal band, inconspicuous dark carpal patches beneath wings, and unfeathered yellow tarsi. Soars circling for hours, on broad motionless wings, with tips of primaries upcurved and tail widely spread; wings held straight, slightly raised; short neck gives distinctive *blunt appearance* unlike eagles', whose heads project. Flight rather heavy. Hovers occasionally. Hunts by pouncing from low altitude on small animals, beetles, rarely small birds; also fond of carrion. Often seen in small groups. See also Honey Buzzard.
Voice: A high, plaintive mewing *'pee-oo'*, often long-drawn; also a short croaking note.
Habitat: Secluded rocky coasts, moors, plains, mountain slopes, cultivated and wooded regions. Nests on rock ledges, in trees and on broken ground. Map 80.

LONG-LEGGED BUZZARD   *Buteo rufinus*   Pls. 23, 24
Du – Arendbuizerd   Fr – Buse féroce
Ge – Adlerbussard   Sw – Örnvråk

Identification: 24–26″. Extremely difficult to distinguish from occasional very similar form of Buzzard. Has familiar wide variation of plumage, from rich rufous-brown, with broadly streaked creamy under-parts, to rare melanistic form with very dark brown under-parts. Adult's head is usually *pale* and the tail *unbarred, often cinnamon*, but Buzzards, particularly *B. b. vulpinus* of E. Europe, often have similar tails with scarcely detectable barring. In flight looks conspicuously whitish below, except for dark wing-tips, carpal patches and thighs. Immature inseparable from young Buzzard.
Voice: Buzzard-like, but less querulous.
Habitat and Range: Dry, open plains and steppes; locally in mountains. Nests on cliffs or in isolated tree, occasionally on ground. A few breed in Greece. Vagrant elsewhere in S., C., N. and W. Europe.

ROUGH-LEGGED BUZZARD   *Buteo lagopus*   Pls, 23, 24
Du – Ruigpootbuizerd   Fr – Buse pattue
Ge – Rauhfussbussard   Sw – Fjällvråk
N. Am – Rough-legged Hawk

Identification: 20–24″. Normally distinguished from Buzzard by *longer, narrower wings, white tail with broad dark terminal band*; usually much whiter beneath wings and on under-parts, with dark belly; head looks pale. *Conspicuous dark carpal patches* beneath pale wings and dark tips to primaries are distinctive. Legs feathered whitish to base of toes (Buzzard has unfeathered yellow tarsi). Immature resembles young Buzzard, but has some white on tail. Behaviour, voice and flight are similar, but hunts close to ground and *hovers frequently*, on slowly beating wings, pouncing on prey. Feeds chiefly on rabbits and small rodents, occasionally birds. See also Honey Buzzard and Booted Eagle.
Voice: A fairly loud, cat-like *'mee-oo'*, but seldom vocal.
Habitat: Usually barren open country and mountain slopes, also marshes and sand-dunes. Nests on cliff ledges, or on ground in high tundra. Map 81.

LESSER SPOTTED EAGLE   *Aquila pomarina*   Pl. 25
Du – Schreeuwarend   Fr – Aigle pomarin
Ge – Schreiadler   Sw – Mindre skrikörn

Identification: 24–26″. Very similar to Spotted, though slighter in shape: often a

little paler on crown and wing-coverts. Upper tail-coverts may be marked with
a little white; immature has fewer and smaller white spots and usually has a
rusty patch on nape. Can be separated in flight by narrower *base* to tail,
narrower wings *held slightly forward* and *sixth* primary just discernible. Has
similar droop to wings when gliding. Hovers occasionally.
Voice: Less vibrant than Spotted's, a thin '*kyeep, kyeep*'.
Habitat: Often found near water, though to lesser extent than Spotted.
Frequents remote wooded country, with open ground accessible for hunting.
Nests in tree. Map 82.

SPOTTED EAGLE   *Aquila clanga*   Pls. 25, 26
    Du – Bastaardarend   Fr – Aigle criard
    Ge – Schelladler   Sw – Större skrikörn
Identification: 26–29″. Adults very dark purplish-brown, slightly paler below; a
little white often visible on upper tail-coverts. When soaring does so on *straight-
edged wings* (not held forward), which *droop slightly from carpal joints when
gliding*; *seventh* spread primary just discernible; rather short, slightly rounded
tail; *small head with small bill* projects conspicuously on slender neck. Wings
proportionately broader than Golden's. See distinctions from Lesser Spotted.
Immature has *copious, large whitish spots* on upper-parts and noticeable white,
often in V, at base of tail; in flight shows two or several pale bands on wings.
Behaviour sluggish.
Voice: Like shrill yapping of small dog: '*kyak, kyak, kyak*'.
Habitat: A tree-loving species; usually near inland lakes, rivers, marshes. Nests
in forest tree or bush. Map 83.

TAWNY EAGLE   *Aquila rapax*   Pl. 25
    Du – Steppenarend   Fr – Aigle ravisseur
    Ge – Raubadler   Sw – Stäppörn
Identification: 26–31″. Adults almost uniform dark brown, with indistinct grey
bars on short, rounded tail. Very easily confused with adult Lesser Spotted, but
Tawny often has *rusty-yellow patch* on nape and *never* has the white on upper
tail-coverts of some (not all) Lesser Spotteds. Juvenile is *café au lait* coloured,
with blackish primaries, and shows two pale wing-bars in flight. Behaviour very
sluggish, often perching for long periods on ground and usually flies close to
ground; seldom soars, but when doing so holds wings slightly flexed. Feeds on
carrion, frogs, etc. Adults distinguished from Golden Eagle by smaller size,
smaller head and bill and smaller, only faintly barred tail, without broad dark
terminal band; from Imperial by *dark crown* and smaller size. Steppe Eagle *A. r.
nipalensis* (an accidental straggler from Asia) is indistinguishable in the field
from Tawny and is probably conspecific.
Voice: Usual note a high '*kow, kow, kow*'.
Habitat and Range: Open bushy plains or steppes. Nests on ground, on small
mound. Rare on passage Romania; vagrant S., C., N. and W. Europe.

IMPERIAL EAGLE   *Aquila heliaca*   Pl. 25
    Du – Keizerarend   Fr – Aigle impérial
    Ge – Kaiseradler   Sw – Kejsarörn
Identification: 31–33″. A large, rather heavy-looking eagle with blackish-
brown plumage and a pale yellowish crown and nape (almost white in old

birds). Usually has *a few pure white feathers on scapulars*. Tail rather square-cut and shorter than Golden's, with 5–7 grey bars. When soaring, wings held *straight*, not in shallow V or forward; upper surfaces uniformly dark (unlike adult Golden). Immature varies from yellowish-brown to mottled blackish-brown according to age; normally shows dark streaking and has ochreous or pale rufous crown. Adult of Spanish form *A. h. adalberti* has conspicuous *pure white shoulders*, showing in flight as short white band along leading edge of wing. Immature is pale yellowish-brown with darker tail and flight-feathers; fairly distinct pale patch in centre of wing and on lower back; but distinguished from rather similar Tawny by bold streaking on under-parts. Behaviour sluggish. See also Tawny and Golden.

Voice: A quick, barking, '*owk-owk-owk*'.

Habitat: Plains, steppes and marshes. Builds huge conspicuous nest in isolated tall tree. Map 84.

GOLDEN EAGLE *Aquila chrysaetos*   Pls. 25, 26
Du – Steenarend   Fr – Aigle royal
Ge – Steinadler   Sw – Kungsörn

Identification: 30–35″. Large size, majestic gliding and soaring flight with occasional wing-beats, broadly spread upcurved primaries and ample, squarish tail are characteristic. Plumage of adult uniformly dark, except for *golden tinge* on head, nape and across upper surface of secondary coverts. Immature birds show *conspicuous* white at base of primaries and secondaries and have *white tail with broad dark terminal band*, the white diminishing with age. Hunts by quartering mountainsides and pouncing on Ptarmigan, Hare, etc., from very low altitude. When soaring, holds wings well forward and in shallow V. Distinguished in flight from young White-tailed Eagle by longer, squarer tail, and less rectangular wing-shape; when perched, by less bulky appearance and, at close range, by smaller bill and feathered tarsi. Variations of immature plumage can cause confusion with Imperial, Spotted, Lesser Spotted and Tawny Eagles. Apart from size, boldly projecting head and more ample tail prevent confusion with soaring Buzzard.

Voice: Has very occasional yelping '*kya*' and a few whistling notes.

Habitat: Barren mountainsides, locally also mountain forests, sea cliffs and plains. Nests on rocky ledge, sometimes in tree. Map 85.

BOOTED EAGLE *Hieraaetus pennatus*   Pl. 24
Du – Dwergarend   Fr – Aigle botté
Ge – Zwergadler   Sw – Dvärgörn

Identification: 18–21″. A Buzzard-size, long-tailed eagle. Dimorphic; light-phase most plentiful. *White below, with dark flight-feathers and uniform pale cinnamon-buff tail*, which is longish and square-ended. Seen from above, body and wing-coverts are buffish, flight-feathers darker. Dark-phase birds less distinctive, a rich, uniform dark brown *except for pale tail*. Soars on level wings held slightly forward; wing-beats *quicker* than Buzzard's, flight more graceful and rapid, often weaving among trees. Feeds on small birds and other animals.

Voice: Usual notes, a thin, high '*keee*', with downward inflection, and various chattering cries.

Habitat: Deciduous and pine forests, near clearings for hunting. Seldom far from trees. Breeds in tall trees. Map 86.

BONELLI'S EAGLE   *Hieraaetus fasciatus*   **Pl. 24**
   Du – Havikarend   Fr – Aigle de Bonelli
   Ge – Habichtsadler   Sw – Hökörn
Identification: 26–29″. Upper-parts dark brown, almost black on wing-tips, paler on nape, usually showing whitish patch on back. Longish tail has faint bars and a *broad dark terminal band.* Seen from below, the narrowly streaked, *silky-white or creamy under-parts* contrast with the *long, dark, narrow wings,* distinguishing adult from all other eagles. Juvenile has rusty head, closely streaked rufous-brown under-parts and closely barred tail. Second-year birds are confusing, almost uniform brown; under-parts lose rufous tinge, but are not yet white. Behaviour aggressive. Hunts rabbits, birds, etc. Flight rapid and dashing; stoops on prey like falcon.
Voice: Recalls Goshawk; a chattering *'kie, kie, kikiki'*.
Habitat: Rocky mountainous country, but seldom at great altitudes; descends to plains and deserts in winter. Nests on precipitous rock-face, occasionally in tree. Map 87.

OSPREYS: Pandionidae

OSPREY   *Pandion haliaetus*   **Pl. 26**
   Du – Visarend   Fr – Balbuzard pêcheur
   Ge – Fischadler   Sw – Fiskgjuse
Identification: 20–23″. No other eagle-like birds (except Short-toed Eagle) have contrast of *dark upper-parts and snow-white under-parts,* with dusky breast-band. Has slightly crested *white head, with broad black patch through eye.* Wings long, narrow and *decidedly angled;* under-surfaces are white *with black carpal patches* and rows of small dark spots. Tail barred. Hovers heavily above water and *plunges feet first for fish.* Usually perches on dead tree, or rock, near water.
Voice: A short, whistling *'pew-pew'*, sometimes slightly declining.
Habitat: Invariably near water; lakes, large rivers, or sea coasts. Nests on small remote islands, rocky cliffs, trees, ruins, occasionally on sandy or rocky ground. Breeds in scattered groups in some localities. Map 88.

FALCONS: Falconidae

Falcons have long, pointed wings and longish tails. Flight fast, with rapid wing-beats and glides. Large falcons kill their prey by stooping on it at terrific speed. Sexes sometimes similar. Tree, cliff and ground nesting.

LESSER KESTREL   *Falco naumanni*   **Pls. 27, 28**
   Du – Kleine torenvalk   Fr – Faucon crécerellette
   Ge – Rötelfalke   Sw – Rödfalk
Identification: 12″. Looks like small, brightly coloured Kestrel; distinguishable by *more fearless, noisier behaviour* and *sociable nesting.* Flight more supple than Kestrel's and tail more slender, particularly at base; hovers seldom but glides frequently. Male has *unspotted* bright chestnut-red upper-parts, and bluer head

and tail than Kestrel; female and juvenile more similar to Kestrel. Viewed overhead, wings and tail look very pale, with black edges; viewed from above, secondaries show large slate-blue patch; claws are white (Kestrel's are black). Feeds chiefly on flying insects.

Voice: Much more vocal and varied than Kestrel. Usual notes, a chattering '*chet-che-che*', and a plaintive, rising '*wheee*'.

Habitat: Frequents old buildings, rocky gorges, etc., but usually hunts over open country. Breeds in colonies in holes in high walls, roofs, crevices in cliffs, often among pigeons, sparrows, etc. Map 89.

KESTREL *Falco tinnunculus* Pls. 27, 28
Du – Torenvalk   Fr – Faucon crécerelle
Ge – Turmfalke   Sw – Tornfalk

Identification: 13½". Pointed wings, slim tail, mark it as a falcon; small size and *habit of protracted hovering*, as this species. Male has *spotted chestnut* upper-parts, warm buff under-parts with scattered black spots. Head, rump and tail grey, latter with broad black band near white tip. Female has rusty-brown upper-parts, barred instead of spotted, and rusty barred tail. Perches on trees, telegraph poles, rocks, etc. Flies with rapid wing-beats, occasional short glides and frequent periods of hovering, head to wind; slants steeply down to catch mice, beetles, etc. See Merlin, Lesser Kestrel and Sparrowhawk for differences.

Voice: A shrill repeated '*kee, kee, kee*', and a more musical double note '*kee-lee*'. Usually silent outside breeding season.

Habitat: Moors, coasts, farmlands, open woodlands, locally cities. Breeds in old nests of crows, Magpies, etc., and on cliffs, buildings, occasionally in split trees. Map 90.

RED-FOOTED FALCON *Falco vespertinus* Pls. 27, 28
Du – Roodpootvalk   Fr – Faucon kobez
Ge – Rotfussfalke   Sw – Aftonfalk

Identification: 12". A small, gregarious falcon with long wings reaching nearly to tip of short tail, and *bright reddish-orange bill, eye-patches and legs*. Males, usually outnumbering females, are uniform blackish-grey with chestnut under tail-coverts. Female has rufous crown, sandy under-parts, short dark moustachial stripe, barred grey upper-parts and tail. Juvenile resembles brownish young Hobby, with paler, more closely barred upper-parts and longer tail, *pale forehead* and less boldly streaked buff under-parts. Hovers like Kestrel, but with body at steeper angle. Hunts flying insects until late dusk; takes grasshoppers, small rodents, etc., from ground. See also Hobby, Merlin, Kestrel and Lesser Kestrel.

Voice: A shrill '*kikikiki*', higher than Kestrel's cry.

Habitat: Open plains dotted with scrub and coppices, edges of woods, and around farmsteads. Breeds colonially in old nests of Rooks, Magpies, etc. Map 91.

MERLIN *Falco columbarius* Pls. 27, 28
Du – Smelleken   Fr – Faucon émerillon
Ge – Merlin   Sw – Stenfalk

Identification: 10½-13". A very small falcon, dashing after prey at low altitude over open country. Flight buoyant and erratic, with rapid, stiff wing-beats and occasional short glides. Male slate-blue above, with *broad black terminal band* *on tail and heavily rufous-striped under-parts.* Female larger, with dark brown upper-parts and barred brown and creamy tail. No moustachial stripe. Sparrowhawk has short rounded (not pointed) wings. Kestrel has chestnut upper-parts, slimmer tail.

Voice: Male has quick high chatter '*ki-ki-ki-ki*'. Female has a slow, plaintive '*eep-eep*'.

Habitat: Open, hilly and marshy moors, sea cliffs and sand-dunes. Breeds on open ground among heather, coarse grass, or on sand, or in trees in old nests of crows. Map 92.

HOBBY *Falco subbuteo*   Pls. 27, 28

Du – Boomvalk   Fr – Faucon hobereau
Ge – Baumfalke   Sw – Lärkfalk

Identification: 12–14″. The most aerial of the falcons, with dashing flight like Peregrine's, but wings look longer and *tail shorter* (suggesting large Swift). Preys on swallows, larks, etc., and, particularly at dusk, on flying insects. When perched looks slender and compact, *with chestnut on thighs and beneath tail*; pointed 'moustaches' are narrower than Peregrine's and *under-parts more heavily streaked (not barred)*. Juvenile blackish-brown above, more heavily streaked below and lacking chestnut on thighs and below tail. Distinguished from Kestrel by longer, narrower, more back-swept wings, moustachial stripe, chestnut on thighs and beneath tail. See also Red-footed Falcon.

Voice: A clear, repeated '*kew*', or '*ket*', and a rapid '*kikiki*', often with varying pitch.

Habitat: Downs and commons with scattered trees, coppices, light woodlands. Breeds in trees, in old nests, particularly of crow family. Map 93.

ELEONORA'S FALCON *Falco eleonorae*   Pls. 27, 28

Du – Eleonora's valk   Fr – Faucon d'Eléonore
Ge – Eleonorenfalke   Sw – Eleonorafalk

Identification: 15″. About size of Peregrine but more slender. In silhouette resembles *long-tailed* Hobby. Dimorphic. Dark form is *uniform dark brown* with paler streaks on breast, occasionally all black. Light form has paler slate or dark brown upper-parts, buff or creamy breast heavily streaked with black. Under-parts increasingly rufous towards tail. Cere pale lemon or whitish. Stoops like Peregrine on small birds, hawks for insects like Hobby (particularly at dusk) and hovers occasionally like Kestrel. Foraging-flight has characteristic slow wing-beat. Gregarious. See also Red-footed Falcon.

Voice: A harsh '*keya*', sometimes repeated rapidly.

Habitat and Range: Rocky Mediterranean islands and sea cliffs. Migratory, breeding mainly in late summer on Greek islands, Sardinia, Balearics. Vagrant elsewhere in S., W. (including Britain) and C. Europe.

LANNER *Falco biarmicus*   Pl. 27

Du – Lanner valk   Fr – Faucon lanier
Ge – Feldeggsfalke   Sw – Slagfalk

Identification: 17″. Looks like pale Peregrine; distinguishable at close quarters by *buff or sandy crown*, small black moustachial stripe (not broad and lobe-shaped like Peregrine's), whitish ear-coverts and *very lightly spotted* (not barred) whitish under-parts. Immature is darker above than adult and much more heavily marked below. Less bold than Peregrine, preying on smaller birds;

looks more slender in flight, which is less rapid; wings and tail slightly longer. See also Saker.

Voice: A shrill '*kri, kri, kri*' and various wailing cries during breeding season.
Habitat: Cliffs, ruins, rocky mountain slopes, extending to stony plains and semi-desert. Nests among rocks, sometimes in trees. Map 94.

SAKER *Falco cherrug*   Pl. 27
Du – Saker valk   Fr – Faucon sacre
Ge – Würgfalke   Sw – Tatarfalk

Identification: 18″. Distinguished from Peregrine by *earth-brown* (not slate-blue) upper-parts and wings, with buffish emarginations, *whitish crown and nape streaked with dark brown*, narrow, indistinct moustachial streak, white under-parts lightly spotted or streaked (not barred) with brown. Wings slightly longer and broader than Peregrine's. Tail also slightly longer, dark brown, barred with white. Immature has more closely streaked crown and under-parts than adult, particularly on flanks. Very bold and ferocious, attacking prey far larger than itself. Frequently used for falconry. See also Lanner.
Voice: A harsh, high-pitched '*i-jack*'.
Habitat: Open plains, semi-deserts and deserts. Usually nests high in large tree, occasionally among rocks. Map 95.

GYRFALCON *Falco rusticolus*   Pl. 28
Du – Giervalk   Fr – Faucon gerfaut
Ge – Gerfalke   Sw – Jaktfalk

Identification: 20–22″. Distinguished in flight from Peregrine by larger size, slightly longer tail, *broader wing-bases*, slightly blunter wing-tips and slower wing-beats. When perched, *considerably paler, more uniform coloration* and absence of, or only vestigial, moustachial stripe are noticeable. Some individuals of the Greenland race (*F. r. candicans*) look almost totally white, except for dark primaries. (Snowy Owl is larger-headed, round-winged.)
Voice: Usually silent. Occasional wailing '*aaahi*' and a high, yapping chatter are slightly lower-pitched than similar notes of Peregrine.
Habitat: Wild rocky open country, sea coasts and islands. Locally also around edges of coniferous forests. Breeds on rocky cliff-faces. Map 96.

PEREGRINE *Falco peregrinus*   Pls. 27, 28
Du – Slechtvalk   Fr – Faucon pèlerin
Ge – Wanderfalke   Sw – Pilgrimsfalk
N. Am – Duck Hawk

Identification: 15–19″. Distinguished as a falcon by *long pointed wings, slightly tapered tail*, and rapid pigeon-like flight, but with shallower wing-beats, broken by long glides. Identified as this species by *crow-size* and, when perched, by *heavy, black, lobe-shaped 'moustaches'*. Male has blackish crown, slate-grey upper-parts contrasted with buffish-white under-parts, narrowly barred with black. Female considerably larger and often darker. Juvenile dark brown above, with streaked (not barred) buffish under-parts. Hunts by stooping on prey almost vertically at terrific speed, with wings nearly closed. Feeds chiefly on birds up to size of pigeon, grouse, etc. See also Gyrfalcon, Saker and Lanner.
Voice: Has wide range of notes during breeding season: a repeated '*we-chew*', a loud, menacing '*kek-kek-kek*', a short '*kiack*', a thin squeal, etc.

Habitat: Open wild country, cliffs, mountains, moors; in winter, also marshes, locally high spires and towers. Breeds on steep cliffs, mountain crags, etc., sometimes on buildings. Map 97.

GROUSE: Tetraonidae

Plump, chicken-like, chiefly ground-dwelling birds, without the long tails of pheasants. Tarsi and often the toes are feathered. Sexes sometimes similar. Ground nesting.

HAZEL GROUSE   *Bonasa bonasia*   **Pl. 29**
   Du – Hazelhoen   Fr – Gelinotte des bois
   Ge – Haselhuhn   Sw – Järpe
Identification: 14″. A woodland species. Typical grouse shape, but with longish tail and slightly crested crown. In flight both sexes show *conspicuous black band on grey tail*. Upper-parts greyish to rusty-brown (greyest in north of range, more rufous in south), richly spotted and barred black and brown. Broad white bands down side of throat and across scapulars. Under-parts whitish, closely marked with brown, more heavily on flanks. Male has *conspicuous black throat, broadly bordered with white*. Female has whitish throat. Perches freely in trees.
Voice: A high, whistling *'tsissi-tseri-tsi, tsi, tsiu'*.
Habitat: Mixed hill woodlands and thickets, particularly among aspen and birch; locally also in wooded plains. Map 98.

WILLOW GROUSE and RED GROUSE   *Lagopus lagopus*   **Pl. 30**
   Du – Moerassneeuwhoen   Fr – Lagopède des saules
   Ge – Moorschneehuhn   Sw – Dalripa
   N. Am – Willow Ptarmigan
Identification: 15–16″. A stout, short-winged, blackish-tailed bird, with rufous-brown plumage. Like all game-birds flight is rapid, with alternate whirring wing-beats and gliding on down-curved wings; when flushed, looks back in flight. Willow (N. Europe) and Red *L. l. scoticus* (British Isles) now regarded as conspecific.

Willow Grouse and Ptarmigan both have white wings and are often indistinguishable except by voice and habitat. Both very variable, but Willow has darker rufous breeding plumage; at short range *stouter bill* is obvious. In autumn, Willow becomes patchy white and brown; Ptarmigan becomes grey above. In winter, where ranges overlap, a white grouse with black tail and unmarked white head may be male or female Willow, or female Ptarmigan; if it has *black face-patch* it is male Ptarmigan (see diagram, Pl. 30).

Red Grouse is dark rufous-brown *with darker brown wings*. Summer plumage paler than winter, female paler and smaller than male. Irish race yellower than British. Distinguished from female Black Grouse (Greyhen) by smaller size, more rufous colour and unforked tail; from summer Ptarmigan by dark wings and belly.
Voice: Willow crows a rapid *'kowk, ok, ok, ok'*, often preceded by a quiet *'ow . . . ow . . .'*. Red has similar loud crowing call; during breeding season a strident *'go-bak, bak-bak-bak'*.

Habitat: Willow inhabits moors, heather, with willow, birch and juniper scrub, at lower altitudes than Ptarmigan; nests in scrub. Red prefers moors and peat-bogs with crowberry and cranberry, descending in autumn to lower levels and stubble fields; nests among heather and rough grass. Map 99.

PTARMIGAN   *Lagopus mutus*   **Pl. 30**
   Du – Sneeuwhoen   Fr – Lagopède des Alpes
   Ge – Alpenschneehuhn   Sw – Fjällripa
   N. Am – Rock Ptarmigan

Identification: 14″. A grouse of the high mountain slopes, which at all seasons shows *white wings* and white belly. Small red wattle over eye; feet feathered white. In breeding plumage male has richly mottled blackish-brown upper-parts, breast and flanks; female is tawnier. In autumn male's upper-parts, breast and sides are grey, closely marked with black and white, belly mainly white; female is yellowish-grey and looks darker than male. In winter both sexes are *pure white with exception of black tail* (which is largely hidden at rest by white tail-coverts) but male has *black mark from bill through eye* – a clear distinction from Willow Grouse (see diagram, Pl. 30). At short range Ptarmigan's bill looks more slender than Willow Grouse's; both species are very variable, with three distinct changes of plumage.

Voice: A low, harsh croak; '*aar-aar-ka-ka-ka*' in flight and a rattling '*kar-r-rk*' alarm.

Habitat: Barren stony mountain slopes (usually higher than Willow Grouse), except when driven down by weather; breeds at lower levels in Arctic. Nests in shelter of rock or clump of vegetation. Map 100.

BLACK GROUSE   *Tetrao tetrix*   **Pl. 29**
   Du – Korhoen   Fr – Tétras lyre
   Ge – Birkhuhn   Sw – Orre

Identification: Male 21″, female 16″. Male (Blackcock) easily distinguished by glossy *blue-black* plumage with *lyre-shaped tail*, conspicuous *white under tail-coverts and white wing-bar*. Female (Greyhen) distinguished from Red Grouse by larger size and *less rufous plumage*; from female Capercaillie by smaller size and *less boldly barred plumage*; from both by narrow, pale wing-bars and forked tail (neither easy to observe). Both sexes have scarlet wattle above eye. Male in autumn eclipse looks dingy, mottled above, with white throat; tail lacks distinctive shape until full grown. Usually flies higher than Red Grouse with longer glides; longer neck and tail give distinctive silhouette. Perches freely in trees. Confusing hybrids with Capercaillie, Red Grouse and Pheasant occur occasionally.

Voice: Male has a deliberate, sneezing '*tchu-shwee*'. Song at 'lek' (display ground) a rapid, protracted, musical chorus of pigeon-like or '*roo-koo*' bubbling notes.

Habitat: Near trees bordering moors, marshy ground with rushes and scattered trees, peat-mosses, rocky heather-covered hills, plantations, etc. Nests on ground. Map 101.

CAPERCAILLIE   *Tetrao urogallus*   **Pl. 29**
   De – Auerhoen   Fr – Grand tétras
   Ge – Auerhuhn   Sw – Tjäder
Identification: Male 34″, female 24″. A huge grouse-like bird. Male distinguished from all other game-birds by *very large size, dark colouring and ample tail.* General coloration grey, with rich brown wing-coverts, glossy blue-green breast, shaggy 'beard', whitish bill and scarlet skin over eye; under-parts and tail boldly marked with white. White carpal-patch conspicuous during display. Female may be confused with female Black or Red Grouse, but is much larger, with broad tail and *rufous patch on breast* contrasting with paler under-parts. Usually seen on ground in coniferous forests in summer; in trees in winter. Flight usually brief, with alternate spells of quick wing-beats and long glides; bursts out of cover noisily. Hens may hybridize with Blackcock.
Voice: Male at display ground has guttural retching call; female, a Pheasant-like '*kok-kok*'. Male's song is quiet, with '*tik-up, tik-up, tik-up*' accelerating rapidly and ending with a '*pop*' (like withdrawing a cork), followed by a short phrase of grating, whispering notes.
Habitat: Coniferous hilly woodlands. Nests among undergrowth at foot of pine, or in scrub on open high ground. Map 102.

PARTRIDGES AND PHEASANTS:
Phasianidae

Chicken-like terrestrial birds, with unfeathered legs. Pheasants have long, sweeping tails (females shorter). Partridges and Quail are much smaller, more rotund, with very short tails; sexes similar. Ground nesting.

CHUKAR   *Alectoris chukar*   **p. 84**
   Du – Aziatische steenpatrijs   Fr – Perdrix choukar
   Ge – Chukarhuhn   Sw – Berghöna
Identification: 13″. Very similar to Rock Partridge; best distinguished by *clucking or cackling voice, like barnyard fowl.* Lores are *white* (black in Rock); black 'mask' is *narrower* and broken; throat more buff, less grey; centre of gorget *flecked* (not clean-cut); flank-bars bolder and fewer; upper-parts browner.
Voice: A chuckling, decelerating '*tchouk-tchouk-tchoukor-tchoukor*'.

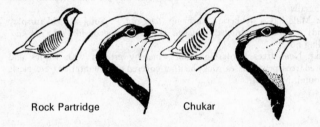

Rock Partridge   Chukar

PARTRIDGES AND PHEASANTS 85

Habitat and Range: Similar habitat to Rock Partridge, but also in more arid regions. Resident E. Greece, E. Bulgaria, Aegean.

ROCK PARTRIDGE *Alectoris graeca* **Pl. 30**
Du – Steenpatrijs Fr – Perdrix bartavelle
Ge – Steinhuhn Sw – Stenhöna

Identification: 13″. Indistinguishable at long range from Red-legged Partridge and Chukar. Best identified by *distinctive voice*. White throat-patch is slightly larger, with black lower border *clean-cut*, instead of merging into upper breast; forehead is ash-grey; upper-parts are grey-brown instead of brown.

Voice: Call-note, a Nuthatch-like '*whit-whit-whit*'; alarm, an explosive '*k-k-kwowk*'; song (spring and autumn), a staccato, grating '*tchertsi-ritt-chi*', with many variants.

Habitat: Stony and rocky slopes and lightly wooded high ground, descending to lower altitudes in winter. Nests among rocks. Map 103.

RED-LEGGED PARTRIDGE *Alectoris rufa* **Pl. 30**
Du – Rode patrijs Fr – Perdrix rouge
Ge – Rothuhn Sw – Rödhöna

Identification: 13½″. At a distance can be confused with Grey Partridge, but adult easily distinguished by *long white stripe over eye, black-bordered white gorget*, lavender flanks *heavily barred chestnut-black-white*, chestnut crown and red bill and legs. Juvenile is very like young Grey Partridge. Voice is very different; runs more swiftly than Grey Partridge; flocks are less compact. See also Rock, Chukar and Barbary Partridges.

Voice: Usual note of male '*chuck, chuck-er*', or a slow harsh '*tschreck . . . tschreck . . .*'; when flushed, calls '*kuk-kuk*'.

Habitat and Breeding: Much as Grey Partridge. Although often on marshy ground, normally prefers dry localities, sandy soil, chalk downs, stony wastes. Map 104.

BARBARY PARTRIDGE *Alectoris barbara* **Pl. 30**
Du – Barbarijse patrijs Fr – Perdrix gambra
Ge – Felsenhuhn Sw – Klipphöna

Identification: 13″. At long range looks paler and pinker than Red-legged Partridge and at short range is easily identified by broad *chestnut* collar, speckled with whitish and by *blue-grey* 'face', throat and upper breast. 'Inflamed' pink eye-ring. Broad buffish streak behind eye; upper-parts pinkish brown, with slate-blue scapulars, broadly margined with crimson. Under-parts resemble Red-legged, flanks boldly barred with grey, black, white and chestnut. Legs reddish.

Voice: Noisy at dawn and dusk. Typical song a loud, slow '*kakelik,kakelik*'.

Habitat and Range: Scrub-covered hillsides, wadis, semi-deserts with a certain amount of water and cover. Resident Gibraltar, Sardinia.

GREY PARTRIDGE *Perdix perdix* **Pl. 30**
Du – Patrijs Fr – Perdix grise
Ge – Rebhuhn Sw – Rapphöna
N. Am – Hungarian Partridge

Identification: 12″. Like all the partridges, a rotund, chicken-like bird, with short rounded wings and short rufous tail; flies low and rapidly, with alternate

spells of whirring wing-beats and gliding on deeply arched wings. Easily confused with larger Red-legged Partridge, but distinguished by *pale orange-chestnut 'face'*, grey neck and breast. Male has *conspicuous dark chestnut horse-shoe mark on lower breast* (female shows trace of similar mark, juvenile is streaky); upper-parts streaked with buff, flanks barred with chestnut. Walks in crouched attitude, squatting when alarmed and running swiftly with head well up in preference to flight. Much shorter-tailed than young Pheasant. Much larger and less sandy than Quail. See also Red-legged Partridge.
Voice: A penetrating, grating '*kree-arit*' and a rapid '*eck-eck-eck*'.
Habitat: Farmlands, pastures, wasteland, moors, sand-dunes, etc. Nests well hidden in hedge bottoms, in growing corn, etc. Map 105.

QUAIL *Coturnix coturnix*   **Pl. 30**
   Du – Kwartel   Fr – Caille des blés
   Ge – Wachtel   Sw – Vaktel
Identification: 7″. Looks like tiny Grey Partridge. Usually first identified by male's *distinctive voice*. General colour *sandy, strongly streaked* with whitish-buff and black above, paler below, with light and dark streaks (not bars) on flanks. Crown dark brown, with creamy stripe down centre and a long creamy stripe above eye. Male has blackish stripes on throat. Female has unmarked buff throat and closely spotted breast. Flight is slower and usually much briefer than Grey Partridge's. Very difficult to flush in breeding season.
Voice: Ventriloquial. Characteristic trisyllabic call of male has accent on first syllable: a repeated '*whic, whic-ic*'. Female has wheezing double note '*queep. . . queep*'. Heard day and night.
Habitat: Seldom seen in open. Frequents and breeds in rough pastures, crops, grass tussocks, etc. Map 106.

PHEASANT *Phasianus colchicus*   **Pl. 29**
   Du – Fazant   Fr – Faisan de chasse
   Ge – Fasan   Sw – Fasan
Identification: Male 30–35″, female 21–25″. A familiar game-bird with a *long, pointed tail*. Male highly coloured, with glossy dark green head, scarlet wattles around eyes and short ear-tufts. Plumage very variable owing to variety of introduced stock, but usually has *white neck-ring*. Female soberly mottled buff and blackish, with shorter but still lengthy tail. Runs swiftly to cover rather than taking wing. Flight strong (take-off noisy), but seldom long sustained or high.
Voice: Crowing male has strident double note '*korrk-kok*', usually followed by brief whirr of wing-flapping. Female has thin whistling note on taking off.
Habitat: Woodland borders, parkland, farmland, shrubberies, reeds. Nests on ground, beneath low vegetation and bracken. Map 107.

GOLDEN PHEASANT *Chrysolophus pictus*   **Pl. 77**
   Du – Goudfazant   Fr – Faisan doré
   Ge – Goldfasan   Sw – Guldfasan
Identification: Male has unmistakable *scarlet under-parts*, golden crest and rump, a fan-shaped gold and black 'hood', green and blue wings and a long, drooping tail. Female resembles female Pheasant, but with longer, more boldly barred tail. Rasping cry like that of Lady Amherst's but higher-pitched. Crosses

between the two occur. Escaped birds now feral in several parts of Britain, breeding in parkland shrubberies. Resident.

LADY AMHERST'S PHEASANT *Chrysolophus amherstiae* **Pl. 77**
  Du – Lady Amherst-fazant   Fr – Faisan de Lady Amherst
  Ge – Diamantfasan   Sw – Diamantfasan
Identification: Size and form of Golden but with longer tail. Male easily distinguished by *white* under-parts and long, barred black and white tail. Crown, throat and wings dark blue-green. Black-and-white scalloped 'hood'. Gold and red rump. Female distinguished from female Golden by blue-grey legs and blue-green instead of reddish eye-rim. Crosses between the two occur. Rasping calls similar. Escaped birds now feral in several parts of England, breeding in parklands. Resident.

BUTTON-QUAILS: Turnicidae

ANDALUSIAN HEMIPODE *Turnix sylvatica* **Pl. 30**
  Du – Vechtkwartel   Fr – Turnix d'Andalousie
  Ge – Laufhühnchen   Sw – Springhöna
Identification: 6″. A small, Quail-like bird, very likely to be confused with Quail when flushed. Crown dark, with buffish centre stripe; sides of head and throat pale buffish, with small dark speckles. Chief distinction from Quail is the *bright orange-rufous patch* on the breast and the *bold black spotting* on the sides. Eye-ring and eye are pale blue. Sexes similar. Extremely shy. Difficult to flush. Runs swiftly in zig-zag. Flight reluctant, low and rapid, with whirring wings, which are briefly held upright on alighting. Solitary.
Voice: A very distinctive '*crooo*', increasing in intensity, resembling distant fog-horn; heard particularly at dawn and dusk; when calling often 'blows itself up' like a ball. Also quiet whistling notes.
Habitat and Range: Sandy plains with palmetto scrub, brush-covered wastes, extensive low thickets, stubble and sugar-beet fields. Nests in dense vegetation. Bred very locally in Spain, S. Portugal, now perhaps extinct.

RAILS, CRAKES AND COOTS: Rallidae

Rails and crakes are compact, skulking marsh-birds, more often heard than seen; wings short and rounded; tails short and often cocked; flight usually brief and reluctant, with legs and long toes dangling. Moorhens and coots have stout bodies, small heads and long toes for walking on aquatic vegetation; heads often jerked while swimming. Sexes usually similar. Reed or ground nesting.

WATER RAIL *Rallus aquaticus* **Pl. 31**
  Du – Waterral   Fr – Râle d'eau
  Ge – Wasserralle   Sw – Vattenrall
Identification: 11″. Difficult to observe; usually identified by *very distinctive voice*. Distinguished from all the 'crakes' by *long red bill*. Upper-parts olive

brown, patterned with blackish feather-centres; face, throat and breast dark blue-grey; *flanks conspicuously barred black and white*; under tail-coverts *whitish*; legs pinkish-brown. Juvenile has mottled under-parts. Nervous and skulking behaviour as Corncrake, but occasionally perches on bushes in open.
Voice: A hard, persistent 'gep . . . gep . . . gep . . .'; a piglet-like, squealing 'tjuir-r-r'; a diminishing series 'krui, krui, krui' and an astonishing variety of groaning, grunting and purring notes, including a sharp 'zik, zik, zik' which can be confused with other crakes. Often heard at night.
Habitat: Dense aquatic vegetation, reed- and osier-beds, sewage-farms, overgrown ponds, ditches, river banks. Nests among reeds or sedges above shallow water. Map 108.

SPOTTED CRAKE   *Porzana porzana*   Pl. 31

Du – Porceleinhoen	Fr – Marouette ponctuée
Ge – Tüpfelsumpfhuhn	Sw – Småfläckig sumphöna

Identification: 9″. Body near size of Water Rail, but bill much shorter. Very difficult to observe, but voice is distinctive. Resembles small, dark Corncrake, with *dark* olive-brown upper-parts *streaked and spotted with white* and short *dark brown* (not chestnut) wings. Legs greenish. Bill yellowish with red base. Breast grey, with white speckles. Jerks tail when suspicious, revealing *conspicuous buff under tail-coverts.* Immature Sora (see Accidentals) shows paler buff. Solitary and largely crepuscular. Little and Baillon's are much smaller, with barred under tail-coverts.
Voice: A high, whipping 'whitt . . . whitt . . . whitt', long repeated on the same note. Male also has monotonous hard ticking note 'tchit-a, tchit-a', recalling Snipe's clock-like note.
Habitat: Rather less aquatic than Baillon's or Little Crakes. Swamps and fens, overgrown ditches, margins of ponds, rivers, etc. Nests in boggy locations. Map 109.

LITTLE CRAKE   *Porzana parva*   Pl. 31

Du – Klein waterhoen	Fr – Marouette poussin
Ge – Kleines Sumpfhuhn	Sw – Liten sumphöna

Identification: 7½″. Little and Baillon's Crakes are very similar in appearance, voice and habitat and can seldom be seen closely. Both are *much smaller* than Spotted Crake. Male Little differs from male Baillon's in having *olive-brown upper-parts, no white streaks on wing-coverts* (only indistinct pale flecks on mantle) and *lack of black bars on flanks*, though rest of under-parts are slate-grey and under tail-coverts are barred like Baillon's. Females easily separated, Little having *buff* under-parts (not grey) and a *whitish throat.* Both sexes have green bill *with red base.* Legs *green* (Baillon's are dull flesh coloured). Juveniles of both species resemble female Little, but young Little is less heavily barred below than young Baillon's. Behaviour and flight as Spotted Crake. See Baillon's.
Voice: A sharp 'quek, quek, quek', gradually dropping in scale and accelerating to a short trill. Call-note an explosive 'kirrook'.
Habitat: As Spotted, but with fondness for high *Phragmites* reeds and lagoons with floating vegetation. Map 110.

BAILLON'S CRAKE *Porzana pusilla* **Pl. 31**

Du – Kleinst waterhoen   Fr – Marouette de Baillon
Ge – Zwergsumpfhuhn   Sw – Dvärgsumphöna

Identification: 7″. Smaller than Starling. Both sexes resemble male Little Crake, but when seen well (which rarely occurs) distinguished by smaller size (the smallest European crake), *rufous upper-parts, boldly and closely etched with white, strongly barred black and white flanks, dull flesh legs* and green bill *without* red base. (Little Crake is olive-brown above.) In flight narrow white edge to first primary is a further distinction. Males of both species have slaty blue-grey face, throat and under-parts and barred black and white under tail-coverts. Juveniles very similar (resembling Little Crake), though under-parts of Baillon's are often more strongly barred and upper-parts have more distinct pale markings. Behaviour as Little Crake. See also Spotted Crake.

Voice: Easily confused with Little Crake, but Baillon's is a quicker, more jarring trill, sometimes with 2–4 slower introductory notes. Also a sharp, high chirp.

Habitat: Usually prefers lower, denser vegetation and smaller pools than Little Crake, in swamps, fens and overgrown ponds. Map 111.

CORNCRAKE *Crex crex* **Pl. 31**

Du – Kwartelkoning   Fr – Râle de genêts
Ge – Wachtelkönig   Sw – Kornknarr

Identification: 10½″. Difficult to observe. Presence usually indicated by male's *distinctive rasping voice*. Looks *short-necked*. Plumage *yellowish-buff*, marked with blackish above; greyish on head and breast; flanks and under tail-coverts barred with chestnut. *Chestnut wings conspicuous in flight*. Behaviour solitary, crepuscular and very skulking, hiding in long grass. Distinguished from all other crakes by larger size and buffer appearance.

Voice: In breeding season male has penetrating and persistent call, a rasping, disyllabic *'rerrp-rerrp'* (often written *'crex-crex'*), usually at night, but often also by day. Also a loud, high squealing note.

Habitat: Frequents and nests in meadows, lush vegetation, crops. Map 112.

MOORHEN *Gallinula chloropus* **Pl. 31**

Du – Waterhoen   Fr – Poule d'eau
Ge – Teichhuhn   Sw – Rörhöna
N. Am – Florida Gallinule

Identification: 13″. A stout blackish bird of pond margins. Distinguished from Coot by smaller size, *bold irregular white streak along flanks and conspicuous white under tail-coverts* with black centre stripe. Legs green, with red 'garter' above joint. Red frontal shield and bill, latter with yellow tip. Juvenile dark grey-brown, with whitish belly, greenish-brown bill and frontal shield. Jerks tail when nervous. Swims buoyantly with jerking head. Dives occasionally. Rises from water by pattering along surface. Flight usually low, legs dangling. Often feeds in flocks in winter.

Voice: A harsh, penetrating *'kr-r-rk'* or *'kittick'*, and various chattering and squeaking notes.

Habitat: Ponds, slow streams, marshes, tarns, sewage-farms and meadows, even farmyards. Nests in reeds and bushes near water, occasionally in trees and old nests of other species. Map 113.

PURPLE GALLINULE   *Porphyrio porphyrio*   **Pl. 31**
   Du – Puperkoet   Fr – Poule sultane
   Ge – Purpurhuhn   Sw – Purpurhöna
Identification: 19″. Upper-parts rich, dark *blue-purple*, glossed with turquoise
on throat and breast; under tail-coverts *pure white*. *Very deep bill*, frontal shield,
legs and eyes are *bright red*. Much larger and heavier-bodied than Coot, *with
longer legs*. Juvenile is dusky bluish-slate, with grey throat and sides of head.
Climbs among reeds; seldom in open. Easily distinguished in flight by long,
dangling *red* legs. Coot is uniform blackish, with white frontal shield and grey
legs; Moorhen is much smaller, has green legs.
Voice: Weird hooting and shrieking noises.
Habitat and Range: Swamps with extensive reed-beds, borders of lakes fringed
with dense cover. Nests in reeds, cane-brakes, etc. Breeds in S. Spain, Sardinia,
Portugal. Vagrant elsewhere in W. and C. Europe.

COOT   *Fulica atra*   **Pl. 31**
   Du – Meerkoet   Fr – Foulque macroule
   Ge – Blässhuhn   Sw – Sothöna
Identification: 15″. A stout, slaty-black water-bird with jet-black head. Distinguished from Moorhen by larger size, bulkier body and *conspicuous white
frontal shield and bill*; also by lack of white stripe across flanks and of white on
under tail-coverts. In flight shows narrow white edge to secondaries. Legs
green, with large 'scalloped' toes, projecting in flight like long 'tail'. Juvenile
dusky-grey, with white throat and upper breast, sometimes confused with
young Great Crested Grebe. Stays closer to water than Moorhen and 'plop-
dives' frequently for food, staying submerged up to half a minute. Gregarious in
winter. Distinguished at long range when swimming with ducks by rounded
back and small head. Flight is laboured, alighting on water with big splash.
Patters along surface when taking off.
Voice: A loud, short '*tewk*'; also various disyllabic calls '*kt-kowk*', etc., and a
hard, explosive '*skik*'.
Habitat: Usually prefers larger areas of open water than Moorhen. Packs
occur on reservoirs and salt water in winter. Nests among reeds and other
aquatic vegetation. Map 114.

CRESTED COOT   *Fulica cristata*   **Pl. 31**
   Du – Knobbelmeerkoet   Fr – Foulque à crête
   Ge – Kammblässhuhn   Sw – Kamsothöna
Identification: 16″. Closely resembles Coot, but at medium range can usually be
distinguished (especially when breeding) by contrast between white frontal
shield and *blue-grey* bill (both are white in Coot). When breeding, Crested has
red knobs either side of frontal shield; these are obscure in winter. Has
distinctive voice. Lacks white on secondaries. Legs bluish-grey. Behaviour,
flight and habitat as Coot, with which it mingles, but is more shy and keeps
closer to cover.
Voice: Usual note a loud, almost human '*hoo-hoo*', and loud clucking notes.
Range: Rare S. Spain, apparently resident. Vagrant elsewhere in S. Europe.

CRANES: Gruidae

Large, stately, terrestrial birds, superficially resembling storks. Inner secondaries much elongated, drooping over the tail. Long neck and legs extended in flight. Usually migrate in V or line formation. Voices trumpet-like. Sexes similar. Ground nesting.

CRANE *Grus grus*   **Pl. 5**
  Du – Kraanvoge   Fr – Grue cendrée
  Ge – Kranich   Sw – Trana

Identification: 45″. Distinguished from storks and herons by much elongated inner secondaries, forming *drooping blackish 'tail'*. General colour slate-grey, with *curving white stripe* on side of head and neck, contrasting with black face and throat. At short range *red crown* is visible. Bill is shorter than in storks and herons. Immature has brown head and upper-parts, lacking the white head pattern of adult and with much less bushy 'tail'. Behaviour extremely shy. Walks slowly and gracefully. When suspicious stretches upright, with long neck erect. Very rarely perches on trees. Flight slow but powerful, neck and legs extended, wing-tips square-ended. Migrating flocks assume V or line formations. (Storks usually fly in shapeless flocks.)

Voice: A strident, trumpeting '*kr-rooh*' and a quieter guttural '*kror-r-r*'; various grating and hissing notes.

Habitat: In winter, avoids wooded regions, occurring on river banks, lagoons, fields and steppes. Breeds on ground in wet bogs, lightly wooded swamps, reedbeds, etc. Map 115.

DEMOISELLE CRANE *Anthropoides virgo*   **Pl. 5**
  Du – Jufferkraan   Fr – Demoiselle de Numidie
  Ge – Jungfernkranich   Sw – Jungfrutrana

Identification: 38″. Easily distinguished from Crane by much smaller size (stands 12″ shorter) and by *large crest-like tuft of white feathers behind each eye* and much smaller bill. Plumage mostly ashy blue-grey, with black on lores, much of neck, elongated breast-feathers and wing-quills. Black-tipped inner secondaries much elongated, drooping right over tail, but *without Crane's bushy effect*. Flight as Crane, with neck extended; not distinguishable at high altitude unless both together, when smaller size and shriller voice are discernible.

Voice: A harsh, grating '*kar-r-r*' and a loud, musical trumpeting, noticeably higher-pitched than Crane's.

Habitat and Range: Open plains and high plateaux, visiting fresh water regularly in hot weather. Nests on dry ground. Formerly bred Romania. Vagrant to S., E., C., N. and W. Europe.

BUSTARDS: Otididae

Chiefly terrestrial, frequenting grassy steppes and extensive cultivated fields. Gait a stately walk. Behaviour very shy, crouching or running swiftly at first sign of danger. Flight is powerful, wings broad, bodies stout. Ground nesting.

LITTLE BUSTARD   *Tetrax tetrax*   **Pl. 32**
   Du – Kleine trap   Fr – Outarde canepetière
   Ge – Zwergtrappe   Sw – Småtrapp
Identification: 17″. Less than half size of Great Bustard. Extreme shyness
makes observation difficult. Male in breeding plumage distinguished by *bold
black and white neck*; upper-parts and crown finely vermiculated sandy-buff,
with blue-grey face; under-parts white. Female is paler above, streaked and
barred with black, buffish-white below, with barred breast and flanks, no
distinctive markings on face or neck. Behaviour as Great Bustard, but runs
readily and hides by crouching flat. Flight very swift, recalling grouse; male has
rapid whistling wing-beats. *Looks chiefly white in flight*, with bold black wing-
tips; flies much higher than Great Bustard. Usually in small flocks, but large
groups occur in autumn. See also Houbara.
Voice: A short '*dahg*', or '*kiak*', and a snorting '*ptrrr*' or '*prett*' which carries
considerable distance.
Habitat: Grassy plains, large fields of corn, clover and other crops. Map 116.

HOUBARA BUSTARD   *Chlamydotis undulata*   **Pl. 32**
   Du – Kraagtrap   Fr – Outarde houbara
   Ge – Kragentrappe   Sw – Kragtrapp
Identification: 25″. Size between Great and Little Bustards, in shape resembling
female turkey. Neck and rufous tail noticeably long. Both sexes distinguished at
all seasons by *tufts of long black and white feathers drooping down each side of
neck*, which can be displayed conspicuously or partly hidden; short black and
white crest; large eyes. Upper-parts pale vermiculated sandy-buff, under-parts
white, with greyish throat. In flight shows uniform sandy mantle and wing-
coverts, black flight-feathers with bold white patch near base of primaries, but
much less white than Great or Little Bustards. Wing-beats slow; wings long and
comparatively narrow.
Voice: An occasional low grunting bark.
Habitat and Range: Bare stony or sandy steppes, or semi-desert. Also occurs in
corn and other crops. Vagrant to most of Europe (including Britain).

GREAT BUSTARD   *Otis tarda*   **Pl. 32**
   Du – Grote trap   Fr – Outarde barbue
   Ge – Grosstrappe   Sw – Stortrapp
Identification: Male 40″, female 30″. Easily distinguished by *very large size,
stout body and long thick neck and legs*. Head and neck *pale grey* (male has long
'moustaches' of whitish bristles); upper-parts rich buff barred with black,
under-parts white with rich chestnut breast; female less stout, lacking breast-
band. In flight wings look *chiefly white*, with widely spread black tips; neck and
legs are extended, wing-beats slow, regular, but powerful. Walks sedately, with
head erect. Distant male looks all white when displaying. Exceptionally shy.
Usually in small flocks, females predominating; in breeding season males
remain in flocks. Distinguished from other bustards by much larger size and
lack of black on neck.
Voice: In breeding season an occasional deep bark; more rarely a squeal.
Habitat: Frequents and breeds on open treeless plains, grassy steppes,
extensive fields of corn, maize, etc. Map 117.

OYSTERCATCHERS: Haematopodidae

OYSTERCATCHER   *Haematopus ostralegus*   **Pls. 36, 37**
   Du – Scholekster   Fr – Huitrier pie
   Ge – Austernfischer   Sw – Strandskata

Identification: 17″. A large *pied* shore-bird with a *long orange-red bill and stout pink legs*. Has black head, breast and upper-parts contrasting with pure white under-parts. Bill flattened laterally, often slightly uptilted. Broad white wing-bar, white rump, black and white tail, conspicuous in flight. Non-breeders have a white band across throat. Very noisy. Flocks rest on islets and sand-bars between tides; feed among rocks and on mud-flats. Flight strong, with shallow wing-beats.

Voice: A loud *'pic, pic, pic'*. Alarm, a strident *'kleep, kleep'*. Song, a long piping trill, beginning slowly, varying in volume and pace.

Habitat: Mainly sea-shores, islands, estuaries. Locally inland on grass. Usually breeds on sea-shores, locally inland by lakes and streams in northern Britain, occasionally far from water. Map 118.

STILTS AND AVOCETS: Recurvirostridae

BLACK-WINGED STILT   *Himantopus himantopus*   **Pls. 36, 37**
   Du – Steltkluut   Fr – Echasse blanche
   Ge – Stelzenläufer   Sw – Styltöpare

Identification: 15″. Unmistakable. In flight, *grotesquely long pink legs* project nearly 7 inches beyond tail. *Black upper-parts contrast with gleaming white under-parts*. Male in summer usually but not always has black on back of head or crown; female usually has white head and neck (sometimes mottled black) and dark brown mantle and wings. Juvenile and winter adults have dusky markings on head and neck. *Black under-surfaces of narrow, sharply pointed, triangular wings conspicuous in flight*. Gait, a deliberate long-paced walk, often wades deeply. Behaviour nervous and noisy.

Voice: A very shrill, yelping *'kyik, kyik, kyik'*, a sharp, Coot-like *'kek'* and a tern-like *'kee-arr'*.

Habitat: Wet marshes, lagoons, flood waters. Breeds colonially, building nest in shallow water, or on tussock or mud. Map 119.

AVOCET   *Recurvirostra avosetta*   **Pls. 36, 37**
   Du – Kluut   Fr – Avocette
   Ge – Säbelschnäbler   Sw – Skärfläcka

Identification: 17″. Unmistakable. Identified by *long, slender, upcurved* bill, contrasting *black and white* plumage and long, *lead-blue* legs. Immature birds more or less suffused with brownish. In flight legs project well beyond tail. Gait, a graceful, fairly quick walk; feeds in shallows with side-to-side sifting motion of head, but also wades deeply; swims readily and 'up-ends' like duck.

Voice: A high fluty *'kleep'*, or *'kloo-it'*, and a yelping *'kyik'* or *'kew'*.

Habitat: Exposed mud-flats, estuaries and sandbanks. Breeds colonially among scrub and tussocks near shallow water, on sandbanks, low islands in river deltas and in brackish lagoons. Map 120.

THICK-KNEES: Burhinidae

STONE CURLEW *Burhinus oedicnemus*   **Pls. 32, 41**
  Du – Griel   Fr – Oedicnème criard
  Ge – Triel   Sw – Tjockfot
Identification: 16″. A large, rather ungainly bird, distinguished from all other waders by round-headed appearance *with large yellow eyes*. Has short, stout, yellow and black bill, long, heavy, pale yellow legs and streaked sandy-brown and white plumage. Shows conspicuous wing pattern in flight, with *two bold whitish bars* (one fairly conspicuous on closed wing). Runs furtively with head low and body hunched. Rests on horizontal tarsi, flattening itself with head on ground to hide. Flight usually low, with deliberate wing-beats and occasional long glides, but may be erratic in flock evolutions at dusk.
Voice: A wailing, Curlew-like '*coo-ree*', or a high, shrill '*kee-rrr-eee*', the middle syllable dropping. Chiefly vocal in evening.
Habitat: Frequents and breeds on stony, sandy and chalky open ground, bare downs, heaths, etc., with scant vegetation, occasionally among scattered pines, marshes, etc., increasingly in cultivation. May occur in winter on sea coasts. Map 121.

COURSERS AND PRATINCOLES: Glareolidae

CREAM-COLOURED COURSER *Cursorius cursor*   **Pls. 33, 39**
  Du – Renvogel   Fr – Courvite isabelle
  Ge – Rennvogel   Sw – Ökenlöpare
Identification: 9″; looks larger in flight. A slim, *pale sandy-coloured* bird, with long, *pale creamy legs*, a short, sharply pointed down-curved bill, *very conspicuous black primaries* and *black* under-surfaces of wings. Broad *black and white stripe* curving from eye to pale grey nape. Behaviour plover-like, running swiftly but spasmodically and crouching to escape detection. Flight rapid, with regular beats of distinctively black wings. Easily distinguished from pratincoles by paler appearance, longer whitish legs, prominent eye-stripe and short rounded tail.
Voice: Call-notes a deep barking '*praak-praak*' and a quieter '*tuk, tuk*'.
Habitat and Range: A desert-haunting species, occurring as vagrant on sandy beaches, dunes, etc., in most European countries, north to British Isles, Scandinavia, Finland.

COLLARED PRATINCOLE *Glareola pratincola*   **Pls. 36, 39**
  Du – Vorkstaartplevier   Fr – Glaréole à collier
  Ge – Brachschwalbe   Sw – Vadaresvala
Identification: 10″. Looks unusual, perched or flying. Has long, pointed dark wings and *deeply forked black tail with white base*, black legs and short, slightly down-curved bill. Upper-parts olive-brown, under-parts buffish with white belly and *black-bordered creamy throat-patch*. In winter, throat-patch has

indistinct border. Juvenile has a broad breast-band of dark brown steaks. Has rapid, tern-like flight. On take-off or landing can show chestnut wing-pits, but they normally look black in flight. Outer halves of upper wing-surfaces darker than inner. See also Black-winged Pratincole and Cream-coloured Courser. Large noisy flocks hawk for flying insects. Gregarious and often crepuscular.
Voice: Noisy in flight. Call-note a hard, rather tern-like, '*kyik*', or a chattering '*kitti-kirrik-kitik-tik*'.
Habitat: Sun-baked mud-flats, with low vegetation, marshes, plains, often near water. Breeds colonially. Map 122.

BLACK-WINGED PRATINCOLE   *Glareola nordmanni*   **Pl. 36**
   Du – Steppenvorkstaartplevier   Fr – Glaréole à ailes noires
   Ge – Schwarzflügelige Brachschwalbe   Sw – Svartvingad vadaresvala
Identification: 10″. Difficult to distinguish from Collared Pratincole owing to rare opportunities for seeing black wing-pits, which can only be noted with certainty when bird takes off or lands. However, upper-parts and wings of Black-winged are almost uniformly dark, *lacking Collared's white edges to secondaries*. Wing-pits of both species look black in flight; intermediate forms occur. Behaviour, flight, voice and habitat much as Collared Pratincole. Breeds Danube delta. Vagrant to N., C. and W. Europe (including Britain).

PLOVERS: Charadriidae

Wading birds, more compactly built, thicker-necked and more boldly patterned than sandpipers; bills are shorter and stouter, eyes larger. Distinctive tilting action when feeding. Plumage patterns in flight, and call-notes, are important in identification. Immatures of many species summer on coasts south of breeding range. Sexes usually similar. Ground nesting.

LITTLE RINGED PLOVER   *Charadrius dubius*   **Pls. 33, 34**
   Du – Kleine plevier   Fr – Petit gravelot
   Ge – Flussregenpfeifer   Sw – Mindre strandpipare
Identification: 6″. Resembles small Ringed Plover, but distinguished by *lack of white wing-bar*, flesh-coloured or yellowish legs (not orange, but colour not reliable when muddy), *different voice* and usually different habitat; also by white line *above* black forehead-band. At short range *yellow eye-ring* can be seen. Juvenile often has incomplete brown gorget, giving resemblance to Kentish Plover, but is distinguished by pale flesh legs and lack of wing-bar.
Voice: A high, piping '*tee-u*'. Trilling song rather like Ringed Plover's but lacks its richness, chiefly repetition of '*tree-a, tree-a*'.
Habitat: Fresh-water localities, particularly flooded gravel-pits and gravelly river islands; on coasts in winter. Breeds on gravel or sand shores of inland waters, locally on coasts. Map 123.

RINGED PLOVER   *Charadrius hiaticula*   **Pls. 33, 34**
   Du – Bontbekplevier   Fr – Grand gravelot
   Ge – Sandregenpfeifer   Sw – Större strandpipare
Identification: $7\frac{1}{2}$″. A plump, lively little shore-bird, with a *broad black band* across its white breast and *orange legs* (which can look black when muddy).

Behaviour active, running with brief pauses, *tilting* distinctively to pick up food. Upper-parts hair-brown with white collar, black mark through eyes and *prominent white forehead*. Bill orange with black tip. White wing-bar conspicuous in flight. Immature scaly-brown above, without black on head; blackish-brown breast-band often incomplete (resembling Kentish); legs yellowish; tail white-tipped. Flight rapid, with regular wing-beats.
Voice: A melodious '*too-li*', or '*coo-eep*'. Song begins slowly, becoming a trilling repetition of the phrase '*quitu-weeoo*'.
Habitat: Sandy and muddy shores, visiting inland waters, etc., on migration. Breeds on beaches, among dunes, salt-marshes, locally inland on tundra, sandy ground and dry stream-beds. Map 124.

KILLDEER   *Charadrius vociferus*   **Pl. 35**
  Du – Killdeerplevier   Fr – Gravelot à double collier
  Ge – Keilschwanzregenpfeifer   Sw – Skrikstrandpipare
Identification: 10″. Superficially resembles Ringed Plover, but is very much larger and has *two* black breast-bands. Long rufous tail has black subterminal band with white tips. In flight shows a *golden-rufous rump, long, wedge-shaped tail* and strong white wing-bars. Bill slender and black; legs pale flesh.
Voice: Usually noisy; a loud, insistent and repeated '*kill-dee*', or '*kill-deea*'; also a plaintive '*dee-ee*', with rising inflection.
Habitat and Range: Usually seen on ploughed fields and pastures, on which it also breeds (like an American counterpart of the Lapwing); in winter also frequents sea-shore. Vagrant from N. America to W. (including Britain), N. and C. Europe.

KENTISH PLOVER   *Charadrius alexandrinus*   **Pls. 33, 34**
  Du – Strandplevier   Fr – Gravelot à collier interrompu
  Ge – Seeregenpfeifer   Sw – Swartbent strandpipare
  N. Am – Snowy Plover
Identification: 6¼″. Distinguished from Ringed and Little Ringed Plovers by paler upper-parts, less plump form, *blackish bill and legs*, narrower dark patch through eye and *small dark patch* each side of upper-breast (instead of complete black band). Adults occasionally have yellow legs. Narrower white wing-bar recalls Ringed Plover, but upper-parts are paler and dark tail shows more conspicuous white at sides. Male has narrow white supercilium, blackish patch on front of *rufous* crown. Female is paler, with brownish instead of black patches on sides of breast and lacks black on crown. Juvenile can be confused with young Ringed and Little Ringed, which have incomplete breast-bands and yellowish or flesh-coloured, not black, legs. Leg-action much faster when running than Ringed.
Voice: A soft '*wit-tit-tit*', a fluty '*poo-eet*', or '*po-it*'. Alarm, '*kittup*'. Song, a long trill, beginning slowly and accelerating.
Habitat: Mainly coastal. Frequents and nests on shingle, or mixed sand and mud beaches, dry mud-flats. Map 125.

GREATER SAND PLOVER   *Charadrius leschenaultii*   **Pl. 35**
  Du – Woestijnplevier   Fr – Gravelot mongol
  Ge – Wüstenregenpfeifer   Sw – Ökenpipare
Identification: 8½″. Dun-brown above, white below, with *heavy tern-like black bill* and dark olive legs. Male in breeding plumage has *broad rusty breast-band,*

black ear-coverts and narrow black band across white forehead; fore-crown and nape pale cinnamon (no white neck-ring). Female has paler, more diffuse breast-band and grey in place of black on head. In winter sexes similar, with greyish mottling on sides of upper breast, but male retains faint traces of black on head and shows broad white supercilium; distinguished from winter Lesser by larger size, much heavier and longer bill, larger head and longer legs. Immature has pale fringes to feathers of upper-parts and rusty fringes on breast. See Lesser Sand and Caspian Plovers (Accidentals).

Voice: A musical, whistling *'peeph'*. Less vocal than most plovers.

Habitat and Range: Frequents sandy coasts and coastal mud-flats. Vagrant from C. and W. Asia to N., E., C., W. (including Britain) and S. Europe.

DOTTEREL   *Charadrius morinellus*   Pls. 33, 34

Du – Morinelplevier   Fr – Pluvier guignard
Ge – Mornellregenpfeifer   Sw – Fjällpipare

Identification: 8½″. Male smaller. Very tame. Distinguished by *white band* between brown breast and *orange-chestnut under-parts*, and blackish crown with very broad *white eye-stripes*, joining in distinctive V on nape. Belly black. Winter adults and juveniles are paler, with indistinct markings and ash-brown breasts. In overhead flight the white throat, pectoral band and tail-coverts contrast sharply with dark breast and black belly; in winter, markings are less clear, but the eye-stripes and pectoral band are always diagnostic though sometimes difficult to see. Has 'chunky', short-tailed appearance in flight. Legs yellowish.

Voice: A repeated, soft *'titi-ri-titi-ri'*, becoming a rapid trill.

Habitat: Stony heights and tundra; on migration on lowland heaths, coastal fields. Breeds on bare high ground. Map 126.

LESSER GOLDEN PLOVER   *Pluvialis dominica*   Pl. 35

Du – Aziatische goudplevier   Fr – Pluvier doré asiatique
Ge – Sibirischer Goldregenpfeifer   Sw – Arktisk ljungpipare

Identification: 10″. Smaller and more slightly built than Golden, with *longer legs*, relatively larger head, often with more prominent supercilium, and narrower wings extending well beyond tail when closed. Distinguished in all plumages by *dusky-buff under-wings and grey axillaries* (Golden has white under-wings). Adult in summer shows more black on upper- and under-parts, flanks usually lacking white borders. Immature recalls Dotterel of same age; has whiter face and supercilium and buffer under-parts than immature Golden.

Voice: Musical single, double and treble notes, the most distinctive (from Golden) a Lapwing-like *'pee-wit'* and *'klee-e-eet'*.

Habitat and Range: On migration as Golden. Breeds on arctic tundra. Vagrant to W. (including Britain), N., C. and E. Europe.

GOLDEN PLOVER   *Pluvialis apricaria*   Pls. 33, 34

Du – Goudplevier   Fr – Pluvier doré
Ge – Goldregenpfeifer   Sw – Ljungpipare

Identification: 11″. Distinguished in all plumages by dark upper-parts *richly spotted with gold*. Northern birds in summer usually have *jet-black face and under-parts*, cleanly divided by broad white stripe from forehead, down neck (almost meeting at breast) and down sides to flanks. Southern birds are much less clean-cut, with partly obscured black face and under-parts and the white

blurred and yellowish. In winter, face and under-parts whitish, mottled golden-brown on breast. No wing-bar, but tail and rump are *uniform with rest of upper-parts,* and centre and base of under-surfaces of wings are *white* (Lesser Golden's are dusky-buff). Can be confused in juvenile plumage with Grey.
Voice: Call-note (usually in flight) a clear liquid '*tlui*'; alarm, a melancholy '*tlu-i*'. Song, in display flight, a varied rippling trill, embodying repeated phrases '*toori*', '*tirr-peeoo*', etc.
Habitat: Hilly and lowland moors, and, in winter, also fields, sea-shores and estuaries; nests among heather. Map 127.

GREY PLOVER *Pluvialis squatarola* **Pls. 33, 34**
Du – Zilverplevier   Fr – Pluvier argenté
Ge – Kiebitzregenpfeifer   Sw – Kustpipare
N. Am – Black-bellied Plover
Identification: 11″. In breeding plumage, *black below and whitish above.* Resembles no other wader except Golden Plover, but distinguished in any plumage by heavier build and bill, larger eyes, *conspicuous black axillaries* ('wing-pits') contrasting with whitish under-surfaces of wings and by *whitish wing-bar, rump and tail.* Adults in summer have upper-parts spangled with *whitish* (not gold); in winter, upper-parts are more uniform brownish-grey, under-parts look whiter than Golden Plover's; immature is yellowish, can be confused with Golden Plover. Has dejected, hunched appearance.
Voice: Call-note a plaintive, *trisyllabic,* slurred whistle '*tlee-u-ee*'.
Habitat: Chiefly coastal mud-flats, sandy beaches and shores. Breeds on arctic tundra. Map 128.

SPUR-WINGED PLOVER *Hoplopterus spinosus* **Pl. 35**
Du – Sporenkievit   Fr – Vanneau éperonné
Ge – Spornkiebitz   Sw – Sporrvipa
Identification: 10½″. Very striking *black and white* appearance. Slightly crested, jet-black crown, *black centre of throat,* breast and under-parts. Cheeks, neck and under tail-coverts white. Upper-parts dun brown with drooping dark-edged scapulars. Wings and tail strongly patterned black and white, with small spur on bend of wing. Behaviour resembles Lapwing's.
Voice: Usual note, a noisy '*zac-zac-zac*'.
Habitat and Range: Open ground and marshes, often saline. A North African and Asiatic species, breeding in NE Greece and Black Sea coast. Vagrant S. and C. Europe.

SOCIABLE PLOVER *Chettusia gregaria* **Pl. 35**
Du – Steppenkievit   Fr – Pluvier sociable
Ge – Steppenkiebitz   Sw – Stäppvipa
Identification: 11½″. A rather large, long-legged plover. Looks pinkish-grey in distance, but at close range *black crown contrasts with broad white supercilia joining in V at nape.* In flight the *white secondaries, black primaries and white tail* with broad black subterminal band are conspicuous. In summer, cheeks and lower throat warm buff, breast and back pinkish-grey, belly shading to *dark chestnut, contrasting with white under-tail coverts* in flight. In winter, head and belly markings are less distinct and breast has some dark streaking. Immature looks like brownish winter adult but under-parts buffish with stronger streaking. Flight recalls Lapwing, but wings are narrower and less rounded.

Voice: In winter a shrill, short whistle and a harsh rasping 'etch-etch-etch', sometimes becoming a long chatter.
Habitat and Range: Open sandy or grassy plains, wastelands near upland cultivation; also occurs near coasts. Breeds in steppe. Vagrant from Asia to E., C., N., W. (including Britain) and S. Europe.

WHITE-TAILED PLOVER   *Chettusia leucura*   Pl. 35

Du – Witstaartkievit   Fr – Vanneau à queue blanche
Ge – Weisschwanzsteppenkiebitz   Sw – Sumpvipa

Identification: 11″. Size of small Lapwing, but with longer bill and much longer, *conspicuously yellow legs*, which project well beyond tail in flight. *Pale greyish-white head and pure white tail* are best field marks. Upper-parts bronze-brown, under-parts pale with white throat, grey breast and white belly tinted buffish. In flight, black and white wing pattern (resembling Spur-winged Plover), conspicuous white tail and projecting legs are diagnostic.
Voice: Usual call a shrill '*kit-kit*'.
Habitat and Range: Fresh-water marshes and lagoons. Vagrant from W. Asia to E., S. and W. Europe (including Britain).

LAPWING   *Vanellus vanellus*   Pls. 33, 34

Du – Kievit   Fr – Vanneau huppé
Ge – Kiebitz   Sw – Tofsvipa

Identification: 12″. Typical of farming country. A large iridescent *greenish-black and white* plover, distinguished by a *long wispy crest* and *black breast* contrasting with pure white under-parts and cheeks; also by distinctive voice and, in flight, by *broad, very rounded wings*. Tail white, with broad black terminal band and chestnut under tail-coverts. Flight often wildly erratic, with slow 'flapping' wing-beats and headlong plunges during acrobatic display-flight. Gregarious, often in huge, straggling flocks in winter.
Voice: A loud, nasal "*peese-weet*', or a longer '*pee-r-weet*', with variants.
Habitat: Farmlands, sewage-farms, marshes and mud-flats. Breeds on arable land, moors, marshes, etc. Map 129.

SANDPIPERS, STINTS, GODWITS, CURLEWS, SNIPE, PHALAROPES:
Scolopacidae

Legs longish, or very long; wings usually pointed and angular; bills long and slender; plumages often differ in summer and winter. Stints and small sandpipers are often very difficult to identify. Wing-bars, rump and tail patterns important diagnostically. Many species summer on coasts south of breeding range, some occurring in large flocks. Sexes similar. Usually ground nesting.

KNOT   *Calidris canutus*   Pls. 40, 41

Du – Kanoetstrandloper   Fr – Bécasseau maubèche
Ge – Knutt   Sw – Kustsnäppa

Identification: 10″. *Noticeably stocky and short in neck, bill and legs*. In summer, upper-parts strongly mottled chestnut and black; head and under-parts *russet*

(Curlew Sandpiper is similar in coloration, but is much smaller, longer in leg and has longer, curved bill). In winter is nondescript 'scaly' ash-grey above, whitish below. Identified in flight by large size, *uniform pale rump and tail* and pale wing-bar. (Dunlin and Sanderling in flight have blackish centre to their rumps and sharper wing-bars, and are much smaller.) Often in *densely packed flocks*.

Voice: A low '*nut*'; flight-call a whistling '*twit-wit*'.

Habitat: Frequents sandy and muddy sea-shores, occasionally on inland waters. Breeds on high arctic barrens. Map 130.

SANDERLING   *Calidris alba*   Pls. 40, 41
Du – Drieteenstrandloper   Fr – Bécasseau sanderling
Ge – Sanderling   Sw – Sandlöpare

Identification: 8″. A plump, small, extremely active, whitish bird which races after the retreating waves like a clockwork toy. In flight *long white stripe on dark wing* contrasts more boldly than in other small shore-birds. Dark tail has white sides. In summer, upper-parts, head and breast chestnut, speckled blackish, contrasting with pure white belly. (See also Little Stint and Baird's Sandpiper.) In winter, is *whitest of the small waders*; head and under-parts white; upper-parts pale grey with dark 'shoulder-patch'; distinguished from much slimmer winter phalaropes by lack of dark eye-patch and different behaviour. Bill and legs black. Distinguished in winter from darker Dunlin by larger size, *much bolder wing-bar and stouter, straight bill*; in summer also by *paler upper-parts and lack of black patch on belly*. Immature chequered black and white above, with pinkish-buff head and breast.

Voice: A short '*twick*', or '*quit*'.

Habitat: Winters on sandy beaches; a few occur inland on passage. Breeds on stony arctic tundra. Map 131.

SEMIPALMATED SANDPIPER   *Calidris pusilla*   Pl. 42
Du – Kleine grijze strandloper   Fr – Bécasseau semi-palmé
Ge – Sandstrandläufer   Sw – Dvärgsnäppa

Identification: 5½–6¾″. Can be confused with two other N. American vagrants, the Western and Least Sandpipers and, in winter, also with Little Stint. In summer is much *less rufous* than Western or Least. Bill is shorter and straighter than Western's and with thicker tip; is thicker and slightly longer than Least's. Western often has rusty scapulars, whereas Semipalmated's are paler. Least is smaller, browner, thinner-billed and has yellowish legs (Semipalmated's and Western's are black). In autumn Semipalmated, especially juvenile, is extremely difficult to distinguish from Little Stint in winter plumage. Juvenile Little Stint may be separated by prominent white V on back. Chief distinctions of Semipalmated are plumper body, slightly shorter and thicker-tipped bill, different call-note and more plover-like start-and-stop feeding style. At very close range the semipalmation between the toes may be visible.

Voice: A short, soft '*chewp*', or '*chirrup*', lacking the '*ee*' sound of the Western and Least calls.

Habitat and Range: Beaches and mud-flats. Vagrant from N. America to W. Europe (including Britain).

LITTLE STINT *Calidris minuta*   **Pls. 40, 41**
  Du – Kleine strandloper   Fr – Bécasseau minute
  Ge – Zwergstrandläufer   Sw – Småsnäppa
Identification: 5¼″. Smallest common wader. Distinguished from Dunlin by *straight short bill* and smaller, neater appearance. Adult in summer has rufous upper-parts and crown, rufous-tinged and streaked breast, white supercilium and belly. In winter has cold grey upper-parts and whiter neck and breast. Immature like pale summer adult with cleaner breast and two distinctive pale Vs on back. In flight shows narrow wing-bar and white *sides* to rump, like Dunlin. See also Temminck's, summer Sanderling, and Semipalmated Sandpiper, and other stints in Accidentals.
Voice: A sharp '*tit*', or '*tirri-tit-tit*'. Song, a long undulating trill.
Habitat: On passage, much as Dunlin. Breeds in coastal marshes and on tundra, among willow scrub, etc. Map 132.

TEMMINCK'S STINT *Calidris temminckii*   **Pls. 40, 41**
  Du – Temminck's strandloper   Fr – Bécasseau de Temminck
  Ge – Temminckstrandläufer   Sw – Mosnäppa
Identification: 5½″. Distinguished from similar Little Stint by *more uniform, greyer appearance* above and on breast, different voice and different behaviour. In flight, shows an inconspicuous white wing-bar and white on outer tail-feathers (Little Stint shows grey). A short range *pale greenish or brownish legs* are also diagnostic (Little Stint's are black). When flushed, 'towers' like Snipe. See also other Stints and Common Sandpiper.
Voice: A short trilling '*tirrr*' and a buzzy, prolonged tittering, in display-flight and from ground.
Habitat: Seldom on sea-shore. On passage frequents wet marshes, lakes with vegetation, occasionally saltings and estuaries. Breeds among low vegetation on tundra, shores and islets. Map 133.

LEAST SANDPIPER *Calidris minutilla*   **Pl. 42**
  Du– Amerikaanse kleinste strandloper   Fr – Bécasseau minuscule
  Ge – Wiesenstrandläufer   Sw – Amerikansk småsnäppa
Identification: 5″. The smallest of the stint group. General appearance dark, tiny and rather square-headed. Darker than Semipalmated, duller than Little or Western, more uniform than Long-toed. Best distinguished by small size, *needle-fine* blackish bill with a slight droop, *dark* brown upper-parts with a very narrow pale V on mantle edges, well-streaked breast and throat with very white belly. Legs can look either pale or blackish, varying from yellowish-green to dark brown. In flight wings look relatively short and small, with a thin whitish bar. Has distinctive *crouched appearance* when feeding or running. 'Towers' when disturbed.
Voice: Calls a high, drawn-out '*kreet*', or variations on '*trrip-trip*' and '*quee*'.
Habitat and Range: Tidal flats, shores, marshes. Vagrant from N. America to W. (including Britain), N. and C. Europe.

WHITE-RUMPED SANDPIPER   *Calidris fuscicollis*   **Pl. 40**
Du – Bonaparte's strandloper   Fr – Bécasseau de Bonaparte
Ge – Weissbürzelstrandläufer   Sw – Piplärksnäppa
Identification: 7″. A small, streaked sandpiper, more slender than Dunlin, with
a *neat curved white patch on upper tail-coverts* contrasting with dark tail. Upper-
parts rufous in spring with dark feather-centres; greyer in autumn. Immature
resembles autumn adult, but has rufous and whitish feather-margins. In flight
shows thin, obscure whitish wing-bar. Distinguished from Curlew Sandpiper
by smaller size, shorter, *straight* bill and smaller white rump-patch.
Voice: A thin, mouse-like '*jeet*'.
Habitat and Range: Beaches, mud-flats. A vagrant from N. America to W.
(including Britain), N., C. and E. Europe.

BAIRD'S SANDPIPER   *Calidris bairdii*   **Pl. 40**
Du – Baird's strandloper   Fr – Bécasseau de Baird
Ge – Baird-Strandläufer   Sw – Gulbröstad snäppa
Identification: 7″. Smaller than Pectoral, larger than stints, with *long wings
overlapping tail when perched*. Lower back and central tail-feathers are *black*.
Adult in summer recalls Sanderling, but with less bold wing-stripe. First-winter
birds have dark 'scaly' upper-parts and white under-parts with buff breast-
patches. Bill slightly decurved. Legs blackish. Call '*churrut*' or '*kreep*', recalling
Curlew Sandpiper. Somewhat similar to Least, Semipalmated, Western. White-
rumped and Pectoral are more or less *striped* above; Baird's looks more 'scaly'
and mostly buffish-brown; Buff-breasted is all buff below (not only on breast)
and has yellow (not blackish) legs. Vagrant from N. America to W. (including
Britain), N., C. and E. Europe.

PECTORAL SANDPIPER   *Calidris melanotos*   **Pls. 40, 41**
Du – Gestreepte strandloper   Fr – Bécasseau tacheté
Ge – Graubruststrandläufer   Sw – Tuvsnäppa
Identification: 7½″. A little larger than Dunlin, smaller than Knot. Crown, neck
and upper-parts streaked black and rusty-brown, with buff snipe-like *stripes
down back*. Rich brown cap and ear-coverts contrast with long, creamy
supercilium and chin. Neck and breast closely streaked, *ending abruptly against
pure white of lower breast*. When alert, neck looks longer than in most similar
shore-birds (more like small Reeve). *Legs ochre.* Flight erratic when flushed,
showing virtually no wing-bar and very dark centre tail-feathers. See also
Sharp-tailed and Baird's Sandpipers.
Voice: A rather hoarse '*krrik*' or '*tchree-eep*'.
Habitat and Range: Occurs on passage on grassy mud-flats and marshes,
occasionally on sea-shores. Autumn visitor from N. America to Britain,
Ireland. Vagrant elsewhere in W., N., C. and E. Europe.

SHARP-TAILED SANDPIPER   *Calidris acuminata*   **Pl. 42**
Du – Siberische gestreepte strandloper   Fr – Bécasseau à queue pointue
Ge – Spitzschwanzstrandläufer   Sw – Spetsstjärtad snäppa
Identification: 8½″. Easily mistaken for Pectoral, but distinguished in all
plumages by *lack of sharp contrast between dark breast and white belly* and by
whiter, more prominent eye-ring. Legs greenish-grey or blackish. Summer
adults have even dark brown scalloping (not streaks) on buff breast *merging*

into white belly and flanks. (Pectoral's streaking ends abruptly, does not extend to flanks.) In autumn breast is greyish-tawny or rich buffish, with some streaks on sides which may also form a collar on lower throat. Immature in winter has rich buff breast.

Voice: A rather rasping '*trrit-trrit*', or a more Swallow-like '*chree-creep*', less harsh than Pectoral's cry.

Habitat and Range: Sea-shores and grassy edges of salt-marshes. Vagrant from Siberia to W. (including Britain), N. and C. Europe.

CURLEW SANDPIPER   *Calidris ferruginea*   **Pls. 33, 40, 41**
   Du – Krombekstrandloper   Fr – Bécasseau corcorli
   Ge – Sichelstrandläufer   Sw – Spovsnäppa

Identification: 7½″. In breeding plumage mainly brick-red, resembling much larger Knot; crown and upper-parts richly marked black and chestnut; sides of head, neck and under-parts *bright brick-red* with some mottling; white rump partly obscured by blackish tips. In winter, looks very similar to Dunlin, with which it associates; best distinguished by *white rump*, which is conspicuous in flight (Dunlin's has dark centre); also by longer legs and neck, more elegant, upright carriage, clearer breast (washed rosy-buff in immature), brighter supercilium, different voice and *more slender, longer, evenly down-curving bill.* Shape of bill is not always diagnostic, as Dunlin's is sometimes similar.

Voice: A liquid '*chirrip*'.

Habitat and Range: On passage, as Dunlin. Breeds in E. Arctic Asia. On passage throughout Europe; in winter occasionally north to British Isles.

PURPLE SANDPIPER   *Calidris maritima*   **Pls. 40, 41**
   Du – Paarse strandloper   Fr – Bécasseau violet
   Ge – Meerstrandläufer   Sw – Skärsnäppa

Identification: 8¼″. Size between Dunlin and Knot. Distinguished by rock-haunting habits, stocky build and, in winter, by *very dark head, breast and upper-parts*, contrasting with white belly and scalloped flanks; in summer upper-parts look paler, light rufous emarginations giving patterned effect. Has white throat and 'spectacles'. Tame behaviour usually permits sight of *short yellow legs and yellow base to bill*. Shows narrow white wing-bar and secondary edges.

Voice: When flushed, a high-pitched trilling '*tritt, tritt*', or a piping '*weet-wit*'.

Habitat: In winter frequents rocky coasts and offshore islets. Breeds on hillsides in tundra. Map 134.

DUNLIN   *Calidris alpina*   **Pls. 33, 40, 41**
   Du – Bonte strandloper   Fr – Bécasseau variable
   Ge – Alpenstrandläufer   Sw – Kärrsnäppa
   N. Am – Red-backed Sandpiper

Identification: 7″. Commonest British shore-bird. Distinguished in summer by *large black patch on lower breast*; upper-parts and crown *chestnut*, streaked black; upper breast white, finely streaked. Bill fairly long, slightly down-curved at tip. In winter, streaked brownish-grey above, white below, with finely streaked greyish breast and flanks. White wing-bar and white *sides* of rump and tail fairly conspicuous in flight. (Sanderling in winter is larger, with whiter plumage and a brighter wing-bar; Curlew Sandpiper in winter, though more graceful, with longer legs and whiter under-parts, is best distinguished by it conspicuous white rump.) Feeding attitude is 'hunched up'.

Voice: A short, high, nasal '*dzee*'. Song, a purring trill.

Habitat: Sea-shores, estuaries, also inland waters, sewage-farms, etc. Breed near water on high moors, bogs, salt-marshes. Map 135.

BROAD-BILLED SANDPIPER *Limicola falcinellus* Pl. 40
Du – Breedbekstrandloper   Fr – Bécasseau falcinelle
Ge – Sumpfläufer   Sw – Myrsnäppa

Identification: $6\frac{1}{2}''$. Smaller than Dunlin, with disproportionately short legs and long bill with heavy base and kinked tip. Distinguished in breeding plumage by *very dark upper-parts*, with bold Jack Snipe-like *creamy streaks on back*; *bol double supercilium forking behind eye*, giving head a distinctive *striped appearance*; at rest, *copper edges* of secondaries can be conspicuous; streaked breast contrasts with white under-parts. Looks very dark in flight, with sligh wing-bar. In winter, is greyish above, with streaked breast, very like Dunlin, bu upper fork of eye-stripe is sometimes indistinct and has blackish patch at carpa joint on closed wing. Often less active than most shore-birds.

Voice: A deep, trilling '*chr-r-eek*'.

Habitat: On passage, usually in salt-marshes, mud-flats, sewage-farms, les often on sea-shore. Nests in tussocks in wet bogs and morasses. Map 136.

BUFF-BREASTED SANDPIPER *Tryngites subruficollis* Pl. 40
Du – Blonde strandloper   Fr – Bécasseau rousset
Ge – Grasläufer   Sw – Prärielöpare

Identification: $8''$. Recalls immature Ruff, but smaller. Has distinctive *smal round head on long neck, pale eye-ring, short bill and chrome-yellow legs*. Upper parts like Ruff, but lacks black or white markings above tail; no wing-bar. Fac and under-parts rich clear buff, often fading to whitish on belly. Under-surface of wings, scalloped with blackish. Very tame. See also Baird's.

Voice: A low, trilled '*pr-r-r-reet*' and a clicking '*tik*'.

Habitat and Range: Dry fields with very short grass, in preference to shores. vagrant from N. America. Recorded chiefly in British Isles; also elsewhere i W., C., N. and E. Europe.

RUFF *Philomachus pugnax* Pls. 38, 4
Du – Kemphaan   Fr – Chevalier combattant
Ge – Kampfläufer   Sw – Brushane

Identification: Male $11\frac{1}{2}''$, female $9''$. Male unmistakable in breeding plumage with *enormous erectile ruff and ear-tufts* in various combinations of black white, purple, chestnut, buff, giving thick-necked appearance in flight. Femal (Reeve) and male in winter have bold 'scaly' dark and sandy upper-parts, bu breast, no ruff or ear-tufts. Adults in early or late breeding plumage are brow above, with copious dark mottling around breast, contrasting sharply with pal chin and white belly. In winter resembles Redshank, but distinguished b shorter bill, 'scaly' plumage, *dark tail with conspicuous oval white patch each sid* (occasionally joined), lack of white on secondaries and more erect stance. Leg vary from grey-brown to green or orange. Juvenile resembles Reeve, but wit more richly marked upper-parts and pinkish-buff breast; can be very puzzling

Voice: A low '*chut-ut*'; has occasional deep guttural gobbling note, at displa mounds, where sexually promiscuous.

Habitat: In winter and on passage on inland marshes, lake shores, occasionally estuaries. Breeds on northern tundra: in southern range in water-meadows and marshes. Map 137.

JACK SNIPE   *Lymnocryptes minimus*   **Pls. 38, 39**

Du – Bokje   Fr – Bécassine sourde
Ge – Zwergschnepfe   Sw – Dvärgbeckasin

Identification: 7½″. Smallest snipe. Difficult to observe on the ground, but quickly distinguished from Snipe by *smaller size, relatively much shorter bill and lower, more direct flight* (though it may dodge a little occasionally). Breaks over at last moment and drops again quickly, instead of 'towering' after wild zig-zag flight, like Snipe. *Usually silent when flushed.* At short range lack of buff centre-stripe on crown, brighter stripes contrasting with purplish gloss on back, *lack of white on tail* and of barring on flanks are further distinctions from Snipe.
Voice: Muffled throbbing note, like sound of galloping horse, delivered in display-flight and on ground.
Habitat: As Snipe. Breeds in wet swamps and bogs. Map 138.

SNIPE   *Gallinago gallinago*   **Pls. 38, 39**

Du – Watersnip   Fr – Bécassine des marais
Ge – Bekassine   Sw – Enkelbeckasin
N. Am – Wilson's Snipe

Identification: 10½″. A secretive, tight-sitting, brown marsh-bird, with a long straight bill. Difficult to observe closely, but quickly identified by characteristic *zig-zag flight and hoarse rasping cry when flushed.* Much larger than shorter-billed Jack Snipe, near size of Great Snipe but less bulky; smaller than Woodcock. Black and rufous back *strongly striped* with golden-buff. Tail shows *a little* white on outer edges and tips (adult Great Snipe shows *conspicuous* white corners, Jack Snipe none; young Great Snipe also shows none and is difficult to distinguish in the field from Snipe except by behaviour). Stripes on head are *lengthways* (Woodcock's are *across*). Long, slender bill carried downwards in flight. Flies in small parties, or 'wisps'.
Voice: When flushed, a dry, rasping 'schaap'. Song, a rhythmic monotonously repeated 'chic-ka'. In oblique dives during display-flight a vibrating sound (so-called drumming) is produced by the widely spread outer tail-feathers, like rapidly repeated 'huhuhuhuhu'.
Habitat: Marshes, water-meadows, sewage-farms, boggy moors, etc. Nests in coarse grass or rushes, occasionally in heather. Map 139.

GREAT SNIPE   *Gallinago media*   **Pls. 38, 39**

Du – Poelsnip   Fr – Bécassine double
Ge – Doppelschnepfe   Sw – Dubbelbeckasin

Identification: 11″. Distinguished on the ground with difficulty from Snipe by deeper-chested, *darker and more barred appearance*, including belly (which is white on Snipe), and shorter bill with deeper base. More easily distinguished in flight, when wing shows long blackish central panel with white borders, whereas Snipe's secondaries form darkest area; adult Greats (but not immatures) show *much more white on outer tail-feathers*. Flight is slower and heavier and usually direct (not twisting), with wings more bowed; *usually rises silently*; bill held more horizontally.

Voice: An occasional brief croak. Males at display grounds in spring indulge in remarkable bubbling, popping, croaking chorus-singing.
Habitat: Except in breeding season often frequents drier localities than Snipe: stubble fields, bracken-covered heaths, etc. In breeding season usually in marshy country, banks of rivers, etc. Map 140.

LONG-BILLED DOWITCHER   *Limnodromus scolopaceus* **Pls. 38, 39**
Du – Noordelijke grizze snip   Fr – Bécasseau à long bec
Ge – Langschnabel-Schlamläufer   Sw – Större beckasinsnäppa

Identification: 11½″. A bulky, short-tailed bird of snipe-like proportions. In any plumage recognized by the combination of long, *snipe-like bill* and white back, rump and tail. The white extends *up the back* in a long point. Might be mistaken for Greenshank but legs are much shorter and wings have white stripe on rear margin. In summer plumage has breast washed with cinnamon-red. Feeds with 'sewing-machine' motion, rapidly jabbing its long bill perpendicularly into the mud. Hard to separate from Short-billed *L. griseus* (Accidentals), but is larger, bill is longer, closed wings do not reach tail-tip and under tail-coverts are *barred* (not spotted).
Voice: Long-billed Dowitcher: a long, shrill '*keeek*', repeated when flushed in a long rippling trill. Short-billed Dowitcher: a rapid triple '*kut-kut-kut*' recalling Lesser Yellowlegs.
Habitat and Range: Long-billed on passage usually in muddy fresh-water pools with marginal vegetation. Short-billed on coastal mud-flats. Autumn vagrant most years from N. America to British Isles; vagrant N. and E. Europe.

WOODCOCK   *Scolopax rusticola*   **Pls. 38, 39**
Du – Houtsnip   Fr – Bécasse des bois
Ge – Waldschnepfe   Sw – Morkulla

Identification: 13½″. A rather solitary woodland species. Perfect 'dead leaf' camouflage and retiring habit make observation difficult. Distinguished from Snipe by larger, stouter form, thicker bill, *more rounded wings, finely barred* buffish under-parts and *transverse black bars* on back of head and neck. Passes day in thick shelter, taking wing with distinctive swishing sound (but without calling), quickly dropping to cover again. Flight usually rapid and dodging. In flight looks stout, short-tailed and 'neckless', with bill pointing downward at an angle. Crepuscular.
Voice: During slow display-flight (known as 'roding') above trees, at dawn and dusk, male has soft, croaking '*orrrt-orrrt*', followed by a louder, high sneezing '*tsiwick*'.
Habitat: Wooded regions particularly with wet, overgrown rides and patches of evergreen. Usually nests at foot of tree. Map 141.

BLACK-TAILED GODWIT   *Limosa limosa*   **Pls. 36, 37**
Du – Grutto   Fr – Barge à queue noire
Ge – Uferschnepfe   Sw – Rödspov

Identification: 16″. A tall, upstanding wader. Distinguished from Bar-tailed by longer, *straighter* bill, *longer legs* trailing well beyond tail in flight, *broad white wing-bar and bold black band* on pure white tail. In summer, head and breast are chestnut, flanks and belly white with blackish bars. Winter plumage more like dark Bar-tailed, but wing and tail pattern are unchanged. Juvenile has rufous-buff neck and breast.

Voice: Flight-call a clear *'reeka-reeka-reeka'*; notes on breeding ground include a nasal *'quee-yit'* recalling Lapwing; song a clear repeated *'wheddy-whit-o'*.

Habitat: In winter, estuaries, marshes; on passage, inland lakes and sewage-farms. Nests in water-meadows, moors and dunes. Map 142.

BAR-TAILED GODWIT *Limosa lapponica* Pls. 36, 37

Du – Rosse grutto	Fr – Barge rousse
Ge – Pfuhlschnepfe	Sw – Myrspov

Identification: 15″. Bar-tailed is slightly smaller than Black-tailed and distinguished by lack of white wing-bar, *closely barred tail*, more upturned bill, dull white rump and *considerably shorter legs*, which barely project beyond tail in flight. In summer, male looks rich reddish-chestnut, particularly about head, neck and breast; female is much duller. In winter, both look strikingly pale, with mottled grey upper-parts, whitish under-parts; in distance, colour is not unlike Curlew's. Juvenile has more strongly streaked buffish breast.

Voice: Usually silent outside breeding season. Flight-note a harsh *'kirrik'*; alarm, a shrill *'krick'*. Song higher-pitched and faster than Black-tailed's.

Habitat: Usually coastal. Often seen in winter in dense packs at water's edge. Breeds on swampy peat-moss, in marshes near or beyond tree limits. Map 143.

WHIMBREL *Numenius phaeopus* Pls. 36, 37

Du – Regenwulp	Fr – Courlis corlieu
Ge – Regenbrachvogel	Sw – Snåspov

Identification: 16″. Smaller than Curlew. Distinguished by neater appearance, darker, more contrasting upper-parts, relatively shorter bill more kinked than curved, and *boldly striped crown*. Call is entirely different. Wing-beats are quicker. See also Slender-billed Curlew. Hudsonian Whimbrel *N. p. hudsonicus* (an N. American race, accidental Iceland, Scotland, Ireland, Spain) lacks the white rump and is darker.

Voice: An even tittering of about seven whistling notes. Song resembles the fluty, bubbling part of Curlew's song.

Habitat: As Curlew. In breeding season frequents boggy moors; nests among heather and rough grass. Map 144.

SLENDER-BILLED CURLEW *Numenius tenuirostris* Pl. 36

Du – Dunbekwulp	Fr – Courlis à bec grêle
Ge – Dünnschnabel-Brachvogel	Sw – Smalnäbbad spov

Identification: 16″. Smaller and slimmer than Curlew, slightly longer-billed than Whimbrel. A pale, Whimbrel-size bird, uniformly chequered above, without striations but with *distinctive spots on breast and flanks* (spots heart-shaped, but look round at distance). Crown *finely* streaked, giving capped appearance above white supercilium. Distinguished in flight by combination of *snow-white under-parts and rump*, pale tail and contrast between dark primaries and pale, barred secondaries. Flight recalls Curlew, but can be very swift and erratic.

Voice: Resembles Curlew's *'cour-lee'*, but shorter and less deep; alarm, a sharp *'kew-ee'*.

Habitat and Range: In winter as Curlew. Breeds in marshy steppes. Occurs on passage in Balkans and Italy. Vagrant to S., C. and W. Europe.

CURLEW *Numenius arquata* **Pls. 36, 37**
Du – Wulp Fr – Courlis cendré
Ge – Grosser Brachvogel Sw – Storspov
Identification: 21–23″. Largest European wader. Easily recognized by *very long, down-curved bill* and distinctive voice. Plumage greyish or buffish-brown, closely streaked; whitish rump extends to lower back. Flight strong and rather gull-like, with measured beat; flocks usually fly high, in lines or chevrons. Whimbrel is smaller, with shorter curved bill and boldly striped crown. See also Slender-billed Curlew.
Voice: A pure, ringing '*cour-li*', or '*crwee*' '*croo-ee*'. Song is loud, slowly delivered and remarkably liquid, embodying long bubbling trill. Sings almost all the year.
Habitat: Mud-flats and estuaries. Occurs inland during migration. Nests on moors, marshes, meadows, sand-dunes. Map 145.

UPLAND SANDPIPER *Bartramia longicauda* **Pl. 42**
Du – Bartram's strandloper Fr – Bartramie à longue queue
Ge – Bartrams Uferläufer Sw – Höglandssnäppa
Identification: 11″. A large, streaked, buffish-brown wader, near size of Ruff, with graceful, slender appearance. The general brown coloration, rather short bill (shorter than head), comparatively small-headed, thin-necked appearance, *long wings* lacking wing-bars but with white-tipped secondaries, *rather long tawny tail* and habit of holding wings elevated upon alighting are helpful points (under-wing surfaces are strongly barred). See also Pectoral Sandpiper.
Voice: A mellow whistle in flight, '*kip-ip-ip-ip*'.
Habitat and Range: Extensive fields, burnt ground, etc. (not sea-shores). A vagrant from N. America. Has been recorded chiefly in British Isles; also C. and S. Europe.

SPOTTED REDSHANK *Tringa erythropus* **Pls. 38, 39**
Du – Zwarte ruiter Fr – Chevalier arlequin
Ge – Dunkler Wasserläufer Sw – Svartsnäppa
Identification: 12″. Distinguished in summer from all other waders by *sooty-black plumage*, speckled with white on upper-parts, looking at a distance darker below than above. Long white streak up rump and back; tail barred. In winter, looks more like Redshank, but distinguished by *lack of wing-bar*, longer and thinner bill, longer legs projecting well beyond tail in flight, and *cleaner ash-grey upper-parts* copiously spotted with white. Legs dark red in summer, orange in winter. Voice is very distinctive. When seen with Redshank, Spotted has more upright stance with longer neck and is more active in feeding. See also Greenshank.
Voice: A loud, distinctive '*tchuit*', and a quiet contact-note '*gek, gek*'.
Habitat: As Redshank. Breeds in open areas in northern forests. Map 146.

REDSHANK *Tringa totanus* **Pls. 38, 39**
Du – Tureluur Fr – Chevalier gambette
Ge – Rotschenkel Sw – Rödbena
Identification: 11″. Distinguished in flight by conspicuous *white hind-edges of dark wings and white back and rump*; when perched, by long *orange-red* legs. Bill long, reddish, with black tip. Upper-parts strongly marked with black and grey. Tail barred black and white. Under-parts closely streaked and speckled.

Juvenile buffer above, with orange-yellow legs; sometimes confused with Lesser Yellowlegs (which see). Behaviour suspicious and noisy; when uneasy, often 'bobs'. See also Spotted Redshank.

Voice: When flushed, a volley of high-pitched notes. Usual call a musical, down-slurred 'tleu-hu-hu'. Alarm, an incessant yelping 'teuk'. Song has various repeated musical phrases, notably 'taweeo'.

Habitat: Marshes, moors, saltings, water-meadows, sewage-farms. Winters on estuaries and mud-flats. Nests in tussock. Map 147.

MARSH SANDPIPER *Tringa stagnatilis*   Pl. 38

Du – Poelruiter	Fr – Chevalier stagnatile
Ge – Teichwasserläufer	Sw – Dammsnäppa

Identification: 9″. Slender and long-legged, in winter plumage recalling Greenshank, but distinguished, apart from size, by *very fine straight bill, white face and forehead* and proportionately longer, spindly, greenish legs. In summer, feathers on mantle have black centres with buffish edges, giving *boldly spotted effect*. In flight, shows dark and white pattern similar to Greenshank's, but *feet project farther beyond tail*. Voice is quite different. Movements noticeably more graceful than Greenshank's.

Voice: Usual notes (none very loud), 'tew', 'teea', 'chik', 'chick-cleuit', etc., and a twittering trill.

Habitat: Seldom on sea-shore. Winters around inland waters and marshes. Breeds (occasionally in small groups) on grassy borders of lakes and on marshy steppes. Map 148.

GREENSHANK   *Tringa nebularia*   Pls. 38, 39

Du – Groenpootruiter	Fr – Chevalier aboyeur
Ge – Grünschenkel	Sw – Gluttsnäppa

Identification: 12″. Distinguished from Redshank by whiter face and under-parts, *lack of white on wing*, longer greenish legs, which project well beyond tail in flight. Also by slightly larger size, very slightly upturned blackish bill and *extensive white up back*. In winter upper-parts are paler and greyer. See also Spotted Redshank, Lesser Yellowlegs and Marsh Sandpiper.

Voice: A ringing 'tew-tew-tew', less shrill than Redshank; a repeated scolding 'tyip', etc. Song a mellow, repeated 'tew-i'.

Habitat: As Redshank. Breeds on moors or in patches of grass or heath in forest, usually not far from water. Map 149.

GREATER YELLOWLEGS   *Tringa melanoleuca*   Pl. 42

Du – Grote geelpootruiter	Fr – Grand chevalier à pattes jaunes
Ge – Grosser Gelbschenkel	Sw – Stor gulbena

Identification: 13–15″. About one-third larger than very similar Lesser. Best distinction is *relatively longer, stouter bill* which is usually *slightly upcurved* (like Greenshank's); stouter and longer than Redshank's. Looks much like Greenshank though more spotted above and lacking the long white wedge up lower back (the whitish rump is lightly speckled). Rather stout, rich yellow legs; bill black with olive base. Immature in winter is whiter below and on rump.

Voice: A 3–4 syllable 'heu-heu-heu', very like Greenshank, but louder, higher and more ringing than Lesser Yellowlegs.

Habitat and Range: Outside breeding season usually on grassy marshes, around pools and on coastal mud-flats. Vagrant from N. America to W. (including Britain) and N. Europe.

LESSER YELLOWLEGS *Tringa flavipes*   Pl. 38
  Du – Kleine geelpootruiter   Fr – Petit chevalier à pattes jaunes
  Ge – Gelbschenkel   Sw – Gulbena

Identification: 10″. Slightly smaller than Redshank; delicate proportions recall Wood Sandpiper, but is larger, with longer, more slender bill and longer *bright yellow legs*. No white on wings. Square white rump-patch *not extending up back* distinguishes it from Redshank and Greenshank. White supercilia meet on forehead. Greater Yellowlegs is larger, with longer, more upcurved bill.

Voice: A soft whistle of one, two or occasionally three notes, '*cu*', or '*cu-cu*'. Song, a rapidly repeated '*tootle-to-to*'.

Habitat and Range: Frequents mud-flats, marshes. A vagrant from N. America, chiefly to British Isles; recorded C. and N. Europe.

SOLITARY SANDPIPER *Tringa solitaria*   Pl. 42
  Du – Amerikaanse bosruiter   Fr – Chevalier solitaire
  Ge – Einsiedelwasserläufer   Sw – Amerikansk skogssnäppa

Identification: 7½–9″. A dark-backed, blackish-rumped sandpiper with all-dark wings and *conspicuous white sides to dark-centred tail* crossed by bold black bars. Blackish undersides of wings and olive-green legs recall Green Sandpiper, but *dark rump* is quick distinction. Distinguished from somewhat similar Lesser Yellowlegs by dark legs and rump; from Spotted Sandpiper by lack of white wing-stripe. Has nodding head action and a darting flight with almost Swallow-like wing action.

Voice: Usual call a high '*peet*', or '*peet-weet-weet*'.

Habitat and Range: Fresh-water marshes, ponds, streamsides. Vagrant from N. America to W. (including Britain) and N. Europe.

GREEN SANDPIPER *Tringa ochropus*   Pls. 38, 39
  Du – Witgatje   Fr – Chevalier culblanc
  Ge – Waldwasserläufer   Sw – Skogssnäppa

Identification: 9″. Larger and stouter than Wood or Common Sandpipers. Easily distinguished in flight by *blackish* beneath wings (Wood Sandpiper has buffish-white) and by *blackish upper-parts*, contrasting strongly with *brilliant white rump*, most of tail and under-parts. Neck and breast streaked greyish-brown, particularly on sides. No wing-bar. Tail barred with black near tip. In summer, upper-parts are speckled with whitish-buff, but much less boldly than in Wood Sandpiper (though juveniles are more speckled); faintly speckled in winter. Legs greenish and do not project beyond tail. Behaviour shy and solitary. 'Bobs' head and tail. Flight rapid, with jerky, snipe-like wing-beats.

Voice: When flushed, a ringing '*weet, tluitt, weet-weet*'. Song, a medley of high, fluty trilling '*titti-looi, titti-looi*', etc.

Habitat: Outside breeding season on marshes, sewage-farms, lakes and streams, seldom on sea-shore. Breeds in swampy forest regions, often in old nests in trees. Map 150.

WOOD SANDPIPER   *Tringa glareola*   **Pls. 38, 39**
  Du – Bosruiter   Fr – Chevalier sylvain
  Ge – Bruchwasserläufer   Sw – Grönbena

Identification: 8″. A delicately built sandpiper. Distinguished in summer by dark olive-brown upper-parts, *closely spotted with white*; head, neck and breast finely streaked; bold whitish supercilium. In flight, *whitish rump and buffish-white beneath wings* contrast with upper-parts less boldly than in Green. No wing-bar. In winter, white speckles are faint, giving resemblance to Green Sandpiper, but latter is stouter and blacker, with contrasting white on rump and tail and has blackish beneath wings. Legs are long, yellow or yellowish-green.

Voice: Habitually noisy; parties making high liquid trilling. When flushed a shrill, rapid '*chiff-chiff-chiff*'. Also a rising, liquid '*tlui*'. Song embodies a musical '*tleea-tleea-tleea*', in high song-flight.

Habitat: On passage frequents marshes, sewage-farms, lake shores, etc. Breeds in fairly open ground near water in northern forest regions, and on tundra. Map 151.

TEREK SANDPIPER   *Xenus cinereus*   **Pl. 40**
  Du – Terek strandloper   Fr – Bargette de Térek
  Ge – Terekwasserläufer   Sw – Tereksnäppa

Identification: 9″. Distinguished by long, dark, *noticeably upcurved bill and bright orange legs*. In winter, crown and upper-parts pale greyish; in summer browner, with two broad, irregular black stripes converging down back. Under-parts white, with faint streaks on neck and breast. In flight, pale rump and white rear edge of wings are conspicuous. 'Bobbing' action strengthens similarity to large, short-legged Common Sandpiper, but dashing, jinking gait and front-heavy appearance are distinctive.

Voice: Rather noisy. A fluty '*dudududu*', or piping '*twita-wit-wit-wit*'. In breeding season, '*too-lee*' and other melodious notes, some recalling Whimbrel.

Habitat and Range: Occurs along shores of large rivers, saltings, coastal flats. Breeds in marshes among willow scrub. Breeds Finland (? regular). Vagrant elsewhere in Europe (including Britain).

COMMON SANDPIPER   *Actitis hypoleucos*   **Pls. 40, 41**
  Du – Oeverloper   Fr – Chevalier guignette
  Ge – Flussuferläufer   Sw – Drillsnäppa

Identification: 7¾″. Distinguished by *olive-brown upper-parts* (faintly speckled with black in summer), brown rump and tail with white sides, white under-parts, faintly streaked on neck and breast. Has characteristic low flight over water, with rapid, *shallow* wing-beats alternating with brief glides on *down-curved wings* showing conspicuous white wing-bar. Also distinguished by *constant bobbing of head and tail* and by shrill voice. Runs among riverside stones. Distinguished from other sandpipers by combination of small size, dark upper-parts *and dark rump*. See also Temminck's Stint.

Voice: When flushed, a shrill piping '*twee-see-see*'. Song, a high, rapid '*titti-weeti,titti-weeti*'.

Habitat: Clear-running rivers, hill streams and lakes; on passage at sewage-farms, estuaries, etc. Breeds on banks of streams and lakes, river shingle-bars, etc. Map 152.

SPOTTED SANDPIPER *Actitis macularia*   P
    Du – Amerikaanse oeverloper   Fr – Chevalier grivelé
    Ge – Drosseluferläufer   Sw – Amerikansk drillsnäppa
Identification: 7½″. Generally separable from Common Sandpiper by v
which usually *lacks ringing quality* of Common and includes a hard '*chwit*' a
'*peet-weet*' flight-call. Plumage differences most marked in summer when b
spotted under-parts and black-tipped *yellow* bill are diagnostic. Imma
distinguishable by stronger whitish barring on wing-coverts, darker
secondaries (without Common's whitish patch), usually yellowish legs
cleaner under-parts. Adults in winter are greyer than Common. Vagrant
N. America to W. (including Britain), C. and S. Europe. Has bred Scot

TURNSTONE *Arenaria interpres*   **Pls. 3**
    Du – Steenloper   Fr – Tournepierre à collier
    Ge – Steinwälzer   Sw – Roskarl
Identification: 9″. A robust shore-bird with '*tortoiseshell*' plumage.
orange legs and a stout, pointed, black bill. In summer, upper-parts are
chestnut and black, head black and white, under-parts white with *broad*
breast-band. In winter, 'tortoiseshell' replaced by dusky brown, with
throat. See Pl. 34 for unique flight pattern. Turns over stones and shells
seeking food.
Voice: A quick, staccato '*tuk-a-tuk*' and a long rapid trill.
Habitat: Winters along rocky or pebbly coasts. Usually breeds on ex
rocky ground on coastal islands, but in Arctic also occasionally on river isl
Map 153.

WILSON'S PHALAROPE *Phalaropus tricolor*
    Du – Wilson's franjepoot   Fr – Phalarope de Wilson
    Ge – Wilsons Wassertreter   Sw – Wilsons Simsnäppa
Identification: 9″. Phalaropes are dainty birds, *conspicuously tame, swin*
habitually and buoyantly, often far out at sea. When feeding on shallow
they 'spin' characteristically. Females larger and brighter than males. Wi
is a fairly large, dark-winged phalarope, with *no wing-bar* and a *white*
Breeding female has broad neck-stripe from black eye-stripe through
chestnut on neck to paler chestnut along back; crown, hind-neck and bac
grey; under-parts white with reddish suffusion on front of neck. Male is d

Phalarope Swimming

with dark crown and back. In winter, sexes alike, pale grey-brown above, the unstreaked breast and flanks gleaming white; sides of head and neck mainly white, sometimes with dark mark through eye. Black bill *longer than in other phalaropes*, needle-fine; legs black in summer, often yellowish in winter. In flight shows white rump and tail like Yellowlegs but easily distinguished by actions, unspotted plumage and shorter legs. Very active, running on mud with lurching gait, darting bill from side to side.

Voice: A nasal, grunting '*aangh*' and a Yellowlegs-like '*chu*' in flight.

Habitat and Range: Less aquatic than other phalaropes, usually seen on muddy shores or in shallows. Vagrant from N. America to W. (including Britain), N. and C. Europe.

RED-NECKED PHALAROPE *Phalaropus lobatus*   Pls. 33, 40, 41
Du – Grauwe franjepoot   Fr – Phalarope à bec étroit
Ge – Odinshühnchen   Sw – Smalnäbbad simsnäppa

Identification: 7″. Similar in habits to Grey Phalarope, but distinguished in breeding plumage by smaller size, *white throat* and under-parts, with *bright orange patch down side of neck* (less evident in male). In autumn, distinguished by *darker*, more streaked upper-parts, *more brightly contrasting white wing-bar on darker wing*; at short range also by *needle-fine* bill. Bill, legs and feet blackish, *never showing yellow*. Immature resembles winter adult, but with much darker crown and upper-parts. Distinguished from winter Sanderling by characteristic dark mark through eye, much finer bill, and swimming habit.

Voice: Similar to Grey, but lower-pitched.

Habitat: As Grey Phalarope. Breeds in small scattered groups in wet marshes, lake shores and river islands. Map 154.

GREY PHALAROPE *Phalaropus fulicarius*   Pls. 33, 40, 41
Du – Rosse franjepoot   Fr – Phalarope à bec large
Ge – Thorshühnchen   Sw – Brednäbbad simsnäppa
N. Am – Red Phalarope

Identification: 8″. In summer, Grey Phalarope has *dark chestnut under-parts* (blackish at a distance), *white face, dark crown, yellow bill*; upper-parts have bold snipe-like pattern; white wing-bar conspicuous in flight. In winter, pale blue-grey above, with white head and under-parts, resembling Sanderling, but distinguished by *dark mark through eye*, long-bodied appearance and different behaviour. Very like Red-necked Phalarope in autumn, but is slightly larger, paler and less streaked above; distinguished at short range by thicker, shorter bill; in flight by less contrasting white on grey wings. Bill is black, sometimes yellowish at base; legs horn, grey or black; yellow webs on toes are diagnostic when visible.

Voice: A shrill '*whit*', or '*prip*', resembling Sanderling, and a quiet '*eeee*'. Courting female makes trilling mixture of musical and grating notes.

Habitat: Pelagic outside breeding season, but occurs occasionally on passage on coasts and inland waters. Breeds on tundra around pools or coastal lagoons. Map 155.

SKUAS: Stercorariidae

Large, rather hawk-like sea-birds with dark plumage and narrow, angled wings. Centre tail-feathers usually elongated in adults. Plumage very variable and confusing, occurring in light, intermediate and dark phases; but all show flash of white on the wing created by white wing-quills. Behaviour piratical, chasing other birds until they disgorge. Settle freely on water. Sexes similar. Ground nesting.

POMARINE SKUA   *Stercorarius pomarinus*   **Pl. 43**
   Du – Middelste jager   Fr – Labbe pomarin
   Ge – Mittlere Raubmöwe   Sw – Bredstjärtad labb
   N. Am – Pomarine Jaeger

Identification: 20″, including 2″ tail projection. Smaller than Great Skua, larger, *heavier* and deeper breasted than Arctic and Long-tailed. Adults distinguished by elongated but *blunt and twisted* centre tail-feathers, giving very thick-ended appearance in flight; but projections may be broken short. Occurs in light and dark forms. Light form has blackish face and cap, yellowish white cheeks and collar, white under-parts, barred flanks and wing-tips and usually a dark breast-band. Dark form is fairly uniform dark brown. Both forms have whitish patches on upper and lower wing-surfaces, but not as white as in Great Skua. Immature uniformly mottled dark brown and buffish, heavily barred below, without tail elongations; indistinguishable in the field from young Arctic and Long-tailed, except by larger size, much heavier build and broader, more rounded wings.

Voice: A harsh, barking '*gek-gek*' and a squealing '*yee-e-e*'.

Habitat and Range: Chiefly offshore, but also pelagic. Breeds in small widely scattered colonies on Russian tundra. On passage W. European coasts (including Britain) and Baltic. Vagrant to C. Europe and Mediterranean.

ARCTIC SKUA   *Stercorarius parasiticus*   **Pl. 43**
   Du – Kleine jager   Fr – Labbe parasite
   Ge – Schmarotzerraubmöwe   Sw – Labb
   N. Am – Parasitic Jaeger

Identification: 18″, including 3″ tail projection. Smaller and slighter than Pomarine, larger and heavier than Long-tailed. Distinguished by elongated but *straight and pointed* centre tail-feathers; Pomarine's are blunt and twisted; Long-tailed's are usually much longer and thinner. Bill more slender than Pomarine's. Light form has blackish cap, contrasting with yellowish-white cheeks and hind-neck, dark brown upper-parts, white under-parts, usually with dusky breast-band. Intermediate forms pale brown below, with varying whitish-buff sides of head. Dark form is uniform blackish-brown. Immature light form is closely barred and mottled above and below. See Pomarine for similarities. Behaviour piratical, chasing other sea-birds until they disgorge. Normal flight steady and graceful, otherwise hawk-like and dashing. Adults and particularly immatures show white flash on wing.

Voice: Higher than Great Skua's; also a nasal, wailing '*eee-air*'; alarm, '*ya-wow*' repeated.

Habitat: Offshore and pelagic waters, occurring occasionally in large numbers on coasts on migration. Breeds colonially on tundra and moors. Map 156.

LONG-TAILED SKUA *Stercorarius longicaudus*   Pl. 43
Du – Kleinste jager   Fr – Labbe à longue queue
Ge – Kleine Raubmöwe   Sw – Fjällabb
N. Am – Long-tailed Jaeger

Identification: 20–22″, including 5–8″ tail projection. Distinguished from pale form of commoner Arctic Skua by smaller size, lighter build and usually *much longer, thinner, very flexible centre tail-feathers* (but streamers may be broken short in both species). Long-tailed is much whiter on breast than Arctic, lacking breast-band but with dusky lower belly (pale-phase Arctic has white belly) and has *more clean-cut black cap, contrasting with broad white collar* and pale back; cheeks are cleaner yellow; bill *black* (not brown); legs *grey* (not black); also has less white on wings. The uniform dark brown form apparently unknown in recent years. Immature usually indistinguishable from young Arctic, but is greyer and has little, if any, white on wings. When swimming, erect neck and long cocked tail are characteristic. Flight more buoyant and graceful than other skuas.
Voice: Seldom vocal. At breeding grounds a shrill '*kreee*', or '*kree-ep*'.
Habitat: More pelagic than Arctic Skua. Breeds in widely scattered colonies on high tundra and stony fells. Map 157.

GREAT SKUA *Stercorarius skua*   Pl. 43
Du – Grote jager   Fr – Grand labbe
Ge – Grosse Raubmöwe   Sw – Storlabb
N. Am – Skua

Identification: 23″. Larger and stockier than Herring Gull. Plumage fairly uniformly dark, rustier below. Distinguished in flight from all other adult skuas and from immature gulls by heavier build, *short tail*, stout hooked black bill and very *conspicuous* white patch across base of primaries. Wings broad and rounded, *not pointed* as in other skuas. Legs blackish. Juvenile has less white on wings. Normal flight gull-like, but dashing and hawk-like in pursuit of other birds, which it forces to disgorge and occasionally kills. Solitary outside breeding season. Settles frequently on water.
Voice: When attacking, a guttural '*tuk-tuk*'; also a harsh, nasal '*skeerrr*' and a deep barking '*uk-uk-uk*'.
Habitat and Range: Pelagic and coastal waters. Breeds in scattered colonies on moors near sea, Iceland, Faeroes, Shetland, Orkney, Outer Hebrides, N. Scotland and N. Norway. Mainly migrant, in winter extending south over Atlantic and western North Sea to S. Spain (and beyond). Vagrant elsewhere in N., C. and S. Europe.

GULLS: Laridae

Gulls are long-winged sea-birds; some are seen regularly over land. Mostly white, with grey or black backs and wings. More robust, wider-winged and longer-legged than terns, walking readily. White-headed species often have dusky streaks on heads in winter; dark-hooded species have mainly white heads in winter, more or less mottled with brown. Sexes similar. Ground or cliff nesting.

GREAT BLACK-HEADED GULL   *Larus ichthyaetus*   Pl. 46

Du – Reuzenzwartkopmeeuw   Fr – Goéland à tête noire
Ge – Fischmöwe   Sw – Svarthuvad trut

Identification: 26″. Size of Great Black-backed. The only *big* gull with black head in breeding season and with white half-rings above and below red-rimmed eye. Distinguished at all seasons by *massive yellow bill with black band and reddish tip*. Legs yellowish-green. In winter, head is white with dusky marks on crown and near eye; distinguished from rather similar winter Herring Gull by massive bill and extensive white on wings. Immature has white tail with broad black band and distinctive black and white wing pattern.
Voice: A harsh '*kraaka*'. Various yapping and laughing notes at nest.
Habitat and Range: Normally coastal, occurring inland on passage. Vagrant from Russia, Asia to Europe (including Britain).

MEDITERRANEAN GULL   *Larus melanocephalus*   Pls. 44, 45

Du – Zwartkopmeeuw   Fr – Mouette mélanocéphale
Ge – Schwarzkopfmöwe   Sw – Svarthuvad mås

Identification: 15½″. Larger and stouter than Black-headed. Adult distinguished at all seasons by *white primaries without black tips* and *heavier, droop-tipped bill*. Legs and bill *rich red*, latter crossed by dark band. In summer, head is *really black* (not brown), hood extending well down nape with striking white broken eye-ring. In winter, head resembles winter Black-headed. First-year birds easily confused with young Common Gull, but black tail-band is narrower; wings have whitish central band after primaries extending to inner primaries (Common has similar but less contrasting pattern). Subadult has black on outer primaries. Behaviour as Black-headed.
Voice: Deeper and more wailing than Black-headed. A nasal '*ayeea*' and a guttural '*kwow*'.
Habitat: As Black-headed, but less often seen inland. Breeds on islets in lagoons and lakes. Map 158.

LAUGHING GULL   *Larus atricilla*   Pl. 46

Du – Lachmeeuw   Fr – Goéland atricille
Ge – Aztekenmöwe   Sw – Sotvingad mås

Identification: 16–17″. Near size of Common Gull but looks more slender. Best field marks are the *dark mantle blending into the black wing-tips* and the conspicuous white border along the trailing edge of the wing. In breeding season the head is black; in winter, white with dark markings around eye and back of head. Long, slightly drooping bill and legs dark red to blackish. First-year birds very dark, with white rump; the white rear edge of wings, dark breast, blackish legs and flat forehead are useful marks.
Voice: A strident, laughing '*ha-ha-ha-ha-haah-haah-haah*' and '*ka-ha, ka-ha*'.
Habitat and Range: Coastal, beaches, salt-marshes. Vagrant from N. America to W. Europe (including Britain).

LITTLE GULL *Larus minutus*   **Pls. 44, 45**
    Du – Dwergmeeuw   Fr – Mouette pygmée
    Ge – Zwergmöwe   Sw – Dvärgmås
Identification: 11″. World's smallest gull, with wing-span 20 per cent less than Black-headed. Wing-tips slightly rounded. Tail square-ended. Agile in flight, feeding tern-like from water surface. First-year birds identified by small size, *prominent dark zig-zag W* on upper wings, black tail-band and blackish cap. First-year Kittiwake has rather similar pattern but has slightly forked tail, grey instead of Little's brownish back, black instead of Little's reddish legs and longer, more pointed wings. Second-winter Little has narrow black and white wing-tips. Adult and second-year birds easily recognized in flight by *all-blackish* under-wings, pale grey upper-wings and, in summer, by *complete jet-black hood* extending to nape. See also Sabine's, Ross's and Bonaparte's.
Voice: A rather low '*kek-kek-kek*' and a repeated '*kay-ee*'.
Habitat: As Black-headed. Nests in small scattered colonies, often with terns or other gulls, usually around inland marshes. Map 159.

SABINE'S GULL *Larus sabini*   **Pls. 44, 45**
    Du – Vorkstaartmeeuw   Fr – Mouette de Sabine
    Ge – Schwalbenmöwe   Sw – Tärnmås
Identification: 13″. Size between Kittiwake and Little. The only European gull with a *forked tail* (young Kittiwake's is only slightly forked). Distinguished in flight by sharply contrasting *triangular black, white and grey wing pattern* and all-white forked tail. Bill black with *yellow tip*. Legs dark grey. In summer has dark greyish head and uniform grey upper-parts. In winter has narrow blackish half-collar on nape. At long range wing pattern can be confused with first-year Kittiwake or Little, but the contrasting black primaries, mainly white secondaries and grey coverts of the Sabine's are more clear-cut and the tail obviously forked. Juveniles (most likely to be seen in European waters) have extensive grey-brown on head and breast-sides, giving impression of dark front; at close range look for very scaly pattern of upper-parts, dark bar on under-wing secondaries, pale pinkish legs, all-black bill and broad white tail-band.
Voice: Has a grating tern-like cry.
Habitat and Range: Northern coastal waters and, in breeding season, also on arctic tundra. Breeds on swampy islets in tundra and along low-lying coasts. Occurs annually in British Isles, occasionally Iceland, Faeroes and coasts of W. Europe. Vagrant in C. and N. Europe.

BONAPARTE'S GULL *Larus philadelphia*   **Pl. 46**
    Du – Kleine Kokmeeuw   Fr – Mouette de Bonaparte
    Ge – Bonaparte-Möwe   Sw – Bonapartes mås
Identification: 12½″. Smaller than Black-headed, which it resembles in white fore-wing with black tips to primaries, but has *thinner, black bill* and, in summer, a dark, *slate-coloured* 'hood'. Has darker grey mantle than Black-headed and *grey* (not white) nape. In winter, head resembles Black-headed. Best field mark at all ages is *white undersides to primaries* (Black-headed's are dark greyish in adult, dusky in first-winter birds). Adult legs *orange* (not red); dusky in juvenile. Juvenile looks like small juvenile Black-headed, but black patches near tips of inner primaries and secondaries form prominent dark trailing edge. *Flight noticeably buoyant and tern-like.*

Voice: Rather silent, but has occasional nasal rasping 'cheeer'.
Habitat and Range: Habitat much as Black-headed. Nests near coasts in spruce
forest belt. Vagrant from N. America to W. (including Britain) and C. Europe

BLACK-HEADED GULL   *Larus ridibundus*   Pls. 44, 45
Du – Kokmeeuw   Fr – Mouette rieuse
Ge – Lachmöwe   Sw – Skrattmås

Identification: 15″. A smallish, active gull, frequently seen inland. Distinguished in flight by *pure white leading edges of pointed wings.* Under-surfaces
of primaries dark grey. Slender crimson bill and legs. In summer, head is
chocolate-brown; in winter, white with blackish marks before and behind eye.
Immature has patterned brown upper-parts and crown and a black-tipped
white tail, but still shows characteristic white leading edge to wing; head pattern
as winter adult; bill yellowish with dark tip; legs dark yellowish. Flight more
agile than in larger gulls; often follows plough. Adult Common Gull is slightly
larger, and is distinguished at all seasons by greenish bill and legs, and by
different wing and head patterns. See also Mediterranean, Slender-billed, Little
and Sabine's.
Voice: Noisy in breeding season. Usual notes, a harsh 'kwarr', a short 'kwup'
etc.
Habitat: Common inland and on coast, rarely far from land. Frequents lakes
sewage-farms, harbours, farmlands. Breeds colonially on marshes, moors
shingle-banks, lake islands. Map 160.

SLENDER-BILLED GULL   *Larus genei*   Pl. 44
Du – Dunbekmeeuw   Fr – Goéland railleur
Ge – Dünnschnäblige Möwe   Sw – Smalnäbbad mås

Identification: 17″. Can be confused with Black-headed owing to *similar wing
pattern,* but has longer neck, longer tail and usually *distinctively down-tilted
head and bill.* Bill longer, more pointed but heavier than Black-headed's; look
black, though actually dark red. Legs dark red. In breeding plumage head and
neck *pure white.* Under-parts have faint rosy tinge. Immature more like adult
than in other gulls, but has black terminal bar on tail; grey smudge usually
visible on ear-coverts; pale brown markings on upper-parts fainter than in
young Black-headed; legs dirty yellowish.
Voice: A nasal 'yep, yep' and high chattering notes.
Habitat: Coastal waters and estuaries. Nests in small groups or colonies
sometimes among terns, on dry mud-banks, islands in lagoons, in marshes
along river banks. Map 161.

AUDOUIN'S GULL   *Larus audouinii*   Pl. 4
Du – Audouin's meeuw   Fr – Goéland d'Audouin
Ge – Korallenmöwe   Sw – Rödnäbbad trut

Identification: 19¾″. Size near Herring Gull, but less bulky; wings appear longer
and *narrower.* Bill heavy, *coral-red with black subterminal band and yellow tip*
upper mandible has pronounced feather cloak, looking like dark blob at a
distance. Red eye-rim. Legs olive. Under-wing and belly of adult suffused with
grey, so that head appears very white. In flight adult shows *black outer primaries*
(white tips very restricted) forming *wedge-shaped patch* in sharp contrast with
pale grey inner wing. Subadults and immatures have black wedge extending to

carpal joint, pale grey crown, dark mark behind eye and brownish upper-parts. Feeds more skilfully than Herring Gull, in surf and open water.
Voice: A weak but harsh *'gi-errk'*.
Habitat: A deep-sea species. Locally around islands, occasionally along rocky mainland coasts. Nests colonially on sloping cliffs or among rocks on small Mediterranean islands. Map 162.

RING-BILLED GULL *Larus delawarensis*   Pl. 46
Du – Ringsnavelmeeuw   Fr – Goéland à bec cerclé
Ge – Ringschnabelmöwe   Sw – Ringnäbbad mås
Identification: 18–20″. Slightly larger than Common Gull, with noticeably paler mantle, *conspicuous black ring on longer and thicker yellow bill* and yellowish or greenish legs. Eye pale. In flight shows more black beneath primaries than larger Herring Gull. Immature often has pinkish legs, but distinguished from young Herring by narrower black tail-band; from young Common Gull by paler mantle, greyer tail and less sharply defined tail-band.
Voice: A shrill *'kyow'*, various squealing notes and an anxious *'ka-ka-ka'*.
Habitat and Range: Coasts, estuaries, lakes, refuse dumps, breeding on lake islands. Vagrant from N. America to W. (including Britain) and N. Europe.

COMMON GULL *Larus canus*   Pls. 44, 45
Du – Stormmeeuw   Fr – Goéland cendré
Ge – Sturmmöwe   Sw – Fiskmås
N. Am – Short-billed Gull
Identification: 16″. Adult Common and Herring look rather alike, with pale grey upper-parts and black wing-tips with white spots, but Common is much smaller and longer-winged, with more delicate *greenish-yellow bill and legs*. Herring Gull's legs are pale flesh (yellow in Mediterranean and eastern Scandinavian forms) and its heavier yellow bill has a red spot; its back is also paler. In winter, head more strongly streaked with grey than Herring. Immature distinguished from second-year Herring Gull by *clean-cut black band on white tail* (see Pl. 45). Juvenile largely grey-brown, with blackish bill and flesh-brown legs. See also Kittiwake (same size) and Black-headed (smaller).
Voice: Much higher and shriller than Herring Gull's. A squealing *'kee-a'*, or *'hieea'*.
Habitat: As Herring Gull, but more often inland. Breeds colonially on moors, hillsides and around lochs. Map 163.

LESSER BLACK-BACKED GULL *Larus fuscus*   Pls. 44, 45
Du – Kleine mantelmeeuw   Fr – Goéland brun
Ge – Heringsmöwe   Sw – Silltrut
Identification: 21″. About size of Herring Gull; smaller than Great Black-headed from which (apart from size, which is often difficult to judge) distinguished in summer by *yellow* legs; but in winter some adults and near-adults have flesh or pallid legs. British form *L. f. graellsii* has slate-grey upper-parts; Scandinavian *L. f. fuscus* is as black as Great Black-backed. Juvenile and first-year birds are mottled dark brown, with blackish bills and brownish-flesh legs, usually indistinguishable from young Herring Gull. Older immature birds have progressively darker backs, whiter heads and under-parts, yellower legs and bills.
Voice: Like deep-toned Herring Gull.

Habitat: As Herring Gull, but more frequent inland and out at sea. Nests colonially on inland moors and bogs, grassy sea islands, cliff-tops. Map 164.

HERRING GULL *Larus argentatus*   Pls. 44, 45
Du – Zilvermeeuw   Fr – Goéland argenté
Ge – Silbermöwe   Sw – Gråtrut

Identification: 22″. Commonest coastal gull. Looks rather like Common, with similar *black and white wing-tips*, but is much larger, paler above and has a heavier yellow bill with a red spot and *flesh-pink legs* (except in Mediterranean form *L. a. michahellis* and eastern Scandinavian form *L. a. omissus* which have *yellow* legs and *darker backs*). Best distinguished from adult Lesser Black-backed (which see) by *paler* grey upper-parts; Glaucous and Iceland Gulls have no black on wings. Juvenile uniform brown with darker primaries and tail and blackish bill, indistinguishable from young Lesser Black-backed. Second-year bird has greyer back and whiter base to tail, with darker tip.

Voice: A repeated, strident '*kyow*'; anxiety-note when breeding, a dry '*gah-gah-gah*'; also varied mewing, barking and laughing notes.

Habitat: Coasts, estuaries, also waters and fields often far inland. Breeds usually colonially, on cliffs, islands, beaches, occasionally in marshes. Map 165.

ICELAND GULL *Larus glaucoides*   Pl. 44
Du – Kleine burgemeester   Fr – Goéland à ailes blanches
Ge – Polarmöwe   Sw – Vitvingad trut

Identification: 22″. Nearly size of Herring Gull. Closely resembles Glaucous (see below), but is smaller, less bulky, with *much shorter, less heavy bill*, larger and darker eyes and more domed crown. Wing-tips project noticeably beyond tail when perched. Breeding adult has *red* eye-ring. Looks long-winged in flight, which is more rapid and buoyant than Glaucous. First- and second-year birds have extensive black bill-tips, *merging* into greyish or pinkish bill (young Glaucous has basal two-thirds of bill bright pinkish or yellowish, with short, clear-cut black tip). Juvenile plumage has neater pattern of barring than Glaucous and appears *greyer*-brown, with broader whitish fringe to tail. Voice higher-pitched than Herring's. Winter visitor from high Arctic to Iceland, Britain, Scandinavia. Vagrant elsewhere in W., C. and S. Europe.

GLAUCOUS GULL *Larus hyperboreus*   Pls. 44, 45
Du – Burgemeester   Fr – Goéland bourgmestre
Ge – Eismöwe   Sw – Vittrut

Identification: 25–29″. Glaucous and Iceland Gulls are the only western Palearctic gulls with *no black on wings or tail*, showing conspicuous white primaries and secondaries at all ages. Glaucous is between Herring and Great Black-backed in size, with a long, massive bill and sloping forehead giving an aggressive appearance. When perched, wing-tips project beyond tail less than in Iceland Gull, which is smaller, less bulky, with much smaller bill and more rounded head. Adult Glaucous looks all-white at a distance, but has pale grey mantle, *yellow* eye-ring, pinkish legs and a yellowish bill with red spot. See Iceland for juvenile comparisons. Young Glaucous looks pale coffee-coloured, rather than grey-brown as in Iceland.

Voice: Resembles Herring Gull's, but usually shriller.

Habitat: As Great Black-backed. Breeds colonially above and below sea cliffs, on stacks and islands in Arctic. Map 166.

GREAT BLACK-BACKED GULL   *Larus marinus*   Pls. 44, 45
Du – Mantelmeeuw   Fr – Goéland marin
Ge – Mantelmöwe   Sw – Havstrut

Identification: 27″. Much larger than Herring and Lesser Black-backed. Distinguished in breeding season from latter (apart from size) by *whitish-pink legs* and deeper voice. Adult is *almost black* above, not slate-grey as in British Lesser Black-backed, though Scandinavian Lesser Black-backed is also blackish. Bill is more massive than in Lesser Black-backed. Juvenile has more chequered, clearer-cut markings than young Herring, with paler head and under-parts, latter becoming progressively whiter and mantle darker in second and third years. Behaviour fiercely predatory.

Voice: Usual note a curt, deep '*owk*'.

Habitat: Offshore waters, coasts and estuaries. Locally inland in winter. Breeds either singly or colonially, sometimes with Lesser Black-backed, on rocky coastal islands, moors, also cliffs and lake islands. Map 167.

ROSS'S GULL   *Rhodostethia rosea*   Pl. 46
Du – Rose Meeuw   Fr – Mouette de Ross
Ge – Rosenmöwe   Sw – Rosenmås

Identification: 12½″. Slightly larger than Little, which in some plumages it resembles, but *longish tail is conspicuously wedge-shaped*. Flight buoyant, long wings pointed (not rounded like Little). Hovers taking food from water and feeds phalarope-fashion when swimming. When perched, the round head, small black bill and short red legs give dove-like impression, but wings project far beyond tail. Summer adult has unmistakable *black neck-ring* and *pink under-parts*; some pink often retained in winter. Adult also differs from Little in having narrow black leading edge to outer wing, a broad white band on trailing edge of inner wing and (in winter) no dark cap. First-year bird has striking W pattern across wings in flight, like Little, but wedge tail is diagnostic; black on tail is confined to elongated central feathers (not almost complete band as in most Littles). Winter adult lacks Little's dark cap; under-wing is grey (not blackish) and the white rear edge on upper-wing does not extend to outer primaries as in Little. Immature wing pattern recalls young Sabine's, but latter has wholly white inner primaries and forked tail.

Voice: Variable; high-pitched and more melodious than most gulls; typical calls are a bubbling '*e-wo, e-wo, e-wow*', or '*kliaw*'.

Habitat and Range: Strays frequent sea coasts and coastal lagoons. Seen regularly perched on ice-floes and glacier edges, seldom swimming. Breeds in swampy arctic tundra. Vagrant from NE Siberia to W. (including Britain), N., C. and S. Europe.

KITTIWAKE   *Rissa tridactyla*   Pls. 44, 45
Du – Drieteenmeeuw   Fr – Mouette tridactyle
Ge – Dreizenmöwe   Sw – Tretåig mås

Identification: 16″. An open-sea species. A little smaller than Common Gull, with short, blackish legs and a rather upright posture when perched. Scavenges round fishing boats, picking food from surface and plunging tern-like. Adult has white head in summer (dusty marks in winter), white tail, greenish-yellow bill. Distinctive flight pattern with grey mantle and wing-coverts (darker than Common Gull), white trailing edge and pale grey primaries shading to white

before *bold black triangle* (without white spots) at wing tips. Juvenile has black
bill, blackish ear-spot and rear half-collar, striking dark W pattern across wings
in flight and a black band at end of slightly forked tail. In first summer the half-
collar and wing pattern are partly obscured and the bill yellowish at base.
Young Little Gull has similar flight pattern but is smaller, with squared tail and
no neck-band. See also Sabine's and Ross's.

Voice: Noisy only at breeding grounds. A loud *'kitti-wake'*, or *'kaka-week'*,
with rising inflection.

Habitat: Usually well out at sea, often at northern fishing grounds: rare inland.
Breeds in close colonies on steep cliff-faces and in sea caves; locally on
buildings. Map 168.

IVORY GULL   *Pagophila eburnea*   Pl. 44

Du – Ivoormeeuw   Fr – Goéland sénateur
Ge – Elfenbeinmöwe   Sw – Ismås

Identification: 17½″. Distinguished by *all-white plumage*, short *black* legs and,
when perched, by very plump, *pigeon-like appearance*. Head small and
rounded, bill rather short, mainly greyish with orange-yellow tip. Eye large and
dark. First-winter birds have irregular grey smudges on face and chin, often
with a small white crescent around eye, a light sprinkling of dark spots on
upper-parts (sometimes also below), small black tips to primaries and a very
narrow black terminal band to tail. Flight buoyant, almost tern-like. Much
larger Glaucous and Iceland Gulls also have unmarked white primaries, but
have pinkish legs. Distinguished from occasional albino Common Gull or
Kittiwake by black legs, yellow-tipped grey bill and larger size.

Voice: Harsh shrill cries *'kee-er'*, etc., are tern-like.

Habitat and Range: An Arctic species usually seen on fringe of pack-ice, but
wanders south occasionally in winter. Breeds colonially on more or less ice-
bound rocky cliffs and ground. Regular Iceland in winter. Vagrant elsewhere in
N. and W. (including Britain), C. and S. Europe.

TERNS: Sternidae

Terns are slender, narrower-winged than gulls and more graceful in flight; bills
more slender, sharply pointed, often carried downward in flight; tails forked.
Most terns are whitish, with black caps; in winter, foreheads are white. Usually
hover and plunge for fish. Poor walkers. Sexes similar. Ground or pond nesting.

GULL-BILLED TERN   *Gelochelidon nilotica*   Pls. 47, 4

Du – Lachstern   Fr – Sterne hansel
Ge – Lachseeschwalbe   Sw – Sandtärna

Identification: 15″. Resembles Sandwich Tern both in summer and winter
plumage, but distinguished by *'swollen'*, *much shorter, wholly black bill* and
much less forked *grey* tail; in flight is broader-winged and heavier-bodied. Legs
black, noticeably longer than in other terns. Black cap is lost in winter, head
becoming much whiter than in Sandwich. Juvenile has buffish crown with dark
patch around eye. Behaviour much as other terns, but *habit of hawking for
insects over land* is certain distinction from Sandwich; seldom plunges into
water.

Voice: A throaty, rasping '*cahac, cahac*', or '*za-za-sa*', and rapid laughing notes, quite distinct from Sandwich Tern's higher note.

Habitat: Salt-marshes, sandy coasts and inland waters. Breeds colonially on sandy shores and islets in saline lagoons. Map 169.

CASPIAN TERN *Sterna caspia*   Pls. 47, 49

Du – Reuzenstern	Fr – Sterne caspienne
Ge – Raubseeschwalbe	Sw – Skräntärna

Identification: 21″. Almost as big as Herring Gull; distinguished by large black cap, forked tail and *heavy, bright orange-red bill*. Black cap extends just below eye, but in winter looks greyish, darkest around eye. Juvenile like winter adult with brownish mottling on upper-parts. Looks gull-like in flight, much less buoyant than other terns, but is quickly identified by huge bill; dark under-surfaces of primaries are conspicuous. See also Royal Tern (Accidentals).

Voice: A loud, deep, corvine '*kraa-uh*', or a hoarse '*scheeg*' and various cackling notes.

Habitat: Chiefly coastal, but occurs also on lakes and large rivers. Breeds singly or colonially on sandy coasts or islands. Map 170.

SANDWICH TERN *Sterna sandvicensis*   Pls. 47, 49

Du – Grote stern	Fr – Sterne caugek
Ge – Brandseeschwalbe	Sw – Kentsk tärna
N. Am – Cabot's Tern	

Identification: 16″. Distinguished by rather large size, long wings, short forked tail and *long black bill with yellow tip*. Legs black. Under-parts may have pinkish tinge, like Roseate, but latter's very long tail streamers and bright red legs are distinctive. *Elongated feathers at back of crown* erected when excited, giving shaggy appearance; in winter, crown is chiefly white, with streaky black crest; may assume winter plumage while still breeding. Immature looks very white, with much less forked tail and can lack yellow on bill, causing confusion with Gull-billed. Flight more gull-like than in smaller terns.

Voice: Noisier than most terns. A strident, rasping '*keer-reck*', a sharp '*tripp*', or '*kirr-kit*'.

Habitat: Almost exclusively maritime. Nests in crowded colonies on sandy or shingle beaches, rocky or sandy islands, occasionally on shores of inland waters. Map 171.

ROSEATE TERN *Sterna dougallii*   Pls. 47, 49

Du – Dougall's stern	Fr – Sterne de Dougall
Ge – Rosenseeschwalbe	Sw – Rosentärna

Identification: 15″. Distinguished in mixed flock with Common or Arctic by very different voice, *much whiter* appearance and shorter wings. Bill *black* with red base in summer, all-black in winter. Rosy tinge on breast visible in spring, but soon disappears. Sandwich also often has pinkish tinge, but Roseate is easily distinguished in spring by *red legs* and long tail-streamers. When perched, tail-streamers in spring extend *far beyond* wing-tips; in Common and Arctic they seldom project. Juvenile just distinguishable from young Common and Arctic by bolder markings on crown and upper-parts. Behaviour as in Common Tern, but wing-beats shallower and faster.

Voice: A long rasping '*aaak*', a soft, very characteristic '*chu-ick*' and a long angry chattering '*kekekekek*', like Common or Arctic.

Habitat and Range: As Common Tern, but exclusively maritime. Nests sociably with Common or Arctic Terns, on islets, occasionally on beaches. Summer visitor, breeding very locally in Britain from Clyde and Tay southwards, also on coasts of Ireland and off Brittany. Vagrant elsewhere in W., N., S. and C. Europe.

COMMON TERN *Sterna hirundo*   **Pls. 47, 49**
  Du – Visdiefje   Fr – Sterne pierregarin
  Ge – Flussseeschwalbe   Sw – Fisktärna
Identification: 14″. Common, Arctic and Roseate are easily confused and their usual differences are seldom completely reliable. In summer, Common usually distinguishable at short range by *black tip to orange-red bill* (Arctic's is wholly blood-red, Roseate's is mainly black). In winter, Common's bill is blackish with red base (Arctic's and Roseate's are wholly blackish). All three have red legs in summer, but when perched together Arctic usually shows noticeably shorter legs; in winter, Common's legs are still reddish (Arctic's are blackish, Roseate's orange-red, though blackish when juvenile). Common's tail-streamers *do not project beyond closed wing-tips* (Arctic's project slightly, Roseate's go far beyond wings). In winter and immature plumage all three have incomplete black caps, with white foreheads, but Common has darker 'shoulder' patches. In summer look for contrast on trailing edge of outer wing: tips of outer primaries are dark, but those of inner primaries are pale (Arctic lacks this contrast). In overhead flight Arctic's primaries are *all semi-transparent*; in Common only innermost four make *light patch* behind wing angle.
Voice: Noisy and varied. A long, grating '*kree-errr*' with downward inflection, '*kirri-kirri*' and a chattering '*kikikikik*'.
Habitat: Coastal and some inland waters, beaches and islands. Breeds colonially on beaches, sand-dunes and islands. Map 172.

ARCTIC TERN *Sterna paradisaea*   **Pls. 47, 49**
  Du – Noordse stern   Fr – Sterne arctique
  Ge – Küstenseeschwalbe   Sw – Silvertärna
Identification: 15″. Distinguished from Common Tern by *wholly blood-red bill* (wholly blackish in winter, and tip may still be black in spring); when perched, usually by *shorter legs*. Under-parts and neck usually greyer than in Common and Roseate, often showing by contrast a *white streak below the black cap*. Tail-streamers usually project *a little* beyond the wing-tips when perched, but never as far as in Roseate. See Common Tern for detailed comparison between the three species.
Voice: As Common Tern, but whistled '*kee-kee*', with rising inflection, said to be characteristic. Most notes higher and harder than Common.
Habitat: As Common Tern, but more maritime and more frequently on rocky offshore islets. Map 173.

SOOTY TERN *Sterna fuscata*   **Pl. 4**
  Du – Bonte stern   Fr – Sterne fuligineuse
  Ge – Russseeschwalbe   Sw – Sottärna
Identification: 16″. No other tern on the European list is *black above and white below* (adult at all seasons). Crown, back, wings and tail black; under-parts, cheeks and patch on forehead white; bill long and black; feet black. The much smaller Black Tern is blackish-grey above, never completely black, and has a

Sooty Tern

slightly forked grey tail. The Sooty has a very deeply forked black tail with white outer margins. Immature is sooty-brown above, flecked with white on back, grey-brown below. See also Bridled Tern (Accidentals).

Voice: A nasal '*ker-wacky-wack*'.

Habitat and Range: Oceanic, breeding on islands in warm southern oceans. A vagrant to W. (including Britain), S., C., and N. Europe.

LITTLE TERN   *Sterna albifrons*   Pls. 48, 49
Du – Dwergstern   Fr – Sterne naine
Ge – Zwergseeschwalbe   Sw – Småtärna
N. Am – Least Tern

Identification: 9½". Easily distinguished from other terns by *diminutive size*, *black-tipped yellow bill, yellow legs and white forehead*, the last contrasting sharply in summer with black crown and black stripe through eye. In winter back of crown is ash-grey merging to black at nape. Immature resembles winter adult but has darker bill and legs. Tail-streamers are short. In flight, wings are relatively narrower, *wing-beats quicker* and periods of hovering before diving longer than in other terns.

Voice: A high rasping '*kree-ik*', a sharp repeated '*kitt*' and a rapid chattering '*kirri-kirri-kirri*'.

Habitat: Sand and shingle beaches, occurring inland on migration. Breeds in small scattered colonies on beaches; on Continent also on shores of lakes and rivers. Map 174.

WHISKERED TERN   *Chlidonias hybridus*   Pls. 48, 49
Du – Witwangstern   Fr – Guifette moustac
Ge – Weissbartseeschwalbe   Sw – Skäggtärna

Identification: 9¾". Whiskered, Black and White-winged Black are all small marsh terns with generally dark breeding plumage and distinctively *dipping feeding-flight*. In summer, Whiskered is distinguished from Black Tern and White-winged Black Tern by *white cheeks and sides of neck*, contrasting with black crown and *dark grey under-parts*; in flight, *white beneath wings and white under tail-coverts* are fairly conspicuous. Looks very much paler than other 'black' terns; but forked tail, flight and plunging for food recall Common Tern. Winter adult distinguished from Black by paler upper-parts, *absence of dark patches on sides of breast* and *less black on crown*; from White-winged Black by *greyish* (not white) on nape, longer bill and uniform upper-parts. Immature distinguished from young Black by *variegated* 'saddle' contrasting with pale wings, absence of breast-patches; from young White-winged Black by *pale grey* (not white) rump and longer bill. Bill dark red in summer, blackish in winter, as long as head and deeper than other marsh terns.

Voice: A rasping '*zeck*' or '*ky-ik*' and other raucous notes.
Habitat: Like Black, but prefers deeper waters. Map 175.

BLACK TERN *Chlidonias niger*   **Pls. 48, 49**
Du – Zwarte stern   Fr – Guifette noire
Ge – Trauerseeschwalbe   Sw – Svarttärna

Identification: 9½″. The only tern with *all-blackish-grey* breeding plumage, except for conspicuous *white under tail-coverts*. During moult looks mottled and patchy. In winter has white forehead, neck and under-parts, with small blackish patch on sides of breast in front of wings. Immature like winter adult but with darker 'saddle'. Bill black, slender, almost as long as head. See Whiskered and White-winged Black Terns for winter and immature comparisons. Flies back and forth over water, dipping erratically to pick insects off surface, but very rarely plunges. See also Sooty Tern.

Voice: Seldom vocal. Usually a rather squeaky '*kee-pee*' or '*kreek*'.
Habitat: Inland waters, also coastal on passage. Breeds in scattered colonies, building floating nest in shallows of marshes and lagoons. Map 176.

WHITE-WINGED BLACK TERN *Chlidonias leucopterus*   **Pl. 48**
Du – Witvleugelstern   Fr – Guifette leucoptère
Ge – Weissflügelseeschwalbe   Sw – Vitvingad tärna

Identification: 9¼″. Unmistakable in summer, with startling *black plumage and conspicuous white wing-coverts and tail*; further distinguished from Black by *white tail* and *black* (not pale grey) under wing-coverts. Adult in winter distinguished from Black by *absence of dark patches on breast*, less black on crown, stouter build and steadier flight; from Whiskered by *complete* white collar, paler rump and squarer tail. Immature distinguished from young Black by *contrasting* dark brown 'saddle' and pale grey wings; from young Whiskered by *uniform* dark 'saddle' and clear white rump. Bill red in summer, blackish in winter; shorter and stubbier than Black or Whiskered.

Voice: A rasping '*cherr*', or '*kerr*'.
Habitat: As Black Tern, with which it frequently associates throughout the year. Map 177.

AUKS: Alcidae

Black and white salt-water diving birds with short necks, very short, narrow wings, and legs set far back. Flight is whirring, large feet jutting out sideways before alighting. Carriage usually upright when standing. Sexes similar. Cliff or hole nesting.

GUILLEMOT   *Uria aalge*   **Pl. 56**
Du – Zeekoet   Fr – Guillemot de Troïl
Ge – Trottellumme   Sw – Sillgrissla
N. Am – Common Murre

Identification: 16½″. Distinguished from Razorbill by *slender pointed bill and thinner neck*. Upper-parts of northern race *U. a. aalge* usually look as black as Razorbill's, though head is browner; but southern *U. a. albionis* is dark chocolate-brown in summer, grey-brown in winter. Fairly frequent 'Bridled' form (not separate species) has narrow white eye-ring and a white line extending back from eye. In winter, sides of head and throat are white, as in winter Razorbill, but with conspicuous *black line* from eye across ear-coverts. Behaviour like Razorbill, but in flight head and neck look thinner and longer and tail shorter. See also Brünnich's Guillemot.

Voice: Very noisy in breeding colonies. A long, harsh '*arrrr*', or '*arra*'.

Habitat: As Razorbill. Breeds in dense colonies on ledges on steep cliff-faces and on flat tops of isolated stacks, often with Razorbills and Kittiwakes. Map 178.

BRÜNNICH'S GUILLEMOT *Uria lomvia* Pl. 50

Du – Kortsnavelzeekoet Fr – Guillemot de Brünnich
Ge – Dickschnabellumme Sw – Spetsbergsgrissla
N. Am – Brünnich's Murre

Identification: 16½". Closely similar to Guillemot, but distinguished at close range at all seasons by *noticeably shorter and thicker bill* (but much less deep than Razorbill's) and by *narrow pale line along basal sides of bill*. In winter also by black of crown extending *well below eye*, without dark stripe through ear-coverts. Young Razorbill may be confused with Brünnich's Guillemot, but its bill is more stubby and rounded. Flight, behaviour and voice as Guillemot.

Habitat and Range: As Guillemot, but roams farther out to sea in winter. Breeds Iceland, N. Norway; winters south to Norway, occasionally Faeroes. Vagrant on coasts south to British Isles, N. France, also inland in C. Europe.

RAZORBILL *Alca torda* Pl. 50

Du – Alk Fr – Petit pingouin
Ge – Tordalk Sw – Tordmule
N. Am – Razor-billed Auk

Identification: 16". Black above, white below. Distinguished from Guillemot by rather heavy head, short thick neck and *laterally compressed bill*, crossed midway by a conspicuous *white line*. Looks more squat than Guillemot when swimming and usually carries pointed tail *cocked up*. Both species have curved white bar on closed wing and conspicuous white rear edge to wings in flight. Throat and sides of head of adult are white in winter. Juvenile has smaller bill, without white stripe; young Guillemot has longer, more pointed bill and distinctive black line running back from eye. Sociable, perching upright or horizontally, on ledges with Guillemots.

Voice: A weak whirring whistle and a protracted querulous growling, at breeding grounds.

Habitat: Spends most of time in coastal and offshore waters. Breeds in colonies, usually with Guillemots, on sea cliffs. Map 179.

BLACK GUILLEMOT *Cepphus grylle* Pl. 50

Du – Zwarte zeekoet Fr – Guillemot à miroir
Ge – Gryllteiste Sw – Tobisgrissla

Identification: 13½". Much smaller than Guillemot. Easily distinguished in summer by *all-black plumage, with large white wing-patch and bright red feet*. In winter, under-parts are white, black portions of upper-parts closely mottled with white. Juvenile darker above than winter adult, with whites indistinctly mottled with brown. Behaviour as Guillemot, but is usually seen in very small numbers. In summer and at distance on water might be confused with Velvet

Scoter, which is much larger and shows only small white bar on closed wing and *white on rear* (not front) of wing in flight. See also winter grebes.

Voice: Very distinctive – a weak, whistling cry, occasionally becoming a trilling twitter, during which brilliant vermilion gape is conspicuous.

Habitat: Stays closer to shore than other guillemots, often among rocky, even well-wooded, islands. Nests singly or in small scattered groups, in holes or under boulders on rocky shores, cliff ledges, islands. Map 180.

LITTLE AUK *Alle alle* **Pl. 50**
Du – Kleine alk Fr – Mergule nain
Ge – Krabbentaucher Sw – Alkekung
N. Am – Dovekie

Identification: 8″. Smallest winter sea-bird. Not much larger than Starling. Easily distinguished by *chubby, 'neckless' form and very short bill*. Under-wing blackish, preventing confusion with juvenile Puffin or other auks, all of which have pale under-wings. In summer, head and upper breast blackish-brown and upper-parts black; narrow white wing-bar; white under-parts. In winter, ear-coverts, throat and upper breast become dirty white.

Voice: Noisy at breeding grounds. A high, shrill chatter.

Habitat and Range: Offshore to pelagic. Occasionally 'wrecked' on shore during severe gales. Breeds in vast colonies, in holes among rocks, on high arctic sea cliffs, locally among mountains. Nests N. Iceland. Partial migrant. In winter extends south from Arctic to North Sea and N. Atlantic; irregular English Channel; vagrant elsewhere in N., C. and S. Europe.

PUFFIN *Fratercula arctica* **Pl. 50**
Du – Papegaaiduiker Fr – Macareux moine
Ge – Papageitaucher Sw – Lunnefågel

Identification: 12″. Easily distinguished in summer by *triangular, red, blue and yellow laterally flattened bill*, stumpy big-headed form, black and white plumage and *bright orange feet*. In winter, bill is somewhat smaller, but still recognizably Puffin-shaped; cheeks greyer. Juvenile has much smaller, blackish bill, but shows typical Puffin face pattern (see Pl. 50). In flight looks distinctively big-headed. Perches upright, but rests horizontally.

Voice: Usually silent, but has long growling notes '*ow*', or '*arr*', at breeding site.

Habitat: Coastal and offshore waters. Breeds colonially in rabbit or shearwater burrows, or in holes excavated in turf, on cliffs or grassy islands. Map 181.

SANDGROUSE: Pteroclididae

Plump, pigeon-like terrestrial birds, with very short, feathered legs and toes. Wings and tails long and pointed. Flight very rapid. Gait mincing and dove-like. Habitat usually deserts and arid ground. Noisy. Ground nesting.

BLACK-BELLIED SANDGROUSE *Pterocles orientalis* **Pl. 32**
Du – Zwartbuikzandhoen Fr – Ganga unibande
Ge – Sandflughuhn Sw – Ringflyghöna

Identification: 14″. Larger and bulkier than Pin-tailed. Distinguished even at a distance by less elongated tail and *very conspicuous black belly*. Male has sandy-grey head, greyish upper-parts speckled with orange, orange wing-coverts and secondaries, chestnut throat with black patch below, pinkish-grey breast, crossed with a narrow black band. Female is sandy, closely spotted on head and upper-parts, throat is yellow with a blackish patch, breast warm ochreous, closely spotted with black and crossed below with a black band.

Voice: Usual note a deep rattling '*churr-rur-rur*'.

Habitat and Range: Semi-desert, or undulating stony country. Nests on ground. Resident Spain, Portugal. Vagrant elsewhere in S. and C. Europe.

PIN-TAILED SANDGROUSE   *Pterocles alchata*   Pl. 32
    Du – Witbuikzandhoen   Fr – Ganga cata
    Ge – Spiessflughuhn   Sw – Långstjärtad flyghöna

Identification: 12½″. On ground resembles squat, pale Grey Partridge, but quickly distinguished by long, needle-pointed centre tail-feathers; in flight also by long, sharply pointed wings and 'neckless' silhouette. Smaller than Black-bellied and Pallas's. Distinguished from both (particularly in flight) by *white belly* and *white under-wing with black tip*. Male in breeding plumage has upper-parts boldly spotted with lemon-yellow on dark grey-brown, chestnut wing-coverts, grey crown, orange-yellow face, *black chin and throat, broad chestnut breast-band*. Female has yellowish upper-parts, finely barred with black and lavender; throat and under-parts white, with two or three narrow black bands across the breast. Male in winter resembles female, but lacks lavender barring. Rapid flight recalls Golden Plover; flocks usually much larger than Black-bellied, often executing massed evolutions. See Black-bellied, Pallas's, and Spotted (Accidentals).

Voice: A loud, croaking '*catarr, catarr*', usually in flight.

Habitat and Range: Dry, dusty plains, high stony plateaux, sun-baked mud-flats, and edges of marismas. Nests on ground. Resident S. France, Spain, Portugal. Vagrant elsewhere in S. Europe.

PALLAS'S SANDGROUSE   *Syrrhaptes paradoxus*   Pl. 32
    Du – Steppenhoen   Fr – Syrrhapte paradoxa
    Ge – Steppenhuhn   Sw – Stäpphöna

Identification: 14–16″. Distinguished by long, needle-pointed centre tail-feathers (longer than Pin-tailed) and conspicuous *black patch* on belly (less extensive than in Black-bellied). Male has orange head and throat, with curved grey mark from eye down side of neck; barred sandy upper-parts; pale greyish breast and primaries. Female has narrow black border to throat-patch and black spots on crown and neck, which lack orange. See Black-bellied and Pin-tailed.

Voice: Flocks very noisy. Usual notes a deep '*kerki*', or '*kerkerki*'.

Habitat and Range: Sandy semi-desert regions. During periodic irruptions into Europe usually occurs on sandy coasts, stubble fields, etc. Nests on ground. Has occurred sporadically throughout Europe, west to Britain (where it has bred, also in Denmark) and has reached Ireland, Faeroes. Last big invasion 1908.

PIGEONS AND DOVES: Columbidae

Plump, fast-flying birds, with small heads and characteristically deep, crooning voices. The terms 'pigeon' and 'dove' are loosely used and interchangeable, but in a general way 'pigeon' refers to the larger species with ample, squared or rounded tails, 'dove' to the smaller, more slender species with longer, graduated tails. Sexes similar. Tree or hole nesting.

ROCK DOVE *Columba livia*   **Pl. 51**
    Du – Rotsduif   Fr – Pigeon biset
    Ge – Felsentaube   Sw – Klippduva
Identification: 13″. The ancestor of the familiar 'domestic pigeon'. Distinguished from Stock Dove and much larger Woodpigeon by *whitish rump, two broad black bands right across secondaries, and white beneath wings.* Tail has black terminal band, usually with some white on outer feathers. Plumage bluegrey, paler on back, with glossy green and lilac on sides of neck. Domestic varieties vary from typical ancestral form to white, tan and blackish varieties. Flight faster than Woodpigeon's and usually low.
Voice: Song indistinguishable from domestic pigeon's '*oo-roo-coo*'.
Habitat: Usually in small numbers around rocky sea cliffs and adjacent fields. On Continent also locally around inland cliffs. Nests in crevices or caves among rocks. Domestic forms abundant in cities and farms, nesting in buildings. Map 182.

STOCK DOVE *Columba oenas*   **Pl. 51**
    Du – Holenduif   Fr – Pigeon colombin
    Ge – Hohltaube   Sw – Skogsduva
Identification: 13″. Rather *smaller and darker* than Woodpigeon, from which easily distinguished in flight or when perched by *absence of white on wings and neck.* Upper-parts bluer grey. Glossy green patch on side of neck. Two short broken black wing-bars. Juvenile lacks green on neck. Behaviour like Woodpigeon, with which it often associates in winter, but less gregarious and flight is more rapid. Rock Dove has distinctive whitish rump and two very broad black wing-bars; but some feral domestic pigeons have rumps like Stock Dove.
Voice: Distinguished from Woodpigeon's by more monotonous delivery: '*ooo-roo-oo*', etc., the first syllable being usually emphasized.
Habitat: As Woodpigeon, but prefers more open parkland with old trees, also cliffs, sand-dunes, etc. Nests in holes in old trees, rocks, rabbit burrows, buildings, etc. Map 183.

WOODPIGEON *Columba palumbus*   **Pl. 51**
    Du – Houtduif   Fr – Pigeon ramier
    Ge – Ringeltaube   Sw – Ringduva
Identification: 16″. Larger than other pigeons, with *broad white band across wing* (conspicuous in flight) and glossy green and purple on vinous neck, with *white patch each side.* Juvenile lacks neck markings. Often roams in huge flocks in winter. Mingles freely with town pigeons and Stock Doves. 'Explodes' noisily from trees when alarmed. See also Stock and Rock Doves.

Voice: Muffled cooing song, a repeated phrase of five notes, '*co-cooo-co, coo-coo*'.

Habitat: Occurs almost anywhere, including town centres, but not often in treeless regions or extreme north. Nests in trees, hedges, old nests, etc. Map 184.

COLLARED DOVE   *Streptopelia decaocto*   Pl. 51
Du – Turkse tortel   Fr – Tourterelle turque
Ge – Türkentaube   Sw – Turkduva

Identification: 11″. Distinguished from Turtle Dove by *impression of longer tail*, uniform *pale* dusty-brown upper-parts and narrow black half-collar at *back* of neck. From below, *white terminal half of black tail* is diagnostic; from above, closed tail looks uniform with upper-parts. Head and under-parts paler and greyer, with vinous-pink flush, particularly on breast. Blackish primaries contrast with rest of plumage. Eyes red. Barbary Dove *S. risoria* (often domesticated) is rather similar but has paler creamy-buff plumage and lacks contrasting dark primaries.

Voice: A deep, '*coo-cooo, coo*', usually accented on second syllable (*S. risoria* usually accents first syllable). Flight-call, a very nasal '*kwurr*'.

Habitat: Mainly towns and villages. Usually nests in trees; locally on buildings. Map 185.

TURTLE DOVE   *Streptopelia turtur*   Pl. 51
Du – Tortelduif   Fr – Tourterelle des bois
Ge – Turteltaube   Sw – Turturduva

Identification: 11″. Smaller than other common pigeons; recognized by much more slender shape and *well-graduated black tail with white edges.* Upper-parts *sandy-rufous* with black centres to feathers; black and white striped patch on side of neck; soft pinkish throat and breast. Juvenile lacks neck-patches and vinous tinge. Usually in pairs or small parties. Flight swift and direct, wing action more jerky than Woodpigeon's. See also Collared, Laughing, and Rufous (Accidentals).

Voice: Softer and 'sleepier' than that of other pigeons: a repeated, almost purring, '*roor-r-r*'.

Habitat: Open bushy country with uncut hedges and small woods. Nests in bushes, thickets, orchards, etc. Map 186.

LAUGHING DOVE   *Streptopelia senegalensis*   Pl. 75
Du – Palmtortel   Fr – Tourterelle de Sénégal
Ge – Palmtaube   Sw – Palmduva

Identification: $10\frac{1}{4}$″. A smallish dove with a *frontal* neck-ring. Head and neck vinous-pink, with *broad, speckled black and copper collar at base of fore-neck*; chin paler, belly and under tail-coverts white; upper-parts dark rufous, with greyish rump; *pale blue-grey wing-coverts are conspicuous in flight*; tail blackish, with broad white tips to outer feathers; legs and eye-ring crimson. Sexes similar, immature duller.

Voice: A rapidly repeated '*coo*', each series of notes ascending and descending.

Habitat and Range: Widespread in and around towns and villages in parts of Africa and SW Asia, nesting in thorn bushes, small trees and on buildings. Breeds European Turkey; vagrant S. and N. Europe.

PARROTS: Psittacidae

RING-NECKED PARAKEET   *Psittacula krameri*   **Pl. 77**
  Du – Halsbandparakiet   Fr – Perruche à collier
  Ge – Halsbandsittiche   Sw – Halsbandsparakit
Identification: 16″. Unmistakable emerald-green with very long tail and
hooked red bill. Male has narrow red and black neck-ring; sexes otherwise
similar. Gregarious, fast-flying and noisy. Usual call a loud, rasping screech.
Nests in holes in trees, under loose roof-tiles, etc. (Asia.) Escaped birds now
feral in parts of England; recorded Scotland, Wales.

CUCKOOS: Cuculidae

Rather slim, long-tailed, slender-winged birds, with two toes forward and two
behind. Brood-parasitic in nesting. Sexes similar.

GREAT SPOTTED CUCKOO   *Clamator glandarius*   **Pl. 54**
  Du – Kuifkoekoek   Fr – Coucou-geai
  Ge – Häherkuckuck   Sw – Skatgök
Identification: 15½″. Easily distinguished by *conspicuous crest*, 'capped' appearance, long graduated dark grey tail with *bold white edging*, brown upper-parts
boldly spotted with white. Under-parts and sides of head creamy-white,
yellowish on throat. Bright orange orbital ring. Juvenile has blackish head, no
crest, *rich chestnut* primaries. Conspicuous and noisy when breeding, often
perching on fences; Magpie-like in some attitudes. Flight fairly strong and
direct. Sociable.
Voice: A chattering, tern-like '*kittera, kittera, kittera*', followed by gobbling
notes; a harsh, rising '*zhree*' (recalling Azure-winged Magpie), a crow-like
'*kark*' of alarm, etc.
Habitat and Range: Outskirts and glades of woods, olive groves, bushy plains
with occasional trees. Brood-parasitic, eggs usually laid in nests of crow family,
particularly Magpie; often lays several eggs in same nest. Summer visitor to
Spain, Portugal, S. France, Yugoslavia, perhaps Greece, Bulgaria. Vagrant
elsewhere in Europe (including Britain).

CUCKOO   *Cuculus canorus*   **Pl. 54**
  Du – Koekoek   Fr – Coucou gris
  Ge – Kuckuck   Sw – Gök
Identification: 13″. Long-tailed, rather sharp-winged; in flight sometimes
confused with Sparrowhawk (which has broad, *rounded* wings). *Call-note is
unmistakable.* Upper-parts and throat blue-grey; under-parts whitish, barred
dark grey; tail long, rounded, slate-grey, spotted and tipped with white. Legs
yellow. Juvenile is variable; upper-parts either red-brown strongly barred
(suggesting female Kestrel), or grey-brown with faint bars; both forms have
barred buffish-white under-parts and white patch on nape. Rufous females,
similar to red-brown juvenile, occur occasionally. Flight direct, gliding before
alighting. Solitary outside breeding season.

Voice: A mellow, penetrating '*cuc-coo*', sometimes single or treble notes; also a deep '*wow-wow-wow*'. Female has long, bubbling note.
Habitat: Edges of woodlands, bushy commons, etc., also in treeless areas, locally on open high ground. Polyandrous and brood-parasitic; individual birds usually parasitizing only one species, laying single egg in each nest. Map 187.

YELLOW-BILLED CUCKOO   *Coccyzus americanus*   **Pl. 75**
  Du – Geelsnavelkoekoek   Fr – Coulicou à bec jaune
  Ge – Gelbschnabelkuckuck   Sw – Gulnäbbad regengök
Identification: 12″. Smaller, slimmer and more dove-like than Cuckoo; dull brown above and whitish below. Distinctive marks are *yellow* lower mandible, *large white spots* at the tips of the dark tail-feathers and *rufous* in the wings, conspicuous in flight. See also Black-billed Cuckoo (Accidentals).
Voice: A rapid, throaty '*ka-ka-ka-ka-ka-kow-kow-kowp-kowp-kowp*' (slower towards end).
Habitat and Range: Copses, thickets, woodlands. A vagrant from N. America to W. (including Britain), N., C. and S. Europe.

BARN OWLS: Tytonidae

BARN OWL   *Tyto alba*   **Pl. 52**
  Du – Kerkuil   Fr – Chouette effraie
  Ge – Schleiereule   Sw – Tornuggla
Identification: 13½″. A long-legged, very pale owl, with a white face. *Pale golden-buff upper-parts*, finely speckled; *unstreaked white under-parts*. Eyes black. No ear-tufts. Nocturnal, but occasionally hunts by day. Perches upright, when 'knock-kneed' long legs and large head are distinctive. Flight wavering and, at dusk, distinctly ghostly. Feeds chiefly on small rodents. Dark-breasted form *T. a. guttata* of N. and E. Europe is darker above and rich buff below.
Voice: A long, wild shriek. Hissing, snoring and yapping notes also occur.
Habitat: Very partial to human habitation, breeding in farm buildings, church towers, ruins, etc. Also frequents parks with old timber, occasionally cliffs. Map 188.

OWLS: Strigidae

Largely nocturnal birds of prey, with large heads, flattened faces forming 'facial discs', and forward-facing eyes. Half-hidden hooked bills and powerful claws. Flight noiseless. Some species have conspicuous feather-tuft 'ears'. Most owls have large eyes and closely feathered feet. Sexes usually similar. Nest in holes, old nests, or on ground.

SCOPS OWL   *Otus scops*   **Pl. 52**
  Du – Dwergooruil   Fr – Hibou petit-duc
  Ge – Zwergohreule   Sw – Dvärguv
Identification: 7½″. Identified by combination of very small size and *ear-tufts* (latter not always conspicuous). Plumage closely vermiculated and speckled

grey-brown. Has smaller, less flat head than Little Owl and is slimmer, with more tapered shape and longer tail. *Monotonous song* is very distinctive. Chiefly nocturnal. Feeds mainly on insects.

Voice: Usual note a soft, penetrating, persistently repeated '*pew*', closely resembling voice of Midwife Toad, which often causes confusion.

Habitat: Trees near human habitation, plantations, gardens, etc.; also among old buildings. Nests in holes, occasionally in old nests of other birds. Map 189.

EAGLE OWL *Bubo bubo*   Pl. 52

Du – Oehoe	Fr – Hibou grand-duc
Ge – Uhu	Sw – Berguv

Identification: 26–28″. Largest European owl (twice the size of Long-eared Owl), with *prominent ear-tufts*, broadly streaked tawny breast, *large orange eyes*. Upper-parts tawny, mottled with dark brown. Kills prey up to size of Hare and Capercaillie. Hunts at dawn and dusk, roosting in cleft rocks or hollow trees, or perched upright on branch close to tree trunk. Solitary.

Voice: A deep, but brief '*ooo-hu*', second syllable falling slightly, sometimes followed by a quiet, guttural chuckling. Female has a fox-like barking call.

Habitat: Rocky promontories in forests, crags, mountainsides and open steppes. Breeds in hollow among rocks and scrub, in hollow trees, or old nests of birds of prey. Map 190.

SNOWY OWL *Nyctea scandiaca*   Pl. 52

Du – Sneeuwuil	Fr – Chouette harfang
Ge – Schneeule	Sw – Fjälluggla

Identification: 21–26″. A *very large, white, round-headed* owl, flecked or barred with dusky brown; some much whiter than others; males whiter than females. Chiefly diurnal and solitary. Glides slowly, or dashes swiftly after passing birds. Takes prey up to size of Arctic Hare and Eider. Perches in open on post, rock, haystack, dune, or other low vantage point. Irrupts from Arctic every four years or so. Distinguished from white Gyrfalcon by larger, rounder head, rounded wings and less vigorous flight; from white-breasted Barn Owl by much larger size, white upper-parts and *yellow eyes*.

Voice: Usually silent. Flight-notes when breeding, a repeated loud '*krow-ow*', or a repeated '*rick*'.

Habitat: Arctic tundra and barren hills. During irruptions frequents open country, dunes, marshes, sea and lake shores, etc. Nests on mossy hummocks in tundra. Map 191.

HAWK OWL *Surnia ulula*   Pl. 53

Du – Sperweruil	Fr – Chouette épervière
Ge – Sperbereule	Sw – Hökuggla

Identification: 14–16″. Distinguished from other owls by *long tail* and rather short, pointed wings, which give hawk-like silhouette in flight, and by *closely barred* under-parts. Face whitish, *heavily bordered with black*. Crown and upper-parts blackish-brown, barred with white. Hunts chiefly by day. Perches conspicuously on tree-top or telegraph pole, often in un-owl-like, *inclined posture* and frequently jerks tail. Flight recalls Sparrowhawk, usually low, sweeping upward to perch. Often bold and indifferent to man.

Voice: A chattering '*kikikiki*', more like hawk than owl. Song, a sonorous, deep bubbling sound.

Habitat: Coniferous forests and open birch scrub. Breeds in shelter of broken tree-top, in hollow trees, old nests of hawks, etc. Map 192.

PYGMY OWL *Glaucidium passerinum*   **Pl. 53**
   Du – Dwerguil   Fr – Chouette chevêchette
   Ge – Sperlingskauz   Sw – Sparvuggla

Identification: $6\frac{1}{2}''$. Smallest European owl – smaller than Starling. Distinguished by *very small size* and relatively small head. Upper-parts dark brown, spotted with whitish-buff; grey-white under-parts streaked with blackish; whitish face with small yellow eyes beneath short white 'eyebrows'. Tail closely barred brown and whitish, *frequently elevated or jerked upward.* Behaviour bold and active. Partly diurnal. Hunts and kills small birds in flight. Little Owl is much larger and paler, with flattened crown. See also Tengmalm's.

Voice: Very vocal. A whistling '*keeoo*', '*kitchick*', etc. Song, a monotonously repeated Bullfinch-like '*whee . . . whee . . . whee . . .*'.

Habitat: Mature secluded forests, usually coniferous, in mountainous regions. Nests in hollow trees, and woodpecker holes. Map 193.

LITTLE OWL *Athene noctua*   **Pl. 53**
   Du – Steenuil   Fr – Chouette chevêche
   Ge – Steinkauz   Sw – Minervauggla

Identification: $8\frac{1}{2}''$. Distinguished by *small size* and *squat, flat-headed appearance.* Upper-parts dark brown, closely spotted and barred with white. Under-parts whitish, broadly streaked with dark brown. Flattened head and face and yellow eyes give fierce, frowning expression. Often seen in daylight. Perches upright on telegraph poles, fences, etc. Bobs and bows when suspicious. Flight low and rapid, *deeply undulating.* Feeds chiefly on insects and small rodents, less often on small birds. See also Tengmalm's Owl.

Voice: A shrill, rather plaintive '*kiu*', a sharp, barking '*werro*', etc.

Habitat: Varied, but usually fairly open farming country and stony wasteland. Nests in holes in trees, especially pollarded willows, and in rocks, buildings, burrows. Map 194.

TAWNY OWL *Strix aluco*   **Pl. 53**
   Du – Bosuil   Fr – Chouette hulotte
   Ge – Waldkauz   Sw – Kattuggla

Identification: 15″. *Mottled and streaked, large round head, black eyes, no ear-tufts.* Upper-parts vary from warm brown to tawny or greyish. Under-parts buffish-brown with bold dark streaks. Facial discs grey-brown. Strictly nocturnal. Feeds chiefly on small rodents, birds, insects, etc. Distinguished from Long-eared by heavier build, black eyes and absence of ear-tufts; from Short-eared by darker, less buff appearance and black eyes; from Barn Owl by larger size and much darker appearance, particularly of face and under-parts.

Voice: A shrill '*ke-wick*'. Song, a deep musical '*hoo-hoo-hoo*', followed at an interval by a long, tremulous '*oo-oo-oo-oo*'.

Habitat: Mature woods, parks, large gardens. Nests in hollow trees, old nests of large birds, occasionally in buildings and rabbit burrows. Map 195.

URAL OWL *Strix uralensis*   **Pl. 53**
   Du – Oeraluil   Fr – Chouette de l'Oural
   Ge – Habichtskauz   Sw – Slaguggla

Identification: 24″. Resembles very large, *pale, long-tailed* Tawny. General colour greyish-white, broadly streaked with dark brown; wings and rather long, well-rounded tail are boldly barred. Head rounded, without ear-tufts. Facial discs greyish-white *without lines*. Eyes *blackish-brown*. Behaviour much as Tawny Owl. Great Grey is larger, with smaller *yellow* eyes and heavily lined facial discs. Tawny is much smaller and darker, with larger eyes.

Voice: A rather high, barking 'wow . . . wow . . . wow . . .' at irregular intervals, and a harsh '*kawveck*'. Song a deep, rising and falling '*oo-hoo*'.

Habitat: Mixed woods, coppices and forests. Nests in fractures of broken-off trees, occasionally in old nests of birds of prey. Map 196.

GREAT GREY OWL *Strix nebulosa*   **Pl. 53**
   Du – Laplanduil   Fr – Chouette lapone
   Ge – Bartkauz   Sw – Lappuggla

Identification: 27″. Near size of Eagle Owl, but easily distinguished by *grey colour, very round head without ear-tufts* and longer tail. Plumage dusky grey, irregularly marked with dark and white on upper-parts and broadly streaked below. Facial discs very large and heavily lined; *dark patch on chin*; *eyes noticeably small and yellow*. In flight shows distinctive pale band across base of primaries. Ural Owl is somewhat smaller and browner, with *dark* eyes and *unlined* facial discs.

Voice: A deep-toned, booming '*hu-hu-hu-hoo*', often rising and repeated at regular intervals; also a high, shrill '*ke-wick*'; both calls not unlike Tawny's.

Habitat and Range: Dense northern coniferous forests. Lays in old nests of large birds of prey. Resident in arctic Norway, Sweden, Finland; has bred Poland. In 'invasion' years, extends south over much of Scandinavia, Finland, Estonia, occasionally East Germany.

LONG-EARED OWL *Asio otus*   **Pl. 52**
   Du – Ransuil   Fr – Hibou moyen-duc
   Ge – Waldohreule   Sw – Hornuggla

Identification: 14″. Only medium-size owl with *long ear-tufts*. Upper-parts streaked and mottled buff and grey-brown; under-parts somewhat paler below. Distinguished from bulbous-headed Tawny by more angular head, long ear-tufts (when visible), more slender body and *orange-yellow* (instead of black) eyes. In flight, wings and tail look longer than Tawny's; wing-tips look more rounded (less 'fingered'). See also Short-eared, which is stockier, with much shorter ear-tufts, and, unlike Long-eared, often glides with wings in a shallow V. Roosts by day in thick foliage, or in upright elongated posture on branch, close to tree trunk. Feeds on small mammals, birds and insects. Locally roosts in small parties in autumn or winter.

Voice: A low, sighing '*oo-oo-oo*', much more moaning than cry of Tawny. Female has barking '*wick*' call. Several yelping and wailing notes and wing-clapping also occur. Normally silent in second half of year.

Habitat: Coniferous forests, also small coppices of conifers, locally in deciduous woods. Breeds in old nests, and occasionally on ground in wood, or on moorland, Map 197.

SHORT-EARED OWL *Asio flammeus* **Pl. 52**
　Du – Velduil　　　　　　　　Fr – Hibou des marais
　Ge – Sumpfohreule　　　　　　Sw – Jorduggla
Identification: 15″. Hunts at dusk and in daylight in open country. In flight resembles Long-eared (when neither show ear-tufts), but is generally paler, more mottled. Both have large dark carpal patch on upper wing-surface set off by buff bases of primaries; in Short-eared, which also has pale barring on secondaries, the contrast is more prominent. Short-eared has *pale trailing edge to upper-wing* and tail is *strongly barred* (Long-eared's tail looks more uniformly dark). Under-parts variable in both, but in Short-eared the belly is *noticeably paler than the breast*. Both have small dark carpal patch on under-wing. Distinguished from Long-eared when perched by more 'bulbous' head, almost invisible ear-tufts, tawnier colour and 'fiercer' expression. Perches freely on ground. Flight rolling; frequently glides *on slightly raised wings*. Seen in parties during rodent 'plagues'.
Voice: A high sneezing bark *'kee-aw'*. Song, a repeated, deep *'boo-boo-boo'*, usually during circling display-flight. Wing-clapping also occurs. Female has grating *'gweek'* call.
Habitat: Open marshy country, sand-dunes, moors. Breeds on ground among heather, sedges, clumps of marram grass, etc. Map 198.

TENGMALM'S OWL *Aegolius funereus* **Pl. 53**
　Du – Ruigpootuil　　　　　　Fr – Chouette de Tengmalm
　Ge – Rauhfusskauz　　　　　Sw – Pärluggla
　N. Am – Boreal Owl
Identification: 10″. Slightly larger than Little Owl, but distinguished by more erect posture, larger, *much more rounded head, with deeper facial discs* (not flattened over eyes as in Little Owl). Has *blacker borders* to facial discs, broader white eyebrows, *chocolate-brown* coloration, and white, well-feathered legs and feet, crown finely spotted (not streaked) with white. Juvenile almost uniform mahogany colour with broad white eyebrows. Strictly nocturnal except in Arctic. Roosts by day in conifers. Flight wavering, not dipping like Little Owl.
Voice: A fairly rapid phrase of 3–6 similar, high, but musical notes *'poo-poo-poo'*, etc., the final note often diminishing in emphasis, sometimes accelerating almost to a trill. Alarm, *'ja-week'*.
Habitat: Coniferous forests in mountainous regions, locally in mixed woods. Winters in valleys and lowlands. Nests in woodpecker holes or natural holes in trees. Map 199.

NIGHTJARS: Caprimulgidae

Nocturnal insectivorous birds, with large eyes, huge gapes, tiny bills and feet, long wings and ample tails. Plumage beautifully camouflaged with 'dead leaf' pattern. Usually pass day immobile, on ground or perched lengthways along branch. Sexes similar. Ground nesting.

NIGHTJAR *Caprimulgus europaeus* **Pl. 54**
　Du – Nachtzwaluw　　　　　　Fr – Engoulevent d'Europe
　Ge – Ziegenmelker　　　　　　Sw – Nattskärra
Identification: 10½″. Best known for remarkable nocturnal *churring song*. General appearance elongated, grey-brown, closely speckled and barred with

dark brown and buff, affording perfect camouflage. Broad head is flattened, with very small bill and very large gape. Wings and tail are long. Male has three white spots near wing-tips and conspicuous white tips to outer tail-feathers. Spends day crouched motionless along (occasionally across) branch, or on ground. Feeds on wing at night, pursuing moths in floating, erratic and silent flight. Loud 'wing-clapping' is frequent during breeding season. See also Red-necked and Egyptian Nightjars.

Voice: Flight-call, a soft nasal '*goo-ek*'; alarm, a high '*quick-quick-quick*'. Song, at night, a loud, rapid churring, *rising and falling* and sometimes long sustained, sometimes 'running down' with a few clucking notes. Beware similar noise of Mole Crickets.

Habitat: Moors, commons, open woodland glades with bracken and sand-dunes. Lays eggs on bare ground. Map 200.

RED-NECKED NIGHTJAR   *Caprimulgus ruficollis*   **Pl. 54**
   Du – Moorse nachtzwaluw   Fr – Engoulevent à collier roux
   Ge – Rothalsziegenmelker   Sw – Rödhalsad nattskärra

Identification: 12″. Looks very similar to the Nightjar, but distinguished by somewhat larger size, *heavier head, sandy-rufous collar and larger white throat-patch*. In flight looks more rufous and heavier than Nightjar; *both* sexes show more conspicuous white marks on primaries and on outer tail-feathers.

Voice: Far-carrying song consists of double, or sometimes single, incessantly repeated notes, '*kutuk-kutuk-kutuk*', etc., like hard rapping on hollow wood, up to 100 notes per minute.

Habitat and Range: Pine woods, bushy, semi-desert regions and pine-clad hillsides. Lays eggs on bare ground. Summer visitor Spain and Portugal. Has bred S. France. Vagrant elsewhere in S. and W. Europe (including Britain).

EGYPTIAN NIGHTJAR   *Caprimulgus aegyptius*   **Pl. 75**
   Du – Egyptische nachtzwaluw   Fr – Engoulevent d'Egypte
   Ge – Ägyptischer Ziegenmelker   Sw – Ökennattskärra

Identification: 10″. *Much paler* and noticeably sandier than Nightjar, appearing almost uniform in flight, though plumage is finely pencilled. Neither sex has well-defined white spots on wings or tail, though webs of inner primaries are whitish.

Voice: A repeated single knocking note '*tok, tok, tok*'.

Habitat and Range: A desert species, of casual occurrence in Mediterranean area. Also recorded C. and W. Europe (including Britain).

SWIFTS: Apodidae

Essentially aerial. Slim, with long, scythe-like wings and short tails. Flight extremely rapid. Sexes similar. Hole nesting.

SWIFT   *Apus apus*   **Pl. 57**
   Du – Gierzwaluw   Fr – Martinet noir
   Ge – Mauersegler   Sw – Tornsvala

Identification: $6\frac{1}{2}$″. Distinguished from all swallow family by *long, scythe-shaped wings*; *sooty, blackish plumage*, with whitish chin (seldom visible); short, forked tail. Sociable and exclusively aerial in habit. Flight very rapid and distinctive, on extremely quickly beaten, stiffly held wings. Noisy during breeding season, when screaming groups chase wildly around roof-tops. See also Alpine and Pallid Swifts.

Voice: A shrill, prolonged, piercing screech; also a rapid chirruping.

Habitat: Aerial. May occur anywhere, but especially in areas with suitable nesting sites. Usually nests in buildings under eaves, occasionally in rocky cliffs; in holes in trees in N. Europe. Map 201.

PALLID SWIFT   *Apus pallidus*   Pl. 57

Du – Vale gierzwaluw   Fr – Martinet pâle
Ge – Fahlsegler   Sw – Blek tornsvala

Identification: 6½″. In good light can be distinguished from Swift by paler, milkier-brown coloration; outer wing is darker than inner, above and below (the opposite of Swift); *dark mantle creates distinct 'saddle' effect*; white throat *extends to upper breast, sides of neck and forehead*; dark eye-spot contrasts with paler head. Tail looks blunter, with a shallow fork. Flight more deliberate than Swift's, with which it often associates. Voices and habitats similar. Map 202.

ALPINE SWIFT   *Apus melba*   Pl. 57

Du – Alpengierzwaluw   Fr – Martinet alpin
Ge – Alpensegler   Sw – Alpseglare

Identification: 8¼″, with 21″ wing-span. *Much larger*, paler and browner than Swift, with *white under-parts and brown breast-band*. Size is conspicuous when seen together. Very distinctive voice. Behaviour and flight like Swift, but often glides with wings deeply depressed. Sociable. See also Needle-tailed Swift (Accidentals).

Voice: Has loud, rising and falling, trilling flight-call, resembling distant cry of falcon; usually in chorus while wheeling around nesting places.

Habitat: Chiefly in high, rocky mountainous regions, locally also along sea cliffs and among old buildings. Builds cup-shaped nest in cleft rocks, natural crevices and beneath rafters. Usually nests in colonies. Map 203.

WHITE-RUMPED SWIFT   *Apus caffer*   Pl. 75

Du – Witstuitgierzwaluw   Fr – Martinet à croupion blanc
Ge – Weissburzelsegler   Sw – Kafferseglare

Identification: 5½″. Distinguished from Little Swift (Accidentals) by slightly larger size, *much narrower white rump-patch and deeply forked tail*. In young birds rump-patch can be difficult to see. Plumage otherwise uniform blackish, paler on lower belly and with well-defined whitish throat-patch. Has almost bat-like twittering song, but slightly deeper-toned than Little Swift. Usually associates with Red-rumped Swallows, whose old nests are preferred for breeding, but also feeds with Little Swifts and can therefore easily be overlooked. A tropical African species which has bred S. Spain since 1966.

KINGFISHERS: Alcedinidae

KINGFISHER   *Alcedo atthis*   **Pl. 54**
  Du – IJsvogel   Fr – Martin-pêcheur
  Ge – Eisvogel   Sw – Kungsfiskare

Identification: 6½″. Unmistakable. Brilliant *iridescent blue and emerald-green upper-parts*, white throat and neck-patch, *chestnut cheeks and under-parts, long dagger-shaped bill*. Head large, body stumpy, wings and tail short, feet small and bright red. Perches alertly, with nervous 'bobbing' action, plunging after small fish or insects, occasionally hovering. Normal flight low, direct and very rapid. Solitary.

Voice: A high, piping '*chee*', or '*chee-kee*', repeated rapidly when excited. Infrequent song, a short trill, of similar quality to call-notes.

Habitat: Streams, rivers, canals, lakes. In winter also sea coast and tidal marshes. Nests in holes bored in stream banks, sometimes far from water. Map 204.

BEE-EATERS: Meropidae

BLUE-CHEEKED BEE-EATER   *Merops superciliosus*   **Pl. 75**
  Du – Groene bijeneter   Fr – Guêpier de Perse
  Ge – Blauwangenspint   Sw – Blåkindad biätare

Identification: 12″. Easily distinguished from common Bee-eater by *almost uniform bright green plumage* without any yellow or brown on upper-parts. Has *coppery-orange* throat-patch but no black band below. In flight shows flashing coppery under-surfaces of wings. Central tail-streamers much longer than in Bee-eater. Call-notes very similar but huskier. Habitat and breeding behaviour similar. Vagrant from Africa, Asia to S., W. (including Britain), C. and N. Europe.

BEE-EATER   *Merops apiaster*   **Pl. 54**
  Du – Bijeneter   Fr – Guêpier d'Europe
  Ge – Bienenfresser   Sw – Biätare

Identification: 11″. Unmistakable. *Vivid colours*, long curved bill and projecting middle tail-feathers are conspicuous even at long range. Both sexes have *chestnut and yellow upper-parts*, blue-green primaries and tail, *blue-green under-parts* with *brilliant yellow throat*. Juvenile lacks long middle tail-feathers. Behaviour essentially gregarious; often perches on telegraph wires. Flight graceful, with gliding turns.

Voice: Very distinctive. Usual note a throaty but far-carrying and constantly repeated '*prruip*'.

Habitat: Prefers open bushy country with a few trees, telegraph poles, but also occurs in woodland glades. Breeds colonially in holes bored in cuttings, sand-pits, river banks, sometimes level ground. Map 205.

ROLLERS: Coraciidae

ROLLER *Coracias garrulus*   **Pl. 54**
  Du – Scharrelaar   Fr – Rollier d'Europe
  Ge – Blauracke   Sw – Blåkråka
Identification: 12". A heavy Jay-like bird with a powerful bill. Plumage is *pale azure-blue, with bright chestnut back, vivid blue wings with black borders* (in flight), greenish-blue tail with brown centre feathers. Behaviour rather shrike-like, pouncing from exposed perch or overhead wires on passing insects. Flight Jackdaw-like, gliding occasionally; 'tumbles' from considerable height during nuptial display.
Voice: A loud, deep, corvine '*kr-r-r-r-ak*' or '*krak-ak*', and a harsh chatter.
Habitat: Mature forests and fairly open country with a few trees. Breeds in old hollow trees, holes in banks, ruins, etc. Map 206.

HOOPOES: Upupidae

HOOPOE *Upupa epops*   **Pl. 54**
  Du – Hop   Fr – Huppe fasciée
  Ge – Wiedehopf   Sw – Härfågel
Identification: 11". Unmistakable. Both sexes have pale pinkish-brown plumage, *boldly barred black and white wings and tail,* long black-tipped *erectile crest* (which is usually depressed) and long curved bill. Feeds chiefly on ground in open. Flight weak and undulating, with distinctive slow 'open-and-shut' action of rounded wings.
Voice: A low, far-carrying '*poo-poo-poo*'; also several mewing notes and a quiet chattering alarm.
Habitat: Open woodlands, orchards, parklands, etc. Winters in more open bushy country. Nests in holes in old trees, occasionally in ruins. Map 207.

WOODPECKERS: Picidae

Chisel-billed birds, with powerful feet (usually two toes front, two rear), remarkably long tongues, and short, stiff tails which act as props in climbing tree trunks. Flight usually strong, but undulating. Most males have some red on head. Nest in holes excavated in trees.

WRYNECK *Jynx torquilla*   **Pl. 55**
  Du – Draaihals   Fr – Torcol fourmilier
  Ge – Wendehals   Sw – Göktyta
Identification: 6½". Although related to woodpeckers, appearance and attitudes are rather passerine. At a distance looks *uniform grey-brown, with paler under-parts*; at short range vermiculated plumage resembles Nightjar's. Upper-parts and long, rounded tail closely patterned grey, brown and buff. Under-parts buffish, closely chequered with grey-brown. Feet like woodpecker's: two toes forward, two behind. Crown feathers erectile. More often heard than seen.

Feeds on ground, hopping with raised tail; perches across branches, but clings like woodpecker to tree trunks. Flight undulating, looking rather like long-tailed lark.

Voice: A nasal, repeated '*kyee kyee*', louder and less shrill than Lesser Spotted Woodpecker's call, resembling distant Hobby.

Habitat: Gardens, orchards, parks, hedgerows with trees. Nests in natural holes in trees, masonry, nest-boxes, etc. Map 208.

GREY-HEADED WOODPECKER *Picus canus*   Pl. 55
Du – Kleine groene specht   Fr – Pic cendré
Ge – Grauspecht   Sw – Gråspett

Identification: 10″. Easily mistaken for rather small, greyish Green Woodpecker, but distinguished by *grey head and neck* with thin black stripe through eye and *narrow* black moustachial stripe. Male has bright crimson forehead (not crown). Female lacks red. Juvenile is browner and has flanks barred with brown; young males show some crimson on forehead. Behaviour as Green Woodpecker. Spanish race of Green has little black on face and greyish coloration and can therefore be confused with Grey-headed.

Voice: Call-notes resemble Green Woodpecker's, but 'laughing' song is much less harsh and becomes *progressively deeper and slower*. Drums for long periods in spring.

Habitat: As Green Woodpecker, but also occurs locally in deciduous mountain forests up to tree limits. Less often in coniferous woods. Map 209.

GREEN WOODPECKER *Picus viridis*   Pl. 55
Du – Groene specht   Fr – Pic vert
Ge – Grünspecht   Sw – Gröngöling

Identification: 12½″. A large woodpecker with *dull green upper-parts*, pale grey-green under-parts, crimson crown, *conspicuous yellowish rump and lower back*. Sides of head and moustachial stripe are black; male has crimson centre to very broad moustachial stripe. Juvenile is paler, distinctly spotted and barred. Frequently feeds on ground, at ants' nests. Hops heavily, in upright position. Flight deeply undulating, with long wing-closures between each upward bound. See also Grey-headed for reference to Spanish race.

Voice: A very loud ringing 'laugh'. Very seldom drums.

Habitat: Deciduous woods, parks, farmlands, commons with scattered trees. Nests in holes bored in trees. Map 210.

BLACK WOODPECKER *Dryocopus martius*   Pl. 55
Du – Zwarte specht   Fr – Pic noir
Ge – Schwarzspecht   Sw – Spillkråka

Identification: 18″. Largest European woodpecker (big as a Rook) with *uniform black plumage*. Male has slightly crested crimson crown; female has crimson confined to patch on back of head. Eyes pale yellow. Bill pale. Flight heavy and undulating.

Voice: A loud, whistling '*klea*' and a high, grating '*krri-krri-krri-krri*'. Song, usually in flight, a strident, ringing '*choc-choc-choc*', recalling Green Woodpecker, but usually slower and shorter. Drums occasionally and very loudly.

Habitat: Mature coniferous forests in northern and mountainous regions and in beech woods. Excavates very large oval nest-hole, sometimes at considerable height. Map 211.

GREAT SPOTTED WOODPECKER *Dendrocopos major* **Pl. 55**
   Du – Grote bonte specht   Fr – Pic épeiche
   Ge – Buntspecht   Sw – Större hackspett
Identification: 9″. Considerably smaller than Green, but much larger than Lesser Spotted, from which it is distinguished by black back with *large white shoulder-patches* and *crimson under tail-coverts*. (Upper-parts of Lesser Spotted give closely barred impression.) *Unbroken black bar across white cheek.* Under-parts are unstreaked white, with *sharply defined* red below tail. Male (not female) has crimson nape-patch, but immatures of both sexes have *entire crown crimson*. Seldom feeds on ground, but often on bird-tables. See also White-backed, Middle Spotted and Syrian Woodpeckers.
Voice: A very loud, sharp '*tchick*' or '*kik*', much louder and more frequent than similar call of Lesser Spotted. Both sexes drum very rapidly on resonant dead branches.
Habitat: More a woodland and garden bird than Green, but also in pine woods in north. Map 212.

SYRIAN WOODPECKER *Dendrocopos syriacus* **Pl. 55**
   Du – Syrische bonte specht   Fr – Pic syriaque
   Ge – Blutspecht   Sw – Syrisk hackspett
Identification: 9″. Very similar to Great Spotted (large white shoulder-patches and black cap), but *lack of black cheek-bar gives white-faced appearance.* Tail shows less white than Great Spotted, but wings show more white. Under tail-coverts are paler crimson than in Great Spotted. Juveniles, because of their red caps, may be confused with Middle Spotted, but have reddish collar and black moustachial stripe joining bill.
Voice: Softer than Great Spotted: a quiet '*chig*', '*kirrook*' (not unlike Moorhen) and a song recalling Middle Spotted.
Habitat: Chiefly around villages and near cultivation. Map 213.

MIDDLE SPOTTED WOODPECKER *Dendrocopos medius* **Pl. 55**
   Du – Middelste bonte specht   Fr – Pic mar
   Ge – Mittelspecht   Sw – Mellanspett
Identification: $8\frac{1}{2}$″. Can be confused with Great Spotted and Syrian, which are only other European woodpeckers with *white shoulder-patches*. Distinguished by slightly smaller size, conspicuous and slightly crested light crimson crown without any black edging; *conspicuous white sides to head* have very narrow black moustachial stripe, but no black eye-stripe; whole head looks pale; white under-parts with heavily streaked flanks *merge gradually* into rose-pink on belly (instead of contrasting sharply with crimson under tail-coverts as in Great Spotted). Wings boldly barred black and white, with narrower white shoulder-patches than Great Spotted. Female is duller, with paler crimson crown. See also Syrian.
Voice: Resembles Great Spotted's quick chatter, but is slightly lower in pitch and the first note is usually higher: '*ptik-teuk-teuk-teuk-teuk*'. In spring has slow, nasal cry, '*wait . . . wait . . .*' repeated in descending or ascending scale. Drums rarely.
Habitat: Usually in hornbeam and beech forest, in high branches. Excavates nest-hole high up in deciduous tree. Map 214.

WHITE-BACKED WOODPECKER *Dendrocopos leucotos*   Pl. 55

Du – Witrugspecht   Fr – Pic à dos blanc
Ge – Weissrückenspecht   Sw – Vitryggig hackspett

Identification: 10″. Larger, more slender-looking than Great Spotted and with paler head. Distinguished by combination of *uniform black back and shoulders and white or barred rump*. Male has whitish forehead and scarlet crown extending to nape. Under-parts white, boldly streaked with black on flanks, *merging into* pink under tail-coverts. Wings boldly barred black and white, *without white shoulder-patches*. Female has black crown. Juveniles show trace of red on crown and under tail-coverts. Three-toed is only other European woodpecker with white rump, but is much smaller and is white from nape to rump.

Voice: Infrequent call resembles Great Spotted's '*tchick, tchick*' but is deeper-toned.

Habitat: Hilly deciduous woods with plenty of old rotting trees; locally in dense coniferous forests; around towns in winter. Nests in holes bored in rotted trees. Map 215.

LESSER SPOTTED WOODPECKER *Dendrocopos minor*   Pl. 55

Du – Kleine bonte specht   Fr – Pic épeichette
Ge – Kleinspecht   Sw – Mindre hackspett

Identification: $5\frac{3}{4}$″. Smallest European woodpecker. Distinguished from all other 'pied' woodpeckers by *sparrow-size, closely barred* black and white upper-parts and *absence of any red on under tail-coverts*. Forehead, cheeks and under-parts whitish, with a few dark streaks on flanks. Male has dull crimson crown; female's is whitish; juveniles show some crimson on crown and have browner under-parts. Behaviour retiring; spends most of time in small upper branches *fluttering among twigs*.

Voice: A repeated, high '*pee-pee-pee*', not unlike Wryneck's call, but weaker and less ringing. Also a rather weak '*tchick*', resembling cry of Great Spotted. Drums much less powerfully than Great Spotted.

Habitat: Old orchards and open woodlands. Map 216.

THREE-TOED WOODPECKER *Picoides tridactylus*   Pl. 55

Du – Drieteenspecht   Fr – Pic tridactyle
Ge – Dreizehenspecht   Sw – Tretåig hackspett

Identification: $8\frac{3}{4}$″. About size of Great Spotted, with large head. Feet have only three toes. Distinguished from all other European woodpeckers by *complete lack of crimson markings* (even in male), nearly all-black wings, *broad whitish stripe down back from nape to rump* and black cheeks. Male has *yellow* centre to crown; female's is black, with whitish forehead. Under-parts white, *barred with black* on flanks. Juveniles are greyer, with white backs considerably mottled with black. White-backed Woodpecker also has white lower back, but its upper back is black and it has rosy under tail-coverts and white bars on wings. Less active than other woodpeckers, passing long periods at one spot.

Voice: Seldom vocal, but resembles weak Great Spotted; sometimes a chattering '*kek-ek-ek-ek*'. Drums occasionally, but slowly.

Habitat: Mountain and arctic forests, with preference for burnt tracts. Nests in holes bored in trees and telegraph poles. Map 217.

The Colour Plates

Plate 1

GREBES AND DIVERS

- **SLAVONIAN GREBE**   page
  Summer: Buffish head-tufts; rufous-chestnut neck.
  Winter: Black and white pattern; thin dark bill; black cap above eye.

- **BLACK-NECKED GREBE**
  Summer: Buffish ear-tufts; black neck.
  Winter: Like Slavonian Grebe, but greyer neck; upturned bill; black
    cap to below eye.

- **RED-NECKED GREBE**
  Summer: Reddish neck, white chin and cheek.
  Winter: Greyish neck; no white above eye; yellow-based bill.

- **LITTLE GREBE**
  Summer: Puffy, dark; light patch on bill.
  Winter: Pale below. Identify by shape and bill.

- **GREAT CRESTED GREBE**
  Summer: White neck; black 'horns'; rusty frill.
  Winter: Satiny white; pinkish bill; white above eye.

- **RED-THROATED DIVER**
  Summer: Grey head; dark reddish throat.
  Winter: Pale face; finely speckled back; thin upturned bill.

- **BLACK-THROATED DIVER**
  Summer: Grey crown; back spots in patches.
  Winter: Dark as Great Northern; bill slender, but not upturned.
    Whitish thigh-patch often helpful.

- **GREAT NORTHERN DIVER**
  Summer: Black head, all-chequered back, stout bill.
  Winter: Dark back; stout straight bill.

- ○ **WHITE-BILLED DIVER**
  Plumages like those of Great Northern.
  Recognized by stout, whitish, upturned bill without dark upper
    ridges.

Divers in flight are hunchbacked, with a slight
downward sweep to the neck and the feet
projecting behind.

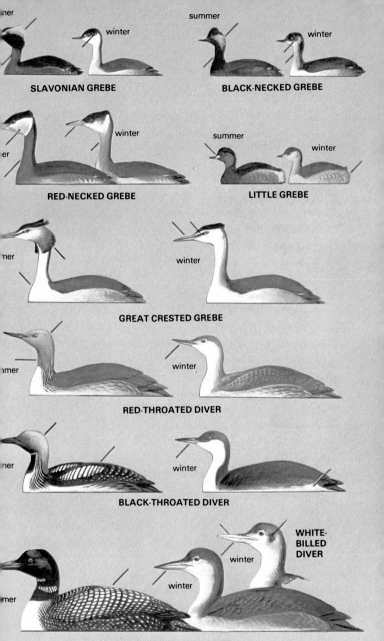

SLAVONIAN GREBE

summer

winter

BLACK-NECKED GREBE

winter

RED-NECKED GREBE

summer

winter

LITTLE GREBE

winter

GREAT CRESTED GREBE

winter

RED-THROATED DIVER

winter

BLACK-THROATED DIVER

WHITE-BILLED DIVER

winter

winter

GREAT NORTHERN DIVER

Plate 2

PETRELS AND SHEARWATERS

Petrels (little dark sea-birds with white rump-patches) are usually seen skimming or flitting low over the waves.

Fulmars and Shearwaters fly with several flaps and a glide, banking on stiff sabre-like wings in the wave troughs.

● **LEACH'S PETREL** page 4
Tail with a slight fork (seldom visible). Diagonal grey on wings. Bounding flight.

△ **WILSON'S PETREL** 4
Square-ended tail; longish legs. Yellowish feet (seldom visible); bat-like wing-beats. Dark under-wing.

● **STORM PETREL** 4
Square-ended tail; whitish bar under wing. Flitting flight.

● **MANX SHEARWATER** 4
Black above, white below; no patch at base of tail. West Mediterranean form browner above and below.

○ **LITTLE SHEARWATER** 4
Like small Manx, but black crown does not extend below eye; feet bluish (not pink).

● **CORY'S SHEARWATER** 4
No sharp head pattern; yellowish bill; flight like Fulmar. May or may not have white at base of tail.

● **GREAT SHEARWATER** 4
Well-defined dark cap, white cheek and white patch at base of tail. Flight rather like Manx.

● **FULMAR** 4
Bull-necked; stubby bill; stiff-winged, gliding flight.
Light phase: White head; light patch at base of primaries.
Dark phase: Smoky grey.

● **SOOTY SHEARWATER** 4
Dark all over except for whitish linings on under-surfaces of wings.

Other sea-birds which spend most of their time flying: skuas (Pl. 43), gulls (Pls. 44, 45, 46), terns (Pls. 47, 48, 49).

LEACH'S PETREL

WILSON'S PETREL

STORM PETREL

MANX SHEAR-WATER

typical form

MANX SHEAR-WATER

Medit. form

LITTLE SHEAR-WATER

CORY'S SHEAR-WATER

GREAT SHEAR-WATER

light phase

dark phase

FULMAR

SOOTY SHEAR-WATER

Plate 3

CORMORANTS

Cormorants are long-billed, dark water-birds, larger (except Pygmy Cormorant) than any duck. In flight the neck is held slightly above the horizontal. They fly in line or V formation, like geese, and stand upright, often with wings half open in a 'spread-eagle' pose. They swim low, like divers, but with the neck more erect.

● **CORMORANT** page 44

Differs from Shag in being larger, with a heavier bill, *white chin and cheeks*. Breeding birds have a *white patch on the thighs*. Continental birds when breeding have much white on the neck. Immature Cormorants can be separated from young Shags by their size, build, and the presence of *much white* on the underparts.

● **SHAG** 44

Smaller and thinner-billed than Cormorant; adult lacks the white cheek-patch and when breeding may have a short erect crest. Immature is much darker on the under-parts than young Cormorant.

PYGMY CORMORANT 44

Smaller, shorter-necked, and shorter-billed than Shag. Tail longer.

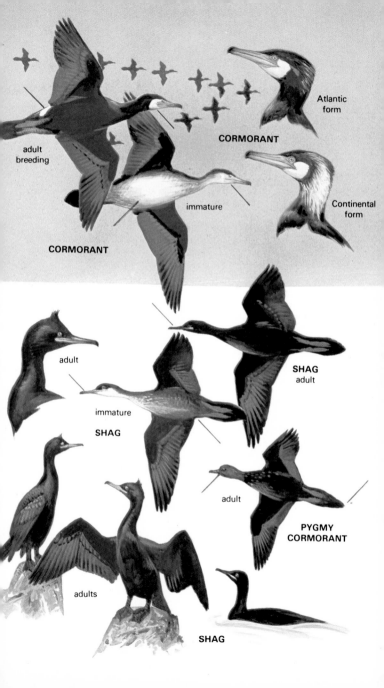

adult
breeding

CORMORANT

CORMORANT

Atlantic
form

immature

Continental
form

adult

SHAG

immature

SHAG

SHAG
adult

adult

**PYGMY
CORMORANT**

adults

SHAG

Plate 4

MISCELLANEOUS LARGE SEA BIRDS

WHITE PELICAN   page 4
Very large; huge bill. Extensive black on primaries and secondaries
  of under-wing. Feet reddish.

DALMATIAN PELICAN   4
Very large. Separated from White Pelican by lack of extensive black
  on under-wing and 'dirtier' white plumage. Feet blackish.

○ **BLACK-BROWED ALBATROSS**
Wing-span 7 ft. Suggests huge, long-winged, large-billed Black-
  backed Gull, but note black tail and wide black borders on under-
  wing. Distinctive gliding flight close to waves.

● **GANNET**
Adult: White; pointed tail; bold black primaries. Plunges headlong
  after fish.
Immature: Dark brown with pointed tail.
Changing immature: White, patched with dark.

WHITE
PELICAN

DALMATIAN
PELICAN

BLACK-BROWED
ALBATROSS

adult

GANNET

immature

changing
immature

GANNET

Plate 5

LONG-LEGGED MARSH BIRDS
(Bitterns, Herons, Cranes)

● **BITTERN** page 4
Tawny-brown; barred and mottled. Bill often pointed upwards.

○ **AMERICAN BITTERN** 4
Smaller than Bittern; more streaked, less barred. Conspicuous black
  neck-patch.

○ **LITTLE BITTERN** 4
Very small; large creamy wing-patch.
Male: Black back.
Female: Brown back.
Juvenile: Brownish; streaked wings.

○ **NIGHT HERON** 4
Adult: White breast, black back, black crown.
Immature: Brown; whitish spots on back and wings.

● **GREY HERON** 4
Large, pale grey; dark flight-feathers.

○ **PURPLE HERON** 4
Darker, more slender than Grey Heron; bulging chestnut neck
  conspicuous in flight. Immature sandier.

○ **CRANE** 9
Long white cheek-stripes; drooping feathers over tail.

DEMOISELLE CRANE 9
Smaller than Crane; black breast; white head-tufts.

Herons (including bitterns and egrets) fl
with their necks tucked back to their
shoulders. Cranes and all other large
long-legged marsh-birds fly with their
necks extended.

NIGHT HERON

BITTERN

AMERICAN BITTERN

juvenile

LITTLE BITTERN

juvenile

adult

juvenile

NIGHT
HERON

adult

juvenile

GREY
HERON

PURPLE
HERON

adult

CRANE

DEMOISELLE
CRANE

Plate 6

LONG-LEGGED MARSH BIRDS
(Herons, Spoonbill, Glossy Ibis, Flamingo, Storks)

● **LITTLE EGRET**   page
  Small, white; yellow feet, slender black bill.

○ **GREAT WHITE EGRET**
  Large, white; blackish feet.

○ **CATTLE EGRET**
  Looks white; heavy 'jowl', reddish legs and bill.
  Buffish plumes lost after breeding; bill and legs may then be
    yellowish or dusky.

○ **SQUACCO HERON**
  Adult: Looks sandy-brown; almost white in flight; greenish legs.
  Juvenile: Striped breast.

● **SPOONBILL**
  Adult: White; long, black, spatulate bill.
  Juvenile: Pinkish spatulate bill; black wing-tips.

○ **GLOSSY IBIS**
  Dark glossy body; decurved bill.

  GREATER FLAMINGO
  Bright crimson on wings; very long neck and legs.

○ **WHITE STORK**
  White, with black on wings; red bill.

○ **BLACK STORK**
  Black, with white belly; red bill.

White Stork   **Flamingo**   **Black Stork**

breeding

LITTLE EGRET

breeding

GREAT WHITE EGRET

breeding

breeding

non-breeding

non-breeding

juvenile

CATTLE EGRET

SQUACCO HERON

adults

SQUACCO HERON

SPOONBILL

juvenile

adult

GLOSSY IBIS

GREATER FLAMINGO

WHITE STORK

BLACK STORK

Plate 7

SWANS AND GEESE
(See also Plate 8)

● **BEWICK'S SWAN**   page 51
  Adult: Rounded head; base of bill yellow.
  Immature: Dingy; bill dull flesh to base.

● **WHOOPER SWAN**   51
  Adult: Flat profile; yellow on bill more extensive, forming point.
  Immature: Larger than Bewick's; longer neck.

● **MUTE SWAN**   51
  Adult: Bill orange, with black knob.
  Immature: Bill flesh, black at base

○ **SNOW GOOSE**   54
  Adult: White, with black wing tips.
  Immature: Dingier; bill dark.

● **BARNACLE GOOSE**   54
  Black chest and neck; white face.

● **CANADA GOOSE**   54
  Black neck, light chest; white throat-patch.

● **BRENT GOOSE**   55
  Black chest and neck; small white neck-spot.
  Immature birds lack the neck-spot.
  Dark-bellied form: Usually E. and S. British coasts.
  Pale-bellied form: In Britain mainly west, especially Ireland.

○ **RED-BREASTED GOOSE**   55
  Chestnut breast; broad white flank-stripe; head pattern.

juvenile   juvenile   juvenile

adult   adult   adult

BEWICK'S   **WHOOPER**   **MUTE**

MUTE SWAN

WHOOPER SWAN

BEWICK'S SWAN

adult

SNOW GOOSE

CANADA GOOSE

BARNACLE GOOSE

BRENT GOOSE

RED-BREASTED GOOSE

light-bellied form

dark-bellied form

Plate 8

SWANS AND GEESE IN FLIGHT
(See also Plate 7)

Most swans and geese fly in
line or V formation

BRENT GOOSE

light-bellied form

dark-bellied form

above

BARNACLE GOOSE

below

above

CANADA GOOSE

WHOOPER SWAN

MUTE SWAN

SNOW GOOSE

Plate 9

GREY GEESE
(See also Plate 10)

The best place in Europe to study geese is the New Grounds of the Wildfowl Trust, at Slimbridge. Captive examples of all birds shown on this plate can be studied there and during winter many can be seen in a wild state. The Director of the Trust, Sir Peter Scott, has guided the preparation of the goose plates.

Grey Geese with ORANGE Legs

● **WHITE-FRONTED GOOSE**   page 53
   Pink bill; white patch above base of bill and black blotches on belly
      are lacking in juvenile.

● **GREENLAND WHITE-FRONTED GOOSE**   53
   A subspecies; winters mostly Ireland and west Scotland. Darker; bill
      yellow (nail horn-colour in immature, not white).
   Juvenile usually shows little or no white at base of bill and often no
      bars on breast.

○ **LESSER WHITE-FRONTED GOOSE**   53
   Smaller; stubby bill; *yellow ring* around eye; white more extensive on
      forehead. A distinct species.

● **BEAN GOOSE**   52
   Dark head and neck; bill orange-yellow with black markings, but
      variable.

Grey Geese with PINK Legs

● **PINK-FOOTED GOOSE**   52
   Small dark head; dark neck; bill black and pink.

● **GREYLAG GOOSE**   53
   Large and pale; orange-yellow bill has no black.

EASTERN GREYLAG   53
Paler, with broad, light feather edges; pink bill.
Feral in W. Europe, including Britain.

WHITE-FRONTED

juvenile

Greenland form

LESSER
WHITE-
FRONTED

BEAN

adult

WHITE-FRONTED
GOOSE

GREENLAND
WHITE-FRONTED
GOOSE

BEAN GOOSE

LESSER
WHITE-FRONTED
GOOSE

eastern form

PINK-FOOTED
GOOSE

western form

GREYLAG
GOOSE

PINK-FOOTED

western   eastern

GREYLAG

Plate 10

CHIEFLY GREY GEESE IN FLIGHT
(See also Plate 9)

For the most part, grey geese on the wing all look very similar and it requires much experience to separate them at a distance. Their voices (below) are useful clues. At close range the bill and leg colours as shown on Pl. 9 are distinctive.

● **WHITE-FRONTED GOOSE**   page 53
  Fore-wing brownish; adult shows black blotches on breast. At close
    range, orange legs, pink bill, white forehead.
  Greenland White-front has yellow bill.
  Voice: Musical, high-pitched, usually disyllabic, sometimes trisyl-
    labic. *'Kow-lyow'* or *'lyo-lyok'*, etc.

● **BEAN GOOSE**   52
  Dark; no fore-wing contrast; orange feet; black and yellow bill.
  Voice: Reedy and bassoon-like *'ung-unk'*, not unlike lower notes of
    Pink-foot. Relatively silent.

● **PINK-FOOTED GOOSE**   52
  Fore-wing blue-grey; pale body; very dark head; pink feet.
  Voice: Musical *'ung-unk'*, higher than Bean. Sometimes *'king-wink'*,
    or often repeated *'wink-wink-wink'*.

● **GREYLAG GOOSE**   53
  Fore-wing strikingly pale grey; rather large; pale head.
  Voice: *'aahng-ung-ung'*, or *'gaahnk'*, very like farmyard goose.

○ **RED-BREASTED GOOSE**   55
  Black belly; rufous chest; white stripes.

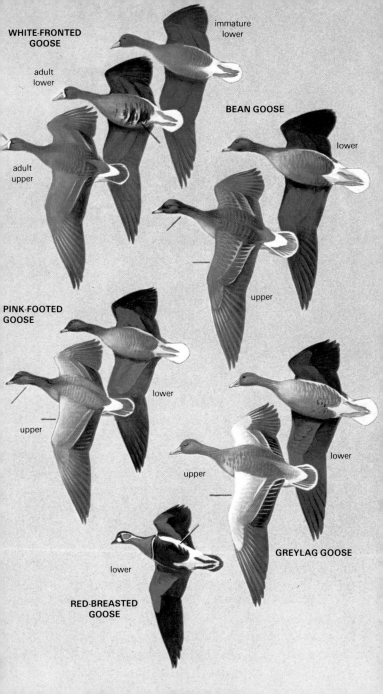

WHITE-FRONTED GOOSE

immature lower

adult lower

adult upper

BEAN GOOSE

lower

upper

PINK-FOOTED GOOSE

lower

upper

lower

upper

lower

GREYLAG GOOSE

lower

RED-BREASTED GOOSE

Plate 11

SURFACE-FEEDING DUCKS
(Marshes and Ponds)

- **MALLARD** page 58
  Male: Green head; white neck-ring;
     purplish-brown breast.
  Female: Some orange on bill;
     whitish tail.

- **PINTAIL** 59
  Male: Needle tail; neck-stripe.
  Female: Grey bill; slender pointed tail.

- **GADWALL** 57
  Male: Grey body; black rear.
  Female: Orange-sided bill; white speculum (in flight).

- **WIGEON** 57
  Male: Chestnut head; buff crown.
  Female: Short blue-grey bill; light shoulders (not often visible when
     swimming).

- **SHOVELER** 60
  Male: Spoon-like bill; dark chestnut sides.
  Female: Spoon-like bill; blue shoulders (in flight).

- **MANDARIN** 56
  Male: Orange 'side-whiskers'; orange 'sails'.
  Female: White mark around eye; white chin.

- **TEAL** 58
  Male: Small; grey with dark head; horizontal white stripe above
     wing.
  Female: Small size, green speculum.

- **GARGANEY** 59
  Male: White stripe on head; bluish shoulder-patch.
  Female: From Teal by greyer wings; obscure speculum.

  MARBLED DUCK 60
  Mediterranean. Dappled plumage.
  Shaggy head; dark smudge through eye; white tail.

MALLARD

♂   ♀

PINTAIL

♂   ♀

GADWALL

♂   ♀

WIGEON

♂   ♀

SHOVELER

♀

♂

MANDARIN

♀

♂

TEAL

♂   ♀

GARGANEY

♂   ♀

MARBLED DUCK

♂

Plate 12

DIVING DUCKS
(Goldeneyes and Pochards, etc.)

Diving ducks (ducks of open waters and sea) patter along the surface when taking flight. Surface-feeding ducks (marsh ducks, Pl. 11) spring directly up from the water.

● **GOLDENEYE** page 66
  Male: Round white spot before eye.
  Female: Grey body; brown head; white collar; white on wing visible when swimming.

BARROW'S GOLDENEYE 66
Iceland.
  Male: White crescent on face; blacker above than Goldeneye.
  Female: Very similar to Goldeneye (see text).

○ **FERRUGINOUS DUCK** 62
  Male: Deep mahogany; white under tail-coverts.
  Female: Similar, but duller.

● **SCAUP** 62
  Male: Black fore-parts; pale back; blue bill. 'Black at both ends, white in the middle'.
  Female: Sharply defined white patch at base of bill.

● **TUFTED DUCK** 62
  Male: Black fore-parts; black back; drooping crest.
  Female: From female Scaup by suggestion of crest. White at base of bill restricted or absent.

● **POCHARD** 61
  Male: Grey; black chest; chestnut head.
  Female: Buff mark around eye and base of bill; blue band on bill.

● **RED-CRESTED POCHARD** 61
  Male: From Pochard by red bill and white sides.
  Female: Pale cheek; from female Common Scoter by paler plumage; white wing-patch; red on bill.

GOLDENEYE

BARROW'S GOLDENEYE

FERRUGINOUS DUCK

SCAUP

TUFTED DUCK

POCHARD

RED-CRESTED POCHARD

Plate 13

SEA DUCKS

● **LONG-TAILED DUCK**
Male in summer: Needle tail; white face-patch.
Male in winter: Needle tail; pied pattern.
Female: Dark wings; white face; dark cheek mark.

△ **HARLEQUIN**
Male: Dark; rusty flanks; harlequin pattern.
Female: Dark; face-spots; small bill.

○ **SURF SCOTER**
Male: Black body; white patches on head and bill.
Female: Light face-spots; no white on wing.

● **VELVET SCOTER**
Male: Black body; white wing-patch.
Female: Light face-spots; white wing-patch.

● **COMMON SCOTER**
Male: All black; orange patch on bill.
Female: Dark body; light cheek; dark crown.

● **EIDER**
Male: White above; black below.
Female: Brown; heavily barred. See diagram below.

○ **KING EIDER**
Male: Whitish fore-parts; black rear two-thirds; orange shield.
Female: See diagram below.

△ **STELLER'S EIDER**
Male: White head; chestnut under-parts; black spot.
Female: See diagram below.

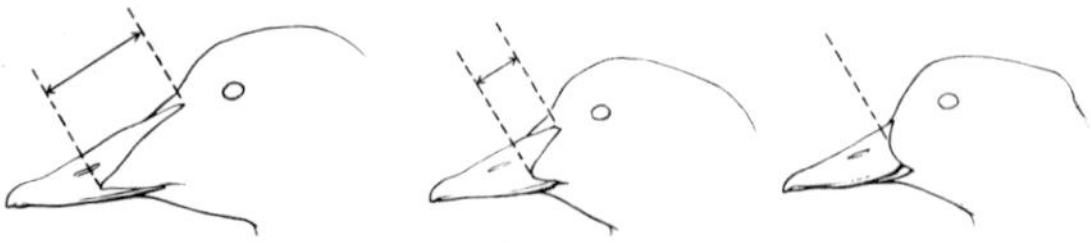

Eider ♀   King Eider ♀   Steller's Eider ♀

Female Eiders can be told by their bills; long and sloping in the Eider, with long lobe extending to the forehead; stubbier in the King Eider, with less lobing; no obvious lobes in the Steller's.

summer   ♂ winter   **LONG-TAILED DUCK**   ♀ winter

HARLEQUIN

SURF SCOTER

VELVET SCOTER

COMMON SCOTER

EIDER

KING EIDER   **STELLER'S EIDER**

Plate 14

SAW-BILLS, SHELDUCKS, STIFF-TAIL

Saw-bills or fish-eating ducks have slender spike-like bills with toothed edges. They swim low in the water.

Shelducks are large and somewhat goose-like.

Stiff-tails are dumpy, with long tails, often cocked.

● **RED-BREASTED MERGANSER**   page 67
   Male: White collar; wispy crest; chestnut breast.
   Female: Crested head; *blended* throat and neck.

● **GOOSANDER**   67
   Male: Long white body; dark head; black back.
   Female: Crested; *sharply defined* throat and neck.

● **SMEW**   66
   Male: White, marked with black; white crest.
   Female: Chestnut cap; white cheeks; thin bill.

● **SHELDUCK**   56
   Chestnut belt encircling white body; red bill.
   Male has knob on bill; female is without knob.

△ **RUDDY SHELDUCK**   56
   Orange-chestnut body; pale head.
   Male with narrow black neck-ring; female without.

   WHITE-HEADED DUCK   68
   Male: Dark body; white head; blue bill (in summer).
   Female: Light cheek crossed by dark line.
   Both sexes have swollen base to bill.

RED-BREASTED MERGANSER

GOOSANDER

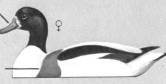

SMEW

SHELDUCK

RUDDY SHELDUCK

summer

WHITE-HEADED DUCK

Plate 15

WATERFOWL RARITIES

Note: Males only are shown in flight.

△ **PIED-BILLED GREBE**   page 21
   Winter: Short stout bill, white under tail-coverts.
   Summer: Black ring on bill, black throat.

● **RUDDY DUCK**   6
   Male in summer: Ruddy body, white cheek, black cap.
   Male in winter: Greyish; white cheek; dark cap.
   Female: Dark lines across white cheek.
   From White-headed by lack of swollen bill and smaller size.

○ **RING-NECKED DUCK**   6
   Male: High-crowned head, white band on bill; white mark in front
   of grey side.
   Female: Indistinct light face-patch; white eye-ring and white ring on
   bill.

○ **BLUE-WINGED TEAL**   6
   Male: White crescent on face, black and white rear.
   Female: Pale face-spot near base of bill; bill longer than Garganey's.

△ **BAIKAL TEAL**   5
   Male: Creamy cheek with circular pattern.
   Female: White spot near bill; broken supercilium.

○ **AMERICAN WIGEON**   5
   Male: Pinkish brown; grey head with dark green patch and white
   crown.
   Female: Differs from female Wigeon by greyer head, whitish
   borders on tertials.

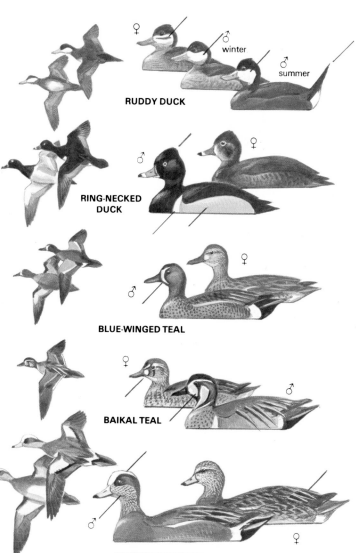

PIED-BILLED GREBE
summer
winter

RUDDY DUCK
♀
♂ winter
♂ summer

RING-NECKED DUCK
♂
♀

BLUE-WINGED TEAL
♂
♀

BAIKAL TEAL
♀
♂

AMERICAN WIGEON
♂
♀

Plate 16

DUCKS IN FLIGHT
(See also Plate 18)

Note: Males only are analysed below. For females, see text.

- **SHELDUCK** page 56
  Black, white and chestnut pattern.

△ **RUDDY SHELDUCK** 56
  Pale cinnamon colour; large fore-wing patches.

- **MALLARD** 58
  Dark head; two white borders on speculum; neck-ring.

- **PINTAIL** 59
  Needle tail; one white border on speculum; dark head.

- **WIGEON** 57
  Large white shoulder-patches; grey back.

- **SHOVELER** 60
  Heavy bill; striking blue shoulder-patches.

- **GADWALL** 57
  Grey-brown; white patch on inner secondaries.

- **GARGANEY** 59
  Small; white head-streak; bluish shoulder-patches.

- **TEAL** 58
  Small, dark-winged; dark head; green speculum.

- **SMEW** 60
  White head and inner wing; black outer wing and mantle.

- **GOOSANDER** 6
  Saw-bill shape; white body and inner wing.

- **RED-BREASTED MERGANSER** 6
  Saw-bill shape; dark chest; white inner wing.

 Saw-bills (Smew, Goosander and Red-breasted Merganser) fly with bill. head, neck and body held in a horizontal line. Compare with divers, Pl. 1.

SHELDUCK

♂

RUDDY
SHELDUCK

♂

MALLARD

PINTAIL

WIGEON

SHOVELER

GADWALL

GARGANEY

TEAL

♂

SMEW

GOOSANDER

RED-BREASTED MERGANSER

Plate 17

DUCKS IN FLIGHT
(See also Plate 19)

Note: Males only are analysed below. Some females have similar wing patterns. See text.

● **TUFTED DUCK** page 6
Black back; white rear wing-stripe.

● **SCAUP** 6
Pale grey back; white rear wing-stripe.

○ **FERRUGINOUS DUCK** 6
Mahogany colour; white rear wing-stripe.

● **POCHARD** 6
Grey back; grey rear wing-stripe.

● **RED-CRESTED POCHARD** 6
Broad white patch extends nearly length of wing.

● **GOLDENEYE** 6
Large white wing-squares; short neck; dark head with white spot. Wings whistle in flight.

● **LONG-TAILED DUCK** 6
Dark unpatterned wings; white on head and body.

△ **HARLEQUIN** 6
Stocky, dark, with white marks; small bill.

○ **KING EIDER** 6
Whitish fore-parts; black back and rear-parts.

● **EIDER** 6
White back; white fore-wings; black belly.

● **VELVET SCOTER** 6
Black body; white secondaries.

○ **SURF SCOTER** 6
Black body; white patches on head and bill.

● **COMMON SCOTER** 6
All-black plumage.

TUFTED DUCK

SCAUP

FERRUGINOUS DUCK

RED-CRESTED POCHARD

POCHARD

GOLDENEYE

LONG-TAILED DUCK

HARLEQUIN

KING EIDER

EIDER

VELVET SCOTER

SURF SCOTER

COMMON SCOTER

Plate 18

DUCKS OVERHEAD
(See also Plate 16)

Note: Only males are analysed below. For females, see text.

● **SHELDUCK**   page 5⬤
Chestnut breast-band across white under-parts.

△ **RUDDY SHELDUCK**   5⬤
Pale cinnamon body; white under-wings.

● **MALLARD**   5⬤
Dark head and chest; paler belly; neck-ring.

● **PINTAIL**   5⬤
Small dark head; white breast; long thin neck; needle tail.

● **WIGEON**   5
Clean-cut white belly; dark pointed tail.

● **SHOVELER**   6⬤
Dark head and belly; thick white neck; big bill.

● **GADWALL**   5⬤
White belly; white inner secondaries.

● **GARGANEY**   5⬤
Small size; pale under-parts; dark fore-parts.

● **TEAL**   5⬤
Small size; white belly; dark head.

● **SMEW**   6⬤
All-white below, except on wings and tail.

● **GOOSANDER**   6⬤
Dark head; white body; white wing-linings.

● **RED-BREASTED MERGANSER**   6⬤
Saw-bill shape; dark breast-band.

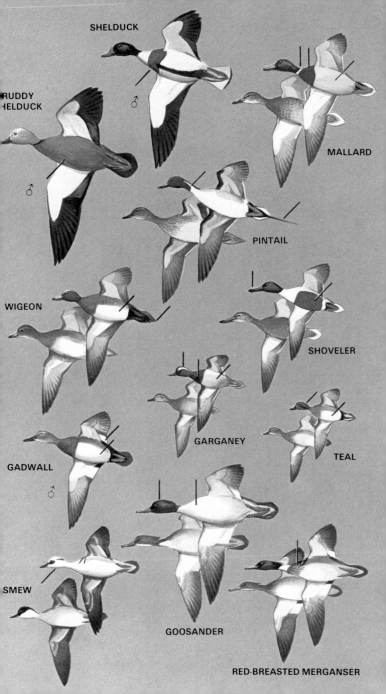

SHELDUCK

RUDDY SHELDUCK

♂

♂

MALLARD

PINTAIL

WIGEON

SHOVELER

GARGANEY

TEAL

GADWALL

♂

SMEW

GOOSANDER

RED-BREASTED MERGANSER

Plate 19

DUCKS OVERHEAD
(See also Plate 17)

Note: Only males are analysed below. For females, see text.

● **TUFTED DUCK** page 62
Similar to Scaup overhead, but less bulky.

● **SCAUP** 62
Black chest; white stripe showing through wing.

○ **FERRUGINOUS DUCK** 62
Mahogany fore-parts and flanks, framing white belly.

● **POCHARD** 61
Chestnut head; black breast; grey belly.

● **RED-CRESTED POCHARD** 61
Black under-parts; bold white flank-patches.

● **GOLDENEYE** 66
Blackish wing-linings; white body.

● **LONG-TAILED DUCK** 64
Uniform dark wings and breast; white belly and head.

△ **HARLEQUIN** 64
Uniform dark colour; white spots; small bill.

○ **KING EIDER** 63
White chest; black belly; blunt head.

● **EIDER** 63
White chest; black belly; pointed head.

● **VELVET SCOTER** 65
Black body; white secondaries.

○ **SURF SCOTER** 65
Black body; white on head and bill.

● **COMMON SCOTER** 65
Black body; silvery flight feathers.

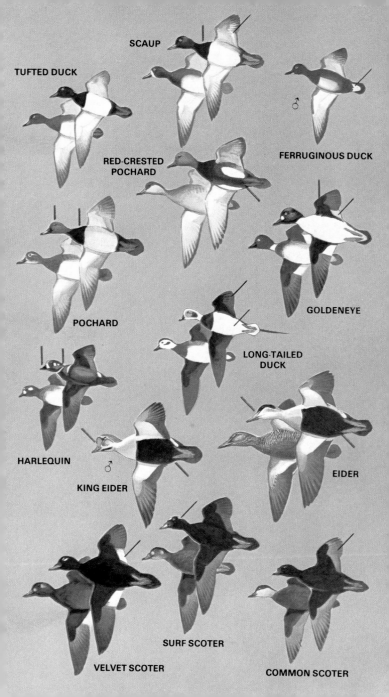

TUFTED DUCK

SCAUP

FERRUGINOUS DUCK
♂

RED-CRESTED
POCHARD

POCHARD

GOLDENEYE

LONG-TAILED
DUCK

HARLEQUIN

KING EIDER
♂

EIDER

VELVET SCOTER

SURF SCOTER

COMMON SCOTER

Plate 20

VULTURES

GRIFFON VULTURE

BLACK VULTURE

LAMMERGEIER

EGYPTIAN VULTURE

EGYPTIAN

LAMMERGEIER

GRIFFON

BLACK

Plate 21

HARRIERS AND KITES
(See also Plate 22)

Harriers have small heads, long bodies, long wings and long tails.

● **MARSH HARRIER**   page 72
Male: Grey on wings and tail; rufous below.
Female: Dark brown; pale crown and throat.
Juvenile: Like female, or with head nearly all dark.

● **MONTAGU'S HARRIER**   73
Male: Black bars across secondaries; greyish rump; rusty marks on under-parts.
Female: Slimmer than Hen Harrier; rump-patch slightly narrower.

● **HEN HARRIER**   72
Male: Grey, with clear white rump-patch; no black bar across wing, but secondaries dark-tipped.
Female: Brown, streaked; white rump-patch.

△ **PALLID HARRIER**   72
Male: Paler than Hen Harrier, with white breast; no white rump-patch; no black wing-bar.
Female: Indistinguishable in field from Montagu's.

Kites are rather similar in shape to harriers, but have notched or forked tails.

○ **BLACK KITE**   69
Dusky; slightly forked tail.

● **RED KITE**   69
Rich rusty, with pale head; deeply forked tail.

BLACK-SHOULDERED KITE   69
Black shoulders; white tail.

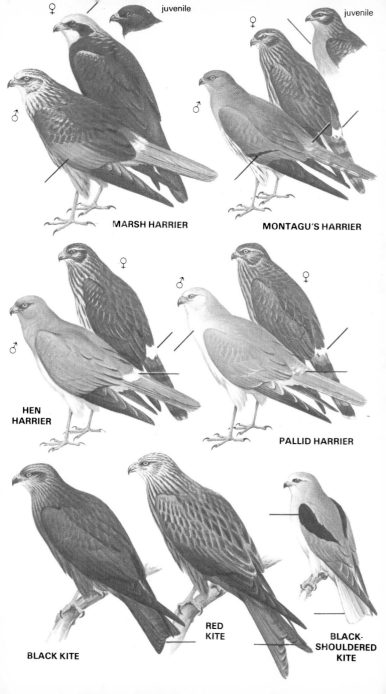

♀
juvenile
♂
MARSH HARRIER

♀
juvenile
♂
MONTAGU'S HARRIER

♀
♂
HEN HARRIER

♂
♀
PALLID HARRIER

BLACK KITE

RED KITE

BLACK-SHOULDERED KITE

Plate 22

HARRIERS AND KITES IN FLIGHT
(See also Plate 21)

Harriers have long wings, long tails and long bodies. Their wings are not as pointed as those of falcons and their flight is more languid and gliding, usually low over the ground. When gliding, their wings (especially Montagu's and Hen Harriers) are usually held in a shallow V.

● **MARSH HARRIER**   page 72
Male: Contrasting grey wing-patches and tail.
Female: Dark; pale crown and pale shoulders.

● **MONTAGU'S HARRIER**   73
Male: Dark bar on wing; greyish rump.
Female: From Hen Harrier by slimmer build and slightly smaller rump-patch.

● **HEN HARRIER**   72
Male: From below, dark tips to secondaries form narrow bar. White rump.
Female: Streaked brown; bold white rump.

Kites are rather similar in shape to harriers, but have notched or forked tails. They are buoyant gliders, making great use of their flexible tails.

● **RED KITE**   69
Rusty; deeply forked tail; distinctive wing pattern.

○ **BLACK KITE**   69
Dusky; slightly forked tail; nearly uniform wings below.
Note: Can be confused with some dark Marsh Harriers.

MARSH
HARRIER

♀

♂

MONTAGU'S
HARRIER

♀

♂

HEN HARRIER

♀

♂

RED KITE   BLACK KITE

Plate 23

BUZZARDS AND HAWKS
(See also Plates 24 and 28)

Buzzards have heavy bodies and short wide tails.

● **ROUGH-LEGGED BUZZARD**   page 75
Dark belly; whitish tail with dark terminal band.

● **BUZZARD**   74
Variable. Usually dark with blotched or barred under-parts. Tail
usually as shown, sometimes almost unbarred cinnamon.

● **HONEY BUZZARD**   68
Head smaller, tail longer than Buzzard's.
Tail has broad black bands near base and at tip.

LONG-LEGGED BUZZARD   75
Tail pale cinnamon, usually unbarred; base sometimes whitish.

Accipiters (bird hawks) have small heads,
short wings and long tails.

● **SPARROWHAWK**   73
Male: Small; under-parts closely barred red-brown.
Female: Under-parts closely barred with grey.

● **GOSHAWK**   73
Adult: Large, barred; dark cheek; white supercilium.
Juvenile: Brown, streaked; pronounced supercilium.

ROUGH-LEGGED
BUZZARD

typical

pale

BUZZARD

dark

pale

typical

adult

HONEY
BUZZARD

LONG-
LEGGED
BUZZARD

immature

adult

♂

♀

SPARROWHAWK

GOSHAWK

Plate 24

BUZZARDS AND SMALL EAGLES OVERHEAD
(See also Plate 23)

Buzzards are bulky, with broad wings and broad tails. They soar and wheel high in the open sky. Certain of the eagles are similar in outline to buzzards, but usually have proportionately longer wings.

● **ROUGH-LEGGED BUZZARD**   page 75
Dark belly; whitish tail with broad black band at tip; black 'wrist-patches' on pale wing-linings.

● **BUZZARD**   74
Variable, usually dark; short-necked; secondaries and tail usually with numerous narrow bars.

LONG-LEGGED BUZZARD   75
Tail pale rusty, usually without bars; rufous wing-linings.

● **HONEY BUZZARD**   68
Head more projecting, tail longer than Buzzard's, with broad black bands near base. Note bars across all flight-feathers.

BONELLI'S EAGLE   78
Adult: Silky-white under-parts; dark wings.
Juvenile: Rufous wing-linings have dark edges.

BOOTED EAGLE   77
Buzzard size; longer tail.
Light phase: White wing-linings; dark flight-feathers.
Dark phase: Dark; pale at base of primaries and tail.

SHORT-TOED EAGLE   71
White under-parts and under-wings usually contrast strikingly with dark upper breast. Some birds lack dark breast-band. Owl-like head.

BUZZARD

ROUGH-LEGGED
BUZZARD

HONEY
BUZZARD

LONG-LEGGED
BUZZARD

BONELLI'S
EAGLE
adult

BONELLI'S
EAGLE
juvenile

BOOTED
EAGLE
light phase

BOOTED
EAGLE
dark phase

SHORT-TOED EAGLE

Plate 25

EAGLES
(See also Plate 26)

● **GOLDEN EAGLE**
  Much larger than Buzzard; different silhouette. Adult is all dark
  with golden feathers on head and hind-neck. See overhead flight
  patterns of adult and immature on Pl. 26.

○ **WHITE-TAILED EAGLE**
  Adult more bulky than Golden Eagle; entire head pale, tail white.
  See overhead flight patterns of adult and immature on Pl. 26.

  TAWNY EAGLE
  Adult almost uniform dark brown, often with rusty-yellow patch on
  nape. Juvenile (not shown) *café au lait* coloured. Two pale wing-
  bars show in flight.

  IMPERIAL EAGLE
  Similar to Golden but pale crown of adult may be almost whitish in
  some birds. Usually some *pure white feathers* on scapulars.
  Spanish form has conspicuous *white shoulders*.

  LESSER SPOTTED EAGLE
  Very similar to Spotted Eagle but less heavily built; wings narrower.
  Immature has fewer spots. See text.

△ **SPOTTED EAGLE**
  Adult dark throughout, usually with white visible on upper tail-
  coverts. Immature with *copious, large whitish spots* forming pale
  bands on wing; a white V at base of tail.

WHITE-TAILED
EAGLE

adult

adult

TAWNY
EAGLE

adult

GOLDEN
EAGLE

adult

adult
Spanish form

adult
eastern form

IMPERIAL EAGLE

adult

adult

immature

SPOTTED
EAGLE

LESSER
SPOTTED
EAGLE

immature

Plate 26

EAGLES AND OSPREY OVERHEAD
(See also Plate 25)

- **GOLDEN EAGLE** page 77
  Much larger than Buzzard, with different silhouette.
  Immature: 'Ringed' tail with white base; large white patches at base
    of primaries and outer secondaries.
  Adult: Almost uniformly dark. When upper side is seen, golden
    feathers on head and wing-coverts are diagnostic.

- ○ **WHITE-TAILED EAGLE** 70
  Immature: From adult Golden by shorter, more wedge-shaped tail,
    huge bill and vulturine wing-shape. Paler than Golden, often
    streaked with white and brown on under-parts.
  Adult: White tail.

- **OSPREY** 78
  White head, clear white belly, black 'wrist-patches'.

Spotted Eagle Immature (*after P. J. Hayman*)

Note: all head-on silhouettes showing gliding, not soaring, attitudes.

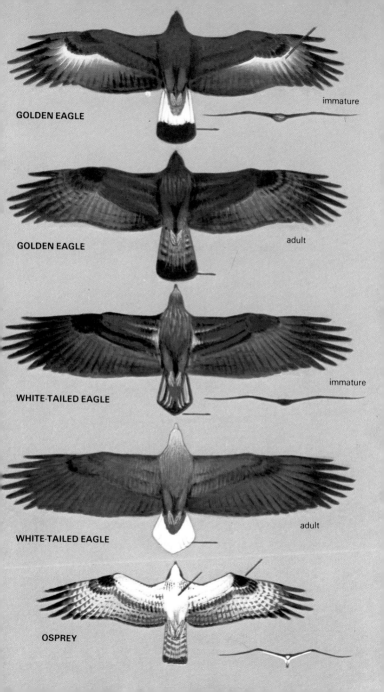

GOLDEN EAGLE immature

GOLDEN EAGLE adult

WHITE-TAILED EAGLE immature

WHITE-TAILED EAGLE adult

OSPREY

Plate 27

FALCONS
(See also Plate 28)

Falcons have rather large heads, broad shoulders, long pointed wings, longish tails.

KESTREL

♂ ♀

LESSER KESTREL

♂

MERLIN

♂ ♀

juvenile

PEREGRINE

LANNER

SAKER

dark form adult

pale form adult

HOBBY

ELEONORA'S FALCON

RED-FOOTED FALCON

♂ ♀

Plate 28

FALCONS AND ACCIPITERS OVERHEAD
(See also Plates 23 and 27)

Falcons have long, pointed wings, long tails. Their wing-strokes are strong, rapid but shallow.

○ **GYRFALCON** page 81
  Grey phase: Larger than Peregrine; broader wing-bases; no contrasting face pattern.
  White phase: Can look as white as a Snowy Owl.

● **MERLIN** 79
  Smaller than Kestrel; darker, more compact.

● **PEREGRINE** 81
  Falcon shape; face pattern; size near that of Crow.

● **HOBBY** 80
  Like small Peregrine, but tail shorter; wings more Swift-like.

○ **RED-FOOTED FALCON** 79
  Male: Very dark; red feet; rusty under tail-coverts.
  Female: Rusty wing-linings; unmarked rusty belly.

● **KESTREL** 79
  Small, slim; black band near tip of tail. Hovers.

△ **ELEONORA'S FALCON** 80
  Pale form: Striped rusty under-parts; dark wings.
  Dark form: All dark, with pale feet.

△ **LESSER KESTREL** 78
  Tail slightly wedge-shaped. White wing-linings. Seldom hovers.

Accipiters (bird hawks) have short, rounded wings and long tails. In flight they alternate several rapid wing-beats with a short glide; they also soar.

● **GOSHAWK** 73
  Very large; under-parts barred with grey; conspicuous white under tail-coverts.

● **SPARROWHAWK** 73
  Under-parts barred with rusty (male) or grey (female).

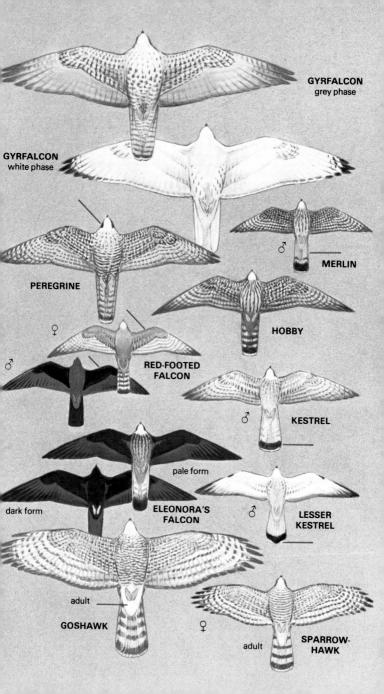

GYRFALCON
grey phase

GYRFALCON
white phase

♂ MERLIN

PEREGRINE

HOBBY

♀

♂ RED-FOOTED
FALCON

♂ KESTREL

pale form

dark form ELEONORA'S
FALCON

♂ LESSER
KESTREL

adult

GOSHAWK

♀ adult SPARROW-
HAWK

Plate 29

GAME BIRDS
(See also Plate 30)

● **PHEASANT**   page 8◖
   Male: Highly coloured; very long tail; usually a neck-ring.
   Female: Large, brown; long pointed tail.

● **BLACK GROUSE**   8
   Male (Blackcock): Glossy black; lyre-shaped tail; white wing-bar.
   Female (Greyhen): Large, brown; long notched tail (notch not
     always evident).

● **CAPERCAILLIE**   8
   Male: Very large size; dusky coloration; broad fan tail.
   Female: Large, brown; fan tail.

HAZEL GROUSE   8
Partridge-size; fan tail with wide black band. Colour phases vary
   from rufous to grey, tending towards rufous in south of range,
   grey in north.

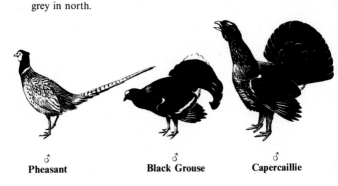

♂   ♂   ♂
Pheasant   **Black Grouse**   **Capercaillie**

See also illustrations of other game-birds, Pl. 30.

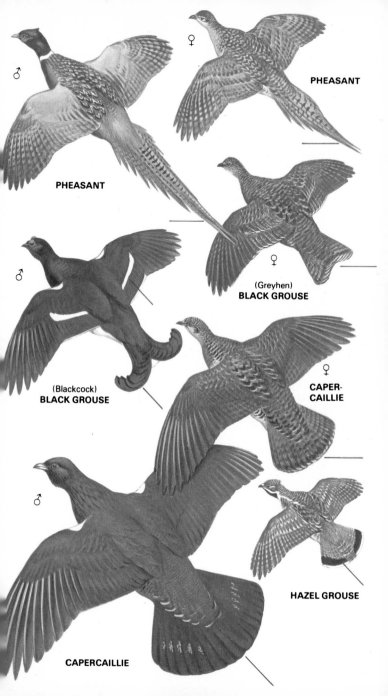

♂

PHEASANT

♀

PHEASANT

PHEASANT

♂

(Greyhen)
BLACK GROUSE

♀

(Blackcock)
BLACK GROUSE

♀

CAPER-
CAILLIE

♂

HAZEL GROUSE

CAPERCAILLIE

Plate 30

GAME BIRDS
(See also Plate 29)

● **RED GROUSE**   page 82
   Dark rufous plumage; dark wings; dark tail.
   Female less rufous, more barred.

   WILLOW GROUSE   82
   Winter: From pale Ptarmigan, see drawing below.
   Summer: Rufous; white wings; black tail.
   Lower altitudes than Ptarmigan.

● **PTARMIGAN**   83
   Winter: White, with black tail.
   Summer: White wings; grey or brown body; black tail.

● **GREY PARTRIDGE**   85
   Rufous tail; rusty head.
   Male with dark horseshoe mark on belly.

Red legs and rufous tails (conspicuous only in flight) characterize the following
three partridges. Best separated by their neck patterns.

● **RED-LEGGED PARTRIDGE**   85
   Necklace black, breaking into short streaks.

   ROCK PARTRIDGE   85
   Necklace black, clean-cut. (See Chukar, p. 84.)

   BARBARY PARTRIDGE   85
   Necklace red-brown, with white spots; grey face.

● **QUAIL**   86
   Small; sandy-brown; striped head.

   ANDALUSIAN HEMIPODE   87
   Quail-like; bright rufous patch on breast; bold spots on sides of
     breast.

         Ptarmigan ♂   **Willow Grouse** ♂ **and** ♀

Note the black face-patch on the male (not female) Ptarmigan in winter. Both
sexes of Willow Grouse lack this, but have thicker bills.

RED GROUSE ♂

♀ **RED GROUSE**

♂ winter

♂ summer

♀ summer

PTARMIGAN

RED-LEGGED PARTRIDGE ♂

below

summer

WILLOW GROUSE

♂

GREY PARTRIDGE

QUAIL

ANDALUSIAN HEMIPODE

PARTRIDGES WITH RED LEGS

ROCK

RED-LEGGED

BARBARY

Plate 31

CRAKES, RAILS, COOTS AND GALLINULES

● **WATER RAIL**   page 87
  Adult: Long red bill; barred flanks; white under tail.
  Juvenile: Dusky; mottled under-parts.

● **CORNCRAKE**   89
  Rusty-red wings; yellowish bill. Often darker than shown, with
    greyish cheeks and breast.

● **SPOTTED CRAKE**   88
  Recalls short-billed rail; often darker than shown. Buff under tail-
    coverts; greenish legs; red base to bill.

△ **BAILLON'S CRAKE**   89
  No red on bill; legs brownish-flesh; bold bars on flanks. Upper-parts
    richer vinous-chestnut than shown, boldly streaked white.

○ **LITTLE CRAKE**   88
  Male: Legs green; no spots on breast; no dark bars on flanks; upper-
    parts olive-brown.
  Female: Buffish breast; green legs; both sexes have red spot on bill.

● **MOORHEN**   89
  Adult: Red bill; white flank-stripe and under tail.
  Juvenile: Brownish with yellowish-green bill.

● **COOT**   90
  Adult: White bill and shield.
  Juvenile: From Moorhen by larger size, no white on tail-coverts.
  Downy young: Orange-red head.

  CRESTED COOT   90
  Bluish bill, white shield; red knobs often inconspicuous.

  PURPLE GALLINULE   90
  Deep purplish-blue; red legs; very large red bill.

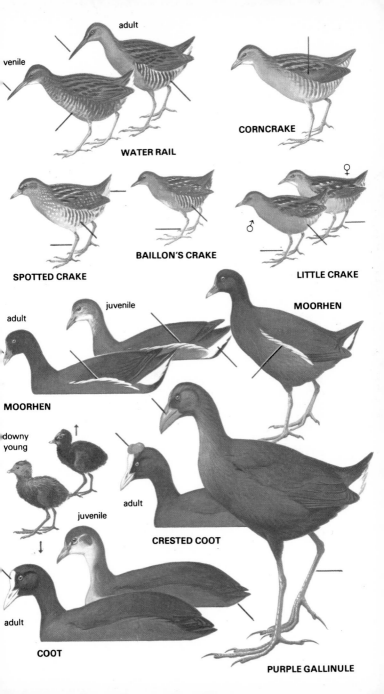

venile

adult

WATER RAIL

CORNCRAKE

SPOTTED CRAKE

BAILLON'S CRAKE

♀

♂

LITTLE CRAKE

MOORHEN

adult

juvenile

MOORHEN

downy young

juvenile

CRESTED COOT

adult

COOT

PURPLE GALLINULE

Plate 32

BUSTARDS, SANDGROUSE AND STONE CURLEW

Bustards are large-bodied, long-legged birds of the open plains.

Sandgrouse are plump, dove-like desert birds with pointed tails.

△ **GREAT BUSTARD**   page 9
   Very large size; head and neck pale grey (no black). White on wing
     extends to primaries.

○ **LITTLE BUSTARD**   9
   Male: Black and white neck pattern; shows much white in flight.
   Female: Streaked brown head and neck.

△ **HOUBARA BUSTARD**   9
   Silhouette recalls hen Turkey with longish tail.
   Long black and white feathers drooping from neck.

  BLACK-BELLIED SANDGROUSE   12
   Black belly; tail less elongated than in other sandgrouse; blackish
    wing-linings.

  PIN-TAILED SANDGROUSE   12
   White belly and under-wings; long needle-pointed tail.

△ **PALLAS'S SANDGROUSE**   12
   Black belly; long needle-pointed tail; pale wing-linings.

● **STONE CURLEW**   9
   Hunched attitude; large pale eyes; broad light bar on closed wing.

GREAT BUSTARD

♂

LITTLE BUSTARD

♀

♂

sexes similar

HOUBARA BUSTARD

BLACK-BELLIED SANDGROUSE

PIN-TAILED SANDGROUSE

STONE CURLEW

PALLAS'S SANDGROUSE

Plate 33

WADERS
(See also Plate 34)

- **RINGED PLOVER** page 95
  Band across breast; yellow legs and base of bill.

- **LITTLE RINGED PLOVER** 95
  Smaller than Ringed Plover; flesh legs; white line above black on
    forehead.

- **KENTISH PLOVER** 96
  Black on sides of breast only; black legs; unbroken supercilium.

- **GREY PLOVER** 98
  Summer: Black below; silvery above.
  Winter: Stout shape; grey above

- **GOLDEN PLOVER** 97
  Summer: Black below, dark above; broad white side-stripe. (Sou-
    thern form has less black.)
  Winter: Less stout than Grey; golden-brown above.

- **LAPWING** 99
  Long wispy crest; black upper breast; iridescent back.

- **TURNSTONE** 112
  Summer: 'Tortoiseshell' back; distinctive face.
  Winter: Dark breast-band; orange legs.

△ **CREAM-COLOURED COURSER** 94
  Sandy; bold eye-stripes; long creamy legs.

- **DOTTEREL** 97
  White stripe over eye and across breast; russet flanks; black belly.

- **DUNLIN** 103
  Summer: Rusty back; black patch on belly.

- **CURLEW SANDPIPER** 103
  Summer: Decurved bill; rufous plumage.

- **GREY PHALAROPE** 113
  Female in summer: Rufous below; white cheeks.
  Male in summer: Duller.

- **RED-NECKED PHALAROPE** 113
  Female in summer: Red neck; white throat.
  Male in summer: Duller.

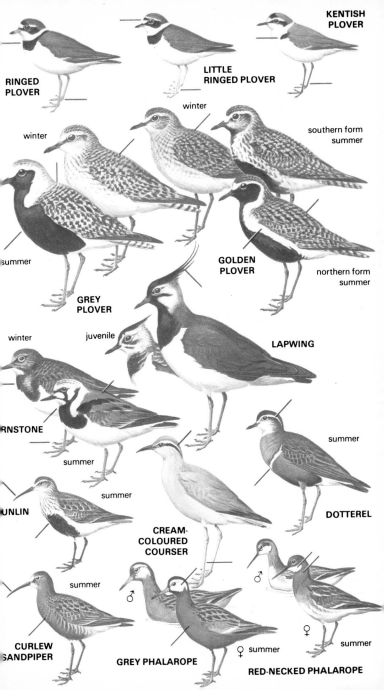

KENTISH PLOVER

RINGED PLOVER

LITTLE RINGED PLOVER

winter

winter

southern form summer

winter

summer

GOLDEN PLOVER

northern form summer

GREY PLOVER

juvenile

LAPWING

winter

RNSTONE

summer

summer

DOTTEREL

UNLIN

summer

CREAM-COLOURED COURSER

summer

summer

♂

♂

♀ summer

CURLEW SANDPIPER

GREY PHALAROPE

♀ summer

RED-NECKED PHALAROPE

Plate 34

PLOVERS AND TURNSTONE IN FLIGHT
(See also Plate 33)

- **RINGED PLOVER** — page 9
  Prominent wing-bar; dark tail with white borders.
- **LITTLE RINGED PLOVER** — 9
  From Ringed Plover by voice and lack of wing-bar.
- **KENTISH PLOVER** — 9
  Sandy-brown above; white sides of tail.
- **GREY PLOVER** — 9
  Summer: Black under-parts; white on wings and rump.
  Winter: Black axillaries; white on wings and rump.
- **GOLDEN PLOVER** — 9
  Summer: Black under-parts; no white above.
  Winter: Lack of pattern above and below.
- **DOTTEREL** — 9
  White face; light breast-bar; dark under-parts; belly paler in winter.
- **LAPWING** — 99
  Black and white; very broad, rounded wings.
- **TURNSTONE** — 112
  Harlequin pattern.

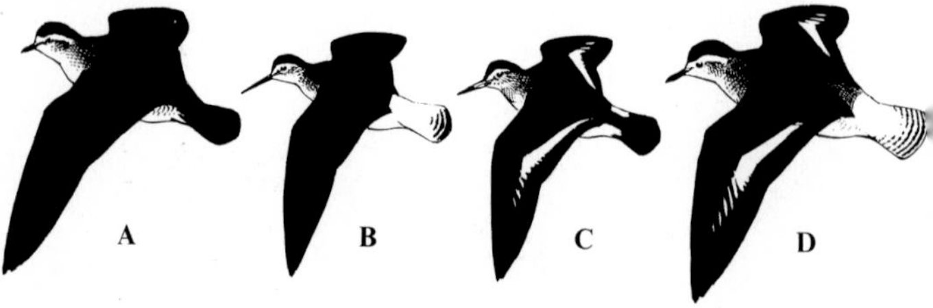

Typical Flight Patterns

A No wing-stripe, no tail pattern
B No wing-stripe, white rump and tail
C Wing-stripe, dark rump and t
D Wing-stripe, white rump and

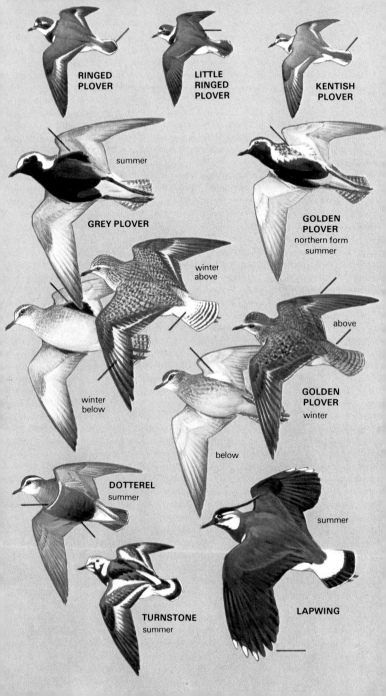

RINGED PLOVER

LITTLE RINGED PLOVER

KENTISH PLOVER

GREY PLOVER
summer

GOLDEN PLOVER
northern form
summer

winter
above

winter
below

above

GOLDEN PLOVER
winter

below

DOTTEREL
summer

summer

TURNSTONE
summer

LAPWING

Plate 35

RARE WADERS (CHIEFLY PLOVERS)

○ **SOCIABLE PLOVER**   page 98
Black crown; white 'eyebrows' join in V at nape; dark belly-patch.

SPUR-WINGED PLOVER   98
Strikingly black and white except for brown back.

△ **GREATER SAND PLOVER**   96
Male: Rusty chest-band; heavy bill. In winter chest-band replaced
by greyish mottling of sides only; face mark fades, supercilium is
white.

△ **WHITE-TAILED PLOVER**   99
White tail, dusky chest, conspicuously black and white wings.

○ **LESSER GOLDEN PLOVER**   97
Breeding: Similar to Golden Plover but is black on sides and under
tail-coverts; dusky-buff (not white) under wings. See text.

○ **KILLDEER**   96
Two black bands across chest; long orange tail.

○ **WILSON'S PHALAROPE**   112
Breeding: Thin bill, strong face pattern, chestnut neck-stripe.
Non-breeding: From other phalaropes by white rump, lack of wing-
bar, and longer, thinner bill. Compare with Lesser Yellowlegs
(Pl. 38).

SPUR-WINGED PLOVER

SOCIABLE PLOVER

breeding

GREATER SAND PLOVER

breeding ♂

WHITE-TAILED PLOVER

non-breeding

KILLDEER

breeding

LESSER GOLDEN PLOVER

WILSON'S PHALAROPE

♀ ♂

breeding

non-breeding

Plate 36

LARGE WADERS
(See also Plate 37)

● **AVOCET**   page 93
Upturned bill; black and white back.

● **OYSTERCATCHER**   93
Large size; black head; orange-red bill.

○ **BLACK-WINGED STILT**   93
Black above; white below; very long pink legs. Both sexes can have
black or white crowns.

● **BLACK-TAILED GODWIT**   106
Summer: Chestnut breast; long straight bill; black tail and flank-
   bars.
Winter: Grey; long straight bill; black tail.

● **BAR-TAILED GODWIT**   107
Summer: Shorter legs than Black-tailed; more upturned bill; barred
   tail; rufous to belly.
Winter: Grey-brown.

○ **COLLARED PRATINCOLE**   94
Rather tern-like; forked tail; white rump; light throat-patch.

△ **BLACK-WINGED PRATINCOLE**   95
Like Collared, but *black* beneath wings, not rufous.

● **CURLEW**   108
Very long, decurved bill; no head-stripes.

● **WHIMBREL**   107
Shorter decurved bill; striped crown.

SLENDER-BILLED CURLEW   107
Bill size close to Whimbrel's, but crown more like Curlew's. Note
   heart-shaped spots on sides.

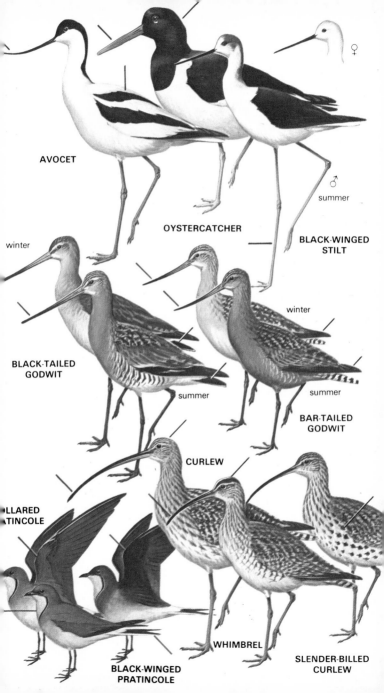

AVOCET

OYSTERCATCHER

♀

♂
summer

BLACK-WINGED
STILT

winter

BLACK-TAILED
GODWIT

summer

winter

summer

BAR-TAILED
GODWIT

CURLEW

LLARED
TINCOLE

BLACK-WINGED
PRATINCOLE

WHIMBREL

SLENDER-BILLED
CURLEW

Plate 37

LARGE WADERS IN FLIGHT
(See also Plate 36)

● **AVOCET** page 93
Black and white pattern above; thin upturned bill.

○ **BLACK-WINGED STILT** 93
White below; wings black above and below; extremely long trailing
   pink legs.

● **OYSTERCATCHER** 93
White wing-bands and rump; black head; orange bill.

● **WHIMBREL** 107
Decurved bill; broad stripes on crown.
Both Whimbrel and Curlew are brown with whitish rump, but
   former is smaller and neater.

● **CURLEW** 108
Very long decurved bill; no bold stripes on crown.

● **BAR-TAILED GODWIT** 107
Long, slightly upturned bill; barred greyish tail; no wing-stripe.

● **BLACK-TAILED GODWIT** 106
Very long bill; bold white rump and wing-stripe; broad black tail-
   band.

Oystercatchers

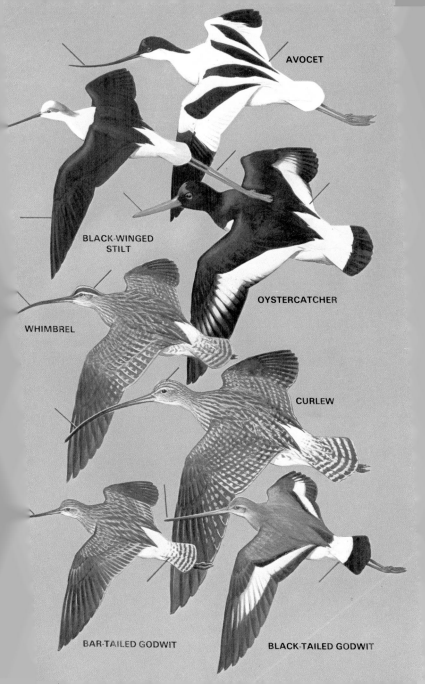

AVOCET

BLACK-WINGED
STILT

OYSTERCATCHER

WHIMBREL

CURLEW

BAR-TAILED GODWIT

BLACK-TAILED GODWIT

Plate 38

WADERS
(See also Plate 39)

page 105
- **SNIPE**
  Long straight bill; striped crown and mantle.

105
- ○ **GREAT SNIPE**
  Larger but stouter-billed; white on tail-corners.

105
- **JACK SNIPE**
  Smaller than Snipe; bill shorter; centre crown dark; pointed tail lacks white.

106
- **WOODCOCK**
  Stout; long bill; barred crown; barred under-parts.

106
- ○ **LONG-BILLED DOWITCHER**
  Snipe-like bill; long white rump; short legs.
  Winter: Grey. *Summer:* Rusty.

110
- **GREEN SANDPIPER**
  Dark above, with square white rump; dark legs.

111
- **WOOD SANDPIPER**
  Paler and browner than Green Sandpiper; legs paler, yellowish at times; slender form.

109
- ○ **MARSH SANDPIPER**
  Like tiny, delicate Greenshank, with very long legs, needle-like bill. White up back extends to shoulders.

110
- ○ **LESSER YELLOWLEGS**
  Long, bright yellow legs; white rump; fine bill.

104
- **RUFF**
  Male (spring): Extraordinary ruff; very variable colours.
  Male (autumn): Brownish 'scaly' upper-parts.
  Female (Reeve): Like small autumn male.

109
- **GREENSHANK**
  Greenish legs; white rump and back; pale head.

108
- **REDSHANK**
  Long orange-red legs; reddish base of bill.

108
- **SPOTTED REDSHANK**
  Adult (summer): Looks blackish; rather dark reddish legs.
  Adult (winter): Much paler than Redshank; white up back; longer bill.

SNIPE

GREAT
SNIPE

JACK
SNIPE

WOODCOCK

summer

winter

LONG-
BILLED
DOWITCHER

summer

GREEN
SANDPIPER

WOOD
SANDPIPER

♂
autumn

RUFF

♂

♂

MARSH
SANDPIPER

LESSER
YELLOWLEGS

♀ (Reeve)

GREENSHANK

summer

winter

SPOTTED
REDSHANK

REDSHANK

Plate 39

WADERS IN FLIGHT
(See also Plate 38)

page 105

● **SNIPE**
Long bill usually held downwards; pointed wings; whitish rim to tail; zig-zag flight.

105

○ **GREAT SNIPE**
Slightly bulkier than Snipe; more white on corners of tail; more direct flight.

105

● **JACK SNIPE**
Smaller than Snipe; shorter bill; no white on tail; rises silently, with less zig-zagging.

106

● **WOODCOCK**
Long bill; rounded wings; dead-leaf colour.

106

○ **DOWITCHER (both species)**
Snipe bill; long narrow white patch on back; white on rear edge of wing.

109

● **GREENSHANK**
Long white patch up back to shoulders; no white wing-stripe.

108

● **REDSHANK**
White rump; broad white stripe on rear edge of wing.

108

● **SPOTTED REDSHANK**
Winter: Pattern similar to Greenshank, but white patch narrower; legs project.

110

● **GREEN SANDPIPER**
Very dark above; white rump; blackish under-wing.

111

● **WOOD SANDPIPER**
From Green Sandpiper by less white on tail and rump; paler under-wing.

94

△ **CREAM-COLOURED COURSER**
Sandy-buff; black primaries above and below.

94

○ **COLLARED PRATINCOLE**
Tern-like; tail forked, white at base.

GREAT SNIPE

SNIPE

JACK SNIPE

WOODCOCK

DOWITCHER

GREENSHANK

REDSHANK

SPOTTED REDSHANK

GREEN SANDPIPER

CREAM-COLOURED COURSER

COLLARED PRATINCOLE

WOOD SANDPIPER

Plate 40

SMALL WADERS
(See also Plate 41)

COMMON SANDPIPER

GREY PHALAROPE
winter

summer

PURPLE SANDPIPER
winter

RED-NECKED PHALAROPE
winter

winter

DUNLIN
winter

autumn

CURLEW SANDPIPER

KNOT
winter

SANDERLING
winter

TEREK SANDPIPER

KNOT
summer

summer

summer

PECTORAL SANDPIPER
autumn

BAIRD'S

WHITE-RUMPED
winter

BUFF-BREASTED

LITTLE STINT
summer   autumn

TEMMINCK'S STINT
winter   summer

BROAD-BILLED SANDPIPER
summer

Plate 41

WADERS IN FLIGHT
(See also Plate 40)

● **DUNLIN** page 103
Autumn: Brownish-grey; near size of Sanderling, but darker, with less conspicuous wing-stripe.

● **PURPLE SANDPIPER** 103
Slaty-brown; white lateral tail-coverts.

● **KNOT** 99
Winter: Stocky; greyish with light barred rump.

● **CURLEW SANDPIPER** 103
Autumn: Suggests elegant Dunlin, but rump white.

● **SANDERLING** 100
Pearly-grey. Has most conspicuous wing-stripe of any small wader.

● **COMMON SANDPIPER** 111
Identify by very short wing-stroke (giving a stiffly bowed appearance when gliding).

● **LITTLE STINT** 101
Very small; narrow wing-stripe; grey sides of tail.

● **TEMMINCK'S STINT** 101
From Little by greyer colour, white sides of tail.

● **RED-NECKED PHALAROPE** 113
Immature: Stripy; bold wing-bars; needle bill.

● **GREY PHALAROPE** 113
Winter: Sanderling-like, but wing-stripe less contrasting; bill thicker than Red-necked Phalarope's.

● **PECTORAL SANDPIPER** 102
Dark brown, with faint narrow wing-bar; tail pattern like Dunlin's.

● **STONE CURLEW** 94
Double white wing-bar.

● **RUFF** 104
Male has ruff on neck in summer; very variable; oval white patches almost join at base of tail.

DUNLIN
autumn

PURPLE
SANDPIPER

KNOT
winter

CURLEW
SANDPIPER
autumn

winter

SANDERLING

COMMON
SANDPIPER

LITTLE
STINT

RED-NECKED
PHALAROPE
immature

GREY
PHALAROPE
winter

TEMMINCK'S
STINT

PECTORAL
SANDPIPER

STONE CURLEW

♀
(Reeve)

RUFF

♂
summer

Plate 42

RARE WADERS (SANDPIPERS)

△ **LEAST SANDPIPER** pa
   Smallest of stints; very thin bill; crouched appearance when feeding.
      See text.
   Note, a distinctive *'kree-eet'*, more of an *ee* sound than Little Stint's.

○ **SEMIPALMATED SANDPIPER**
   Greyish-brown; short thick bill; blackish legs. See text.
   Note, a distinctive *'chewp'* or *'chirrup'*.

○ **SPOTTED SANDPIPER**
   Adult in summer: Thrush-like spots; black-tipped yellow bill..
   Juvenile or winter: Like Common Sandpiper, but tail shorter; breast
      cleaner white in centre, no streaking.

△ **SHARP-TAILED SANDPIPER**
   Suggests Pectoral Sandpiper, but no sharp separation of streaks
      between breast and belly. In autumn has tawny breast with streaks
      confined to sides.

○ **UPLAND SANDPIPER**
   Small head, short bill, shoe-button eye, thin neck, long tawny tail.

△ **SOLITARY SANDPIPER**
   Like Green Sandpiper but with dark (not white) rump.

○ **GREATER YELLOWLEGS**
   Shape of Greenshank, but legs bright yellow. Larger than Lesser
      Yellowlegs; bill longer, and slightly upturned. Leg joints more
      prominent.

breeding

juvenile

LEAST SANDPIPER

breeding

juvenile

SEMIPALMATED SANDPIPER

breeding

SPOTTED SANDPIPER

Juvenile or winter

breeding

juvenile

SHARP TAILED SANDPIPER

UPLAND SANDPIPER

GREATER YELLOWLEGS

SOLITARY SANDPIPER

Plate 43

SKUAS

Skuas are dark, hawk-like sea-birds which pursue other birds in a piratical manner. All show a white flash on the wing. Adults of the three smaller species have elongated central tail-feathers (see drawing). Arctic and Pomarine occur in light, intermediate and dark phases; the tail points are sometimes broken off. Immatures have stubbier central tail-feathers and are difficult to separate.

- **GREAT SKUA**   page 115
  Dark, heavily built; large wing-patches; blunt tail.

- **ARCTIC SKUA**   114
  Pointed central tail-feathers.

- **POMARINE SKUA**   114
  Blunt (and partially twisted) central tail-feathers; broad wing-bases;
    scalloped flanks and under-wings.

- **LONG-TAILED SKUA**   115
  Very long, flexible, pointed central tail-feathers; narrow wings;
    complete white collar.

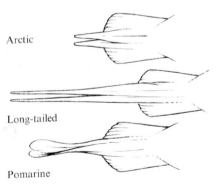

Arctic

Long-tailed

Pomarine

Tails of Skuas (Adults)

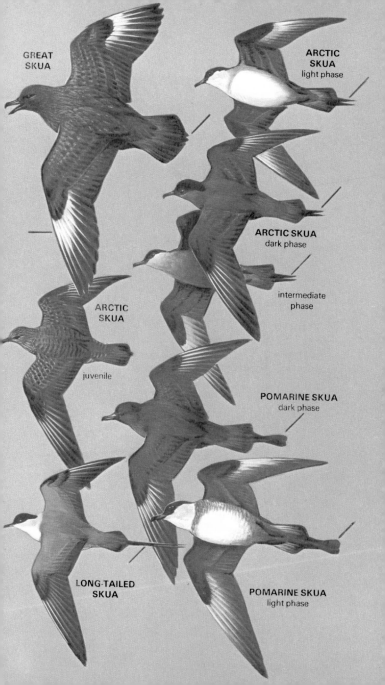

GREAT SKUA

ARCTIC SKUA
light phase

ARCTIC SKUA
dark phase

intermediate
phase

ARCTIC SKUA

juvenile

POMARINE SKUA
dark phase

LONG-TAILED SKUA

POMARINE SKUA
light phase

Plate 44

GULLS (ADULT)

In identifying gulls, look for wing patterns and colour of legs.

- **GREAT BLACK-BACKED GULL**
  Large size; black back and wings; flesh legs.
- **LESSER BLACK-BACKED GULL**
  Size of Herring Gull; legs usually yellow or orange.
  Northern form: Darker (blackish back).
  Southern form: Paler (dark grey).
- **GLAUCOUS GULL**
  Size of Great Black-backed Gull; white primaries; heavy head and bill.
- **ICELAND GULL**
  Size of Herring, but head and bill smaller; white primaries.
- ○ **IVORY GULL**
  Size of Kittiwake; all white; black legs.
- **HERRING GULL**
  Grey back and wings; black on wing-tips; flesh legs.
- **COMMON GULL**
  Smaller than Herring; greenish-yellow bill and legs.
- **KITTIWAKE**
  Solid black 'dipped in ink' wing-tips; black legs.

  AUDOUIN'S GULL
  Heavy red bill with black band; legs olive; black outer primaries contrast with pale grey wing.

- **LITTLE GULL***
  Rounded wings are blackish below.
- **SABINE'S GULL***
  Black outer primaries; white triangle; forked tail.
- **BLACK-HEADED GULL***
  Long wedge of white on primaries; red bill and legs.
- **MEDITERRANEAN GULL***
  White primaries; extensive black hood.
- △ **SLENDER-BILLED GULL**
  Wings as Black-headed, but head white, long bill drooping.

*Adults in winter lose their black heads, which then resemble those of (see Pl. 45).

GLAUCOUS

GREAT
LACK-BACKED

rn

ICELAND

LESSER
LACK-BACKED

IVORY

HERRING

KITTIWAKE

OMMON

below

above

SABINE'S

LITTLE

DOUIN'S

above

ACK-HEADED

below

MEDITERRANEAN

SLENDER-BILLED

Plate 45

GULLS (IMMATURE)

● **GREAT BLACK-BACKED GULL**
Large size; more contrast between chequered back and under-part
than in young Herring Gull.

● **LESSER BLACK-BACKED GULL**
Very similar at first to young Herring Gull; but identification easi
as birds grow older. See text.

● **GLAUCOUS GULL**
First winter: Buffish, with paler primaries.
Second winter: Very white throughout.
(Iceland Gull has similar sequence of plumages.)

● **HERRING GULL**
First winter: Almost uniform muddy-brown.
Second winter: Whiter, with tail broadly black.

● **COMMON GULL**
From second-winter Herring Gull by narrower black band on whi
tail; smaller size; shorter bill.

● **KITTIWAKE**
Dark diagonal band across wing; black hind-collar.

● **BLACK-HEADED GULL**
Dark spots on cheek, narrow tail-band. Whitish outer primarie

● **SABINE'S GULL**
Forked tail and adult's bold wing pattern. No dark diagonal win
bar as in Kittiwake.

● **MEDITERRANEAN GULL**
From Black-headed by blackish (not whitish) leading primari
From Common by narrower tail-band and paler midwing pan

● **LITTLE GULL**
Wing pattern as in immature Kittiwake; wings more rounded; da
cap; lacks bar on nape.

GREAT
BLACK-BACKED

GLAUCOUS
first winter

second winter

GLAUCOUS
second winter

LESSER
BLACK-BACKED

first winter

HERRING

second winter

HERRING

HERRING

COMMON

KITTIWAKE

BLACK-HEADED

SABINE'S

MEDITERRANEAN

LITTLE

Plate 46

RARE GULLS AND TERNS

△ **GREAT BLACK-HEADED GULL**   pa
  Large size; black band on big yellow bill; long flat forehead; black
    band across white primaries.

○ **LAUGHING GULL**
  Adult: Dark mantle blends into black wing-tips. Black hood lost in
    winter.
  Immature: Dusky with *contrasting white rump* and white trailing
    edge of wing.

○ **BONAPARTE'S GULL**
  Breeding adult: Like small Black-headed, but thinner *black* bill.
  Immature: Dark trailing edge on wing.
  At all ages: Primaries white below, with black trailing edge.

○ **ROSS'S GULL**
  Graduated tail; delicate black bill; no black on wing-tips.
  Breeding adult: Tinged with *pink* below; narrow *necklace.*

○ **RING-BILLED GULL**
  Adult: Smaller than Herring Gull with *yellowish or pale greenish legs*
    and *black ring* encircling bill.
  Immature: Suggests small Herring Gull but tail-band narrower and
    usually (but not always) *well defined.*

○ **SOOTY TERN**
  Cleanly patterned; blackish above, white below; white patch on
    forehead.

breeding

adult winter

GREAT BLACK-HEADED GULL

first winter

adult breeding

LAUGHING GULL

adult winter

immature

ling

BONAPARTE'S GULL

immature

ROSS'S GULL

adult winter

adult breeding

first winter

RING-BILLED GULL

adult breeding

SOOTY TERN

adult

Plate 47

TERNS

Terns are more slender in build, narrower of wing and more graceful in flight than gulls. Bills are more slender and sharply pointed, usually held downward towards the water. Tails are usually forked. Most terns are whitish, with black caps in summer. See also Pl. 49.

○ **GULL-BILLED TERN**   page 12
Stout, stubby black bill. The greyish tail is only moderately forked.

● **SANDWICH TERN**   12
Pale; long slender black bill with yellow tip. Shaggy cap.

○ **CASPIAN TERN**   12
Large size; heavy scarlet bill. Dusky underside of primaries.

● **COMMON TERN**   12
Adult in summer: Bill orange-red with black tip. Above, note the dark outer primaries contrasting with paler grey of rest of wing. Overhead, the dark outer primaries contrast with the semi-transparent patch on inner primaries.
Juvenile: White forehead; dark 'shoulders'.

◑ **ROSEATE TERN**   12
Adult in summer: Whiter than Common Tern; longer tail-streamers. Bill largely black.
Juvenile: Paler 'shoulders'; more flecking on wings than Arctic.

● **ARCTIC TERN**   12
Adult in summer: Greyer than Common Tern; bill blood-red to tip. Above, primaries show less contrast than Common's. Overhead, flight-feathers have a translucent look with a well-defined border of black on tips of primaries.
Juvenile: Very similar to Common; see text.

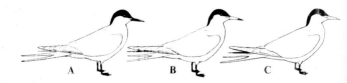

A Roseate Tern. Whitest of the three; tail extends well beyond short wings.
B Common Tern. Tail does not extend beyond wing-tips.
C Arctic Tern. Greyer; shorter legs; tail slightly longer than Common's.

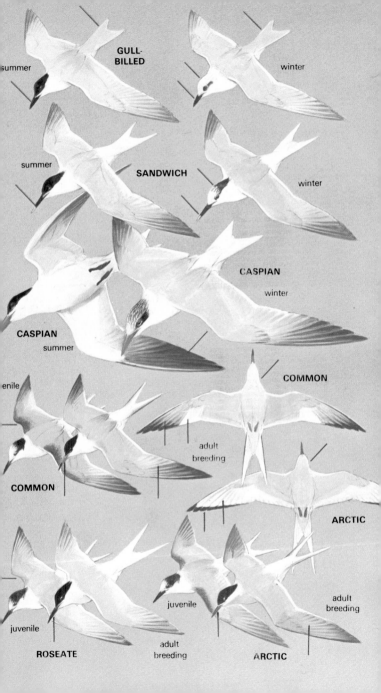

summer

GULL-BILLED

winter

summer

SANDWICH

winter

CASPIAN

winter

CASPIAN

summer

juvenile

COMMON

adult breeding

COMMON

ARCTIC

juvenile

ROSEATE

adult breeding

juvenile

adult breeding

ARCTIC

adult breeding

Plate 48

TERNS

With the exception of the Little Tern, the species shown on this plate are 'marsh terns'. See also Pl. 49.

● **LITTLE TERN**   page 12?
   Adult in summer: Small; yellow bill; white forehead.
   Juvenile: Small; black fore-edge of wing.

○ **WHISKERED TERN**   12?
   Adult in summer: Dusky belly; white cheek.
   Winter: Paler than Black Tern and larger; less black on nape; mantle
      and rump uniform grey.

● **BLACK TERN**   12?
   Adult in summer: Black body and head; grey wings.
   Winter: From White-winged Black by dark mark on side of neck;
      dark band along fore-wing; no contrast between mantle and
      rump.

● **WHITE-WINGED BLACK TERN**   12?
   Adult in summer: Black body and head; black wing-linings. White
      wing-coverts; white tail.
   Winter: Like Black, but lacks dark mark on neck and dark band
      along fore-wing. Unlike Whiskered or Black, whitish rump
      contrasts with grey mantle.

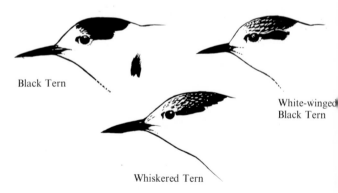

Black Tern

White-winged
Black Tern

Whiskered Tern

Heads of Marsh Terns in Winter

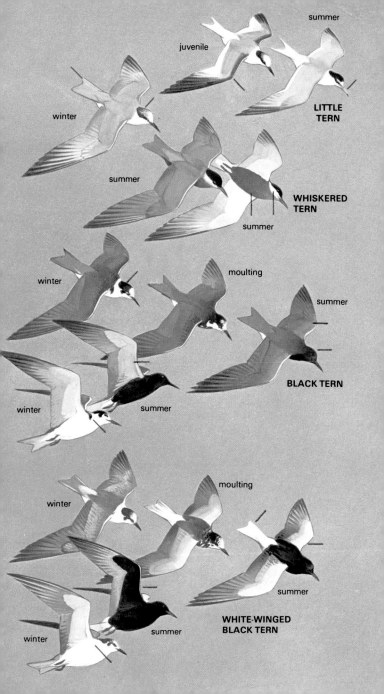

summer

juvenile

summer

winter

LITTLE TERN

summer

WHISKERED TERN

summer

winter

moulting

summer

BLACK TERN

winter

summer

winter

moulting

winter

summer

WHITE-WINGED BLACK TERN

Plate 49

HEADS OF TERNS

The bills of terns are the key features in their recognition. All terns in breedin season have *black caps*. By late summer they begin to get the white forehea typical of winter plumage.

● **BLACK TERN** page 12
Summer: Black head.
Winter: 'Pied' head (see text).
For White-winged Black, see Pl. 48 and text.

○ **WHISKERED TERN** 12
Summer: Dusky throat, white cheeks.
Winter: See text.

● **LITTLE TERN** 12
Summer: Small size; yellow bill; white forehead.
Immature: Small size (see text).

● **COMMON TERN** 12
Summer: Bill orange-red, black tip.
Winter: Black patch from eye around nape.

● **ARCTIC TERN** 12
Summer: Bill blood-red, no black tip.
Winter: Similar to Common Tern (see text).

● **ROSEATE TERN** 12
Summer: Bill mostly black (some have considerable red at base).
Winter: Longer than Common Tern (see text).

○ **GULL-BILLED TERN** 12
Summer: Bill stout and black.
Winter: Black ear-patch; bill stout and black.
Juvenile: Gull-like (see text).

● **SANDWICH TERN** 12
Summer: Crested; bill black with yellow tip.
Winter: Similar, with white forehead.

○ **CASPIAN TERN** 12
Summer: Large size; large scarlet bill.
Winter: Large scarlet bill; streaked forehead.

winter

BLACK

summer

winter

WHISKERED

summer

mature

LITTLE

summer

winter

COMMON

summer

winter

ARCTIC

summer

winter

ROSEATE

summer

juvenile

winter

GULL-BILLED

summer

winter

SANDWICH

summer

winter

CASPIAN

summer

Plate 50

AUKS

Auks are bustling black and white sea-birds with stubby necks. They have a whirring flight and a straddle-legged look when about to land.

● **RAZORBILL**   page 127
   Adult: Heavy head; deep bill with white mark.
   Immature: Smaller bill, with curved ridge.

△ **BRÜNNICH'S GUILLEMOT**   127
   Thicker bill than Guillemot.
   Summer: Light mark on gape.
   Winter: Dark cap to below eye.

● **GUILLEMOT**   126
   Summer: Slender bill; dark head.
   Winter: Black line on white cheek.
   'Bridled' form: White eye-ring and white line.

● **BLACK GUILLEMOT**   127
   Summer: Black body; pointed bill; large white wing-patches.
   Winter: Mottled off-white body; large white patches.

● **PUFFIN**   128
   Summer: Triangular, coloured bill; whitish cheeks.
   Winter: Triangular bill; dusky cheeks.
   Immature: Smaller bill; dusky cheeks.

● **LITTLE AUK**   128
   Starling-size; stubby bill; 'neckless' form.

Puffin   Razorbill   Guillemot   Black
                                                       Guillemot

summer

RAZORBILL

immature

winter

winter

**BRÜNNICH'S
GUILLEMOT**

summer

GUILLEMOT

winter

**BLACK
GUILLEMOT**

summer

winter

summer

GUILLEMOT
'bridled'
form

immature

summer

PUFFIN

PUFFIN

winter

summer

LITTLE AUK

Plate 51

PIGEONS AND DOVES

The terms 'pigeon' and 'dove' are loosely used and often interchangeable, but for the most part 'pigeon' refers to the larger species, 'dove' to the smaller.

● **WOODPIGEON**   page 130
   Large; white wing-patches; white neck-patch.

● **ROCK DOVE**   130
   White rump; two bold black wing-bars.
   The various domestic pigeons are descendants of this species and
      many still closely resemble it.

● **STOCK DOVE**   130
   Short black bars on secondaries; grey rump.

● **TURTLE DOVE**   131
   Slender; rufous back; deeply rounded, white-tipped tail.

● **COLLARED DOVE**   131
   White beneath end half of tail; black collar. The domestic Barbary
      Dove (*S. risoria*) is very similar, but is creamy-buff instead of
      vinous-grey and has pale, not dark, primaries.

Domestic pigeons (descended from the Rock Dove) show a great variety of colour and pattern.

WOOD-PIGEON

ROCK DOVE

STOCK DOVE

TURTLE DOVE

COLLARED DOVE

Plate 52

OWLS

Mainly nocturnal birds of prey, large headed, with large eyes facing front, facial discs, and moth-like, noiseless flight.

● **SNOWY OWL**   page 134
  Large, white; big yellow eyes.

● **BARN OWL**   133
  Heart-shaped face, or round 'monkey' face; no breast streaks; dark
    eyes.
  Light-breasted form: White breast.
  Dark-breasted form: Tawny breast.

● **SHORT-EARED OWL**   137
  Yellowish brown; strongly mottled; marshes.

○ **SCOPS OWL**   133
  Very small. Marbled grey-brown; small head; erects 'ears' when
    alarmed.

● **LONG-EARED OWL**   136
  Slender; heavily streaked; erects long 'ears' when alarmed.

△ **EAGLE OWL**   134
  Huge; 'eared'; rusty, with streaks and bars.

See also illustrations of other owls, Pl. 53.

dark-breasted form

light-breasted form

BARN

SNOWY

SHORT-EARED

SCOPS

LONG-EARED

EAGLE

Plate 53

OWLS

Most owls are nocturnal and therefore seldom seen well unless discovered at their daytime roosts. It is particularly important to learn their voices, which are described in the text. None of the following species has 'ear-tufts'.

● **TAWNY OWL**   page 135
  Heavily built; streaked breast; black eyes; rufous or grey plumage.

● **LITTLE OWL**   135
  Small; spotted above; low frowning 'eyebrows'.

  PYGMY OWL   135
  Hawfinch-size; small-headed; jerks up tail.

△ **HAWK OWL**   134
  Heavy black facial 'frames'; barred under-parts, long tail.

△ **TENGMALM'S OWL**   137
  From Little Owl by larger head, broad 'eyebrows', whiter face, more
    heavily outlined facial discs.

  URAL OWL   136
  Very large, streaked; unlined face; small dark eyes.

  GREAT GREY OWL   136
  Very large, grey; large round head: lined face; small yellow eyes.

See also illustrations of other owls, Pl. 52.

grey phase

LITTLE

PYGMY

rufous phase

TAWNY

HAWK

juvenile

TENGMALM'S

adult

URAL

GREAT GREY

Plate 54

ROLLER, BEE-EATER, HOOPOE, KINGFISHER, CUCKOOS AND NIGHTJARS

Cuckoo

Nightjar

ROLLER

HOOPOE

BEE-EATER

KINGFISHER

CUCKOO

CUCKOO
rufous phase
(♀ only)

GREAT SPOTTED
CUCKOO

NIGHTJAR

RED-NECKED NIGHTJAR

Plate 55

WOODPECKERS AND WRYNECK

● **LESSER SPOTTED WOODPECKER** pa
Sparrow-size; closely barred back.

MIDDLE SPOTTED WOODPECKER
Resembles juvenile Great Spotted, but black face marks not joined.
No black border to red cap.

● **GREAT SPOTTED WOODPECKER**
Large white scapular patches, black crown. Juvenile has red crown.

SYRIAN WOODPECKER
Like Great Spotted, but white cheek lacks bar.

WHITE-BACKED WOODPECKER
White lower back; barred wings.

THREE-TOED WOODPECKER
White back; barred flanks; black cheeks.
Male has yellow cap.

BLACK WOODPECKER
Crow-size; black; male has red crown, female nape only.

● **GREEN WOODPECKER**
Greenish back; yellow rump; dark face with broad pointed 'moustaches'. Juvenile spotted.

GREY-HEADED WOODPECKER
Grey head with narrow black 'moustaches'.
Male only has red cap.

● **WRYNECK**
Long tail; Nightjar-like pattern.

Lesser Spotted   **Middle Spotted**   **Great Spotted**   **White-bac**

LESSER SPOTTED

MIDDLE SPOTTED

SYRIAN

juvenile

GREAT SPOTTED

BLACK

WHITE-BACKED

THREE-TOED

juvenile

WRYNECK

GREEN

GREY-HEADED

Plate 56

LARKS

Streaked, mainly brown ground-birds with aerial songs. They somewhat resemble pipits (Pl. 58) but are heavier, broader-winged.

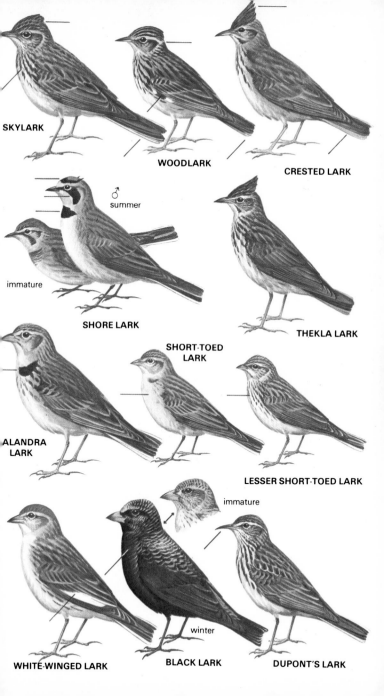

SKYLARK

WOODLARK

CRESTED LARK

♂ summer

immature

SHORE LARK

THEKLA LARK

SHORT-TOED LARK

ALANDRA LARK

LESSER SHORT-TOED LARK

immature

winter

WHITE-WINGED LARK

BLACK LARK

DUPONT'S LARK

Plate 57

SWIFTS, MARTINS AND SWALLOWS

Swallow

House Martin

Sand Martin

● **SWIFT** — page 138
Almost completely blackish; short forked tail.

△ **PALLID SWIFT** — 139
Paler than Swift; dark outer wings and 'saddle'; more white on
throat; dark eye-patch.

○ **ALPINE SWIFT** — 139
Very large; white belly; dark breast-band.

● **HOUSE MARTIN** — 149
White rump-patch; completely white under-parts.

● **SWALLOW** — 149
Deeply forked tail; dark throat.

○ **RED-RUMPED SWALLOW** — 149
Buffish rump-patch; pale throat.

● **SAND MARTIN** — 148
Brown back; band across breast.

CRAG MARTIN — 148
Brown back; no breast-band; squared tail with white spots when
spread; mountains.

Swallow   House Martin   Red-rumped Swallow   Sand Martin

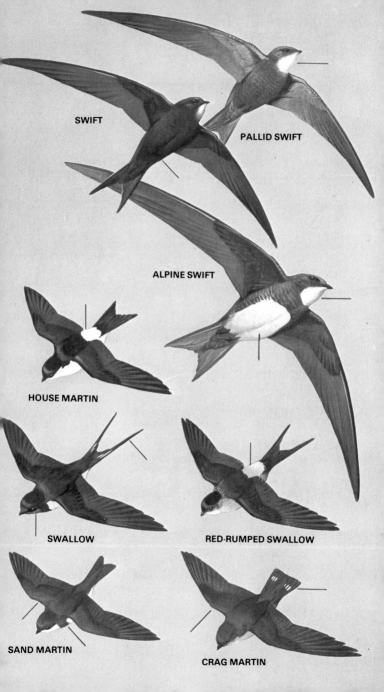

SWIFT

PALLID SWIFT

ALPINE SWIFT

HOUSE MARTIN

SWALLOW

RED-RUMPED SWALLOW

SAND MARTIN

CRAG MARTIN

Plate 58

PIPITS AND WAGTAILS

Pipits are streaked brown ground-birds with white, or whitish, outer tail-feathers and long hind claws. They resemble larks (Pl. 56) but are more slender.

Wagtails are boldly patterned ground-birds, more slender and much longer-tailed than pipits. Some pipits and all wagtails wag their tails. See further analysis of wagtails on Pl. 59.

- **MEADOW PIPIT**   page 151
  Small; streaked above and below; white outer tail-feathers.

- **TREE PIPIT**   151
  From Meadow Pipit by buffer, less olivaceous colour and pinker legs.

- **ROCK/WATER PIPIT**   152
  The only pipits with *dark legs.*
  Rock Pipit: Dark; greyish outer tail. Coasts.
  Water Pipit: *Summer:* (mountains) pinkish unstreaked breast; greyish upper-parts; white outer tail-feathers. *Winter:* (wide-ranging) streaked whitish breast; white eyebrow; white outer tail-feathers.

- **TAWNY PIPIT**   150
  Slim; unstreaked breast; long legs and tail.

- **RICHARD'S PIPIT**   150
  Bulky; dark; very long stout legs; streaked breast.

○ **RED-THROATED PIPIT**   152
  Summer: Variable brick-red throat. *Winter:* From Meadow by blacker, heavier streaks; streaked rump.

- **YELLOW/BLUE-HEADED WAGTAIL**   152
  Yellow under-parts; olive-green back.
  Yellow: Yellow and olive head.
  Blue-headed: Blue-grey cap and cheeks.

- **PIED/WHITE WAGTAIL**   153
  No yellow in any plumage.
  Pied: Black back; black cap and bib joined.
  White: Grey back; black cap and bib separated.

- **GREY WAGTAIL**   153
  Yellow under-parts, grey back. Longest tail of all wagtails. Male in summer has black throat.

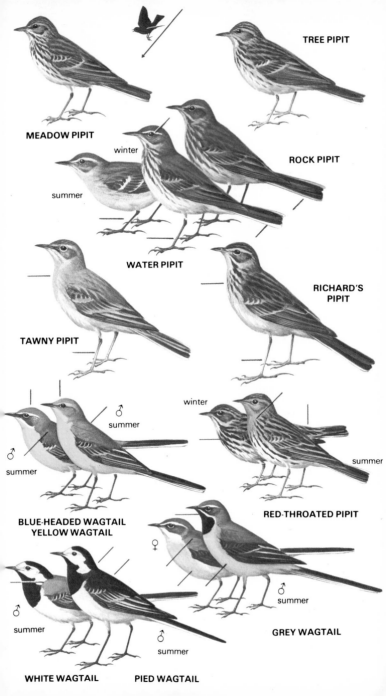

MEADOW PIPIT

TREE PIPIT

winter
summer

ROCK PIPIT

WATER PIPIT

RICHARD'S
PIPIT

TAWNY PIPIT

♂
summer

♂
summer

BLUE-HEADED WAGTAIL
YELLOW WAGTAIL

winter

summer

RED-THROATED PIPIT

♀

♂
summer

GREY WAGTAIL

♂
summer

♂
summer

WHITE WAGTAIL   PIED WAGTAIL

Plate 59

HEADS OF WAGTAILS

WHITE WAGTAIL GROUP Motacilla alba page 153
Distinguished by lack of yellow or olive in plumage.
● **PIED WAGTAIL**
   M. a. yarrellii. Back black (male) or very dark (female).
   Black cap and black bib joined in adults. Breeds British Isles and
      adjacent shores of Continent.
● **WHITE WAGTAIL**
   M. a. alba. Clean grey back. Black cap and black bib separated.
      Breeds on Continent.

GREY WAGTAIL Motacilla cinerea 153
Distinguished by grey back, yellow under-parts.
● **GREY WAGTAIL**
   Male in summer: Black throat; yellow under-parts.
   Female in summer and both sexes in winter: Whitish throat; grey
      back; yellow under-parts.

YELLOW WAGTAIL GROUP Motacilla flava 152
Distinguished by olive-green back; yellow under-parts.
● **YELLOW WAGTAIL**
   M. f. flavissima. Yellow and olive head. Breeds in British Isles, a few
      on adjacent shores of Continent.
● **BLUE-HEADED WAGTAIL**
   M. f. flava. Male in summer: Eye-stripe starting at nostril. C.
      Europe (area not occupied by other races).
   SPANISH WAGTAIL
   M. f. iberiae. Male in summer: White stripe starting from eye. Breeds
      Spain and Portugal, races merging in S. France.
△ **ASHY-HEADED WAGTAIL**
   M. f. cinereocapilla. Male in summer: Grey crown, cheek; no eye-
      stripe. Italy, Corsica, Sardinia, Sicily, Albania.
○ **GREY-HEADED WAGTAIL**
   M. f. thunbergi. Male in summer: Grey crown, blackish cheek; no
      eye-stripe. C. and N. Sweden, Norway, Finland.
△ **BLACK-HEADED WAGTAIL**
   M. f. feldegg. Male in summer: Black cap and cheek; no eye-stripe.
      Balkans, sometimes Austria.

Note: Systematics of the Yellow Wagtail group are complex. Some authors
classify various forms as distinct species. But intergradation occurs where
ranges overlap. Mutants resembling other races breed with birds of normal
appearance. Thus birds identical with Sykes's Wagtail *M. f. beema* of Russia
breed with normal Yellow Wagtails *M. f. flavissima* in England. In field work it
is better to call them all 'Yellow Wagtails'.

PIED

♂ summer ♀ summer winter

juvenile ♂ summer winter

WHITE

♂ summer ♀ summer winter

GREY

juvenile ♂ summer winter

YELLOW

♂ summer ♂ summer winter

SPANISH **BLUE-HEADED**

♂ summer ♂ summer ♂ summer

SHY-HEADED **GREY-HEADED** **BLACK-HEADED**

Plate 60

WHEATEARS, CHATS, ETC.

● **WHEATEAR**   page 160
  Summer male: Grey back; white rump; black mask.
  Autumn: Brown above, buffish below; white rump.

○ **BLACK-EARED WHEATEAR**   161
  Black-throated form: Buff back; black throat.
  White-throated form: Buff back; black mask.

△ **PIED WHEATEAR**   160
  Blackish back; black throat.

△ **BLACK WHEATEAR**   162
  Black, with white rump.

● **REDSTART**   158
  Male: Rusty tail; orange under-parts; black bib.
  Female: Rusty tail; brownish breast.

● **BLACK REDSTART**   158
  Male: Black; rusty tail.
  Female: Slaty; rusty tail.

● **STONECHAT**   159
  Male: Black head; rusty breast; white neck-patch.
  Female: Brownish, with suggestion of male's pattern.

● **WHINCHAT**   159
  White stripes outline dark cheeks; white in tail.

● **ROBIN**   156
  Orange face and breast. Juvenile spotted and barred.

● **BLUETHROAT**   157
  Male: Blue throat; orange tail-patches.
  Female: U-shaped necklace; orange tail-patches.

● **NIGHTINGALE**   157
  Brown back; plain breast; broad chestnut tail.

○ **THRUSH NIGHTINGALE**   157
  Greyer; less chestnut in tail; mottled breast.

△ **ROCK THRUSH**   162
  Male: Blue head; white lower back; orange breast and tail.
  Female: Barred; orange tail.

  BLUE ROCK THRUSH   162
  Male: Slaty blue.
  Female: Barred and spotted.

winter

black-throated
form

white-throated
form

summer

WHEATEAR

BLACK-EARED WHEATEAR

♂

PIED WHEATEAR

♂

♀

♀

sexes
similar

♂

BLACK REDSTART

REDSTART

♂

**BLACK
WHEATEAR**

♀

juvenile

♀

♂

ROBIN

adult

WHINCHAT

ONECHAT

NIGHTINGALE

♂

♂

**THRUSH
NIGHTINGALE**

ed-spotted
form

♀

BLUETHROAT

♂

white- spotted form

♀

♂

ROCK THRUSH

♀

♂

**BLUE
ROCK
THRUSH**

Plate 61

THRUSHES

- **BLACKBIRD**
  Male: All black; yellow bill. *Female:* Dark brown.

- **RING OUZEL**
  Black, with white breast-crescent; pale wing edges.

- **FIELDFARE**
  Grey head and rump; rusty back.

- **SONG THRUSH**
  Brown, with spotted breast; buff wing-linings.

- **MISTLE THRUSH**
  Larger, greyer; rounder spots; white wing-linings.

- **REDWING**
  Reddish flanks and wing-linings; supercilium.

△ **WHITE'S THRUSH**
  Bold 'scaly' pattern above and below.

△ **DUSKY THRUSH**
  Double breast-band; supercilium. Dusky and Naumann's intergrade; are races of same species.

△ **BLACK-THROATED THRUSH**
  Hood and bib contrast with white below. Black-throated and Red-throated are races of same species.

△ **SIBERIAN THRUSH**
  Male: Blackish, with striking white supercilium.
  Female: Brown, see text.

△ **AMERICAN ROBIN**
  Brick-red below; blackish head; broken eye-ring.

NAUMANN'S THRUSH
  Rusty breast; rusty wings. See Dusky.

RED-THROATED THRUSH
  Rufous supercilium, throat, breast. See Black-throated.

△ **EYEBROWED THRUSH**
  Grey upper breast; rusty sides; supercilium.

BLACKBIRD

RING OUZEL

♀

♂

SONG THRUSH

FIELDFARE

MISTLE THRUSH

REDWING

SOME RARE THRUSHES

HITE'S

DUSKY

BLACK-THROATED

♂

SIBERIAN

♀

AMERICAN ROBIN

NAUMANN'S

RED-THROATED

EYEBROWED

Plate 62

SWAMP WARBLERS

Field Marks and Habitat	Song	

NO STREAKS ON BACK

● **REED WARBLER** — page 17

Brown above; clear buffish-white below; pale eye-ring. *Reeds, marshes.* — Tendency to repeat phrases 2–3 times: *'chirruc-chirruc, jag-jag-jag'*, etc.

○ **GREAT REED WARBLER** — 17.

Large size; eye-stripe; large bill. *Reed-beds.* — Strident *'karra-karra, krik-krik, gurk-gurk'*, etc.

● **MARSH WARBLER** — 17●

More olive than Reed; legs flesh-brown, not dark. *Wet thickets, ditches, crops.* — More musical and varied than Reed, with Canary-like trills, mimicry, etc.

● **CETTI'S WARBLER** — 16

Dark rufous; cocked tail. *Dense thickets, bushy ditches.* — A loud abrupt burst, chiefly repetition of *'cheweeoo'*.

● **SAVI'S WARBLER** — 16⑨

Like large Reed, voice like Grasshopper. *Marshes.* — Like reeling trill of Grasshopper, but lower, briefer.

△ **RIVER WARBLER** — 168

Soft streaks on breast. *Thickets, dense herbage.* — Rapid but quiet *'chuffing'* notes, clearly separated.

WITH STREAKS ON BACK

● **SEDGE WARBLER** — 17〇

Streaks; creamy eye-stripe. *Widespread; reeds, wet scrub.* — More varied than Reed; trills, mimicry, chattering.

△ **MOUSTACHED WARBLER** — 16⑨

From Sedge by darker cap, whiter eye-stripe, rustier back. *Reed-beds, swamps.* — Recalls Reed; sweeter, includes phrase suggesting Woodlark's *'lu-lu-lu-lu'*.

● **GRASSHOPPER WARBLER** — 168

Mottled olive-brown upperparts. *Marshy undergrowth, scrub.* — Long reeling trill or buzzing on one high note.

● **AQUATIC WARBLER** — 16⑨

Buff stripe through crown. *Open marshes, sedge, etc.* — Very like Sedge Warbler.

△ **FAN-TAILED WARBLER** — 16⑦

Heavily streaked; short tail. *Marshes, crops.* — Sings in air; lisping *'zip . . . zip . . . zip'*, etc. (or *'dzeep'*).

NO STREAKS ON BACK

REED

GREAT REED

MARSH

CETTI'S

SAVI'S

RIVER

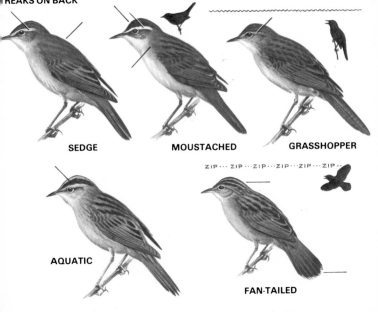

STREAKS ON BACK

SEDGE

MOUSTACHED

GRASSHOPPER

AQUATIC

ZIP···ZIP···ZIP···ZIP···ZIP···ZIP···

FAN-TAILED

Plate 63

SCRUB WARBLERS

Mostly *Sylvia*. With distinctive marks and 'capped' appearance.

Field Marks and Habitat	Song	

● **BLACKCAP**
Black cap to eye, male; brown in female. *Undergrowth, trees.*   Rich warbling notes, more varied than Garden Warbler's.   page 17

△ **ORPHEAN WARBLER**   17:
Black cap to below white eye. *Woodlands, orchards, groves.*   Mellow thrush-like warble, phrases repeated 4–5 times.

△ **SARDINIAN WARBLER**   175
Black cap to below eye; flanks grey; cocks tail. *Dry scrub.*   Recalls Whitethroat's, but longer, with staccato *'cha-cha-cha-cha'*.

● **WHITETHROAT**   17●
White throat, rusty on wing. *Bushes, bramble patches.*   A short, scratchy, urgent chatter, often in display-flight.

● **LESSER WHITETHROAT**   176
Dark mask; not rusty on wing. *Hedgerows, shrubberies.*   Unmusical rattling on one note.

△ **RÜPPELL'S WARBLER**   175
Black throat; white moustache. *Aegean. Rocky scrub.*   Like loud Sardinian: notes interspersed with loud rattle.

△ **SPECTACLED WARBLER**   174
Like small Whitethroat; pinker breast; darker cheek. *Mediterranean; Salicornia, scrub.*   Short and Whitethroat-like; quieter, without grating notes.

○ **SUBALPINE WARBLER**   174
Orange breast; moustache. *Bushes, wood edges.*   Recalls Sardinian; slower, lacks hard scolding notes.

● **DARTFORD WARBLER**   174
Dark vinous breast; cocked tail. *Gorse, low scrub, etc.*   Musical chatter with liquid notes; recalls Whitethroat.

MARMORA'S WARBLER   174
Dark slaty breast. *W. Mediterranean. Low scrub.*   Resembles Dartford's, but is less harsh.

● **BARRED WARBLER**   176
Barred breast; wing-bars. *Thorny thickets, bushes.*   Resembles poor Blackcap; more rapid, briefer phrases.

△ **RUFOUS BUSH ROBIN**   15●
Rufous; large fan tail. *Mediterranean. Gardens, groves.*   Musical, disjointed, some phrases recalling Skylark.

♀ ♂ **BLACKCAP**

ORPHEAN ♂

SARDINIAN ♂

LESSER WHITETHROAT

♀ **WHITETHROAT** ♂

♀ **RÜPPELL'S** ♂

SPECTACLED ♂

SUBALPINE ♂

MARMORA'S ♂

DARTFORD ♂

adult

BARRED

immature

brown-backed form

rufous form

RUFOUS BUSH ROBIN

Plate 64

LEAF WARBLERS

Field Marks and Habitat	Song	
● **WILLOW WARBLER** 'Cleaner' than Chiffchaff and (usually) pale legs. *Bushes, small trees.*	A liquid musical cascade; down scale, ending in flourish.	page 180
● **CHIFFCHAFF** 'Dirtier' than Willow; dark legs. *Trees, thickets.*	Deliberately repeated *'chiff-chaff-chiff-chiff-chaff'*, etc.	180
○ **ARCTIC WARBLER** Wing-bar; pale legs; large bill. *Arctic forests.*	A short, high trill *'ziz-ziz-ziz'*. Call, a husky *'tsssp'*.	177
○ **GREENISH WARBLER** Wing-bar; dark legs; weak bill. *Forests, coppices.*	Loud, high-pitched jingle merging into trill or gabble.	177
● **YELLOW-BROWED WARBLER** Two wing-bars; eye-stripe. *Mixed and coniferous woods.*	Call-note *'weest'*. For song see text.	178
○ **BONELLI'S WARBLER** Pale head; yellow rump. *Pine forest, cork groves, etc.*	Loose trill on same note, flatter than Wood's.	179
● **WOOD WARBLER** Yellow throat; white belly. *Woodlands.*	Repeated notes on one pitch accelerating into dry trill.	179

TREE WARBLERS

● **ICTERINE WARBLER** Long wings; bluish legs. *N., E. and C. Europe; bushes*	Jumble of notes, each repeated, some discordant.	173
● **MELODIOUS WARBLER** Short wings; brownish legs. *SW Europe; bushes.*	Prolonged warbling babble, more musical than Icterine.	173
OLIVE-TREE WARBLER Big bill; pale wing-edging. *Olive groves, oaks.*	Louder, slower, deeper than other *Hippolais*.	172
△ **OLIVACEOUS WARBLER** 'Mousy'; short wings. *Cultivation, scrub.*	Vigorous jumble, at times recalling Sedge Warbler.	172
● **GARDEN WARBLER** Unmarked, brownish. See text. *Woods, hedges, thickets.*	Mellow, suggests Blackcap but much longer, less varied.	177

WILLOW

CHIFFCHAFF

ARCTIC

GREENISH

YELLOW-BROWED

BONELLI'S

WOOD

ICTERINE

MELODIOUS

OLIVE-TREE

OLIVACEOUS

GARDEN

Plate 65

RARE WARBLERS AND FINCHES

○ **LANCEOLATED WARBLER** page 168
Heavily streaked back; band of streaks below white throat.

△ **PALLAS'S GRASSHOPPER WARBLER** 167
Heavily streaked back; rufous rump shading into dark tail. Juvenile
has buffy breast-band with some light streaks.

△ **BLYTH'S REED WARBLER** 170
Greyer than Reed Warbler; bill longer; supercilium indistinct.

△ **BOOTED WARBLER** 172
Pale, sandy; pale buff across breast and flanks.

○ **RADDE'S WARBLER** 179
Larger than Chiffchaff; long, very conspicuous supercilium; yellowish legs, creamy-white under-parts.

○ **DUSKY WARBLER** 179
Smaller than Radde's Warbler; darker, finer-billed; darker auri-
culars and rustier supercilium.

○ **PALLAS'S WARBLER** 178
Striped crown suggests Firecrest, but note yellow rump-patch. See
also Yellow-browed Warbler (Pl. 64).

△ **BLACKPOLL WARBLER** 205
Autumn: Dull greenish; conspicuous light wing-bars, striped back.
Faint streaks on yellowish under-parts.
Male in spring: Black cap and white cheeks. Boldly streaked.

△ **TRUMPETER FINCH** 203
Stumpy pink bill; unmistakable bleating voice.

△ **WHITE-THROATED SPARROW** 205
White throat-patch surrounded by grey. Head-stripes may be black
and white, or tan and buff.

LANCEOLATED
WARBLER

PALLAS'S
GRASSHOPPER
WARBLER

LYTH'S
EED WARBLER

BOOTED
WARBLER

RADDE'S
WARBLER

DUSKY WARBLER

autumn

BLACKPOLL
WARBLER

PALLAS'S
WARBLER

♂

spring

♀

♂

TRUMPETER FINCH

tan-striped
form

white-striped
form

WHITE-THROATED SPARROW

Plate 66

GOLDCRESTS, DIPPER, WREN, CREEPERS AND NUTHATCHES

● **GOLDCREST** page 18
Tiny; orange or yellow crown-stripe.
No stripe through eye.

● **FIRECREST** 18
From Goldcrest by sharp black and white eye-stripes; bronze 'shoulders'.

● **DIPPER** 15
Portly; dark, with white 'bib'; short cocked tail.

● **WREN** 15
Tiny, rotund, brown; tail usually cocked.

● **TREECREEPER** 18
Slender, with curved bill; streaked brown with rusty rump; silvery-white under-parts.

△ **SHORT-TOED TREECREEPER** 18
Nearly identical with Treecreeper, but flanks more brownish. More easily separable by voice and distribution (see text and maps).

△ **WALLCREEPER** 18
Large crimson wing-patches; very rounded wings.

● **NUTHATCH** 18
Stumpy; short tail; sharp bill; blue-grey back.
Scandinavian form is whiter below.

CORSICAN NUTHATCH 18
Small; white stripe over eye; black cap (male).
Corsica.

ROCK NUTHATCH 18
Paler than Nuthatch; larger bill; no spots on tail.
Balkans, Greece.

GOLDCREST

♀ ♂

FIRECREST

♀ ♂

WREN

DIPPER

winter

below

TREE-
CREEPER

SHORT-TOED
TREECREEPER

summer

WALLCREEPER

Scandinavian
form

CORSICAN
NUTHATCH

NUTHATCH

ROCK NUTHATCH

Plate 67

FLYCATCHERS, WAXWING AND SHRIKES

Flycatchers are small birds which sit upright while waiting for passing insects. They frequently flick up their tails.

Waxwings are sleek, crested, Starling-like brown birds.

Shrikes are hook-billed song-birds with the habits of little hawks, catching insects, mice and small birds.

● **SPOTTED FLYCATCHER** page 182
No wing-patch; grey-brown back; streaked breast.

● **PIED FLYCATCHER** 182
Male: Black and white, large white wing-patch. As female in winter.
Female: Brown back; white wing-patch.

△ **COLLARED FLYCATCHER** 182
Male in summer: White collar and rump; large wing-patch extends
along wing. See also Semi-collared Flycatcher, Pl. 76.

● **RED-BREASTED FLYCATCHER** 182
Male: Orange throat; grey cheek; white tail-patches.
Female: Buffish breast; white tail-patches (see Whinchat, Pl. 60).

● **WAXWING** 154
Long crest; yellow tip on tail; scarlet tips to secondaries.

● **GREAT GREY SHRIKE** 191
Light grey forehead; white supercilium; slender bill; long tail; short
wings; white on scapulars.

○ **LESSER GREY SHRIKE** 190
Black forehead; stubbier bill; more upright pose; longer wings.

● **RED-BACKED SHRIKE** 190
Male: Chestnut back; grey crown.
Female: Rusty back; barred breast.

● **WOODCHAT SHRIKE** 191
Adults: Large white scapular-patches; chestnut crown; white rump.
Juvenile: Thickly barred; trace of wing-patch.

MASKED SHRIKE 191
From Woodchat by black crown and rump; white forehead; reddish
flanks.

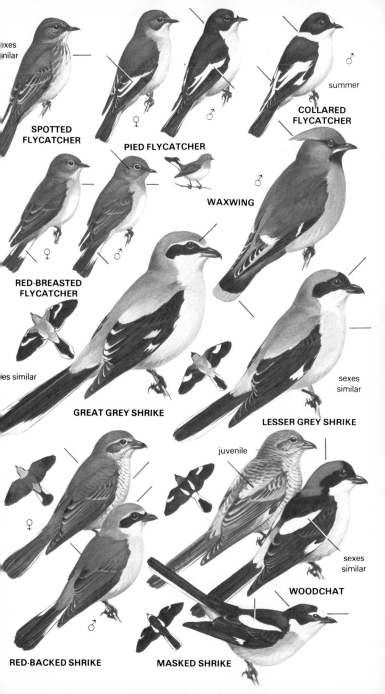

sexes
similar

SPOTTED
FLYCATCHER

♀

♂

PIED FLYCATCHER

♂

summer

COLLARED
FLYCATCHER

WAXWING

♂

♀   ♂

RED-BREASTED
FLYCATCHER

es similar

GREAT GREY SHRIKE

sexes
similar

LESSER GREY SHRIKE

♀

juvenile

sexes
similar

WOODCHAT

♂

RED-BACKED SHRIKE   MASKED SHRIKE

Plate 68

TITS

 Small birds with stubby bills; extremely active, often hanging upside down in their busy search for food. Most true tits (*Parus*, first three rows) have black bibs, white cheeks and black or dark caps. In true tits the sexes are alike.

● **GREAT TIT** page 18(
Black stripe on belly.

● **COAL TIT** 18.
White spot on nape.

● **BLUE TIT** 18:
Blue cap; yellowish under-parts.

● **MARSH TIT** 18·
Glossy black cap; small 'bib'; no light edging on wing.

● **WILLOW TIT** 18
Dull black cap; light area on wing formed by feather edgings; distinctive voice (see text). Scandinavian form is much paler, with whiter cheeks.

AZURE TIT 18·
White cap; white under-parts; much white on wing.

SOMBRE TIT 18·
Large (size of Great Tit); drab, with large bill.

SIBERIAN TIT 18:
Brown cap; 'dusty' appearance.

● **CRESTED TIT** 18:
Crest; 'bridled' face pattern.

● **LONG-TAILED TIT** 18:
White crown-stripe, or white head; very long tail.

△ **PENDULINE TIT** 189
Black mask through eyes; rusty back.

● **BEARDED TIT** 18:
Male: Black 'moustaches'; very long tail.
Female: No 'moustaches'; brown; very long tail.

GREAT

COAL

BLUE

MARSH

WILLOW

northern form

AZURE

SOMBRE

SIBERIAN

CRESTED

BEARDED

♀

LONG-TAILED

northern form

PENDULINE

Plate 69

MAGPIES, NUTCRACKER, CHOUGHS, JAYS, ORIOLE AND STARLINGS

NUTCRACKER

MAGPIE

ZURE-WINGED
MAGPIE

ALPINE CHOUGH

JAY

CHOUGH

GOLDEN ORIOLE

SIBERIAN
JAY

♀

♂

spring ♂

juvenile

POTLESS   STARLING

winter

juvenile

STARLING

adult

ROSE-
COLOURED
STARLING

Plate 70

THE CROW FAMILY

- **CHOUGH**
  Thin red bill; red legs. Mountains; locally sea cliffs. (See also Pl. 69.)

  ALPINE CHOUGH
  Shorter yellow bill; red legs. High mountains. (See also Pl. 69.)

- **HOODED CROW**
  Grey back and belly, black hood.

- **CARRION CROW**
  All black; moderately heavy bill.

- **JACKDAW**
  Small; short bill, grey nape; pale grey eyes.

- **ROOK**
  Bare face-patch, pale bill; shaggy 'trousers'.
  Juvenile: Similar to Carrion Crow but bill more slender.

- **RAVEN**
  Very large; massive bill, shaggy throat; wedge-shaped tail.

ALPINE CHOUGH

CHOUGH

HOODED CROW

CARRION CROW

JACKDAW

ROOK

ROOK

juvenile

RAVEN

Plate 71

FINCHES

Finches (and buntings) have stout bills, adapted for seed cracking. Three types of bills exist within the group: that of the Hawfinch, Bullfinch and grosbeaks, exceedingly thick and rounded in outline; the more ordinary Canary-like bill of most of the finches; and that of the crossbills, the mandibles of which are crossed at the tips.

● **HAWFINCH**   page 205
   Massive bill and head; white wing-bands; short tail.

● **CHAFFINCH**   199
   Double white wing-bars: white sides of tail.
   Male with blue-grey crown, pinkish cheeks and breast.

● **BRAMBLING**   199
   White rump; rusty chest and 'shoulders'.
   Male in summer has black head and back.

● **GOLDFINCH**   200
   Red and white face; broad yellow wing-band.

● **GREENFINCH**   200
   Male: Green; large yellow wing- and tail-patches.
   Female: Duller; dull yellow wing-patches.

△ **CITRIL FINCH**   200
   Unstreaked; greyish nape; dull green wing-bars.

● **SISKIN**   201
   Male: Black crown and chin; yellow on tail.
   Female: Streaked breast; yellow on tail.

○ **SERIN**   199
   Stumpy form; stubby bill; streaks; yellow breast; yellow rump.

Most finches have a strongly undulating flight

HAWFINCH

CHAFFINCH ♂ ♀

BRAMBLING ♂ winter ♀ summer

GOLDFINCH sexes similar

GREENFINCH ♂ ♀

CITRIL FINCH sexes similar

SISKIN ♂ ♀

SERIŃ ♂ ♀

Plate 72

FINCHES

● **BULLFINCH**   page 204
Black cap; white rump; stubby tail.
Male: Rose-red breast.
Female: Warm pinkish-brown breast.

● **LINNET**   201
Male: Red forehead and breast; no black on chin.
Female: Streaked, grey head; browner back.

● **REDPOLL**   202
Red forehead; black chin; buff wing-bars.
Male has pink breast.

○ **ARCTIC REDPOLL**   202
From Redpoll by frostier appearance, unstreaked white rump; white
    wing-bars.

● **TWITE**   201
Rich buff with black streaks; yellow bill in winter.
Male has faintly pinkish rump, like Redpoll.

● **SCARLET ROSEFINCH**   204
Male: Rosy-carmine breast, crown and rump; no white wing-bars.
Female: Yellowish-brown, streaked; round head; bold dark eye;
    pale wing-bars.

△ **PINE GROSBEAK**   204
Male: Large, long-tailed, rosy; white wing-bars.
Female: Golden-brown with brighter crown and rump; wing-bars.

● **CROSSBILL**   203
Male: Dull red; dark wings and tail; crossed bill.
Female: Yellowish-grey; dark wings and tail.

○ **PARROT CROSSBILL**   203
Very stout bill. See text.

○ **TWO-BARRED CROSSBILL**   202
Male: Carmine; white wing-bars; crossed bill.
Female: Yellowish-olive; white wing-bars; streaks.

BULLFINCH

♂

♀

LINNET

♂

♀

ARCTIC REDPOLL

♂

REDPOLL

♂

♀

TWITE

♂

SCARLET ROSEFINCH

♀

♂

PARROT CROSSBILL

♂

PINE GROSBEAK

♀

♂

CROSSBILL

♂

♀

TWO-BARRED CROSSBILL

♀

♂

Plate 73

SPARROWS, ACCENTORS AND BUNTINGS

● **HOUSE SPARROW** page 1
Male: Black bib; grey crown.
Female: Plain dingy breast; dull eye-stripe.

ITALIAN SPARROW (treated under House Sparrow) 19
Male: Chestnut crown; no stripes on sides.
Female: Similar to House Sparrow.

△ **SPANISH SPARROW** 1
Male: Chestnut crown; heavy black streaks.
Female: Similar to House Sparrow, but with faint flank-streaks.

● **TREE SPARROW** 1
Black cheek-spot; chestnut crown. Sexes alike.

△ **ROCK SPARROW** 1
Pale; striped crown; white tail-spots; indistinct yellow spot on breast.

● **DUNNOCK** 1
Streaked brown; grey face and breast; thin bill.

△ **ALPINE ACCENTOR** 1
Chestnut sides; spotted white throat; wing-bars.

○ **RUSTIC BUNTING** 20
Summer: Black and white head; rusty breast-band.
Winter: Brown; trace of head and breast patterns.

● **SNOW BUNTING** 20
Large white wing-patches; head washed with buff.
In summer, male has white head and black back.

SNOWFINCH 19
From Snow Bunting by grey head and black chin.

● **LAPLAND BUNTING** 20
Male in spring: Black face and chest; rusty nape.
Female and winter male: Rusty nape; short tail.
Immature: Light stripe through crown.

● **REED BUNTING** 2
Male: Black head and bib; white moustachial stripe and collar.
Female: Streaked; blackish and creamy moustachial stripes.

HOUSE SPARROW

♂

♀

TREE SPARROW

sexes similar

ROCK SPARROW

sexes similar

♂

♂

ITALIAN SPARROW

SPANISH SPARROW

DUNNOCK

sexes similar

sexes similar

ALPINE ACCENTOR

♂

winter

♀

sexes similar

♂

summer

winter

♂

RUSTIC BUNTING

SNOW BUNTING

SNOWFINCH

immature

♂
summer

♀

♂
summer

LAPLAND BUNTING

REED BUNTING

Plate 74

BUNTINGS

● **CORN BUNTING** page 21
Large; streaked; stubby bill; no white on tail.

○ **LITTLE BUNTING** 209
Rufous crown and cheeks; boldly striped with black.

△ **ROCK BUNTING** 207
Black stripes on grey head; buffish-orange belly and rump.

● **ORTOLAN BUNTING** 208
Olive head and breast; yellow throat and eye-ring.
Immature: Streaked; pink bill; pale eye-ring.

△ **CRETZSCHMAR'S BUNTING** 208
From Ortolan by rusty throat, blue-grey head.
Immature: Resembles immature Ortolan.

● **YELLOWHAMMER** 207
Yellowish, with rufous rump.

● **CIRL BUNTING** 207
Male: Black throat; black and yellow face pattern.
Female: From Yellowhammer by olive-brown rump.

○ **BLACK-HEADED BUNTING** 210
Male: Black hood; yellow below; rufous back.
Female: Unstreaked below; bright yellow under tail-coverts; deep bill.

○ **YELLOW-BREASTED BUNTING** 209
Male: Black face; chestnut band on yellow under-parts; bold white wing-bars.
Female: Strongly striped head; flank streaks only.

RED-HEADED BUNTING 226
Male: Red head and breast; yellow under-parts.

△ **PINE BUNTING** 207
Male: White crown; chestnut throat-patch.

SIBERIAN MEADOW BUNTING 225
Male: Chestnut crown and cheeks; white eyebrow; black 'moustache'.

BLACK-FACED BUNTING 225
Male: Dark grey head; dull yellow under-parts.

CINEREOUS BUNTING 208
Male: Dull yellow head; greyish body and nape.

LITTLE

ROCK

♂

sexes
similar

CORN

sexes
similar

ORTOLAN

CRETZSCHMAR'S

nature

♂

immature

♂

♀

♂

♀

CIRL

YELLOWHAMMER

BLACK-
HEADED

♂

♀

♂

YELLOW-
BREASTED

♀

OCCIDENTAL IN EUROPE

♂

♂

♂

♂

breeds
Greece

♂

RED-HEADED   PINE   SIBERIAN
MEADOW   BLACK-
FACED   CINEREOUS

Plate 75

MISCELLANEOUS RARITIES

WHITE-RUMPED SWIFT page 13
Narrow white rump-patch, deeply forked tail.

LEVANT SPARROWHAWK 7
White under-surface to dark-tipped wings. Reddish (not yellow)
eyes. Male blue-grey above, grey cheeks.

△ **BLUE-CHEEKED BEE-EATER** 14
Green with burnt-orange throat. Narrow black eye-mask bordered
above and below with blue.

LAUGHING DOVE 13
Dark plumage, obscure frontal gorget. Much bluish on wing in
carpal area.

○ **YELLOW-BILLED CUCKOO** 13.
Yellow lower mandible; large white tail-spots; chestnut primaries.

△ **EGYPTIAN NIGHTJAR** 13
Paler, sandier than Nightjar. No clear white on wings or tail.

WHITE-
RUMPED
SWIFT

BLUE-
CHEEKED
BEE-EATER

LEVANT
SPARROW-
HAWK

♂

LAUGHING
DOVE

YELLOW-BILLED
CUCKOO

EGYPTIAN NIGHTJAR

Plate 76

MISCELLANEOUS RARITIES

○ **CITRINE WAGTAIL**   page 153
  Male: Yellow head; black hind-collar.
  Female: Browner, duller; lacks black hind-collar.

○ **PECHORA PIPIT**   151
  From Tree Pipit by voice and pale stripes on back.

○ **OLIVE-BACKED PIPIT**   150
  Smaller than Tree Pipit; back more olivaceous with scarcely
    discernible streaking; more heavily streaked on breast. Postocular
    spot often present.

  SEMI-COLLARED FLYCATCHER   182
  Distinguished from Pied Flycatcher by presence of an upper white
    wing-bar. See also Collared Flycatcher, Pl. 67.

○ **DESERT WHEATEAR**   161
  Tail all black; sandy above and below.

△ **ISABELLINE WHEATEAR**   159
  Sandy-grey above; tail mainly black; large bill.

△ **RED-FLANKED BLUETAIL**   158
  Male: Deep blue above; orange flanks.
  Female: Dusky with dark chest, white throat, orange flanks.

△ **SWAINSON'S THRUSH**   163
  Much smaller than Song Thrush; buff eye-ring, cheek and throat.

  KRÜPER'S NUTHATCH   186
  Bold dark rufous breast-patch.

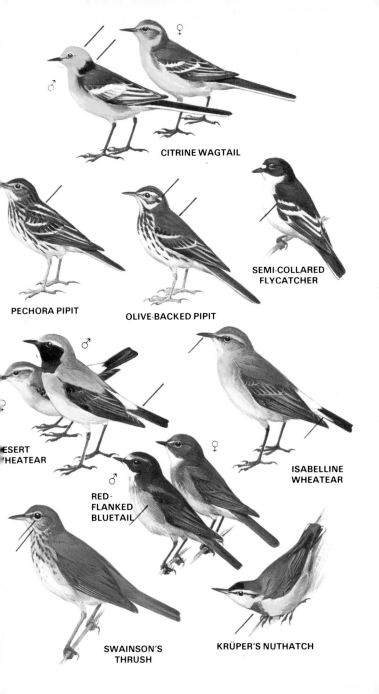

CITRINE WAGTAIL

PECHORA PIPIT

OLIVE-BACKED PIPIT

SEMI-COLLARED
FLYCATCHER

ᐤESERT
ᐤHEATEAR

RED-
FLANKED
BLUETAIL

ISABELLINE
WHEATEAR

SWAINSON'S
THRUSH

KRÜPER'S NUTHATCH

Plate 77

SOME INTRODUCED BIRDS

Many exotic species have been introduced at one time or another into Britain and western Europe, or have escaped. Although most often they were doomed to failure, some, such as those shown here, have succeeded in a limited way. Others introduced as potential game or ornamental species, which seem to have succeeded locally, are Silver Pheasant (Germany), Reeve's Pheasant (France, Germany), California Quail (Germany), Bobwhite (England, Germany), and Wild Turkey (Germany).

● **RING-NECKED PARAKEET**   page 132
A slim, long-tailed, green parrot with a hooked red bill.
Male has a narrow ring on neck.

  COMMON WAXBILL   198
A tiny, finely barred dark finch with a *red belly*, *red bill*, and white
  cheeks. Immature has a black bill.

● **EGYPTIAN GOOSE**   55
Chocolate eye-patch and dark patch on lower breast.

● **GOLDEN PHEASANT**   86
Male: Unmistakable, with scarlet under-parts, golden crest and
  rump.
Female: Similar to female Pheasant but tail longer, more strongly
  barred.

● **LADY AMHERST'S PHEASANT**   87
Male: Unmistakable, with scalloped head-dress, white under-parts,
  barred white tail.
Female: Similar to female Golden Pheasant (see text).

Note: The birds shown on this plate vary in scale. See text for measurements.

RING-NECKED
PARAKEET

COMMON
WAXBILL

EGYPTIAN
GOOSE

GOLDEN PHEASANT

GOLDEN
PHEASANT

LADY
AMHERST'S
PHEASANT

LADY AMHERST'S PHEASANT

LARKS: Alaudidae

Mostly streaked brown ground-birds, with running gait. Fine singers, often high in air. Sexes similar (except Black Lark). Ground nesting.

DUPONT'S LARK *Chersophilus duponti*   **Pl. 56**
Du – Dupont's leeuwerik   Fr – Sirli de Dupont
Ge – Dupont-Lerche   Sw – Smalnäbbad lärka

Identification: 7½". An extremely secretive species, distinguished by rufous appearance, *long, slender, down-curved bill* and absence of white on wings; outer tail-feather white; pale eye-stripe is conspicuous. Rarely seen on wing, except in spring song-flight, when it soars to great height; on landing *runs remarkably swiftly* to hide in thickest available cover; stands very slim and erect.
Voice: Call-note a whistling '*hoo-ee*' and a Greenfinch-like '*dweej*'. Song has short, high musical and nasal phrases, the most distinctive being '*dzee-too-see*'.
Habitat and Range: Semi-desert, with wild thyme, scrub, etc. Breeds S. and C. Spain; vagrant elsewhere.

CALANDRA LARK *Melanocorypha calandra*   **Pl. 56**
Du – Kalanderleeuwerik   Fr – Alouette calandre
Ge – Kalanderlerche   Sw – Kalanderlärka

Identification: 7½". Distinguished by large size, heavy build, *stout yellowish-horn bill and bold black half-collar on each side of neck*. Buffish breast lightly streaked with brown. In flight, tips of secondaries form *conspicuous white rear edges* to large *triangular wings*, which look *almost black below*. No crest. Juvenile buffish; neck-patches partly obscured. Flight very buoyant, often in large winter flocks on stubble. See also White-winged, female Black and Bimaculated Larks.
Voice: A nasal chirrup '*kleetra*'. Rich and varied song similar to Skylark's, but louder, with frequent interjections of mimicry and trilling; sings in high circling flight, often diving silently last few hundred feet to ground.
Habitat: Stony wastelands, farmlands and steppes. Nests on ground. Map 218.

WHITE-WINGED LARK *Melanocorypha leucoptera*   **Pl. 56**
Du – Witvleugelleeuwerik   Fr – Alouette leucoptère
Ge – Weissflügellerche   Sw – Vitvingad lärka

Identification: 7". Distinguished from other larks by *broad white wing-patch*, reaching hind edge, very conspicuous in flight; from Calandra also by lack of black neck-patches and narrower wings. Tawny upper-parts have dark streaks; chestnut on crown, wing-coverts and tail; whitish under-parts and wing-pits, with lightly spotted buffish throat and breast. White outer web of longest primary visible on closed wing. Female has streaked brown crown. See also Snow Bunting.
Voice: Song said to resemble short version of Skylark's, delivered during brief soaring flights and from ground.
Habitat and Range: Mainly arid grass-steppes. Nests on ground. On passage and in hard winters in E. Romania. Vagrant across Europe west to Britain, and south to Malta.

BLACK LARK *Melánocorypha yeltoniensis*   **Pl. 5(**
Du – Zwarte leeuwerik   Fr – Alouette nègre
Ge – Mohrenlerche   Sw – Svart lärka
Identification: 7½″. Male unmistakable: large and *black* with pale sandy
margins to feathers which, in winter, partly obscure the black. Bill short and
stout, yellow with black tip. Female very like *pale* Calandra but distinguished
by *absence of black neck-patches*. Neither sex has white on wings or tail.
Voice: Has clear, piping call-note. Song resembles short spasms of Skylark's
Habitat and Range: Grassy or bushy steppes, often near water, also on deserts
closer to cultivation and roadsides in winter. Vagrant from C. Asia in winter to
C. Europe and west to North Sea coast.

SHORT-TOED LARK *Calandrella brachydactyla*   **Pl. 5(**
Du – Kortteenleeuwerik   Fr – Alouette calandrelle
Ge – Kurzzehenlerche   Sw – Korttålärka
Identification: 5½″. Much smaller than Skylark. Sandy-buff above with dark
streaks and a noticeably pale covert-bar. Whitish below, usually with *small dark
patch* on side of neck (but some are streaked there). No crest, but *reddish cap* i
raised when excited. Short, pointed, yellowish bill gives finch-like character
Juvenile slightly streaked on breast, giving effect of cloudy side-patches. Flight
undulating.
Voice: A short, dry chirrup, '*tchi-tchirrp*', recalling House Sparrow; anxiety
note, '*tee-oo*'. Song, chiefly in high, steeply *rising and falling* flight, a simple
phrase of about eight high-pitched twittering notes, repeated at short intervals
and long-sustained.
Habitat: Open sandy or stony wastes, dry mud-flats with *Salicornia*, steppe
and fields. Nests on ground. Map 219.

LESSER SHORT-TOED LARK *Calandrella rufescens*   **Pl. 5(**
Du – Kleine kortteenleeuwerik   Fr – Alouette pispolette
Ge – Stummellerche   Sw – Dvärglärka
Identification: 5½″. Best distinguished by voice, but western birds are also
greyer than Short-toed, with more uniform dark streaking. *Upper breast usually
finely, copiously streaked*, but some have central gap and thus resemble Short
toed. Crown as mantle, not 'capped'. Covert-bar indistinct. See also Short
toed.
Voice: Has characteristic '*prrit*' which also occurs in song. Song is more
melodious, imitative and continuous than Short-toed, but has similar twittering
character; sings in *rising spiral, or high circling flight*, also on ground.
Habitat and Range: As Short-toed, but also especially dry edges of marshes
Summer visitor, breeding S. Spain. Vagrant elsewhere in S., W. (including
British Isles), C. and N. Europe.

CRESTED LARK *Galerida cristata*   **Pl. 5(**
Du – Kuifleeuwerik   Fr – Cochevis huppé
Ge – Haubenlerche   Sw – Tofslärka
Identification: 6¾″. Plumper and rather paler than Skylark. Distinguished by
long upstanding crest, rather long, slightly curved bill and short tail with dark
centre and *buff* sides. Upper-parts variable sandy- or grey-brown, less strongly
streaked than Skylark; under-parts creamy-buff, streaked on breast; *in flight*
shows orange-buff under wings. Juvenile more spotted above, with shorter crest

Distinguished from Skylark and Woodlark by long narrow crest and absence of white on broad, very rounded wings and short tail. 'Floppy' flight. See also very similar Thekla Lark.

Voice: A liquid '*twee-tee-too*', rising and falling, or a shrill '*quee-tee*'. Song less musical and shorter than Skylark's; usually in short repeated phrases, delivered from ground, low perch and in flight.

Habitat: Generally flat grassy or arid country; often near habitation, dusty mule-tracks, roadsides, etc. Nests on ground. Map 220.

THEKLA LARK *Galerida theklae* **Pl. 56**

Du – Thekla leeuwerik   Fr – Cochevis de Thékla
Ge – Theklalerche   Sw – Lagerlärka

Identification: 6¼″. Difficult to distinguish from Crested unless the two can be compared where they occur together. Thekla is slightly smaller, with paler under-parts. Streaks and spots on breast are more extensive and *extend to nape*. Shows clear *grey* (not buff) beneath wings. Bill is shorter, less pointed. Erected crest more fan-like than Crested's tall spike.

Voice: Calls '*tu-tweeoo*'. Song, often from bush-top, resembles Crested but is more mellow, with longer pauses.

Habitat and Range: Shows some preference for dry, stony hillsides with low, bushy vegetation and dunes with some cover. Occurs up to higher altitudes. Resident in Portugal, S. and E. Spain, Balearics; part of S. France.

WOODLARK *Lullula arborea* **Pl. 56**

Du – Boomleeuwerik   Fr – Alouette lulu
Ge – Heidelerche   Sw – Trädlärka

Identification: 6″. Distinguished from Skylark by smaller size, *very short tail without white sides, conspicuous white eye-stripes joining on nape* behind and below rounded crest, finer bill and distinctive voice. Has characteristic dark mark near bend of wing. Soars in wide spirals during song-flight, finally plunging with closed wings almost to ground. Perches on trees. See also Tree Pipit.

Voice: A melodious '*tooloooeet*'. Song less varied, less sustained and less powerful than Skylark's, but more melodious and more deliberate, consisting of short phrases interspersed with a liquid trilling '*lu-lu-lu-lu*' and '*tee-oo*'; from perch, ground, or in song-flight.

Habitat: Edges of woods, hillsides with a few trees, sandy heaths, etc. Winters in fields. Nests on ground. Map 221.

SKYLARK *Alauda arvensis* **Pl. 56**

Du – Veldleeuwerik   Fr – Alouette des champs
Ge – Feldlerche   Sw – Sånglärka

Identification: 7″. Upper-parts brown, strongly streaked blackish; under-parts buffish-white with boldly streaked breast. *Longish tail with conspicuous white on outer feathers.* Hind margins of long, pointed wings show whitish in flight. Short, rounded crest often prominent. Walks in crouched position. Flight strong and slightly undulating, with alternate spells of wing-beats and 'shooting' with closed wings; soars and hovers in song-flight. See also Wood and Crested Larks.

Voice: A clear, liquid '*chir-r-up*'. Song, a high-pitched, musical outpouring,

very long sustained, in hovering and ascending or descending flight; occasionally from ground or low perch.
Habitat: Moors, fields, marshes, sand-dunes. Nests on ground. Map 222.

SHORE LARK   *Eremophila alpestris*   **Pl. 56**
   Du – Strandleeuwerik   Fr – Alouette hausse-col
   Ge – Ohrenlerche   Sw – Berglärka
   N. Am – Horned Lark
Identification: $6\frac{1}{2}''$. Easily distinguished from all other larks by *pale yellow face and throat, bold black breast-band and cheeks*. Pinkish-brown above, whitish below. Male has black band across crown and *small black 'horns'*. Female has less black. Juvenile appears spotted and duller. Adult head markings partly obscured in winter.
Voice: Clear, pipit-like, or wagtail-like: '*tsee-ree*', '*tiali-ti*', etc. Song, tinkling, irregular and high-pitched, often long-sustained, sometimes high in air in manner of Skylark.
Habitat: Winters on coast on shingle strands, salt-marshes and adjacent stubble fields. Breeds above tree limit in dry tundra. Map 223.

MARTINS AND SWALLOWS:
Hirundinidae

Slim, streamlined form and graceful flight are distinctive. Forked tails, long pointed wings and short bills with very wide gapes. Insect food caught in flight. Sexes similar. Build mud nests on rocks or buildings (except Sand Martin).

SAND MARTIN   *Riparia riparia*   **Pl. 57**
   Du – Oeverzwaluw   Fr – Hirondelle de rivage
   Ge – Uferschwalbe   Sw – Backsvala
   N. Am – Bank Swallow
Identification: $4\frac{3}{4}''$. Smallest European swallow. Distinguished by *earth-brown* upper-parts, white under-parts with *brown breast-band*. Strongly gregarious. Feeds chiefly over water. Flight more flitting, less swooping, than Swallow's. See also Crag Martin.
Voice: A dry '*tchrrip*'; alarm, a short '*brrit*'. Song, a weak twittering.
Habitat: Open country with ponds, rivers, etc. Nests socially, in tunnels bored in sand- and gravel-pits, river banks, cliffs. Map 224.

CRAG MARTIN   *Ptyonoprogne rupestris*   **Pl. 57**
   Du – Rotszwaluw   Fr – Hirondelle de rochers
   Ge – Felsenschwalbe   Sw – Klippsvala
Identification: $5\frac{3}{4}''$. At a distance can be confused with Sand Martin, but distinguished by stockier build and *dark wedge on under-wing from wing-pit*; under-parts dingy white, *without breast-band*, duskier on belly and under tail-coverts; at short range also by *white spots near tip of spread tail*. Alpine Swift is very much larger, with white under-parts and dark breast-band.
Voice: Not very vocal: a rather weak '*chich*', or '*tchrrri*'.
Habitat: Mountain gorges and rocky inland and coastal cliffs. Builds open

half-cup shaped mud nest in cleft rocks or caves in cliff-face, occasionally with House Martins. Map 225.

SWALLOW   *Hirundo rustica*   Pl. 57
Du – Boerenzwaluw   Fr – Hirondelle de cheminée
Ge – Rauchschwalbe   Sw – Ladusvala
N. Am – Barn Swallow

Identification: 7½″. Distinguished by *long tail-streamers*. Has *dark metallic blue upper-parts*, chestnut-red forehead and throat, *dark blue lower throat*, remainder of under-parts creamy white. Juvenile much duller with shorter streamers. Flight swooping and graceful. Gregarious, though less so when breeding. House Martin has white throat and rump, no tail-streamers. Sand Martin and Crag Martin are brown above, with no tail-streamers. Swift is uniformly dark. See also Red-rumped Swallow.

Voice: A high '*tswit*', '*tsee-tsewit*', etc., becoming a rapid twitter when excited. Alarm, a high '*tswee*'. Song, a pleasant, weak mixture of rapid twittering and warbling notes.

Habitat: Open cultivated country with farms, meadows, ponds, etc. Builds open mud and straw nest on rafters or ledges in cow sheds, stables, etc., locally in chimneys. Map 226.

RED-RUMPED SWALLOW   *Hirundo daurica*   Pl. 57
Du – Roodstuitzwaluw   Fr – Hirondelle rousseline
Ge – Rötelschwalbe   Sw – Rostgumpsvala

Identification: 7″. Distinguished immediately by *buff rump, chestnut nape and eye-stripe*, buff throat and under-parts, without dark gorget patch. Crown and back dark metallic blue, wings and forked tail blackish. Lacks Swallow's white tail markings and has rather thicker streamers and *blunter* wing-tips and more lethargic flight. Distinguished from House Martin by buffish, instead of white, rump and under-parts.

Voice: Has distinctive rough, thin, flight-call '*chew-ic*', resembling House Sparrow. Alarm '*keer*'. Song resembles Swallow's, but is less musical.

Habitat: Sea and inland cliffs; less partial to cultivated areas than Swallow, but in flat country usually frequents bridges and buildings. Builds nest like House Martin's, but with spout-shaped entrance, in caves, cleft rocks, under bridges, etc. Map 227.

HOUSE MARTIN   *Delichon urbica*   Pl. 57
Du – Huiszwaluw   Fr – Hirondelle de fenêtre
Ge – Mehlschwalbe   Sw – Hussvala

Identification: 5″. The only European swallow with a *pure white rump*. Under-parts white; head, back, wings and tail blue-black. Tail is short and forked, and without streamers. Short legs and feet are feathered white. Behaviour like Swallow's, but more sociable, nesting in close colonies. Flight less swooping, more fluttering than Swallow's, and often flies higher. See also White-rumped Swift.

Voice: A clear '*tchirrip*', or '*tchichirrip*'; alarm, a shrill '*tseep*'. Song, a weak but pleasant chirruping twitter, less varied than Swallow's.

Habitat: Like Swallow, but more often near human habitation; also in open country. Builds enclosed mud nest, with entrance hole at top, cupped under eaves of houses and barns, locally on cliffs. Map 228.

PIPITS AND WAGTAILS:
Motacillidae

Terrestrial birds, running and walking briskly. Pipits are brown and streaked, with white or whitish outer tail-feathers; less slender than wagtails. Sexes similar. Ground nesting. Wagtails are very slender, strongly patterned, with long tails, slender bills and slender legs. Ground, cranny or rock nesting.

RICHARD'S PIPIT   *Anthus novaeseelandiae*   **Pl. 58**
    Du – Grote pieper   Fr – Pipit de Richard
    Ge – Spornpieper   Sw – Stor piplärka
Identification: 7″. A *large, long-tailed, long-legged* pipit. Upper-parts brown, broadly streaked blackish; breast buffish, *sparsely but boldly streaked*. Pale buff stripes above eye and below cheek. Narrow dark moustachial streak and black line below eye. Legs and hind claws very long. Slightly larger, more erect than Tawny, with shorter, stouter bill; also distinguished in spring by boldly marked back, longer legs and more streaked upper-breast and throat; in early autumn, not safely separated from immature (streaked) Tawny, except by voice and bill.
Voice: A strident, rising '*sh-reep*'. Song quite unlike Tawny's, a mixture of sparrow-like chirping and grating notes.
Habitat and Range: Wet grasslands, marshy steppes and rice fields. Almost annually on passage, or in winter, Heligoland and British Isles; vagrant elsewhere in Europe.

TAWNY PIPIT   *Anthus campestris*   **Pl. 58**
    Du – Duinpieper   Fr – Pipit rousseline
    Ge – Brachpieper   Sw – Fältpiplärka
Identification: 6½″. More slim and wagtail-like than other pipits. Pale, *almost uniform* sandy above, apart from line of dark spots on coverts near bend of wing, and with paler, usually *unstreaked* under-parts. *Conspicuous creamy supercilium.* Indistinct brown moustachial stripe. Legs long and yellowish, though shorter than Richard's. Further distinguished from Richard's by *paler*, less boldly marked plumage and slightly smaller size. In early autumn young birds with streaked breasts resemble young Richard's (see above).
Voice: More variable call-notes than other pipits, usually a drawn-out '*tsweep*', a brief '*chup*', or a sparrow-like '*chirrup*'. Song, a repeated, metallic '*chivee, chivee, chivee*', usually in high song-flight.
Habitat: Wastelands, with sand and scrub, in winter also frequents cultivated land. Nests in depression, sheltered by vegetation. Map 229.

OLIVE-BACKED PIPIT   *Anthus hodgsoni*   **Pl. 76**
    Du – Indische boompieper   Fr – Pipit sylvestre
    Ge – Waldpieper   Sw – Sibirisk piplärka
Identification: 5¾″. Unlike most other pipits is *almost unstreaked and dark olive-greenish above*; under-parts whitish suffused with pale buff and with dark streaks most conspicuously across upper breast. Best field mark is distinctive *head pattern*, with black-edged white supercilium most prominent *behind* the eye. At close range note that the dark cheek usually has a white spot towards the rear, with a black spot below. Constantly wags tail like wagtail.

Voice: Calls a loud '*tseet*'. Song weak and twittering.
Habitat and Range: Usually the edges of coniferous forests. Vagrant from Asia to Europe (including Britain).

TREE PIPIT *Anthus trivialis*   Pl. 58
  Du – Boompieper   Fr – Pipit des arbres
  Ge – Baumpieper   Sw – Trädpiplärka

Identification: 6″. Best distinguished from very similar Meadow Pipit by *voice*, slightly plumper form, stouter bill, *yellowish breast and pinkish legs*, with short hind claws. Upper-parts brown, streaked blackish. Creamy-buff below, with blackish moustachial stripe and boldly streaked breast and flanks. Yellowish supercilium. White outer tail-feathers. Perches readily on trees. Rock Pipit is larger and *darker*. See also Red-throated.
Voice: A rather hoarse '*teeze*'; alarm, a persistently repeated '*sip*'. Song, loud and musical, with long trills, ending in characteristic '*seea-seea-seea*', or with very slow '*chew, chew, chew*'; sings during 'parachute' descent to perch from short upward flight (Woodlark plunges to ground).
Habitat: Heaths, clearings in woods, hillsides, fields with scattered trees and bushes. Nests under bracken, in long grass, etc. Map 230.

PECHORA PIPIT *Anthus gustavi*   Pl. 76
  Du – Petchora-pieper   Fr – Pipit de la Petchora
  Ge – Petschorapieper   Sw – Tundrapiplärka

Identification: 5¾″. Resembles Tree Pipit; best distinguished by *call-note, two pale streaks down back and bold double white wing-bar*. Rump boldly streaked like Red-throated. Under-parts boldly streaked; outer tail-feathers buffish (not white). Rather skulking.
Voice: A stony, hard '*pwit*', usually repeated; unlike call of any other British pipit, lower and less sweet than call of Meadow Pipit. Song is in two parts, a trill followed by a low, curiously buzzy warble.
Habitat and Range: Except when nesting, inclined to stay close to cover, seldom perching on posts like Tree Pipit, but on breeding ground perches freely on trees. Vagrant from NE Europe, Asia to W. (including Britain) and C. Europe.

MEADOW PIPIT *Anthus pratensis*   Pl. 58
  Du – Graspieper   Fr – Pipit farlouse
  Ge – Wiesenpieper   Sw – Ängspiplärka

Identification: 5¾″. Very like Tree Pipit, but distinguished by *voice*, more olive upper-parts and usually *whiter, less yellow breast*, with smaller, more numerous streaks. White outer tail-feathers. Legs brownish, with long hind claws. Perches less frequently on trees than Tree Pipit. Rock Pipit is larger and darker. See also Red-throated.
Voice: A faint '*tseep*', rapidly repeated when alarmed; also a louder '*tissip*'. Song, a thin piping, in gradually increasing tempo, ending in a musical trill, in short song-flight and during 'parachute' descent.
Habitat: Moors, dunes, rough pastures; in winter prefers marshes, cultivated land, sea coasts. Nests on ground. Map 231.

RED-THROATED PIPIT *Anthus cervinus*   **Pl. 58**
   Du – Roodkeelpieper   Fr – Pipit à gorge rousse
   Ge – Rotkehlpieper   Sw – Rödstrupig piplärka
Identification: $5\frac{3}{4}''$. Distinguished from Meadow Pipit by darker upper-parts, *boldly streaked rump* and distinctive voice. In breeding season throat tinged *rusty-red*, sometimes extending to upper breast. Distinguished in winter by heavy dark streaking on under-parts.
Voice: A thin, hoarse '*tzeeez*', and a soft '*teu*'. Song, during flight descent, less musical, more twittering and higher-pitched than Meadow Pipit's.
Habitat: Swampy tundra, marshes and moist cultivated land, usually with dwarf vegetation, often near coast. Nests on ground. Map 232.

ROCK PIPIT and WATER PIPIT *Anthus spinoletta*   **Pl. 58**
  Rock Pipit:
    Du – Oeverpieper   Fr – Pipit maritime
    Ge – Strandpieper   Sw – Skärpiplärka
  Water Pipit:
    Du – Waterpieper   Fr – Pipit spioncelle
    Ge – Wasserpieper   Sw – Vattenpiplärka
Identification: $6\frac{1}{2}''$. Slightly larger and longer than Meadow and Tree Pipits, with rather longer bill. Legs *much darker* than in other pipits. The mountain race (Water Pipit, *A. s. spinoletta*) has *white outer tail-feathers*, whitish supercilium, greyish upper-parts and whitish under-parts, which in autumn and winter are streaked, but are unstreaked and flushed pinkish in breeding season. Coastal races (Rock Pipit, *A. s. petrosus*, etc.) have darker, more olive appearance, with closely streaked olive-buff under-parts and *greyish* (not white) outer tail-feathers. Distinguished from Meadow Pipit in winter by browner upper-parts, *dark legs*; from Tawny Pipit by streaked under-parts, darker upper-parts, *dark legs*.
Voice: A thin '*tsip*', '*jeep*', or '*tseep-eep*'. Song much less tuneful than Tree and Meadow Pipits', usually in 'flapping' song-flight.
Habitat: Breeds in mountainous areas (Water Pipit), or near sea-shore (Rock Pipit). Winters in marshy lowlands, inland waterways, mud-flats and sea coasts. Nests in crevices in rocks, etc. Map 233.

YELLOW WAGTAIL (and other races) *Motacilla flava*   **Pls. 58, 59**
  Yellow Wagtail:
    Du – Engelse gele kwikstaart   Fr – Bergeronnette flavéole
    Ge – Englische Schafstelze   Sw – Engelsk gulärla
  Blue-headed Wagtail:
    Du – Gele kwikstaart   Fr – Bergeronnette printaniére
    Ge – Schafstelze   Sw – Gulärla
Identification: $6\frac{1}{2}''$. A slender, long-tailed, long-legged bird with yellow under-parts. Several races occur in Europe and can, with practice, be separated in the field. Male of the yellowest race (*M. f. flavissima*), breeding in British Isles and on adjacent shores of Continent, has bright yellow supercilium, throat and under-parts; yellowish-green upper-parts and cheeks. Females in summer and both sexes in winter are duller and browner above, paler below; juvenile has buff chin and brown bib. Male of central European race (Blue-headed Wagtail, *M. f. flava*), has bluish crown, slightly darker ear-coverts with a few white marks, white supercilium and white chin. Female much duller, with white chin. For

further distinctions between races, see Pl. 59. Note: there is a tendency for populations to produce mutants and occasional individuals virtually identical with those of other subspecies. Most observers will be satisfied to call them all 'Yellow Wagtails'. See also Grey Wagtail.

Voice: A loud, musical '*tsweep*', or a more grating '*tsirr*'. Song, a simple '*tsip-tsip-tsipsi*'.

Habitat: Usually near water, marshes, stream banks, meadows. Nests in depression under grass, crops, etc. Map 234.

CITRINE WAGTAIL *Motacilla citreola*   Pl. 76

Du – Citroenkwikstaart   Fr – Bergeronette citrine
Ge – Zitronenstelze   Sw – Gulhuvad ärla

Identification: $6\frac{1}{2}''$. Male easily identified in breeding plumage by *canary-yellow head and neck*, blue-grey upper-parts with black hind-collar, yellow under-parts. Female browner and duller, without collar. In winter both sexes resemble typical *flava* from in front (with yellow forehead and supercilium), but both resemble *alba* from behind. Wags tail and bobs head less than typical *alba*.

Voice: A slurred, wheezy '*sweep*', recalling Yellow.

Habitat and Range: Near fresh water in open country, moors, marshes. Vagrant from Asia to C., N., W. (including Britain) and S. Europe.

GREY WAGTAIL *Motacilla cinerea*   Pls. 58, 59

Du – Grote gele kwikstaart   Fr – Bergeronnette des ruisseaux
Ge – Gebirgstelze   Sw – Forsärla

Identification: $7''$. Distinguished at any season from all other yellow-breasted wagtails by *very long* black tail with conspicuous white outer feathers *and blue-grey upper-parts*. Breast brilliant yellow in summer, buffish in winter. Rump greenish-yellow. Male has white supercilium and conspicuous white stripe from bill below dark grey cheek. Chin and throat of male *black* in summer, whitish in winter. Female is tinged greenish above, with whitish throat, summer and winter. Juvenile grey-brown above, buffish below; distinguished from Pied by *yellow* under tail-coverts. Not gregarious, except for roosting. See also Yellow Wagtail.

Voice: Call-notes more metallic than in Pied and song more brief and repetitive. Alarm, a shrill '*see-eet*', or '*siz-eet*'.

Habitat: Shallow streams in hill country, but also lowlands, woodland streams, sewage-farms and cultivated land, particularly in winter. Nests in holes in walls, bridges, banks, etc. Map 235.

PIED WAGTAIL and WHITE WAGTAIL *Motacilla alba* Pls. 58, 59

Pied Wagtail:
Du – Rouwkwikstaart   Fr – Bergeronnette d'Yarrell
Ge – Trauerbachstelze   Sw – Engelsk sädesärla
White Wagtail:
Du – Witte kwikstaart   Fr – Bergeronnette grise
Ge – Bachstelze   Sw – Sädesärla

Identification: $7''$. A well-patterned black and white bird with slender legs, long tail. Summer male of British subspecies (Pied Wagtail, *M. a. yarrellii*) has *black back*, crown, throat and breast; blackish wings with double white bar; black tail with white outer feathers; white forehead, sides of head and belly. Female greyer above, less black on head and breast. In winter both sexes have *black* on crown, and white throat, with crescent-shaped black bib and grey back. Continental subspecies (White Wagtail, *M. a. alba*) is similar, but in breeding season has *light grey* back and *rump*. More easily confused in autumn.

Voice: A lively '*tchizzik*'; alarm, an abrupt '*tchik*'; song, a twitter, embodying variants of call-notes.

Habitat: Gardens, farms, open country and towns. Often, but not always, near water. Nests in holes in buildings, rocks, etc. Map 236.

WAXWINGS: Bombycillidae

WAXWING   *Bombycilla garrulus*   **Pl. 67**
  Du – Pestvogel   Fr – Jaseur boréal
  Ge – Seidenschwanz   Sw – Sidensvans
  N. Am – Bohemian Waxwing

Identification: 7″. Identified by unmistakable *pinkish-chestnut crest*, and short, *yellow-tipped tail*. Has black eye-stripe and throat-patch. Upper-parts chestnut, with grey rump; under-parts pinkish-brown, with chestnut under tail-coverts; dark wings *boldy marked white and yellow*, with scarlet waxy tips to secondaries (less evident on female). Juvenile lacks black throat-patch and has soft streaks below. Flight strong and starling-like. Often very tame. Acrobatic feeding habits recall Crossbill. Gregarious.

Voice: Call-note a weak, high trill, '*zhreee*'. Song, a quiet twittering on different pitches, interspersed with call-note.

Habitat: Breeds in open glades of northern coniferous and birch woods. Winters in more open country, seeking berried fruit in hedges and gardens. Map 237.

DIPPERS: Cinclidae

DIPPER   *Cinclus cinclus*   **Pl. 66**
  Du – Waterspreeuw   Fr – Cincle plongeur
  Ge – Wasseramsel   Sw – Strömstare

Identification: 7″. A stout bird, Wren-like in shape but very much larger, with large sturdy legs; short tail often cocked. *Blackish with white breast*, bordered below by dark chestnut merging into black in British race *C. c. gularis*, but some northern populations lack chestnut. Sexes alike. Juvenile slate-grey above, mottled grey and white below. 'Bobs' spasmodically, perched on rock in stream. Plunges or walks into water, remaining submerged to feed on bottom; swims or or under water. Flight usually low, rapid and direct, following streams. Solitary, on same strip of water all the year.

Voice: A short '*zit*', or, in flight, a metallic '*clink*'. Song, a succession of short high, grating and explosive notes sometimes interspersed with liquid warbling. Sings nearly all year.

Habitat: Swift hill streams; occasionally visits coasts in winter. Builds large globular nest in crevices under waterfalls, bridges, banks; invariably very near running water. Map 238.

WRENS: Troglodytidae

WREN *Troglodytes troglodytes*   **Pl. 66**
  Du – Winterkoning   Fr – Troglodyte
  Ge – Zaunkönig   Sw – Gärdsmyg
  N. Am – Winter Wren

Identification: $3\frac{3}{4}''$. A tiny, plump, closely barred brown bird with a *short cocked tail*. Extremely active; forages among litter on ground like a mouse, catches insects among vegetation like a warbler. Flight whirring and direct.

Voice: A loud, hard '*tit-tit-tit*', becoming a harsh churring when alarmed. Song, a prolonged, breathless jingle of strident but not unmusical notes and high trills. Sings almost all the year.

Habitat: Low cover, in gardens, thickets, woods, rocks, etc. Builds globular nest in hedges, hay-ricks, holes in trees, banks or buildings. Map 239.

ACCENTORS: Prunellidae

Rather drab and sparrow-like in appearance, but with slender bills. They have a distinctive shuffling gait, unobtrusive habits and brief, high-pitched jingling songs. Sexes similar. Bush or rock nesting.

DUNNOCK *Prunella modularis*   **Pl. 73**
  Du – Heggemus   Fr – Accenteur mouchet
  Ge – Heckenbraunelle   Sw – Järnsparv

Identification: $5\frac{3}{4}''$. Inconspicuous and rather featureless; combination of *rich brown and dark grey* is the best guide. Upper-parts dark brown streaked with black; head and neck slate-grey, with brownish crown and ear-coverts, *under-parts slate-grey* with darkly streaked flanks. Dark, thin bill. Feeds on ground, seldom far from cover, moving with slow, shuffling gait, with wings frequently twitched. Usually solitary.

Voice: A high, piping '*tseep*' and a high trilling note. Song, a hurried, weak but pleasant jingle, much shorter and weaker than Wren's, but somewhat similar in character. Sings almost all the year.

Habitat: Hedges, bushes, coppices. Nests in bushes, evergreens, wood-piles. Map 240.

ALPINE ACCENTOR *Prunella collaris*   **Pl. 73**
  Du – Alpenheggemus   Fr – Accenteur alpin
  Ge – Alpenbraunelle   Sw – Alpjärnsparv

Identification: $7''$. Larger, plumper and more brightly coloured than related Dunnock, though attitudes and unobtrusive habits are similar. Distinguished by *black-spotted whitish chin and throat*, greyish breast, *chestnut-streaked flanks*, irregular double white wing-bar enclosing an obvious blackish bar, and pale buffish tips to tail-feathers. Upper-parts streaked grey-brown. Legs coral red. Juvenile has unspotted grey throat.

Voice: A trilling, lark-like '*tchir-rip*', and a throaty '*churrg*'. Song, a pleasant, sustained, rapid warbling, from ground or in brief display-flight.

Habitat: Rocky mountain slopes, up to snow-line. Winters lower. Nests in holes among rocks or vegetation. Map 241.

ROBINS, CHATS AND THRUSHES:
Turdidae

Robins, chats and thrushes are mostly colourful, rather upstanding song-birds. Bills fairly slender. Tails mostly square-ended. Sexes usually similar. Robins usually nest near the ground. Chats are hole nesters. Thrushes build substantial cup-nests in bushes, trees, rocks.

RUFOUS BUSH ROBIN   *Cercotrichas galactotes*   **Pl. 63**
    Du – Rosse waaierstaart   Fr – Agrobate roux
    Ge – Heckensänger   Sw – Rödsångare
Identification: 6″. Slim, long-legged and rather thrush-like in some attitudes. Quickly recognized by *long, chestnut fan-tail, strikingly tipped with bold black and white*. Western race *C. g. galactotes* has all upper-parts foxy red-brown; eastern race *C. g. syriacus* (so-called Brown-backed Warbler) has chestnut confined to rump and tail, remainder of upper-parts grey-brown; both have bold creamy supercilium and sandy under-parts. Behaviour much bolder than warblers; perches conspicuously on bushes and ground, with wings drooped, long tail fanned and jerked vertically.
Voice: Call-note a hard '*teck*'. Song very musical but disjointed and varying in volume, recalling Skylark in some short phrases. Sings from prominent perch, telegraph wires, etc., and in slow, descending display-flight.
Habitat: Gardens, vineyards, palm and olive groves. Nests in prickly-pear hedges and palm bushes. Map 242.

ROBIN   *Erithacus rubecula*   **Pl. 60**
    Du – Roodborst   Fr – Rougegorge
    Ge – Rotkehlchen   Sw – Rödhake
Identification: 5½″. A plump, 'neckless' little bird. Adults have *rich orange* breast and forehead and uniform olive-brown upper-parts. Juvenile lacks orange and is strongly mottled with dark brown and buff; distinguished from young Redstart by *dark brown* instead of chestnut tail; from young Nightingale by smaller size, buffer under-parts and *dark brown* tail. Confiding behaviour towards man and characteristically jaunty attitudes are well known in Britain, but Continental birds are usually shy.
Voice: A persistent and often rapidly repeated '*tic*', a weak '*tsip*', or '*tsissip*', and a thin, plaintive '*tseee*'. Song, heard all year, is a varied, deliberate series of short, high warbling phrases.
Habitat: Gardens, hedges, coppices, woods with undergrowth, etc. Nests in holes or crannies in walls, banks, trees, hedge-bottoms, ivy, tin cans, etc. Map 243.

THRUSH NIGHTINGALE *Luscinia luscinia*   **Pl. 60**
  Du – Noordse nachtegaal   Fr – Rossignol progné
  Ge – Sprosser   Sw – Näktergal

Identification: 6½″. Very like Nightingale, but distinguished by darker, more olive-brown appearance *including tail,* and, at close quarters, by *brownish mottled breast.* Behaviour like Nightingale.

Voice: Call-notes like Nightingale's; song equally musical, with typical deep '*chook-chook-chook*' opening; distinguished by absence of rising crescendo phrases.

Habitat: Dense and damp thickets, particularly alder and birch, and in swampy undergrowth. Nesting habits like Nightingale's. Map 244.

NIGHTINGALE *Luscinia megarhynchos*   **Pl. 60**
  Du – Nachtegaal   Fr – Rossignol philomèle
  Ge – Nachtigall   Sw – Sydnäktergal

Identification: 6½″. Rather featureless, except for *brownish-chestnut tail and remarkable song.* Upper-parts uniform warm brown, under-parts whitish brown. Juvenile spotted and mottled like young Robin, but easily distinguished by larger size, chestnut tail and whiter under-parts; distinguished from young Redstart by larger size and much less bright chestnut tail. Behaviour skulking and solitary. Flight and attitudes while feeding on ground, like Robin. See also Thrush Nightingale.

Voice: A liquid '*wheet*', a loud '*tac*', a soft, very short '*tuc*' and a harsh '*kerr*' of alarm. Song is rich, loud and musical, each note rapidly repeated several times; most characteristic notes, a deep, bubbling '*chook-chook-chook*' and a slow '*piu, piu, piu*', rising to a brilliant crescendo. Sings day and night, from deep cover, or from low exposed perch.

Habitat: Deciduous lowland woods, moist thickets, tangled hedges. Nest well hidden near ground in brambles, nettles, etc. Map 245.

BLUETHROAT *Luscinia svecica*   **Pl. 60**
  Du – Blauwborst   Fr – Gorgebleue
  Ge – Blaukehlchen   Sw – Blåhake

Identification: 5½″. Redstart-like in form; tail spread and flirted frequently, showing *conspicuous chestnut panels at base.* Male in spring has *bright blue throat-patch,* separated from lower breast by black and chestnut bands. Scandinavian form (Red-spotted Bluethroat, *L. s. svecica*) has *chestnut spot* in centre of throat-patch; central and southern European form (White-spotted Bluethroat, *L. s. cyanecula*) has *white spot*. In autumn, throat is usually whitish with some blue and a black border and dark breast-band. Female has whitish throat-patch with black streaks at side, merging into an irregular dark necklace or breast-band, often with traces of blue and chestnut. Juvenile like streaky dark young Robin, but distinguished by chestnut at base of tail. Females and immatures of Red-spotted and White-spotted forms indistinguishable in the field; males doubtfully separable in autumn.

Voice: A sharp '*tac*', a soft '*wheet*' and a guttural '*turrc*'. Song, very musical and varied, in parts faintly resembling Nightingale and Woodlark, but much higher-pitched, weaker and less rich; introduces sharp, high note like striking metal triangle, also a cricket-like note. Sings from perch and in zig-zag flight.

Habitat: Swampy thickets and heaths, tangled hedges, etc. Breeds close to ground among birch, willow and juniper scrub, in damp heaths; usually in high mountains, but in W. Central Europe also in lowlands. Map 246.

RED-FLANKED BLUETAIL   *Tarsiger cyanurus*   Pl. 76
Du – Blauwstaart   Fr – Rossignol à flancs roux
Ge – Blauschwanz   Sw – Blåstjärt

Identification: 5½″. Size and shape of Redstart. Male has *blue-grey upper-parts* (bright cobalt on shoulders, rump and tail, darkest on cheeks and sides of neck); creamy under-parts, with *bright orange flanks*; white stripe across forehead and above eyes. Female is olive-brown above, paler below, with narrow white throat-patch, bluish rump and tail and orange flanks. Immature resembles young spotted Robin. Extremely shy. Frequently flicks tail.

Voice: Call-note a Robin-like '*tick-tick*'. Song is distinctive and musical, with simple repeated phrases of 6–7 clear notes of thrush-like quality. Sings day or night, usually from high tree-top.

Habitat and Range: Dense virgin pine or spruce forests and damp thickets. Nests on ground. Now probably established as summer visitor to eastern Finland; has bred Estonia. Vagrant from Russia and Asia to N., C., W. (including Britain) and S. Europe.

BLACK REDSTART   *Phoenicurus ochruros*   Pl. 60
Du – Zwarte roodstaart   Fr – Rougequeue noir
Ge – Hausrotschwanz   Sw – Svart rödstjärt

Identification: 5¼″. Both sexes at all ages have *constantly flickering rusty tail and rusty rump* (like Redstart). Male is sooty black with blackish (not chestnut) under-parts and whitish wing-patch (some young breeding males lack this); plumage is paler in autumn, with partly obscured wing-patch. Female and juvenile resemble dark Redstarts, but have dark greyish instead of buff under-parts. Actions like Redstart, but prefers to perch on buildings or rocks.

Voice: A brief '*tsip*' and a stuttering '*tititic*', more incisive than similar call of Redstart. Short, very rapid song is simpler and less musical than Redstart's, introducing curious spluttering, hissing notes. Sings from roof-top or other prominent perch.

Habitat: Cliffs, buildings, rocky slopes, occasionally vineyards, etc. Breeds in holes in walls, rocks, buildings. Map 247.

REDSTART   *Phoenicurus phoenicurus*   Pl. 60
Du – Gekraagde roodstaart   Fr – Rougequeue à front blanc
Ge – Gartenrotschwanz   Sw – Rödstjärt

Identification: 5½″. Both sexes distinguished at all ages (from all species except Black Redstart) by *constantly flickering rusty tail and rusty rump*. Male has *black face and throat*, white forehead, slate-grey upper-parts, *chestnut* breast and flanks; black throat partly obscured by white fringes in autumn. Female is greyish-brown above, buffish below; juvenile is mottled like young Robin, but with rusty rump and tail; both much paler and browner than female and juvenile Black Redstart. Behaviour like Robin.

Voice: A rather tremulous '*whee-tic-tic*', a liquid '*wheet*' very like note of Willow Warbler and a clear '*tooick*'. Song, a short, pleasing jingle of hurried, Robin-like notes, fading into a feeble twitter.

Habitat: Woodlands, parks, heaths with bushes and old trees, occasionally ruins. Nests in holes in trees, stone walls, sheds, etc. Map 248.

WHINCHAT   *Saxicola rubetra*   **Pl. 60**
   Du – Paapje   Fr – Traquet tarier
   Ge – Braunkehlchen   Sw – Buskskvätta

Identification: 5″. Stocky, short-tailed appearance resembles female Stonechat, but distinguished at all seasons by *prominent eye-stripe, white patches at base of tail* and less upright pose. Male has strongly streaked brown cheeks, crown and upper-parts; *broad white stripes over eye and down side of throat*; white patch across blackish wings; warm buff throat and breast. Female paler, with buff instead of white eye-stripe, smaller white wing-patches. Juvenile lacks wing-patches. Behaviour like Stonechat.

Voice: A short '*tic-tic*', '*tu-tic-tic*', also several clicking and churring notes. Song, a brief, rather metallic, but pleasing warble, recalling Redstart or Stonechat. Sings from bush-top, occasionally in flight.

Habitat: Commons, marshes, railway cuttings, open country, with a few bushes, bracken, gorse, etc. On passage in cultivated fields and bushy country. Nests in coarse grass, often at foot of small bush, or large plant. Map 249.

STONECHAT   *Saxicola torquata*   **Pl. 60**
   Du – Roodborsttapuit   Fr – Traquet pâtre
   Ge – Schwarzkehlchen   Sw – Svarthakad buskskvätta

Identification: 5″. Plumper and more upright than Whinchat. Male has distinctive *black head and throat, with broad white half-collar* and narrow white wing-stripe; upper-parts dark with whitish patch on rump; under-parts rich chestnut, shading to buff; autumn plumage browner and duller. Female and juvenile upper-parts brown with black streaks, no white on rump, but some black markings on throat; distinguished from Whinchat by lack of eye-stripe, reddish instead of buff breast and lack of white on sides of tail. Perches with constantly jerked wings and tail, on tops of bushes or telegraph wires. Flight low and jerky.

Voice: A persistent scolding '*wheet, tsack-tsack*', like hitting two stones together, also a clicking note similar to Whinchat's. Song consists of irregular, rapidly repeated double notes, not unlike Dunnock's. Sings from elevated perch or in 'dancing' song-flight.

Habitat: As Whinchat, but usually more fond of gorse-clad commons and of coastal areas. Map 250.

ISABELLINE WHEATEAR   *Oenanthe isabellina*   **Pl. 76**
   Du – Isabeltapuit   Fr – Traquet isabelle
   Ge – Isabellsteinschmätzer   Sw – Isabellastenskvätta

Identification: 6½″. Sexes similar. Distinguished by *large size and almost uniform pale greyish-sandy appearance*. At first glance resembles very pale female or young male Greenland Wheater, but lacks their darker ear-coverts and *head and bill are noticeably larger*. Prominent black on tail extends *more than half its length*, with very short extension towards rump. Under-wing coverts much paler than in the Wheatear. Has distinctive running gait.

Voice: Call-note a loud '*cheep*', or a whistling '*wheet-whit*'. Song is long, rich, lark-like and unlike other wheatears.

Habitat and Range: Usually in steppe, barren plains, or lower slopes of bare hills; shows preference for sandy locations in winter. Breeds NE Greece and European Turkey. Vagrant elsewhere in E., W. (including Britain) and N. Europe.

WHEATEAR   *Oenanthe oenanthe*   **Pl. 60**
  Du – Tapuit   Fr – Traquet motteux
  Ge – Steinschmätzer   Sw – Stenskvätta

Identification: 5¾″. Both sexes have conspicuous *white rump* and sides of tail, contrasting with black centre and tip of tail (like broad inverted T). Breeding male has blue-grey back, *broad white supercilium*; black ear-coverts and wings (brownish in autumn); buffish under-parts. Male in autumn is buffer, with brownish back. Female like autumn male. Behaviour restless, flitting across open ground, 'bobbing' and waving fanned tail. Greenland race *O. o. leucorrhoa* (which passes through W. Europe) is larger and tends to be richer coloured, but many individuals are not safely identifiable. See also Black-eared Wheatear.

Voice: A hard '*chack*', '*chack-weet*', '*weet-chack*', etc. Song, a brief, lark-like warbling, combining musical and wheezy, rattling notes.

Habitat: Downs, moors, hilly pastures, cliffs, dunes. Nests in holes in walls, rabbit warrens, stone heaps, etc. Map 251.

Wheatear in Flight

PIED WHEATEAR   *Oenanthe pleschanka*   **Pl. 60**
  Du – Bonte tapuit   Fr – Traquet pie
  Ge – Nonnensteinschmätzer   Sw – Nunnestenskvätta

Identification: 5¾″. Male distinguished from other European wheatears by *black back and breast* and whitish under-parts. Crown and nape whitish in summer, earthy-brown in winter. White on outer tail-feathers sometimes extends nearly to tip, but centre pair are black from near base right to tip. Wings and coverts black in summer, edged pale buffish in winter. Female indistinguishable from female Black-eared, though back and wings usually more earthy-brown. Often feeds shrike-fashion from perch on bush or tree.

Voice: A harsh '*zack*'. Song, very brief and variable musical phrases repeated at intervals.

Habitat and Range: 'Soft' coastal cliffs in Europe, elsewhere stony barrens, rocky hillsides with a few bushes. Nests in holes. Summer visitor, breeding coastal Romania and Bulgaria. Vagrant to W. (including Britain), C. and N. Europe.

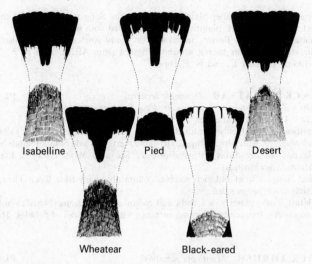

Isabelline   Pied   Desert

Wheatear   Black-eared

Rump and tail patterns of five wheatear species drawn from specimens of males in the British Museum (Natural History)

BLACK-EARED WHEATEAR *Oenanthe hispanica*   **Pl. 60**
  Du – Blonde tapuit   Fr – Traquet oreillard
  Ge – Mittelmeersteinschmätzer   Sw – Rödstenskvätta
Identification: 5¾″. Males are dimorphic, occurring either with a *black patch through eye and cheek and a whitish throat* or with the *black face extending to the whole throat*. Body very pale sandy-buff, with whiter crown and rump, buff breast and whitish under-parts; some birds can look black and white. Wings and scapulars conspicuously black. Tail white with black centre feathers and tip. Autumn plumage buffer. Female resembles Wheatear, but distinguished by darker cheek-patch, *blacker* wings and more white on tail; indistinguishable from female Pied, though usually paler above. Perches readily on trees.
Voice: A rasping note followed by a plaintive whistle. Song rapid and high pitched, '*schwer, schwee, schwee-oo*' in circling display-flight and from perch.
Habitat: Open or lightly wooded arid country and stony mountain slopes. Usually breeds in holes among rocks, walls, etc. Map 252.

DESERT WHEATEAR *Oenanthe deserti*   **Pl. 76**
  Du – Woestijntapuit   Fr – Traquet du désert
  Ge – Wüstensteinschmätzer   Sw – Ökenstenskvätta
Identification: 5¾″. Both sexes distinguished from other wheatears by *black tail almost to base* and noticeable white edges to wing-coverts. Rump and upper tail-coverts white, tinged buffish, particularly in female, which has whitish throat and browner wings than male. Male's *black throat* allows confusion with black-throated phases of Black-eared, but distinguished from latter by buffish instead of black scapulars and lack of conspicuous white on tail. Autumn males have white fringes to throat-feathers.

Voice: Call-note a rather plaintive, soft whistle. Song more mournful than most wheatears: short, plaintive phrases repeated with some variation.

Habitat and Range: Barren and rocky or sandy wastes; in winter also in cultivated areas near barren ground. Vagrant from Africa, Asia to S., W. (including Britain), C. and N. Europe.

BLACK WHEATEAR *Oenanthe leucura*   Pl. 60
Du – Zwarte tapuit   Fr – Traquet rieur
Ge – Trauersteinschmätzer   Sw – Sorgstenskvätta

Identification: 7″. Easily identified by *large size* and striking, slightly glossy, *black plumage*, with white rump, under tail-coverts and side of tail. Female like male but usually duller, brownish-black. See also White-crowned Black Wheatear (Accidentals).

Voice: Song, a brief but rich warble, comparable with Blue Rock Thrush. Anxiety-note '*pee-pee-pee*'.

Habitat: Rocky deserts, sea cliffs and mountainous regions. Nests in holes among rocks, frequently screening entrance with a little wall of pebbles. Map 253.

ROCK THRUSH *Monticola saxatilis*   Pl. 60
Du – Rode rotslijster   Fr – Merle de roche
Ge – Steinrötel   Sw – Stentrast

Identification: 7½″. In all plumages has *short chestnut tail*, with brown centre. Male in summer has *pale slate-blue head, neck and mantle, white lower back*, blackish wings and *chestnut-orange under-parts*; in winter, colours largely obscured by buffish fringes, giving dull mottled effect. Female has strongly mottled brown upper-parts, sometimes with trace of white on back, and mottled buffish under-parts. Behaviour shy and solitary; perches upright, like Wheatear, with loosely swinging tail, before diving out of sight behind rocks. Easily distinguished from Blue Rock Thrush by chestnut tail and white rump.

Voice: A moderate '*chack, chack*'. Song, a clear, fluty warble, from rock or post and in brief vertical display-flight.

Habitat: Breeds in open rocky regions and among trees at 3,000–8,000 ft., in E. Europe down to sea level. Map 254.

BLUE ROCK THRUSH *Monticola solitarius*   Pl. 60
Du – Blauwe rotslijster   Fr – Merle bleu
Ge – Blaumerle   Sw – Blåtrast

Identification: 8″. Slightly larger than Rock Thrush. Male easily distinguished by *deep blue-grey plumage*; in winter looks blackish. Female bluish-brown above, paler below, finely barred with grey-brown. Perches on rocks, with drooped wings and flaunted, relatively short tail, diving out of sight when approached. Solitary. See also Rock Thrush.

Voice: A hard '*tchuck*', or a plaintive '*tseec*'. Song is deliberate, loud and fluty, recalling Blackbird's, but is limited in scope; sings from rock, or in vertical display-flight.

Habitat: Rocky desert regions and bare mountainsides down to sea level. Nests in crevices in rocks, cliffs and buildings. Map 255.

WHITE'S THRUSH *Zoothera dauma* **Pl. 61**
Du – Goudlijster   Fr – Grive dorée
Ge – Erddrossel   Sw – Guldtrast

Identification: 10¾″. Larger than Mistle Thrush. Distinguished by rich, *golden-brown* plumage patterned with *black crescent-shaped* tips to feathers of head and body. In flight, *bold black and white bands beneath wings* are distinctive. Flight deeply undulating. Distinguished from young 'spotty' Mistle Thrush by black and white markings beneath wings and by golden appearance (instead of greyish).

Voice: Song, a single, long, penetrating whistle at different pitches at six-second intervals, each beginning and ending quietly.

Habitat and Range: Normally in deep forest with heavy undergrowth. Vagrant from Asia to C., W. (including Britain), N. and S. Europe.

SIBERIAN THRUSH *Zoothera sibirica* **Pl. 61**
Du – Siberische lijster   Fr – Merle sibérien
Ge – Sibirische Drossel   Sw – Sibirisk trast

Identification: 9″. Male identified by *slaty-black* plumage, *conspicuous white supercilium*, white centre to belly and in flight by white tips to tail. Female has olive-brown upper-parts, buffish eye-stripe, buffish-white under-parts closely spotted with brown. In flight both sexes show *conspicuous white bands across undersides of wings*, providing easy distinction from Dusky and Black-throated Thrushes. Has brief song of two fluty whistles followed by a weak twitter. Vagrant from Asia to N., C., W. (including Britain) and S. Europe.

SWAINSON'S THRUSH *Catharus ustulatus* **Pl. 76**
Du – Dwerglijster   Fr – Grive petite
Ge – Zwergdrossel   Sw – Gråbrun dvärgtrast

Identification: 7″. Resembles very small Song Thrush with *prominent buff eye-ring and buffish cheeks and throat*. These features distinguish it from very similar Grey-cheeked Thrush (Accidentals). Upper breast buffish, spotted with black; faint spots also on upper flanks; under-parts white; mantle and rump olive-brown. Distinguished in flight from Song Thrush by lack of orange beneath wings. Bill blackish, legs pale brownish. Shy and retiring in undergrowth, but seen occasionally in tree-tops. Feeds chiefly on ground, but sometimes by fly-catching.

Voice: A high-pitched, weak '*whit*'. Song musical and fluty, each phrase rising.

Habitat and Range: On passage frequents open woodland glades, gardens, damp woods. Breeds in damp parts of spruce and fir forests. Vagrant from N. America to W. (including Britain), C., N. and S. Europe.

RING OUZEL *Turdus torquatus* **Pl. 61**
Du – Beflijster   Fr – Merle à plastron
Ge – Ringdrossel   Sw – Ringtrast

Identification: 9½″. Unmistakable. Male has uniform dull black plumage, with a *broad white crescent* across breast; winter plumage has light feather edges, giving 'scaly' appearance. Female is browner, with narrower, duller crescent. Juvenile has no crescent and looks like very spotty young Blackbird. Flight rapid, dodging behind rocks when approached. Distinguished from occasional pied Blackbird by *grey patch on closed wing-feathers*.

Voice: A clear, piping '*pee-u*', and a scolding Blackbird-like '*shek-shek-shek*'.

Song, a few double or treble notes, '*tcheru*', '*tchivi*', '*ti-cho-o*', etc., repeated 3– times, between pauses, interspersed with chuckling notes.
Habitat: Hilly moorlands and mountains, usually above 1,000 ft. Breed among heather, juniper, rocks, often by track or stream; also within tree lim. on Continent. Map 256.

BLACKBIRD   *Turdus merula*   **Pl. 61**
Du – Merel   Fr – Merle noir
Ge – Amsel   Sw – Koltrast
Identification: 10″. Male, a sturdy *all-black* bird, with *bright orange-yellow bil and eye-rim*. Female is uniform dark brown above, paler brown below, with speckled whitish chin and brown bill. Juvenile more rufous and more mottled Immature male brownish black with blackish bill. Occasional part-albino males distinguished from Ring Ouzel by lack of pale wing-patch and by difference in voice. Feeds on ground. Tail is raised and fanned and wings drooped on alighting.
Voice: A screeching chatter, when flushed; a persistent mobbing note '*tchink tchink, tchink*'; an anxious '*tchook*'; a thin '*tsee*', etc. Song, a deliberate, loud and melodious warbling, easily distinguished from Song Thrush's by purer, fluty notes, *lack of repetitive habit* and characteristic 'collapse' into weak unmusical ending.
Habitat: Woodlands, hedges, gardens, bushy commons, etc. Nests in hedges, wood-piles, sheds, etc. Map 257.

EYEBROWED THRUSH   *Turdus obscurus*   **Pl. 61**
Du – Vale lijster   Fr – Grive obscure
Ge – Weissbrauendrossel   Sw – Vitbrynad trast
Identification: 7½″. Look for combination of *grey* upper breast and *orange-buff* sides of breast and flanks. Olive-brown upper-parts with greyish crown, *conspicuous white stripe above eye* and a wide white patch below eye to chin. Female is duller. Has simple song of 2–3 thrush-like phrases. Vagrant from Siberia to E., C., W. (including Britain), N. and S. Europe.

DUSKY THRUSH   *Turdus naumanni eunomus*   **Pl. 61**
Du – Bruine lijster   Fr – Grive à ailes rousses
Ge – Rostflügeldrossel   Sw – Sibirisk rödvingetrast
Identification: 9″. Distinguished from commoner European thrushes by *two blackish breast-bands* (the lower incomplete). Flanks have black crescentic markings in winter. Heavy bill. *Conspicuous whitish supercilium.* Broad chestnut areas on *upper and lower* surfaces of wings and rump. Distinguished from Redwing by larger size, blackish breast and flanks and chestnut on upper surfaces of wings; from Naumann's (with which it is conspecific) by blackish instead of chestnut on breast and flanks and blackish instead of chestnut tail. Has grating calls '*spirr*' and '*kvevy*'. Vagrant from Asia to C., W. (including Britain), N. and S. Europe.

NAUMANN'S THRUSH   *Turdus naumanni naumanni*   **Pl. 61**
Du – Naumann's lijster   Fr – Grive de Naumann
Ge – Naumannsdrossel   Sw – Naumanns trast
Identification: 9″. Naumann's and Dusky Thrushes probably interbreed, and are conspecific. Naumann's is distinguished by *chestnut* instead of blackish, on

breast, flanks and tail. Male has grey-brown upper-parts with *chestnut on wings*. Female is browner above, much paler below, with blackish spots on breast and flanks. Has short descending song ending with a weak twitter. Vagrant from Asia to E., C., W. (including Britain), N. and S. Europe.

BLACK-THROATED THRUSH   *Turdus ruficollis atrogularis*   Pl. 61
Du – Zwartkeellijster   Fr – Grive à gorge noire
Ge – Schwarzkehldrossel   Sw – Svarthalsad trast

Identification: 9¼″. Male has striking *black face, throat and breast* (partly obscured by pale fringes in winter), contrasting with whitish under-parts; upper-parts grey-brown. Female browner above, with whitish throat and breast closely spotted or streaked with black. In flight shows rusty-buff beneath wings. Behaviour and shape like Fieldfare. Eastern form, Red-throated Thrush *T. r. ruficollis*, has black throat of *T. r. atrogularis* replaced by brick-red. Both are gregarious in winter.
Voice: Usual note resembles chuckling Blackbird alarm. Bold, short song recalls Song Thrush.
Habitat and Range: Winters in flocks in open country, lower mountain slopes and sheltered areas near cultivation. Vagrant from Asia and Russia to E., C., W. (including Britain), N. and S. Europe.

FIELDFARE   *Turdus pilaris*   Pl. 61
Du – Kramsvogel   Fr – Grive litorne
Ge – Wacholderdrossel   Sw – Björktrast

Identification: 10″. Slightly smaller than Mistle Thrush, much larger than Song Thrush and Redwing. Distinguished by *pale grey head and rump, chestnut back* and almost black tail. Throat and breast rusty-yellow, streaked with black, flanks heavily mottled with black. In flight, blue-grey rump, flashing white beneath wings and flight-call are distinctive. Flight less undulating than Mistle Thrush's. Has alert, upright attitude on ground. Gregarious.
Voice: A harsh, chattering '*tchak-tchak-tchak*' and a quiet '*see*'. Song, a rapid mixture of feeble squeaking, chuckling notes, frequently in flight.
Habitat: Winters in open country, seeking food in fields and along hedges. Breeds usually colonially near clearings or margins of woods, particularly in birch, occasionally on buildings and haystacks; on ground above tree limit. Map 258.

SONG THRUSH   *Turdus philomelos*   Pl. 61
Du – Zanglijster   Fr – Grive musicienne
Ge – Singdrossel   Sw – Taltrast

Identification: 9″. A brown-backed bird, with a spotted breast. Distinguished from Mistle Thrush and Fieldfare by much smaller size, uniform *brown* upper-parts and yellowish-buff breast and flanks with *small spots*; from Redwing by lack of chestnut on flanks and beneath wings and lack of prominent supercilium. Shows *buff* beneath wings. Often feeds on open ground, running spasmodically.
Voice: A loud '*tchuck*', or '*tchick*', repeated rapidly as alarm; flight-call a soft '*sip*' (shorter than Redwing's call). Song loud and musical, the short, varied phrases *repeated 2–4 times*, between brief pauses.

Habitat: Around human habitation, parks, woods and hedges. Nests in bushes, hedges, ivy, etc., occasionally in buildings. Map 259.

REDWING   *Turdus iliacus*   **Pl. 6**
   Du – Koperwiek   Fr – Grive mauvis
   Ge – Rotdrossel   Sw – Rödvingetrast
Identification: 8¼″. Smallest common thrush. Resembles Song Thrush, but distinguished by *conspicuous creamy supercilium*, rich *chestnut* flanks, *streaked* (not spotted) breast and flanks and, in flight, by *chestnut* (not buff) beneath wings. Gregarious, roaming countryside with Fieldfares in winter. See also rare Dusky Thrush.
Voice: Distinctive note (often during night migration) a thin '*see-ip*'; also a harsh '*chittuc*'. Song varies greatly locally; a repeated phrase of 4–6 fluty notes rising and falling, typically '*trui-trui-trui-troo-tri*', followed by a weak, warbling subsong.
Habitat: Winters in open country and light woods. Nests on tree stumps, wood-stacks, in trees or bushes, on ground, etc., in light woods, marshy localities, often on edges of Fieldfare colonies. Map 260.

MISTLE THRUSH   *Turdus viscivorus*   **Pl. 6**
   Du – Grote lijster   Fr – Grive draine
   Ge – Misteldrossel   Sw – Dubbeltrast
Identification: 10½″. Distinguished from much smaller Song Thrush and Redwing by *greyish-brown upper-parts, closely spotted under-parts* and *more upright stance*, with raised head. Shows white beneath wings in flight, like Fieldfare, but readily distinguished from it by *greyish* instead of chestnut back, brownish-grey instead of blue-grey rump, *buffish-white* instead of rusty breast and longer, *paler tail* with whitish tips to outer feathers. Behaviour shy. Strong flight like Fieldfare's, but with longer, more regular wing closures. Juvenile strongly spotted above and can be confused with rare White's Thrush.
Voice: A dry, rasping chatter and a hard '*tuc-tuc-tuc*'. Song is loud, somewhat Blackbird-like, but lacks mellowness and variety, repeating short, rather similar phrases. Sings in all weathers, from tree-tops.
Habitat: Large gardens, orchards, woods. Nests in bare fork in tree. Small flocks roam open country and fields in autumn. Map 261.

AMERICAN ROBIN   *Turdus migratorius*   **Pl. 6**
   Du – Roodborstlijster   Fr – Merle migrateur
   Ge – Wanderdrossel   Sw – Vandringstrast
Identification: 10″. Has character of Blackbird, but with *uniform brick-red breast*, dark grey head and back, *bold white markings around eye* and white tips to outer tail-feathers. Chin white, streaked with black. Bill yellow. Sexes similar, but male has blacker head. See also Naumann's, Red-throated and Eyebrowed Thrushes.
Voice: Harsh, scolding call-notes are typically thrush-like. Song, loud, clear 2–3-note phrases.
Habitat and Range: Woodlands and thickets, often seeking human habitation. Vagrant from N. America to W. (including Britain), N., C. and S. Europe.

WARBLERS: Sylviidae

Warblers are small, active, insectivorous birds, with slender bills. Many confusingly devoid of distinctive markings; plumages wear rapidly, adding to difficulty in identification. Call-notes often rather similar. Voices and behaviour diagnostically important. Usually nest in low vegetation on or near ground, or (in *Acrocephalus*) in reeds. Sexes similar, except in *Sylvia*. For convenience can be divided into four groups: swamp warblers, tree warblers, scrub warblers and leaf warblers. Goldcrests are minute, olive-green arboreal birds, somewhat akin in behaviour to small tits and leaf warblers. Adults have brilliant streak of colour on crown. Sexes nearly similar. Tree-nesting.

CETTI'S WARBLER *Cettia cetti*   Pl. 62
Du – Cetti's zanger   Fr – Bouscarle de Cetti
Ge – Seidensänger   Sw – Cettisångare
Identification: 5½″. Skulking habits make sight identification difficult, but *song is unmistakable*. Upper-parts *dark rufous-brown*, short supercilium, under-parts greyish-white with browner flanks and barred under tail-coverts. Tail full and strongly rounded. Rather rufous appearance may cause confusion with Nightingale, but latter is larger, with longer tail more rufous than upper-parts. Tail often cocked.
Voice: A loud '*chee*', a short '*twic*', a soft '*huit*', and a churring alarm. Song, a very loud, abrupt burst, chiefly a repetition of '*settee*' or '*cheweeoo*' with varying emphasis. Sings from dense vegetation.
Habitat: Low, tangled vegetation, usually near water, ditches, swamps, reed-beds. Nest well hidden in low vegetation. Map 262.

FAN-TAILED WARBLER *Cisticola juncidis*   Pl. 62
Du – Waaierstaartrietzanger   Fr – Cisticole des joncs
Ge – Cistensänger   Sw – Grässångare
Identification: 4″. During breeding season is most easily seen in display-flight, when *distinctive voice* is unmistakable; otherwise skulking. Suggests small, bright Sedge Warbler. Distinguished by *lack of pale eye-stripe* and much smaller size (the smallest European warbler) and *stubby tail*. Upper-parts dark brown, with broad reddish-buff margins and rufous rump, giving heavily streaked buffish impression; throat and under-parts unstreaked whitish, tinged with rufous-buff on breast and flanks; tail short and well rounded, with black and white tips to outer feathers.
Voice: Song a sharp, high, rasping '*dzeep . . . dzeep . . . dzeep . . .*', corresponding with each rise in weak, undulating flight, well up in the air. Call-note '*tew*'.
Habitat: Wet and dry localities, grain fields, rough grassy plains, marshes. Builds deep purse-shaped nest suspended in rushes, long grass, growing corn, or dense undergrowth. Map 263.

PALLAS'S GRASSHOPPER WARBLER *Locustella certhiola* Pl. 65
Du – Siberische snor   Fr – Locustelle de Pallas
Ge – Streifenschwirl   Sw – Starrsångare
Identification: 5¼″. Has skulking character of Grasshopper Warbler, often running on the ground. Plumage recalls Sedge, but with more *marked contrast*

between light and dark areas. Has similar broad whitish supercilium, but crown is darker and forehead much paler; throat and upper breast very white, forming *distinct gorget*; under-parts unmarked greyish-buff with white beneath tail. Grey-buff upper back gives *contrasting pale 'shawl' effect*. Whitish edges to dark-centred wing feathers give chequered impression. Dark spot on wing visible in flight. Bill dark, legs pinkish. Immature has yellow breast and flanks, with faint breast-band of indistinct spots.

Voice: Winter note described as '*chir-chirr*'. Song more like an *Acrocephalus* than a *Locustella*: opens with two notes followed by harsh chattering, ends with a musical trio.

Habitat and Range: Damp meadows with long grass and in rank undergrowth. Winters in rice fields, reeds, swamps. Vagrant from C. Asia, Siberia to C. and W. Europe (including Britain).

LANCEOLATED WARBLER *Locustella lanceolata*   **Pl. 65**
   Du – Temminck's rietzanger   Fr – Locustelle lancéolée
   Ge – Strichelschwirl   Sw – Träsksångare
Identification: 4½". Resembles small Grasshopper Warbler, but is more heavily streaked above, particularly on the brown mantle. Best field mark is the *well-defined gorget of close, parallel streaking on the upper-breast, below the whitish chin and throat*. Indistinct buffish-white streak through eye. Bill dark brown above, pale flesh below; legs pinkish. Behaviour very skulking.

Voice: Winter note described as '*chir-chirr*', resembling Pallas's Grasshopper Warbler. Song resembles Grasshopper but is sharper, slightly lower.

Habitat and Range: Rank vegetation and reeds bordering water, wet meadows and overgrown marshes. Vagrant from NE Russia, Asia to N., C., W. (including Britain) and S. Europe.

GRASSHOPPER WARBLER *Locustella naevia*   **Pl. 62**
   Du – Sprinkhaanrietzanger   Fr – Locustelle tachetée
   Ge – Feldschwirl   Sw – Gräshoppsångare
Identification: 5". Very skulking. Usually identified by *distinctive song*. Upper-parts olive-brown (can be yellowish) *with subdued dark streaking*; less streaked on rump; lightly streaked buffish-white under-parts; well-rounded, faintly barred tail; legs pinkish, variable. Creeps and runs with great agility among undergrowth, but reluctant to fly.

Voice: A short '*twhit*', or '*pitt*', merging into a chatter when alarmed. Far-carrying song is a 'mechanical' churring on one high note, like winding an angler's reel, often for more than two minutes; ventriloquial effect obtained by turning head. Sings day or night. See also Savi's and Lanceolated.

Habitat: Undergrowth in marshes, water-meadows, dry heaths, hedgerows, etc. Nest well concealed on or near ground in long grass, rushes, undergrowth. Map 264.

RIVER WARBLER *Locustella fluviatilis*   **Pl. 62**
   Du – Krekelzanger   Fr – Locustelle fluviatile
   Ge – Schlagschwirl   Sw – Flodsångare
Identification: 5". Distinguished from Grasshopper Warbler by *unstreaked*, dark earth-brown upper-parts; whitish under-parts with faint blurred brown streaking on upper breast; tail shorter, full and rounded, with slightly rufous coverts. Legs pinkish. Juvenile has only faint streaks on throat, more rufous

upper-parts and buffish-white under-parts. Very secretive behaviour and reluctant flight as in Grasshopper Warbler, but differs in song and habitat.

Voice: Has low, harsh call-note. Song recalls Grasshopper Warbler's, but notes are softer and *slower*, with rhythmic 'chuffing' quality, like distant steam-engine running at high speed; ends with 4–5 quiet *'zwee'* notes. Often sings from exposed bush-tops under trees.

Habitat: Moist localities, also often in woodland thickets, or tangled herbage and bramble patches in open ground, or in forest glades, including pine. Nests on or close to ground, in moist undergrowth. Map 265.

SAVI'S WARBLER *Locustella luscinioides* **Pl. 62**
Du – Snor   Fr – Locustelle luscinioïde
Ge – Rohrschwirl   Sw – Vassångare

Identification: 5½″. Superficially resembles large Reed Warbler, but identified by Grasshopper Warbler-like song. Tail broad and well graduated, often faintly barred. Upper-parts *unstreaked* dark reddish-brown; under-parts brownish-white with slightly rufous-brown flanks. Short indistinct buffish supercilium. Distinguished from Grasshopper Warbler by *uniform* plumage; from River Warbler by *unstreaked* breast; from both by distinctive song and larger size. Much less skulking than Grasshopper Warbler, but also runs, mouse-like, through vegetation, with nervous twitching of wings and tail.

Voice: A quiet, persistent *'tswik'* and a scolding chatter. Song very like Grasshopper Warbler's reeling trill, but lower, usually briefer and can be confused with noise made by Bush Cricket. Often preceded by low ticking notes which accelerate until they merge into the typical reeling. Sings from reed-top.

Habitat: Swamps, with wet *Phragmites* reed-beds. Nest well concealed among thick tangle of dead reeds and sedges. Map 266.

MOUSTACHED WARBLER *Acrocephalus melanopogon* **Pl. 62**
Du – Zwartkoprietzanger   Fr – Lusciniole à moustaches
Ge – Tamariskensänger   Sw – Tamarisksångare

Identification: 5″. Distinguished with difficulty from Sedge Warbler by *almost black crown*, contrasting with *whiter supercilium* ending squarely at nape, *dark brown cheeks*, very white throat. Nape and mantle *rustier* than Sedge. Often has *perky habit of cocking its rather short, rounded tail*, but behaviour rather skulking.

Voice: A soft but penetrating *'t-trrt'* and a harsher *'tac-tac-tac'*, which runs into a scolding rattle of alarm. Song recalls Reed Warbler but more varied, including crescendo of clear notes recalling Nightingale.

Habitat: Reed-beds and swamps. Nests in reeds or low bushes above shallow water. Map 267.

AQUATIC WARBLER *Acrocephalus paludicola* **Pl. 62**
Du – Waterrietzanger   Fr – Phragmite aquatique
Ge – Seggenrohrsänger   Sw – Vattensångare

Identification: 5″. Looks like sandy Sedge Warbler, but distinguished by *boldly striped head*. Has *long buff* (instead of whitish) supercilium extending to nape and *conspicuous buff stripe down centre of crown*; prominent black streaks on back, extending less strongly *to rump*; in summer has thin, sparse streaks on breast and flanks. Legs orange-yellow (Sedge's are greyish). Distinguished from

all other *Acrocephalus* and from Moustached Warbler by crown-stripe and
streaked rusty rump. More skulking than Sedge Warbler. Often feeds on
ground. Beware similarity to young Sedge.
Voice: Harsh churring similar to Sedge. Song also rather similar, but less
varied, without mimicry and including a piping '*dee-dee-dee*'.
Habitat: As Sedge Warbler, but prefers open marshes with low vegetation
sedge, etc. Nests near ground. Map 268.

SEDGE WARBLER *Acrocephalus schoenobaenus*   Pl. 6.

Du – Rietzanger   Fr – Phragmite des joncs
Ge – Schilfrohrsänger   Sw – Sävsångare

Identification: 5″. Distinguished from Reed Warbler by *conspicuous whitish
supercilium, boldly streaked upper-parts* except for *unstreaked* tawny rump
Under-parts creamy, with rufous flanks. Adult crown can be very dark, causing
confusion with Moustached. Tail rather pointed. Juvenile yellower, especially
on rump, with faint spots on throat and upper-breast, and a streaked cream
stripe on crown; these features can cause confusion with Aquatic Warbler
Flight and behaviour like Reed Warbler. See also Aquatic and Moustached
Other *Acrocephalus* (Reed Warbler, etc.) have unstreaked upper-parts.
Voice: An explosive '*tuc*', becoming a stuttering rattle when excited; also
harsh churring. Song *more varied* than Reed Warbler's, a loud, rapid sequence
of repeated musical and harsh chattering notes, mingled with long trills and
mimicry. Sings from perch and in short, vertical display flight.
Habitat: Reed-beds and lush vegetation near water, swampy thickets, crops
Builds untidy nest in low, dense vegetation. Map 269.

BLYTH'S REED WARBLER *Acrocephalus dumetorum*   Pl. 6!

Du – Blyth's kleine karekiet   Fr – Rousserolle des buissons
Ge – Buschrohrsänger   Sw – Busksångare

Identification: 5″. Identification difficult, but in fresh plumage has greyer tone
than Reed or Marsh. See also very similar Paddyfield Warbler (Accidentals)
Bill noticeably long and supercilium very indistinct. Short, round wing
exaggerate tail length. Identified with certainty in the hand by wing formula (see
line drawing). Song, day and night, usually from tree, recalls Marsh Warbler's
but is exceptionally long, loud, varied and musical, with phrases repeated 3–8
times. Habitat like Reed. Summer visitor, breeding S. Finland, Estonia, and
Latvia; often singing Sweden. Vagrant C. and W. Europe (including Britain)

MARSH WARBLER *Acrocephalus palustris*   Pl. 6?

Du – Bosrietzanger   Fr – Rousserolle verderolle
Ge – Sumpfrohrsänger   Sw – Kärrsångare

Identification: 5″. Marsh, Reed and Blyth's Reed are easily confused and racial
plumages can vary. Marsh in spring is best distinguished from Reed by its
remarkably musical and varied song; by its slightly shorter and stouter bill; its
more rounded forehead (Reed's is flatter) and its *pale*, flesh-brown legs (Reed's
are darker). Supercilium and eye-ring usually more prominent than Reed's. In
autumn Marsh usually looks greyer-brown, lacking the Reed's more rufous
upper-parts and rump. Can be distinguished from Blyth's Reed by more
distinct supercilium, more olive (less grey) upper-parts, shorter, stouter bill
paler legs and longer wings. See line drawing for differences in wing formula

Voice: A loud, repeated 'tchuc', a quiet 'tuc', a stuttering 'tic-tirric', 'tweek', etc. Song exceptionally musical and varied, with canary-like trills and a wide range of mimicry interspersed with Reed Warbler-like chirrups and a distinctive nasal note 'zaawee'.

Habitat: Dense, low vegetation in ditches, thickets, stream banks, osier-beds, crops, often near water. Builds untidy nest, supported by 'handles' woven around low vegetation. Map 270.

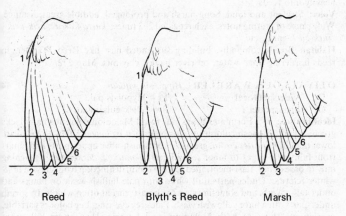

Reed   Blyth's Reed   Marsh

Wing Formulae

Note comparative length of second primary and also depth of notch on inner web

REED WARBLER *Acrocephalus scirpaceus*   Pl. 62

Du – Kleine karekiet	Fr – Rousserolle effarvatte
Ge – Teichrohrsänger	Sw – Rörsångare

Identification: 5″. Uniform brown above, slightly rufous on rump. Whitish below, with buffish under tail-coverts. Leg colour variable, but usually pale brown or greyish flesh. Distinguished from Sedge Warbler by *unstreaked* head and back and very *indistinct* supercilium. Great Reed Warbler is much larger. Very difficult to distinguish from Marsh Warbler (except by voice), but is generally rustier-brown, with longer, finer bill, darker legs and flatter forehead; in autumn juveniles look identical. Rounded tail is spread and depressed during brief flights over water. See also Blyth's Reed Warbler, and Paddyfield Warbler (Accidentals). Line drawing shows wing formula.

Voice: A low 'churr', a harsh 'skurr' of alarm (very like Sedge's), and a weak ticking note. Prolonged song resembles Sedge's, but distinguished by tendency to repeat phrases 2–3 times: 'chirruc-chirruc', 'jag-jag-jag', etc., interspersed with liquid notes and mimicry. Sings day and night.

Habitat: Reed-beds and waterside vegetation; in parts of Europe also found in cultivated land away from water. Breeds colonially, suspending nest in reeds or bushes. Map 271.

GREAT REED WARBLER *Acrocephalus arundinaceus*   **Pl. 62**
Du – Grote karekiet   Fr – Rousserolle turdoïde
Ge – Drosselrohrsänger   Sw – Trastsångare
Identification: 7½″. Easily distinguished from Reed Warbler by *much larger size*, *angular head, longer, much stouter bill, usually bold supercilium* and *strident voice*. Coloration like Reed Warbler. Behaviour less skulking: perches freely on trees or telegraph wires. Flight low, with characteristically spread tail, plunging heavily into reeds.
Voice: Strident and loud. Song harsh and prolonged, audible great distance. Wide range of grating notes, each repeated 2–3 times: '*karra-karra*', '*krik-krik*', '*gurk-gurk-gurk*', etc.
Habitat: Breeds colonially, building suspended nest like Reed Warbler, in reeds bordering open water, on river banks, clay-pits. Map 272.

OLIVACEOUS WARBLER *Hippolais pallida*   **Pl. 64**
Du – Vale spotvogel   Fr – Hypolaïs pâle
Ge – Blassspötter   Sw – Blek gulsångare
Identification: 5¼″. Form and behaviour recall Melodious, but normally lacks greenish and yellowish coloration. Distinguished by *longer bill*, with *yellowish* lower mandible, *flatter crown*, greyish or brownish-olive upper-parts and (apart from faint pale edges to inner secondaries) *unmarked, darker wings* reaching only to base of tail. Last-mentioned feature useful distinction from greyish first-winter Icterine. Under-parts dull white with pale buffish wash on flanks and under tail-coverts and sometimes across breast; throat often whiter. In spring under-parts often have yellowish wash. Pale grey eye-ring. Leg colours variable, overlapping those of both Melodious and Icterine. Has longer bill, more prominent supercilium and flatter crown than Garden Warbler.
Voice: Call-note similar to Icterine's '*tec, tec*'. Alarm, a quiet ticking. Vigorous song consists of a repeated phrase of rapid, babbling notes.
Habitat: Cultivated areas and gardens, with trees and bushes. Nests in bushes, hedges, etc., but sometimes in palm trees. Map 273.

BOOTED WARBLER *Hippolais caligata*   **Pl. 65**
Du – Russische spotvogel   Fr – Hippolaïs russe
Ge – Buschspötter   Sw – Liten gulsångare
Identification: 4½″. A rather nondescript, active, but cover-loving little warbler resembling a *small* Olivaceous, but with a shorter, finer bill and slightly more rounded head. Has rudimentary supercilium extending in front of and behind eye, sometimes also an indistinct dark eye-stripe suggesting a *Phylloscopus*. Shows whitish outer tail-feathers in flight. Under-parts in summer more buffish than Olivaceous, but these look silvery-grey in winter.
Voice: Song, a mixture of babbling and chirruping interspersed with '*shrek-shrek*' notes. Has quiet ticking call-note.
Habitat and Range: Usually in bushy regions or cultivation, locally in semi-desert scrub. Vagrant from Russia, W. Asia to E., N., C. and W. Europe (including Britain).

OLIVE-TREE WARBLER *Hippolais olivetorum*   **Pl. 64**
Du – Griekse spotvogel   Fr – Hypolaïs des oliviers
Ge – Olivenspötter   Sw – Olivgulsångare
Identification: 6″. A large *greyish* warbler with strikingly big, *dagger-like bill*.

yellowish at base. *Bold whitish edges to secondaries* give streaky effect to closed wing. Primaries and tail darker grey-brown. Legs bluish-grey. Crown has peaked appearance at rear. Pale supercilium extends behind eye. Big bill, wing markings and larger size and longer wings easily distinguish it from Olivaceous.
Voice: Call-note '*tuc*'. Distinctive song is louder, *slower*, more contralto and more 'scratchy' than other *Hippolais* warblers.
Habitat: Frequents thorn scrub, olive and oak woods, keeping well out of sight. Nests in fork of branch. Map 274.

ICTERINE WARBLER   *Hippolais icterina*   **Pl. 64**
   Du – Spotvogel   Fr – Hypolaïs ictérine
   Ge – Gelbspötter   Sw – Gulsångare
Identification: 5¼″. A stout, perky, green and yellow warbler. Distinguished with difficulty from Melodious by usually brighter greenish-olive upper-parts (often with yellowish wash), *peaked* rather than rounded crown, *longer, more pointed wings projecting well beyond base of tail*. Except in worn autumn plumage, edges of inner secondaries form *distinct pale patch on folded wing* (whitish in immature, yellowish in adult). Some adults lack yellow below and are often greyer above. Immature greyer and more 'washed-out' than immature Melodious. Legs vary from blue-grey to bluish-black. Bill rather broad and large with dark upper and pinkish lower mandibles. *Voice and range* differ from Melodious.
Voice: A Blackcap-like '*tec*', a characteristic, musical '*deederoid*', a Chiffchaff-like '*hooeet*', and a low churring alarm. Song recalls Marsh Warbler's, a loud, remarkably long-sustained and varied jumble of melodious *and discordant* notes, each *repeated* several times, interspersed with jarring notes.
Habitat: Gardens, parks and cultivated land, but also found in woods, thickets and hedges. Builds snug nest in shrubs, hedges, etc. Map 275.

MELODIOUS WARBLER   *Hippolais polyglotta*   **Pl. 64**
   Du – Orpheusspotvogel   Fr – Hypolaïs polyglotte
   Ge – Orpheusspötter   Sw – Polyglottgulsångare
Identification: 5″. Difficult to distinguish in the field from Icterine except by *voice*. Is slightly smaller, with browner or duller upper-parts, notably on rump. Has distinctly *rounded* crown and *shorter, more rounded wings which do not project beyond base of tail*. In breeding season many adults have yellow wing-patch, but less prominent than Icterine's; browner immature birds lack this. Legs vary from brownish-flesh to blue-grey, but are *usually browner* than Icterine's. Bill colour as in Icterine. Under-parts variable, but usually deeper yellow than Icterine's; some adults and immatures lack yellow and are browner above. Both species and the Olivaceous lack eye-stripe or supercilium, giving featureless face which assists separation from any similar *Acrocephalus* or *Phylloscopus* warblers. Garden Warbler has shorter, thicker bill and lacks any yellow plumage.
Voice: A House Sparrow-like chatter, a Chiffchaff-like '*hooeet*' and an abrupt '*tit, tit*'. Song, often beginning slowly, is a *prolonged*, musical and very varied babbling, more hurried and less harsh than song of Icterine; often introduces sparrow-like chirping notes and mimicry but with litttle repetition.
Habitat: Similar to Icterine, but more often in lush vegetation near water. Builds snug nest in bushes, rarely in trees. Map 276.

MARMORA'S WARBLER   *Sylvia sarda*   **Pl. 63**
   Du – Sardijnse grasmus   Fr – Fauvette sarde
   Ge – Sardengrasmücke   Sw – Sardinisk sångare
Identification: 4¾″. Looks almost black at a distance. Size and shape of
Dartford Warbler, but distinguished by *slate-grey* instead of purplish-brown
throat and under-parts. Upper-parts dark slate-grey, with *almost black head*
wings and tail; belly brownish-white; tail slightly shorter than Dartford's; eye-
ring red. Female slightly browner. Juvenile is paler and greyer above and much
whiter below than young Dartford. Behaviour and habitat as Dartford. See
also Sardinian.
Voice: A single sharp '*tzig*'. Song like Dartford's, but phrases are shorter and
faster.
Range: Resident E. coast of Spain, W. Mediterranean islands, perhaps Sicily

DARTFORD WARBLER   *Sylvia undata*   **Pl. 63**
   Du – Provence-grasmus   Fr – Fauvette pitchou
   Ge – Provencegrasmücke   Sw – Provencesångare
Identification: 5″. Identified by *very dark plumage and long, constantly cocked or*
fanned tail. Male has slate-grey head (with characteristically raised crown
feathers), shading to *dark brown* upper-parts; under-parts *dark purplish-brown*
chin and throat spotted with white in autumn; tail graduated, dark brown with
white border. Eye-ring ruby-red. Behaviour skulking. Flight weak, with
characteristic 'bobbing' action of tail and rapidly whirring wings. See also
Subalpine and Marmora's.
Voice: A scolding metallic '*tchir-r*', a short '*tuc*', '*tchir-r-tuc-tuc*', also a rattling
alarm. Song, a short musical chatter, often in dancing flight, interspersed with
liquid notes, recalling Whitethroat, but more pleasing.
Habitat: Open commons with heather and gorse, dwarf oak, cistus-covered
hillsides, etc. Nests in scrub near ground. Map 277.

SPECTACLED WARBLER   *Sylvia conspicillata*   **Pl. 63**
   Du – Brilgrasmus   Fr – Fauvette à lunettes
   Ge – Brillengrasmücke   Sw – Glasögonsångare
Identification: 5″. Resembles small Whitethroat and also has bright rusty
wings, but *white throat contrasts more strongly with dark head and pinkish-brown*
breast. Narrow white eye-rim not very good field mark. Strikingly pale *straw-*
coloured legs. Crown slate-grey, lores and ear-coverts darker; upper-parts
brown. Juvenile is browner, without grey on head and with more buffish-white
under-parts. Actions recall Whitethroat. Often cocks tail, showing white outer
feathers.
Voice: Song is short and Subalpine-like, but phrases vary in length and begin
with musical, fluty notes; sings from exposed perch, or in dancing song-flight.
Alarm, a characteristic but subdued Wren-like rattle.
Habitat: Chiefly in *Salicornia* on coastal flats and (often with Dartford
Warbler) in low scrub. Nests in low bush. Map 278.

SUBALPINE WARBLER   *Sylvia cantillans*   **Pl. 63**
   Du – Baardgrasmus   Fr – Fauvette passerinette
   Ge – Weissbartgrasmücke   Sw – Rödstrupig sångare
Identification: 4¾″. Distinguished from Dartford, which has similar form and
with which it often occurs, by much paler ash-blue upper-parts, unspotted

throat, and conspicuous white outer feathers of dark rounded tail. Male has *very narrow white moustachial stripe* contrasting with pinkish-chestnut throat and breast. Female and juvenile duller and paler, buffish-pink below, with much fainter moustachial stripes. Eyes appear red at close quarters. Behaviour like Dartford's, raising and spreading tail when excited, but tail is shorter. See also Spectacled.

Voice: A hard but quiet '*tec, tec*', and a quick, chattering alarm. Song recalls Sardinian and Whitethroat, but is more pleasing, slower and lacking hard scolding notes. Sings from bushes and during brief, dancing song-flight.

Habitat: Low bushes and thickets, often with scattered trees; also in open woodland glades and along stream banks. Nests in thick bushes. Map 279.

SARDINIAN WARBLER   *Sylvia melanocephala*   Pl. 63

Du – Kleine zwartkop   Fr – Fauvette mélanocéphale
Ge – Samtkopfgrasmücke   Sw – Sammetshätta

Identification: 5¼″. Male distinguished by *black cap extending well below eye*, pure white throat, grey upper-parts, whitish under-parts *with grey sides. Bright reddish eye-ring* is conspicuous. Frequently cocked, blackish, graduated tail has bold white outer feathers. Female much browner, with grey-brown cap scarcely darker than back. Bobbing flight and restless behaviour recall Whitethroat. See also Marmora's, Orphean, Blackcap and Rüppell's.

Voice: Has loud, staccato alarm-note, '*cha-cha-cha-cha*', like rapidly wound wooden rattle; also '*treek, treek*'. Song, a rapid gabble of harsh and quite musical notes interspersed with staccato alarm-note. Sings from exposed or hidden perches and in brief, dancing display-flight.

Habitat: Dry, fairly open bushy scrub, thickets, pine and evergreen oak woods, etc. Nests in low bushes and undergrowth. Map 280.

RÜPPELL'S WARBLER   *Sylvia rueppelli*   Pl. 63

Du – Rüppell's grasmus   Fr – Fauvette masquée
Ge – Maskengrasmücke   Sw – Svarthakad sångare

Identification: 5½″. Male has *black crown, face and throat, with conspicuous white moustachial stripe*, grey upper-parts, whitish under-parts, black tail with *bold white outer feathers*. Female duller, with pale or dusky throat, but white moustachial stripe still fairly visible. Eyes and legs brilliant red-brown. Male distinguished from Sardinian by *black throat*, and *white 'moustache'*.

Voice: Very easily confused with the Sardinian, though usually louder. Has same rattling alarm-note, but song tends to be shorter, less musical, interrupted by harsh buzzing and rattling notes.

Habitat and Range: Breeds in bushes among low scrub with rocky outcrops. Summer visitor, breeding Aegean region. Vagrant elsewhere in S., E., N. and W. Europe (including Britain).

ORPHEAN WARBLER   *Sylvia hortensis*   Pl. 63

Du – Orpheusgrasmus   Fr – Fauvette orphée
Ge – Orpheusgrasmücke   Sw – Mästersångare

Identification: 6″. Resembles large male Blackcap, but easily separated by *white in outer tail-feathers*; dull, blackish cap *extending clearly below the eye* and merging into grey mantle instead of being clean-cut; also by *white*, instead of grey, throat. Female slightly browner. Eyes are *distinctive pale straw*. Distinguished from Sardinian by much larger size, pale eyes, dull instead of clean-

cut glossy black cap, and different habitat. Immature can be confused with young Barred, but tail is shorter and upper tail-coverts lack light tips.
Voice: A Blackcap-like '*tac, tac*', or '*tyut, tyut*', and a loud, rattling alarm. Song, a loud, mellow, *thrush-like* musical warble, each phrase usually repeated 4–5 times, with few discordant notes.
Habitat: Chiefly arboreal. Wooded districts, orchards, scrub, citrus and olive groves. Nests in bushes, low branches. Map 281.

BARRED WARBLER   *Sylvia nisoria*   Pl. 63
   Du – Gestreepte grasmus   Fr – Fauvette épervière
   Ge – Sperbergrasmücke   Sw – Höksångare
Identification: 6″. Distinguished by whitish under-parts *barred with dark, crescent-shaped markings*, much less distinct in female. Male is ashy grey-brown above, female browner. Dark brown wings have *two whitish bars*. Rather long tail shows some white in outer feathers. Adults have *bright yellow eyes*. Juvenile has slightly buffish under-parts with little or no bars; distinguished from Garden Warbler by greyer appearance, wing-bars and larger size. Appearance is heavy, with stout legs and bill. Behaviour skulking, tail often flicked.
Voice: A hard '*tchack*', a low churring and a distinctive, grating '*tcharr, tcharr*', which also occurs in song. Song resembles Blackcap's in richness and purity, but some more rapid and *briefer harsh phrases* recall Whitethroat.
Habitat: Thorny thickets, bushy commons and hedges, clearings in woods, etc. Usually nests in thorn bushes. Map 282.

LESSER WHITETHROAT   *Sylvia curruca*   Pl. 63
   Du – Braamsluiper   Fr – Fauvette babillarde
   Ge – Klappergrasmücke   Sw – Ärtsångare
Identification: 5¼″. Distinguished from Whitethroat by *shorter tail, much greyer upper-parts, dark ear-coverts* (giving masked appearance), *lack of chestnut on wings* and distinctive song. More skulking than Whitethroat. See also Rüppell's and Sardinian Warblers.
Voice: Call-notes like Whitethroat's. Song begins with subdued warble, followed by outburst of unmusical rattling *on one note*. Sings in thick cover, and lacks Whitethroat's vertical song-flight.
Habitat: As Whitethroat, though usually in taller, denser vegetation, with more trees. Map 283.

WHITETHROAT   *Sylvia communis*   Pl. 63
   Du – Grasmus   Fr – Fauvette grisette
   Ge – Dorngrasmücke   Sw – Törnsångare
Identification: 5½″. A perky little bird with *conspicuously rusty wings* and rather long tail with white outer feathers. Male has *pale grey cap* extending to nape and below eye (brownish-grey in autumn), *pure white throat*. Under-parts very pale pinkish-buff. Female duller, with brownish head and only faint pink on breast. Restless, darting in and out of undergrowth with raised crest and cocked tail. See also Lesser Whitethroat.
Voice: A repeated '*check*', a hoarse, scolding '*tcharr*', and a quiet '*wheet, wheet, whit-whit-whit*' ending hurriedly. Song, a vigorous, urgent chatter, usually from bush, or in brief dancing song-flight.
Habitat: Fairly open country with bushes, brambles, gorse, nettle-beds. Nests near ground in low vegetation. Map 284.

GARDEN WARBLER *Sylvia borin* **Pl. 64**
  Du – Tuinfluiter
  Ge – Gartengrasmücke
  Fr – Fauvette des jardins
  Sw – Trädgårdssångare

Identification: 5½″. A plump, uniform, brownish warbler with pale under-parts and a characteristic *round head* and *stubby bill*. No distinctive plumage features, but may be identified by *sustained and beautiful song*. Distinguished from female and juvenile Blackcap by uniform brownish crown and upper-parts. Legs have bluish tinge.

Voice: Call-note '*check, check*', like Blackcap's, but less hard; a low, harsh '*tchurr-r-r*' and a faint '*whit*'. Song has same mellow quality as Blackcap's, but is quieter and *much longer sustained*. Sings from undergrowth.

Habitat: Woods with abundant undergrowth, thickets, bushy commons with bramble patches, overgrown hedges, fruit bushes. Nests in low bushes and brambles. Map 285.

BLACKCAP *Sylvia atricapilla* **Pl. 63**
  Du – Zwartkop
  Ge – Mönchsgrasmücke
  Fr – Fauvette à tête noire
  Sw – Svarthätta

Identification: 5½″. Male distinguished by *glossy black crown, down to eye-level*; upper-parts greyish-brown, *sides of head* and under-parts ashy-grey. Female has *red-brown crown* and browner under-parts. Juveniles are rustier above, yellow below; young males have blackish-brown crowns. Distinguished from Orphean and Sardinian by *sharply defined cap terminating at eye-level, and absence of white in tail*. See also Garden Warbler.

Voice: An emphatic '*tac, tac*', rapidly repeated when alarmed, and a harsh churring. Song, a remarkably rich warbling, *more varied but less sustained* than Garden Warbler's, often louder towards end.

Habitat: Woodland glades with undergrowth, overgrown hedges, fruit bushes. Nests in brambles, honeysuckle, evergreens, etc. Map 286.

GREENISH WARBLER *Phylloscopus trochiloides* **Pl. 64**
  Du – Grauwe fitis
  Ge – Grüner Laubsänger
  Fr – Pouillot verdâtre
  Sw – Lundsångare

Identification: 4¾″. Very like Chiffchaff, but distinguished by voice, short whitish wing-bar (sometimes indistinct), less yellow under-parts, greyish sides of neck and more pronounced creamy supercilium. Size between Arctic and Yellow-browed, but is *greyer*, less green, and supercilium is less prominent. Legs *dark* grey-brown. Difficult to separate from eastern races of Chiffchaff (with wing-bar) except by longer bill, longer supercilium and voice. (See line drawing for wing formula.)

Voice: Usual note a thin '*chee-wee*'. Song short, high and loud, beginning with rapidly repeated call-note, merging into a gabbled Wren-like trill.

Habitat: Very varied: occurs up to 11,000 ft.; deciduous or coniferous woodlands, coppices, orchards, etc. Nests on or near ground, not necessarily with undergrowth, occasionally in low stone walls. Map 287.

ARCTIC WARBLER *Phylloscopus borealis* **Pl. 64**
  Du – Noordse boszanger
  Ge – Nordischer Laubsänger
  Fr – Pouillot boréal
  Sw – Nordsångare

Identification: 4¾″. Near size of Wood Warbler, but has whitish throat and conspicuous yellowish-white supercilium contrasting with long dark stripe

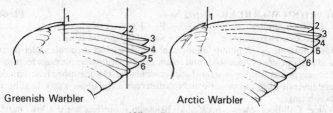

Greenish Warbler   Arctic Warbler

Wing Formulae

Greenish has longer first primary, shorter second primary than Arctic

through eye reaching almost to nape. Plumage variable: greyish-green to greenish-brown upper-parts (darker in first winter); greyish-white under-parts, sometimes with traces of yellow; usually a *narrow whitish wing-bar*, sometimes faint trace of second bar, but both may be lost in worn plumage. Legs *pale* yellowish-brown. Extremely active. See also smaller Greenish Warbler and line drawing for differences in wing formula.

Voice: A husky '*tssp*'; a hard '*zik*'; sometimes a chatter recalling Lesser Whitethroat. Song, a distinctive trill of about 15 notes faintly recalling Bonelli's Warbler, followed by a short '*tseers*'.

Habitat: Usually in lush undergrowth near water, but also in birch and coniferous woods. Nests on ground. Map 288.

PALLAS'S WARBLER *Phylloscopus proregulus*   **Pl. 65**

Du – Pallas' boszanger   Fr – Pouillot de Pallas
Ge – Goldhähnchenlaubsänger   Sw – Kungsfågelsångare

Identification: $3\frac{1}{2}''$. Small size, plumage and behaviour, including hovering, recall Firecrest. Distinguished from Yellow-browed Warbler by brighter green upper-parts, *broad yellow stripe on dark-sided crown*; yellow forehead and supercilium; double *yellow* wing-bars; *primrose-yellow rump-patch* prominent when hovering.

Voice: A soft but shrill, rising '*weesp*', more prolonged than similar call of Yellow-browed; sometimes regarded as two notes '*wee-eesp*', the second higher than the first. Powerful trilling song with many pure notes.

Habitat and Range: Mainly in tree-tops, nesting in birch, conifer and mixed forest. Vagrant from Asia to N., W. (including Britain), C., S. and E. Europe.

YELLOW-BROWED WARBLER *Phylloscopus inornatus*   **Pl. 64**

Du – Bladkoninkje   Fr – Pouillot à grands sourcils
Ge – Gelbbrauenlaubsänger   Sw – Vitbrynad sångare

Identification: $4''$. Distinguished by very small size, whitish *double wing-bars*, the lower one being long, broad and *dark-edged*; broad whitish edges to secondaries, and *very long creamy supercilium*. Upper-parts greenish, becoming paler and yellower on rump. Under-parts whitish. Tail rather short. Sometimes has indistinct pale line down centre of crown. Often chases flies like flycatcher. Distinguished from juvenile Goldcrest by larger size and long, striking supercilium. See also Pallas's Warbler.

Voice: A loud '*weest*', or a very high-pitched '*dzeep*'. Song a repetition of the buzzy double call-note, or a rapid twitter, usually from tree-top.

Habitat and Range: Mixed and coniferous woodlands, often in willows; scrub and undergrowth in winter. On autumn passage fairly regularly in Britain and Heligoland. Vagrant from Asia elsewhere in N., W., C., S. and E. Europe.

RADDE'S WARBLER *Phylloscopus schwarzi*   **Pl. 65**
  Du – Radde's boszanger   Fr – Pouillot de Schwarz
  Ge – Bartlaubsänger   Sw – Videsångare
Identification: 5″. Noticeably larger and longer-tailed than Chiffchaff, recalling Dusky Warbler. Distinguished by *very long, conspicuous creamy supercilium above blackish streak from bill through eye almost to nape*. Rather stout bill, yellowish legs, pale brownish-olive upper-parts, *creamy-white under-parts*. Distinguished from Dusky Warbler by more striking supercilium, larger size, heavier bill and yellowish (not dark) legs.
Voice: A rather weak '*twit-twit*' and a rich, trilling song.
Habitat and Range: Chiefly arboreal, but also skulks in undergrowth. Vagrant from Asia to C., N. and W. Europe (including Britain).

DUSKY WARBLER *Phylloscopus fuscatus*   **Pl. 65**
  Du – Bruine boszanger   Fr – Pouillot brun
  Ge – Dunkellaubsänger   Sw – Brunsångare
Identification: 4½″. Superficially resembles Radde's, but is smaller, *thin-billed* and shorter-tailed. Supercilium much less pronounced and *rusty* (not creamy), without black streak below. Looks darker and browner than other *Phylloscopus* warblers, without any green or yellow. No wing-bar. Under-parts dingy whitish with buffish flanks. Ear-coverts darkly mottled rusty-brown, contrasting with supercilium. Legs brown. Voice very different from Radde's.
Voice: A harsh, Blackcap-like '*tchak-tchak*'.
Habitat and Range: Usually feeds on ground in damp localities. Vagrant from Asia to C., N. and W. Europe (including Britain).

BONELLI'S WARBLER *Phylloscopus bonelli*   **Pl. 64**
  Du – Bergfluiter   Fr – Pouillot de Bonelli
  Ge – Berglaubsänger   Sw – Bergsångare
Identification: 4½″. A very grey warbler, with pale grey-brown upper-parts, *paler grey head and whitish under-parts*. Touch of bright yellow at carpal joint and yellowish wing-patch stand out in contrast. Yellowish rump-patch can be conspicuous but is often difficult to see.
Voice: A soft '*hou-eet*', more clearly disyllabic than Willow Warbler, and '*chee-chee*'; call of eastern race *P.b. orientalis*, in Balkans, a frequent, loud, hard, short '*tsiep*'. Song, a loose trill *on the same note*, slower, more musical and more clearly separated than faintly similar trill of Wood Warbler; can be confused with distant Cirl Bunting, or rattle of Lesser Whitethroat.
Habitat: Dense foliage of trees. Locally in dry pine or deciduous forests, open cork oak groves, or even scattered vegetation up to tree limit in mountains. Nests on ground under trees. Map 289.

WOOD WARBLER *Phylloscopus sibilatrix*   **Pl. 64**
  Du – Fluiter   Fr – Pouillot siffleur
  Ge – Waldlaubsänger   Sw – Grönsångare
Identification: 5″. Larger than Chiffchaff, with much longer wings. Distinguished by brightly contrasted yellowish-green upper-parts, *sulphur-yellow*

throat and breast, and *white belly*. Broad yellow stripe above eye. Wings long, olive-brown, with yellow edges to feathers. Behaviour like Chiffchaff, but does not flick wings, though it often hangs them loosely.

Voice: A liquid '*piu*' and a soft '*whit, whit, whit*'. Has two songs: a piping '*piu*' repeated 5–20 times, and a slowly repeated '*stip*' accelerating to a 'shivering' grasshopper-like trill '*stip, stip stip, stip-stip-stip-shreeeee*'. Sings while moving among tree foliage and in flight.

Habitat: Deciduous woods with light ground cover; also found in coniferous forests in C. Europe. Nests on ground among light undergrowth, usually in beech or oak woods. Map 290.

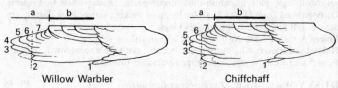

Willow Warbler   Chiffchaff

Wing Formulae

Willow Warbler: 2nd primary longer than 7th.
Chiffchaff: 2nd equal to or shorter than 7th. Note relative lengths of A and B portions of wings. Dotted lines show possible range in position of 2nd primaries
(*After Scott and Grant*)

CHIFFCHAFF　*Phylloscopus collybita*　　　　　　　　　　**Pl. 64**
　　Du – Tjiftjaf　　　　　　　　　　　Fr – Pouillot véloce
　　Ge – Zilpzalp　　　　　　　　　　　Sw – Gransångare
Identification: 4¾″. Similar to Willow Warbler, but plumage dingier, shape more compact and supercilium slightly less pronounced. Best identified by *distinctive song*. *Bill and legs blackish*, but some have pale legs like Willow. Upper-parts olive-brown, under-parts buffish-white faintly washed lemon-yellow. Wing formula (see line drawing) is useful when trapped for ringing. Behaviour less lively than Willow, but wings and tail constantly flicked when feeding. Juveniles yellow below. Vagrants of eastern races often show faint wing-bar and can be mistaken for Greenish Warbler.
Voice: A soft '*hweet*', a louder '*twit*' and a subdued '*tsiff-tsiff-tsiff*'. Song, two notes deliberately repeated in irregular order, '*chiff, chiff, chaff, chiff, chaff*', etc.
Habitat: More arboreal than Willow Warbler. Usually nests just above ground in brambles, evergreens, etc., in light woods and bushy commons. Winters in fairly open vegetation. Map 291.

WILLOW WARBLER　*Phylloscopus trochilus*　　　　　　　**Pl. 64**
　　Du – Fitis　　　　　　　　　　　　Fr – Pouillot fitis
　　Ge – Fitis　　　　　　　　　　　　Sw – Lövsångare
Identification: 4¼″. The most abundant summer visitor to northern half of Europe. Easily confused with Chiffchaff except for *distinctive song*. Is less dumpy, longer-winged and usually looks slightly greener above and yellower below. Base of bill and legs *usually pale brown*, not blackish as in Chiffchaff (but legs are sometimes dark). Juveniles can be very yellow below. Behaviour and

flight lively and acrobatic. See line drawing for comparison with wing formula of Chiffchaff.
Voice: Note very like Chiffchaff's but nearer to two syllables: '*hooeet*', or '*sooee*'. Song, a liquid, musical cadence, beginning quietly and becoming clearer and more deliberate, *descending* to a distinctive flourish '*sooeet-sooeetoo*'.
Habitat: Less arboreal than Chiffchaff, more fond of low vegetation. Nests on ground in open bushy localities. Map 292.

GOLDCREST   *Regulus regulus*   **Pl. 66**
   Du – Goudhaantje   Fr – Roitelet huppé
   Ge – Wintergoldhähnchen   Sw – Kungsfågel
Identification: 3½″. Distinguished from tits and warblers by *very small size, plump form and bright yellow crown with black border*; crest (sometimes concealed) has orange centre in male, is paler yellow in female, absent in juvenile. Upper-parts olive-green; under-parts dull whitish-buff, with greenish flanks. Wings have *two white bars and a broad black band*. Behaviour warbler-like. Roams with tits outside breeding season. Best distinguished from Firecrest by *lack of black eye-stripe*.
Voice: A frequent, shrill, high '*zee-zee-zee*'. Song, a *more varied*, very thin, high, rapid twittering than Firecrest's song. Main phrase '*stit-it-stir-te*' rapidly repeated 3–4 times before terminal flourish. In autumn has longer, musical sub-song of high, soft twittering.
Habitat: Coniferous or mixed woods; in winter also in hedges and under-growth. Builds suspended nest, usually under tip of branch of conifer (but rarely in pine). Map 293.

FIRECREST   *Regulus ignicapillus*   **Pl. 66**
   Du – Vuurgoudhaantje   Fr – Roitelet triple-bandeau
   Ge – Sommergoldhähnchen   Sw – Brandkronad kunsfågel
Identification: 3½″. Distinguished from Goldcrest by *bold white supercilium and black stripe through eye*; upper-parts greener, under-parts whiter; golden tinge on sides of neck visible under good conditions. Male's crest-stripe has more red. Juvenile has rudimentary black and white stripes on head, but lacks crest. Behaviour like Goldcrest.
Voice: Call-notes similar to Goldcrest's, but less persistent. Rather featureless song distinguished from Goldcrest's by high, very rapid double notes being *on same pitch*.
Habitat: As Goldcrest, but less partial to coniferous woods and more often in low undergrowth, bushy swamps, bracken, etc. Builds suspended nest in coniferous or deciduous trees, bushes, creepers, etc. Map 294.

FLYCATCHERS: Muscicapidae

Flycatchers are usually seen perched *upright* on vantage points, from which they make short, erratic flights after passing insects. Bills broad at the base. Sexes similar in Spotted. Hole or tree nesting.

SPOTTED FLYCATCHER *Muscicapa striata*   **Pl. 6**
Du – Grauwe vliegenvanger   Fr – Gobe-mouche gris
Ge – Grauschnäpper   Sw – Grå flugsnappare
Identification: $5\frac{1}{2}''$. Apart from characteristic upright, watchful pose, is identified by ashy-brown plumage, spotted crown and *lightly streaked whitish breast*
Wings and tail often flicked. Sallies from low perch after passing insects with rapid, agile flight, returning to same perch. Rather solitary.
Voice: A very thin, grating '*tzee*' and a rapid '*tzee-tuc-tuc*'. Song, a few thin hasty notes: '*sip-sip-see-sitti-see-see*'.
Habitat: Gardens, parks, edges of woods. Nests on or in buildings, against tree trunks, behind creepers, etc. Map 295.

RED-BREASTED FLYCATCHER *Ficedula parva*   **Pl. 6**
Du – Kleine vliegenvanger   Fr – Gobe-mouche nain
Ge – Zwergschnäpper   Sw – Liten flugsnappare
Identification: $4\frac{1}{2}''$. Smallest European flycatcher. Male only has *bright orange throat*, summer and winter, and greyish head. Insignificant grey-brown above, pale buffish below, but quickly distinguished by *bold white patches* either side of blackish tail, which is often flicked when perched, with drooped wings. Breeding behaviour retiring; occasionally makes sallies in air or to ground after insects, when black and white tail pattern is conspicuous, but more often feeds warbler-fashion among tree-tops. Male suggests tiny Robin, except for white on tail and different colour of face.
Voice: A brisk '*zeek*' and a quiet, Wren-like chatter. Song varied, beginning rather like opening of Willow Warbler's and ending with a quicker trill recalling Redstart.
Habitat: Usually deciduous forests; on passage also in open cultivation. Nesting habits like Pied, but also builds open nest against tree trunk. Map 296.

COLLARED FLYCATCHER *Ficedula albicollis*   **Pls. 67, 76**
Du – Withalsvliegenvanger   Fr – Gobe-mouche à collier
Ge – Halsbandschnäpper   Sw – Halsbandsflugsnappare
Identification: 5″. Resembles Pied, but male distinguished by *bold white collar, whitish rump*, bolder white markings on wings and forehead and less white on sides of tail. In autumn, black markings replaced by dark brown, collar almost disappears and white markings are reduced. Females doubtfully separable, but Collared is usually greyer above, with longer wing markings and some indication of whitish collar and rump. Behaviour and habitat like Pied. The semi-collared eastern form (perhaps species – Semi-collared Flycatcher *F. semitorquata*, see Pl. 76) lacks white collar, has more white on forehead and tail and is more easily confused with Pied.
Voice: Call-notes resemble Pied's. Song is shorter and simpler: '*tsee-tsee-tsee sui-see*', the penultimate note dropping. Map 297.

PIED FLYCATCHER *Ficedula hypoleuca*   **Pl. 6**
Du – Bonte vliegenvanger   Fr – Gobe-mouche noir
Ge – Trauerschnäpper   Sw – Svartvit flugsnappare
Identification: 5″. Male in spring has head and upper-parts *black*; forehead, under-parts, *wing-patch and sides of tail white*; autumn plumage like female, but forehead remains whitish. Female is olive-brown above, buffish-white below

with smaller wing-patches. Juvenile distinguished from young Spotted by white on wings and tail. Flycatching behaviour like Spotted, but seldom returns to same perch and often feeds on ground; tail constantly flirted. Wing-patches prevent confusion with other flycatchers, except Collared. See also Brown Flycatcher (Accidentals).

Voice: A metallic '*whit*', an anxious '*phweet*', a persistent '*tic*' or '*wheetic*' and an explosive '*tschist*'. Song chiefly on two up-and-down notes, a high '*zee-it, zee-it, zee-it*', interspersed with an occasional Redstart-like trill.

Habitat: In British Isles, usually deciduous woods and gardens, often near water. On Continent, also in coniferous forests. Nests in holes in trees, walls, nest boxes. Map 298.

BABBLERS: Timaliidae

BEARDED TIT *Panurus biarmicus*   **Pl. 68**
  Du – Baardmees   Fr – Mésange à moustaches
  Ge – Bartmeise   Sw – Skäggmes

Identification: 6½". A tit-like little bird with *tawny upper-parts, long tawny tail* and pinkish-grey under-parts. Male has ash-grey head with striking *black 'moustaches'* and conspicuous *black under tail-coverts*. Female is paler, with tawny head, no 'moustaches', and no black. Juvenile has dark back, wing-coverts and sides of tail. Flight 'whirring', with loose tail. Acrobatic in reed-beds.

Voice: A distinctive, twanging '*tching*', a scolding '*p'whut*', a squeaky '*cheeu*', etc.

Habitat: Extensive and secluded reed-beds. Nests low down near edge of wet reed-bed. Map 299.

LONG-TAILED TITS: Aegithalidae

LONG-TAILED TIT *Aegithalos caudatus*   **Pl. 68**
  Du – Staartmees   Fr – Mésange à longue queue
  Ge – Schwanzmeise   Sw – Stjärtmes

Identification: 5½" (including 3" tail). Unmistakable *blackish, whitish and pinkish plumage, long graduated tail* and distinctive note. British race *A. c. rosaceus* and the western and southern European races have head white, with bold blackish stripe over eye; mixed pink and black upper-parts; whitish below, with pinkish flanks and belly; black wings and tail with pure white outer tail-feathers. Juvenile has dark cheeks and no pink. Northern race *A. c. caudatus* has pure white head, neck and under-parts. Behaviour restless and acrobatic.

Voice: A distinctive, low '*tupp*', a repeated trilling '*tsirrrup*' and a weak '*tzee-tzee-tzee*'. Infrequent song, a mixture of call-notes and rapid '*see-see-siu*'.

Habitat: Thickets, bushy heaths, coppices, hedgerows; also woods in winter. Builds ovoid mossy, lichen-covered nest, usually in gorse, thorn or bramble bushes, occasionally well up in trees. Map 300.

TITS: Paridae

Small, plump, short-billed birds, very acrobatic when feeding. Most tits roam in mixed bands in winter. Sexes generally similar. Nest in holes.

MARSH TIT *Parus palustris*   Pl. 68
  Du – Glanskopmees   Fr – Mésange nonnette
  Ge – Sumpfmeise   Sw – Kärrmes

Identification: 4¼″. Has black cap and chin. Distinguished from Coal Tit by having *no white patch on nape*, no wing-bars and browner upper-parts; from very similar Willow Tit by *glossy* black crown (instead of dull sooty), smaller black bib, *absence of light patch on closed wing*, and distinctive call-note. Cheeks and under-parts dull greyish-white. Juvenile greyer above, with dull sooty crown, not distinguishable from young Willow Tit. Seldom more than two together in mixed winter flocks of tits.

Voice: Most distinctive. A loud '*pitchew*', or '*piti-chewee*'; other notes are a deep, nasal '*tchair*', and a scolding '*chick-adeedeedee*'. Song varies from a repeated '*tsip*' note to four- or five-note phrases such as '*pitchaweeoo*'.

Habitat: Deciduous woods, hedges, thickets, etc., less often gardens. No particular fondness for marshes. Nests in existing holes in trees, usually willows or alders. Map 301.

SOMBRE TIT *Parus lugubris*   Pl. 68
  Du – Rouwmees   Fr – Mésange lugubre
  Ge – Trauermeise   Sw – Sorgmes

Identification: 5½″. Patterned like Willow Tit, but much larger, sides darker and bill very heavy for a tit, giving impression of Great Tit. *Crown and nape sooty brownish-black* (female's more chocolate-brown), upper-parts grey-brown, *face and sides of neck whitish*, under-parts dull whitish with greyish-brown flanks and large black throat-patch. Behaviour as in Great Tit, but seldom joins mixed flocks in winter.

Voice: A distinctive '*sirrah*', a harsh '*zweet-zweet*', a rather contralto chattering '*chur-r-r-r*' and Great Tit-like notes.

Habitat: Lowland plains and mountain slopes with mixed woods and rocky outcrops. Nests in holes in trees, occasionally among rocks. Map 302.

WILLOW TIT *Parus montanus*   Pl. 68
  Du – Matkopmees   Fr – Mésange boréale
  Ge – Weidenmeise   Sw – Talltita
  N. Am – Black-capped Chickadee

Identification: 4¼″. Very like Marsh Tit, but distinguished by *dull, sooty* black crown, *pale patch* formed by light edges to secondary wing feathers (less visible in summer) and *distinctive call-note*. Flanks darker buff than Marsh, and black bib usually rather larger; juveniles are indistinguishable. Northern race *P. m. borealis* is paler and greyer, with pure white cheeks.

Voice: Usual notes, a nasal buzzing '*eez-eez-eez*', and a very high thin '*zi-zi-zi*' and a loud '*chay*'. Song, a quiet, warbling but Nightingale-like '*chu, chu, chu*' and a Wood Warbler-like '*piu, piu, piu*'.

Habitat: More fond of swampy thickets than Marsh Tit, where it can find

otting stumps. Excavates nest cavities in rotted alder, birch, willow, etc. Map
303.

SIBERIAN TIT *Parus cinctus*   Pl. 68

Du – Bruinkopmees   Fr – Mésange lapone
Ge – Lapplandmeise   Sw – Lappmes

Identification: 5¼″. Has distinctly '*dusty' and fluffy appearance*, unlike neatness
of most tits. Crown and nape *dusky brown*, upper-parts paler, slightly rufous;
face and under-parts dingy white, with slightly rufous flanks and sooty-black
throat-patch merging indistinctly into breast. Juvenile plumage looks 'cleaner'
and neater. Easily distinguished from smaller Marsh and Willow Tits by
obviously brown cap.

Voice: Resembles Willow Tit, but a longer '*eeez*', repeated 4–5 times.

Habitat: Almost exclusively in birch and coniferous forests. Nests in old
woodpecker holes, or excavates holes in soft dead trees. Map 304.

CRESTED TIT *Parus cristatus*   Pl. 68

Du – Kuifmees   Fr – Mésange huppée
Ge – Haubenmeise   Sw – Tofsmes

Identification: 4½″. Easily distinguished by *prominent, speckled black and
whitish crest and distinctive voice*. Face whitish with curved black mark from eye
behind cheek, narrow black collar and bib. Upper-parts warm greyish-brown,
under-parts whitish with buff flanks. Sometimes seeks food on tree trunks, like
Treecreeper. Less sociable than most other tits.

Voice: A short, low-pitched, purring '*choo-r-r*', reminiscent of Long-tailed Tit,
but deeper-toned. Also a repeated, high thin '*tzee-tzee-tzee*'.

Habitat: Usually pinewoods, but also mixed woods and thickets. Nests in holes
in decayed trees, fence posts, etc. Map 305.

COAL TIT *Parus ater*   Pl. 68

Du – Zwarte mees   Fr – Mésange noire
Ge – Tannenmeise   Sw – Svartmes

Identification: 4½″. Slightly smaller than Blue Tit. The only black-crowned tit
with *bold white patch on nape*. Cheeks dingy white; chin to upper breast black;
upper-parts olive-grey, with narrow double white wing-bar; under-parts
whitish, with buff flanks. Juvenile has yellowish cheeks, under-parts and spot
on nape. Less obtrusive than Great or Blue Tits.

Voice: A clear, thin '*tsui*' or '*tsee*' with a short twitter, also a scolding '*chi-chi-
hich*' and a thin '*sissi-sissi-sissi*'. Some notes very like Goldcrest's. Song, a
repeated clear '*seetoo*' or '*seetoooee*', more rapid and less strident than similar
notes of Great Tit.

Habitat: Shows some preference for conifers. Nests in holes in banks and tree
stumps, usually near ground. Map 306.

BLUE TIT *Parus caeruleus*   Pl. 68

Du – Pimpelmees   Fr – Mésange bleue
Ge – Blaumeise   Sw – Blåmes

Identification: 4½″. The only tit with *bright cobalt-blue crown, wings and tail*.
Yellow under-parts; white cheeks with black line through eye and around nape
and cheek to blue-black chin; white edging to crown, white spot on nape;

greenish back. Juvenile has greenish-brown upper-parts, yellow cheeks. Behaviour like Great Tit.
Voice: Varied call-notes, '*tsee-tsee-tsee-tsit*', etc., and a harsh, scolding '*chur-r-r*'. Song, a high '*tsee-tsee*', followed by a long trill.
Habitat: As Great Tit. Map 307.

AZURE TIT *Parus cyanus* Pl. 6

Du – Azuurmees   Fr – Mésange azurée
Ge – Lasurmeise   Sw – Azurmes

Identification: 5¼". Resembles a large, whitish Blue Tit with a rather long tail. Distinguished by *snow-white head*, with narrow dark blue stripe through eye to back of crown, grey-blue upper-parts, *white* under-parts, with small blue streak or patch on breast, *broad white inverted V on dark wing* and conspicuous white on outer tail-feathers. Juvenile has grey crown and is greyer above.
Voice: Call-note recalls Long-tailed Tit's low '*tsirr*'; alarm, a loud '*tcherpink*'.
Habitat and Range: Trees (notably willow) and bushes along stream and river banks and around ponds. Vagrant from Russia to E., C., N. and W. Europe.

GREAT TIT *Parus major* Pl. 6

Du – Koolmees   Fr – Mésange charbonnière
Ge – Kohlmeise   Sw – Talgoxe

Identification: 5½". Largest common tit. Glossy blue-black head and neck, with white cheeks; *yellow under-parts, with black band down centre* (the best field mark). Greenish blue-grey upper-parts. Juvenile has brownish crown and yellowish cheeks. Arboreal and acrobatic.
Voice: Most varied of the tits: a Chaffinch-like '*tsink, tsink*', a nasal, Marsh Tit-like '*tchair, tchair*', a scolding Blue Tit-like '*chi-chi-chi*', etc. Song consists of two- or three-syllable variations on familiar, ringing '*teechew-teechew-teechew*' and occasional mimicry.
Habitat: Mixed woods, hedges, gardens. Nests in holes in trees, walls, drain-pipes, nest-boxes, etc. Map 308.

NUTHATCHES: Sittidae

Nuthatches recall tiny woodpeckers, having strong bills and large feet, but climb trees (or rocks) upwards or downwards, without using their tail as a prop. Sexes similar. Hole nesting.

KRÜPER'S NUTHATCH *Sitta krueperi* Pl. 7

Du – Krüpers boomklever   Fr – Sittelle de Krüper
Ge – Türkenkleiber   Sw – Krüpers nötväcka

Identification: 5". Resembles Corsican Nuthatch, but easily distinguished by *conspicuous dark rufous breast-patch*; black on crown restricted to front half, black and white eye-stripe less conspicuous.
Voice: Resembles Nuthatch's long trilling, also a brief '*puit*' and a harsher '*shwee*'.
Habitat and Range: Found chiefly in outer foliage of conifers. (Asia Minor.) Breeds Greek Islands.

CORSICAN NUTHATCH   *Sitta whiteheadi*   **Pl. 66**
Du – Zwartkopboomklever   Fr – Sittelle corse
Ge – Korsikanischer Kleiber   Sw – Korsikansk nötväcka
Identification: 4¾″. Much smaller than Nuthatch. Distinguished by *black* crown
and broad stripe through eye, and *broad, sharply defined white stripe above eye*.
Under-parts dingy *whitish*. Female is duller, with slate-grey crown.
Voice: More nasal and quieter than Nuthatch; most typical call a short nasal
note recalling distant Jay; also a weak, trilling *'pupupupu'*; a louder, nasal *'pooï'*;
a weak trilling *'tsi-tsi-tsi'*.
Habitat and Range: Confined to mountain forests and groves (particularly of
chestnut) in Corsica. Makes nest holes in rotting trees.

NUTHATCH   *Sitta europaea*   **Pl. 66**
Du – Boomklever   Fr – Sittelle torchepot
Ge – Kleiber   Sw – Nötväcka
Identification: 5½″. A stubby, active, tree-climbing bird, with a powerful
pointed bill. Distinguished by *blue-grey crown and upper-parts, buff under-parts
with chestnut flanks*, white cheeks and throat, bold black streak through eye.
Juvenile lacks chestnut. Climbs trees in short jerks, in any direction including
downwards. Tail is *not* used as support. Hammers nuts wedged in bark. Under-
parts are whiter in Scandinavian race *S. e. europaea*. See also Rock Nuthatch.
Voice: A ringing, metallic *'chwit, chwit, chwit'*, a repeated *'tsit'*, a shrill, trilling
'tsirrr', etc. Song, a repeated, loud *'tuï'*, a long, trilling *'chi-chi-chi-chi'*, *'qui-qui,
qui-qui'*, etc.
Habitat: Old deciduous trees in woods, parks, gardens. Nests in holes in trees,
occasionally in walls, nest-boxes, etc., plastering entrance hole and crevices
with mud. Map 309.

ROCK NUTHATCH   *Sitta neumayer*   **Pl. 66**
Du – Rotsklever   Fr – Sittelle des rochers
Ge – Felsenkleiber   Sw – Klippnötväcka
Identification: 5½″. Very different in habitat from other nuthatches, frequenting
bare rocks, but perches occasionally in trees. Resembles *very faded* Nuthatch,
with *whitish* under-parts, *brownish-buff* (not chestnut) flanks and under tail-
coverts and grey tail *without white markings*. Actions as Nuthatch.
Voice: Shrill, high-pitched and very varied, but lacking rich quality of
Nuthatch. Song, a trilling *'zee-a, zee-a, zee-a'* on a descending scale.
Habitat: Rocky gorges, mountainsides, cliffs. Breeds in caves and crannies in
rocks, plastering entrance with mud, to form short funnel. Map 310.

WALLCREEPERS: Tichodromadidae

WALLCREEPER   *Tichodroma muraria*   **Pl. 66**
Du – Rotskruiper   Fr – Tichodrome échelette
Ge – Mauerläufer   Sw – Murkrypare
Identification: 6½″. Distinguished by *brilliant crimson* on blackish, rounded
wings. Has grey upper-parts, short tail and long, slender, curved bill. *Large
white spots* on edges of wings and tail. Throat and breast black in summer,

whitish in winter. Has spasmodic butterfly-flight; very broad wings constantly flicked while seeking food on rock-faces or old buildings. Juvenile like adults in winter, but brownish, with a straighter bill.

Voice: A clear, piping '*zee-zee-titi-zwee*', in rising cadence.

Habitat: Rocky ravines, earth cliffs, ruins. Breeds in deep crevices, on inland cliff-face, in rocks, occasionally in buildings, usually from about 6,000 ft. to snow-line, wintering in rocky valleys and foothills. Map 311.

TREECREEPERS: Certhiidae

Restless little birds with long, slender, curved bills. Usually seen creeping up tree trunks. Sexes similar. Nest in crevices.

TREECREEPER   *Certhia familiaris*   **Pl. 66**
   Du – Kortsnavelboomkruiper   Fr – Grimpereau des bois
   Ge – Waldbaumläufer   Sw – Trädkrypare

Identification: 5″. A small, *brown*, tree-climbing bird. Easily distinguished from woodpeckers and nuthatches by small size, *thin curved bill* and distinctive behaviour. Brown upper-parts, streaked with buff; silvery white under-parts. Climbs up trees spirally in short spurts, with stiff tail pressed against bark. Travels with tits in winter.

Voice: A thin, high-pitched '*tsee*' or '*tsit*'. Song weak, high-pitched, starting slowly and accelerating: '*tsee-tsee-tsee-tsizzi-tsee*'.

Habitat: Woodlands, parks, gardens with large trees. Nests behind loose bark, in split trees, behind ivy, etc. In C. and S. Europe prefers mountain woodlands and avoids lowlands. Map 312.

SHORT-TOED TREECREEPER   *Certhia brachydactyla*   **Pl. 66**
   Du – Boomkruiper   Fr – Grimpereau des jardins
   Ge – Gartenbaumläufer   Sw – Kortkload trädkrypare

Identification: 5″. Not always safely distinguishable in the field from Tree-creeper, though voice may be helpful, but is less rusty on rump and has *brownish flanks and vent* (a fairly good field mark). Shorter supercilium is less distinct. Bill usually slightly longer and more curved and claws shorter than Treecreeper's.

Voice: At times separable from Treecreeper's by richer quality, recalling Coal Tit. Song is generally slightly louder and shorter, lacking Treecreeper's thin, high-pitched notes: a rhythmic '*teet, teet, teeteroititt*'. Call-note a high, shrill '*srrieh*', or '*zeet*'.

Habitat: Gardens, parks, coppices, avoiding heavy woodlands. In C. and S. Europe Treecreeper usually restricted to mountains and regions above 3,000 ft., whereas Short-toed occurs from 5,000 ft. to sea level. Map 313.

PENDULINE TITS: Remizidae

PENDULINE TIT   *Remiz pendulinus*   **Pl. 68**
  Du – Buidelmees   Fr – Mésange rémiz
  Ge – Beutelmeise   Sw – Pungmes
Identification: 4¼″. Easily distinguished by striking greyish-white head and
throat, with *broad black patch across face*. Back *chestnut*; belly buffish-white.
Juvenile mainly pale ash-brown, without black or chestnut markings.
Voice: Usual note a soft, plaintive '*seeou*', recalling Robin, and a conversa-
tional '*tsi-tsi-tsi*'.
Habitat: Marshy localities, thickets, along dykes, etc., but locally also in dry
regions. Builds ovoid nest with funnel-shaped entrance, suspended in outer
twigs of bush or tree and in reeds. Map 314.

ORIOLES: Oriolidae

GOLDEN ORIOLE   *Oriolus oriolus*   **Pl. 69**
  Du – Wielewaal   Fr – Loriot
  Ge – Pirol   Sw – Sommargylling
Identification: 9½″. Male unmistakable *brilliant yellow, with black wings and
tail*, latter boldly marked with yellow. Female and juvenile yellowish-green with
darker wings and tails and lightly streaked greyish under-parts, difficult to see in
foliage. May be confused with Green Woodpecker, which has yellow rump but
is much heavier, with red on head. Flight rapid, in long undulations with
characteristic upward sweep to regain tree-cover. Normally stays well hidden in
tree-tops.
Voice: A loud, fluty whistle '*weela-weeo*', or '*chuck-chuck-weeo*', from hidden
perch. Alarm, a harsh '*chr-r-r*'. Also several harsh, rather Jay-like notes.
Habitat: Essentially arboreal; well-timbered parks, old orchards, river banks,
woods, seldom in open. Nest usually slung between horizontally forked
branches. Map 315.

SHRIKES: Laniidae

Strikingly patterned, with hook-tipped bills and hawk-like behaviour. Usually
perch watchfully upright on conspicuous vantage points, fanning their rather
long tails. Prey often impaled on thorn-bush 'larders'. Call-notes are harsh, but
songs surprisingly musical. Sexes nearly similar, except Red-backed. Bush or
tree nesting.

ISABELLINE SHRIKE   *Lanius isabellinus*
  Du – Isabelklauwier   Fr – Pie-grièche isabelle
  Ge – Isabellwürger   Sw – Isabellatörnskata
Identification: 6¾″. Care needed in identifying this eastern species as there are
several races, of which *L. i. phoenicuroides* and *L. i. isabellinus* are most likely in

Europe. Males and females rather similar at all ages and can resemble female
and immature Red-backed. Typical adult male *phoenicuroides* has distinctive
rufous crown, tail, upper tail-coverts and rump, contrasting with grey-brown
mantle; under-parts whitish, a prominent black face-mask, white supercilium
and a small white wing-patch (more visible in flight). Typical male *isabellinus*
has *very pallid appearance* and less striking face pattern; tail is paler, more
sandy-rufous, under-parts *creamy*-white, barely visible creamy wing-patch.
Both races sometimes have fulvous flush on flanks. Juvenile Isabelline and Red-
backed very similar, but former have *unbarred* mantle whereas latter retain dark
crescentic markings above and below. Note that female and immature Red-
backed often have rufous on tail and rump. Not illustrated.
Voice: Harsh calls and musical song similar to Red-backed.
Habitat and Range: Open country with scrub, cultivation. Vagrant from Asia
to Europe (including Britain).

RED-BACKED SHRIKE *Lanius collurio*   Pl. 6
   Du – Grauwe klauwier   Fr – Pie-grièche écorcheur
   Ge – Neuntöter   Sw – Törnskata
Identification: 6¾″. Male distinguished by *chestnut back*, separating *pale blue
grey crown and rump*, and broad black face marking through eyes to ear
coverts. Under-parts pinkish-white. Tail black with white sides, often swung
side to side. Female normally lacks black face marks and is dull rufous-brown
above, buffish below, barred with brown crescent markings. Immature
separable from young Woodchat by more rufous plumage, and lack of pale
rump, shoulder-patch and wing-bar. Flight usually direct. Glides and hovers
when hunting along hedges, but usually pounces on prey from elevated perch.
Impales small birds and insects in thorn-bush 'larders' more often than other
shrikes. See also Isabelline Shrike.
Voice: A harsh, grating '*shack*' or '*chee-uk*'. Song, a quiet musical and often
prolonged warbling, interspersed with buzzing notes and a wide range of
mimicry.
Habitat: Bushy commons, uncut hedges, thickets, old quarries. Nests in
bushes, small trees, bramble patches. Map 316.

LESSER GREY SHRIKE *Lanius minor*   Pl. 6
   Du – Kleine klauwier   Fr – Pie-grièche à poitrine rose
   Ge – Schwarzstirnwürger   Sw – Svartpannad törnskata
Identification: 8″. Resembles Great Grey, but is smaller, with *proportionately
longer wings and shorter tail*; broad black face markings *continuing across
forehead* (less evident in female); no white supercilium; pale pinkish under-
parts; *shorter and much deeper bill*; very prominent white wing-bar and white
outer tail-feathers. Juvenile looks *yellowish* at a distance, with relatively
unbarred breast, finely barred dark brown on head and flanks, with brownish-
black wings and tail. Behaviour like Great Grey but *perches more upright*.
Flight usually *direct* (not low and undulating as in Great Grey); hovers
frequently.
Voice: Much as Great Grey; also a clear '*kviell*'.
Habitat: Fairly open cultivated country with scattered trees and bushes,
roadsides, commons, etc. Nests fairly high in trees (even up to 60 ft.); often in
loosely scattered colonies. Map 317.

GREAT GREY SHRIKE   *Lanius excubitor*   **Pl. 67**
  Du – Klapekster   Fr – Pie-grièche grise
  Ge – Raubwürger   Sw – Varfågel
  N. Am – Northern Shrike

Identification: $9\frac{1}{2}''$. Largest of the shrikes. Identified by contrasting *black, white and grey plumage*. Distinguished from Lesser by larger size, grey (not black) forehead, *narrow white supercilium* between black eye-patch and grey crown; *longer, more slender bill*; much more white on scapulars; proportionately shorter wings *meeting at base of tail*; longer, more graduated tail; narrower white area on open wing (closed wing often gives effect of double white bar). Female usually has faint brown wavy bars on breast. Juvenile grey-brown, with brown wavy bars on under-parts. Perches on tree-tops or telegraph pole, from which it attacks small birds, mice, lizards, insects. Tail frequently waved or fanned. Flight low and usually undulating, with steep upward glide to perch; hovers frequently. South European race *L. e. meridionalis* is darker above and pinkish below.

Voice: Characteristic *'shek-shek'* note sometimes prolonged into Magpie-like rattle. Anxiety-note, a grating *'jaaeg'*. Song, a subdued, prolonged mixture of harsh and musical notes.

Habitat: Outskirts of woods, orchards, heaths, hedges, etc. Less fond of open country for breeding than other shrikes. Nest site varied, occasionally in high trees, usually in thorn bushes. Map 318.

WOODCHAT SHRIKE   *Lanius senator*   **Pl. 67**
  Du – Roodkopklauwier   Fr – Pie-grièche à tête rousse
  Ge – Rotkopfwürger   Sw – Rödhuvad törnskata

Identification: $6\frac{3}{4}''$. Distinguished from Great and Lesser Grey Shrikes by *rich chestnut crown and nape*. Has broad black face marking continuing across forehead, pure white throat and under-parts, blackish wings and mantle with *conspicuous white shoulder-patches* and short wing-bar, black tail with white sides, *white rump conspicuous in flight*. Female rather duller. Immature resembles young Red-backed, but with larger, more angular head; is paler and less rufous, with pale rump and shoulder-patch recalling adult pattern; shows traces of whitish wing-bar. Corsican race *L. s. badius* lacks the white wing-bar. See also Masked Shrike.

Voice: Like Lesser Grey, but more varied, with frequent House Sparrow-like chatter. Song, a sustained musical warble, interspersed with harsh notes and mimicry.

Habitat: Dry open country, olive groves, orchards, bushy commons, occasionally large woods. Nests in trees of all sizes. Map 319.

MASKED SHRIKE   *Lanius nubicus*   **Pl. 67**
  Du – Maskerklauwier   Fr – Pie-grièche masquée
  Ge – Maskenwürger   Sw – Masktörnskata

Identification: $6\frac{3}{4}''$. Uniform black above, from crown to tail. Length of Woodchat but slighter; distinguished by *black rump, black crown* with bold white forehead and white supercilium; also by *reddish flanks* (otherwise white under-parts) and more conspicuous white sides to large tail. Wing markings like Woodchat's. Behaviour like Red-backed, but with more graceful flight; seldom adopts prominent perch.

Voice: A harsh, but plaintive, repeated *'keer'*. Song, a subdued monotonou succession of scratchy notes.
Habitat and Range: Olive groves, gardens and lightly wooded country. Nest fairly high in trees. Summer visitor to Turkey, Greece, and S. Yugoslavia irregular Bulgaria. Vagrant elsewhere in S. and W. Europe.

CROWS: Corvidae

The largest of the perching birds, with black or boldly patterned plumage Longish, powerful bills. Sexes similar. Tree, cliff or hole nesting.

JAY *Garrulus glandarius*　　　　　　　　　　　　　　　　　Pl. 6
　　Du – Vlaamse gaai　　　　　　　　Fr – Geai des chênes
　　Ge – Eichelhäher　　　　　　　　　Sw – Nötskrika
Identification: 13½″. Pinkish-brown body, *white rump contrasting with black tail*, bold white patch on wings, *blue and black barred wing-coverts*, streaked black and white erectile crown-feathers. Eyes pale blue. Flight heavy. Often i small noisy parties.
Voice: A penetrating, raucous *'skraaak'*, sometimes in chorus. Various hars notes and subdued chuckling, clicking and mewing.
Habitat: Rarely far from trees. Often in gardens. Usually nests in well-seclude coniferous and deciduous woods. Map 320.

SIBERIAN JAY *Perisoreus infaustus*　　　　　　　　　　　　Pl. 6
　　Du – Taiga gaai　　　　　　　　　Fr – Mésangeai imitateur
　　Ge – Unglückshäher　　　　　　　Sw – Lavskrika
Identification: 12″. *Fox-red wing-feathers, rump and especially outer feathers o well-graduated tail* are conspicuous in flight. Crown and nape dull sooty-brown wings, back, centre tail-feathers and under-parts mouse-grey, with rufou flanks and under tail-coverts. Retiring and usually silent in breeding season otherwise perky and confident, snatching food from humans in winter. Agile i clinging to tips of pine branches to reach cones.
Voice: A cheerful *'kook, kook'*, and a raucous *'chair'*; also *'whisk-ee'* an Buzzard-like mewing notes.
Habitat: Thick northern coniferous and birch woods, resorting to outskirts o camps and villages in winter. Usually nests in spruce or pine, on branch close t trunk. Map 321.

AZURE-WINGED MAGPIE *Cyanopica cyana*　　　　　　　Pl. 6
　　Du – Blauwe ekster　　　　　　　Fr – Pie-bleue
　　Ge – Blauelster　　　　　　　　　Sw – Blåskata
Identification: 13½″. Easily recognized by *rich black cap* extending to nape and below eyes, *blue wings* with black inner edges to primaries, and long, graduated *blue tail*, or by *distinctive voice*. Upper-parts brownish-grey, under-parts pale with white throat. Behaviour confident and perky, roaming the country in noisy bands; more secretive in breeding season. Actions resemble Magpie's.
Voice: A querulous *'zhree'*, with rising inflection, and a harsh *'kraa, kwink-kwink-kwink'*.

Habitat and Range: Gardens, orchards, olive and eucalyptus groves and woods, particularly where ilex and pine are abundant. Builds open nest, usually in fork of pine, ilex, poplar or oak. Breeds in scattered groups. Resident in C. and S. Spain, Portugal.

MAGPIE   *Pica pica*   **Pl. 69**
Du – Ekster   Fr – Pie bavarde
Ge – Elster   Sw – Skata

Identification: 18″. Unmistakably *contrasting black and white plumage and long tail*. Scapulars, flanks and belly white; remainder black, glossed blue, green and purple. Often in small parties; larger gatherings occur in winter.

Voice: A loud, rapid '*chak-chak-chak-chak*'. Various not unmusical chattering and piping notes in breeding season.

Habitat: Farmlands and open country with hedges and some trees. Builds domed nest in tall trees, thorn bushes, hedgerows, wood edges, even bramble-patches. Map 322.

NUTCRACKER   *Nucifraga caryocatactes*   **Pl. 69**
Du – Notenkraker   Fr – Casse-noix moucheté
Ge – Tannenhäher   Sw – Nötkråka

Identification: 12½″. Dark chocolate-brown, *boldly speckled with white*. Long, heavy, blackish bill. Very conspicuous *white under tail-coverts*, with broad white border to underside of shortish black tail (upper side shows only narrow white tip). Wings blackish and very broad in flight. Flight Jay-like. Often in small parties, except in breeding season. Likes perching on tree-tops.

Voice: A harsh '*kror*' and a loud, rasping '*krair*', often repeated fairly quickly 4–6 times, also a Jay-like '*skraaak*'. In breeding season various croaks, clicks and mewing notes.

Habitat: Mainly coniferous forests in mountainous regions, also deciduous woods in winter. Breeds in conifers. Map 323.

ALPINE CHOUGH   *Pyrrhocorax graculus*   **Pls. 69, 70**
Du – Alpenkauw   Fr – Chocard à bec jaune
Ge – Alpendohle   Sw – Alpkaja

Identification: 15″. Distinguished from Chough by much *shorter and straighter yellow bill*. Legs are red. At short range plumage looks blacker, less shot with blue. In gliding flight separable from Chough by backward-curved wing-tips (Chough's wings are straight-edged and broader). Behaviour similar. Juvenile is duller, with blackish legs.

Voice: Less vocal than Chough but generally higher-pitched; a rippling '*chirrish*', a shrill, explosive '*tchiupp*' and harsh, crow-like notes.

Habitat: Mountains. Does not normally descend to lowlands, nor occur on sea coasts. Nests in cleft rocks and in ruins. Map 324.

CHOUGH   *Pyrrhocorax pyrrhocorax*   **Pls. 69, 70**
Du – Alpenkraai   Fr – Crave à bec rouge
Ge – Alpenkrähe   Sw – Alpkråka

Identification: 15½″. Glossy, blue-black plumage, *long, curved red bill and red legs*. Flight strong, buoyant and frequently acrobatic, with widely separated, upcurved primaries when soaring. Sociable. Easily distinguished from Jackdaw by total absence of grey plumage and from yellow-billed Alpine Chough by *longer, red bill* and broader, straighter wings.

Voice: A long, high-pitched '*chweeaw*', not unlike Jackdaw, but more musical. The characteristic '*chuff*' and several gull-like calls '*kwuk-uk-uk*', etc.

Habitat: Mountains and locally cliffs and rocky outcrops near the sea. Nests in cleft rocks, cliff ledges, caves. Map 325.

JACKDAW   *Corvus monedula*   **Pl. 70**
   Du – Kauw   Fr – Choucas des tours
   Ge – Dohle   Sw – Kaja

Identification: 13″. Black, with *grey nape* and ear-coverts. Under-parts dark grey. Eye distinctively pale grey. *Smaller size,* quicker wing-beat, jaunty actions, *shorter bill* and characteristic voice easily distinguish it from Rook and crows. Gregarious, often with Rooks and Starlings. Scandinavian form *C. m. monedula* generally has paler collar and under-parts and a barely discernible white patch either side of neck.

Voice: Unmistakable '*chak*' and, when excited, a chattering '*chaka-chaka-chack*'; also '*kya*' and widely varying breeding calls.

Habitat: Parks, cliffs, old buildings, farmlands. Nests sociably in holes in trees, buildings, cliffs, occasionally in burrows and in branches of trees. Map 326.

ROOK   *Corvus frugilegus*   **Pl. 70**
   Du – Roek   Fr – Corbeau freux
   Ge – Saatkrähe   Sw – Råka

Identification: 18″. Black, with iridescent gloss. Distinguished from crows by *bare, whitish face and more slender, more pointed greyish-black bill*; thighs appear noticeably shaggy when walking. Juvenile is duller, with fully feathered black face; more easily confused with Carrion Crow, but bill is always more slender. Flight direct and regular, with faster wing-beats than Carrion Crow's. Gregarious.

Voice: Has wide vocabulary. Usual notes, '*kaw*' or '*kaaa*'. Voice much less harsh than Carrion Crow's.

Habitat: Prefers agricultural areas with some trees. Nests and roosts *in colonies* in tree-tops. Map 327.

CARRION CROW   *Corvus corone corone*   **Pl. 70**
   Du – Zwarte kraai   Fr – Corneille noire
   Ge – Rabenkrähe   Sw – Svart kråka

Identification: 18½″. All black; glossy in good light. Heavy black bill. Flight direct, slow and regular; soars rarely. Usually solitary or in pairs, except when roosting. Distinguished from immature Rook by heavier, more rounded bill; from Hooded Crow (a subspecies) by uniform black plumage; from Raven by much smaller size, less massive bill, squarer tail, but most readily recognized *by voice*.

Voice: A harsh, croaking '*kraa*' repeated 3–4 times. Also querulous, repeated '*keerk*' and a muffled metallic '*konk*'.

Habitat: Moors, cultivated country with some trees, sea-shores, even town parks. Usually nests in trees, occasionally on cliffs. Map 328.

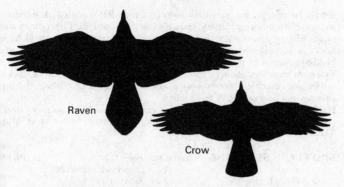

Flight-silhouettes of Raven and Crow
(Carrion Crow and Hooded Crow have same silhouette)

HOODED CROW *Corvus corone cornix* **Pl. 70**

  Du – Bonte kraai   Fr – Corneille mantelée
  Ge – Nebelkrähe   Sw – Grå kråka

Identification: 18½″. Easily distinguished from Carrion Crow (of which it is a subspecies) and Rook by *grey back and under-parts.* Remainder black. Voice, habits and habitat as Carrion Crow, with which it interbreeds where ranges overlap. Northern race is *C. c. cornix;* southern is *C. c. sardonius.* Map 329.

RAVEN *Corvus corax* **Pl. 70**

  Du – Raaf   Fr – Grand corbeau
  Ge – Kolkrabe   Sw – Korp

Identification: 25″. Large size, *massive black bill,* shaggy throat-feathers, *wedge-shaped* end of tail and *deep,* distinctive voice easily distinguish it from smaller crows. Plumage black, iridescent in good light. Powerful, direct flight; often soars and glides; acrobatic flight especially during courtship.

Voice: A repeated, deep '*prruk*'; a deep '*koo-rook*', a tooting note like an old-fashioned motor horn and a high metallic '*tok*'; many other croaking and clucking notes.

Habitat: Frequents and breeds on cliffs, mountains, also in trees. Map 330.

STARLINGS: Sturnidae

Stocky birds, with short tails, long pointed bills. Jaunty, garrulous and very active. Feed on open ground. Sexes similar. Hole nesting.

STARLING *Sturnus vulgaris* **Pl. 69**

  Du – Spreeuw   Fr – Etourneau sansonnet
  Ge – Star   Sw – Stare

Identification: 8½″. Blackish, glossed bronze-green and purple. *Short tail; pointed wings; long sharp bill.* Plumage closely speckled in winter, particularly female. Juvenile mouse-brown, with whitish throat. Bill of adult dark in winter, lemon-yellow in spring. Jaunty, quarrelsome and garrulous. Flight direct and rapid, gliding occasionally. Feeds and roosts gregariously. Occurs in huge flocks in autumn and winter, congregating in dense, noisy throngs on city buildings, woods or reed-beds at dusk.

Voice: A harsh descending '*tcheeer*'. Also a medley of clear whistles, clicks, rattles and chuckles, woven into a long, rambling song, delivered from chimney-pot or tree-top. A good mimic.

Habitat: Equally at home in town or country. Breeds in holes in trees, buildings, thatches, nest-boxes, etc., or holes in ground in barren areas. Map 331.

SPOTLESS STARLING   *Sturnus unicolor*   Pl. 69

Du – Zwarte spreeuw	Fr – Etourneau unicolore
Ge – Einfarbstar	Sw – Svart stare

Identification: 8½". Indistinguishable at a distance from Starling, but at short range male in breeding plumage is obviously *blacker*, glossed with purple and *without spots*; bill yellow. Female is duller. In winter both adults are greyish-black, speckled with small, arrow-shaped white spots. Juvenile like dark young Starling. Behaviour and flight like Starling.

Voice: Louder and shriller than Starling's; notably a whistling '*seeooo*'.

Habitat and Range: Usually in small colonies on cliffs and in towns and villages, locally in wooded regions and around isolated farms. Nests in holes in trees, cliffs, ruins, under eaves, etc. Resident in Spain, Portugal, Corsica, Sardinia, Sicily. Vagrant Greece.

ROSE-COLOURED STARLING   *Sturnus roseus*   Pl. 69

Du – Rose spreeuw	Fr – Martin roselin
Ge – Rosenstar	Sw – Rosenstare

Identification: 8½". Similar to Starling in form and movements, though flight subtly different. Plumage unmistakable *rose-pink, with glossy black head, neck, wings and tail, and a distinctive crest*. Bill more thrush-like than Starling's, orange-yellow in summer, legs pink; in winter bill is brown. Juvenile is sandy-brown, with darker wings and tail and no crest; *paler* than young Starling, even in flight, and further distinguished by *conspicuously pale rump* and *yellowish bill*. (But beware occasional rather similar biscuit-coloured young Starlings.) Gregarious, even when nesting. Often associates with Starlings, particularly when feeding among cattle.

Voice: Flight-notes like Starling; feeding flocks maintain rapid, high-pitched chatter, louder though less varied than Starling's.

Habitat and Range: Open country, agricultural land, cliffs, steppes. Breeds in holes among stones on open ground, and in walls or wood-stacks. Passage in Greece, breeding irregularly in SE Europe, west to Hungary and Italy and occurring in summer and autumn increasingly erratically westwards over rest of Europe to British Isles, Iceland.

SPARROWS: Passeridae

Thick-billed, sturdy little birds, mainly without bright colours. Sexes sometimes similar. Nest in holes, trees, buildings or rocks.

HOUSE SPARROW *Passer domesticus*   **Pl. 73**
    Du – Huismus   Fr – Moineau domestique
    Ge – Haussperling   Sw – Gråsparv
Identification: 5¾″. Perhaps the most familiar bird. Male distinguished by *dark grey crown, chestnut nape, black throat* and whitish cheeks. Female and juvenile lack the black throat and are dull brown above and dingy white below, without distinctive marks. Male Italian Sparrow, the so-called *P. d. italiae* (now regarded as hybrid House × Spanish) has brighter coloration in breeding plumage, with *rich chestnut* crown, *whiter* cheeks and under-parts. See Pl. 73 and map. See also Tree and Spanish Sparrows.
Voice: Garrulous and varied. A loud '*cheep*', '*chissis*' and various grating, twittering and chirping notes.
Habitat: Built-up areas and cultivated land, seldom far from human habitation. Nests in holes or crevices in buildings, ivy, ricks, etc. Map 332.

SPANISH SPARROW *Passer hispaniolensis*   **Pl. 73**
    Du – Spaanse mus   Fr – Moineau espagnol
    Ge – Weidensperling   Sw – Spansk sparv
Identification: 5¾″. Male has rich, *chestnut-red* crown, as in Italian Sparrow (see House Sparrow) but is distinguished by *much more extensive black throat and heavily streaked upper-breast, black-streaked flanks, and much more heavily marked back*. Female and juvenile resemble House Sparrows, but some show faint streaks on flanks. Behaviour and flight much as in House Sparrow, but often seen in dense flocks far from houses.
Voice: A full, rich '*chup*' and other notes resembling House Sparrow's, but all are richer in tone.
Habitat: Not restricted to houses, preferring bushy woods, roadside trees and forests. Breeds colonially and singly, in foundations of occupied or unoccupied nests of storks, eagles, etc., and in old martins' nests and in branches of wayside or forest trees. Map 333.

TREE SPARROW *Passer montanus*   **Pl. 73**
    Du – Ringmus   Fr – Moineau friquet
    Ge – Feldsperling   Sw – Pilfink
Identification: 5½″. Sexes alike. Distinguished from male House Sparrow by rich *chocolate-brown crown, and black spot on purer white ear-coverts* which almost form white collar. Smaller and more slender than House Sparrow and more retiring. See also Spanish Sparrow.
Voice: Higher-pitched than House Sparrow's. A short metallic '*chik*' or '*chop*', a repeated '*chit-tchup*' and a rapid twittering '*tiwi-twit-iwit*'. Unmistakable flight call '*tek, tek*'.
Habitat: In W. Europe more rural than House Sparrow. In south and eastern countries occurs around houses and in the north on tundra. Nests in holes in

trees (particularly pollarded willows), nest-boxes, haystacks, etc., but in houses in S. and E. Europe. Map 334.

ROCK SPARROW *Petronia petronia*   Pl. 73
Du – Rotsmus   Fr – Moineau soulcie
Ge – Steinsperling   Sw – Stenfink

Identification: $5\frac{1}{2}''$. Pale and plump, with short tail. Centre of crown is grey-brown, sides of crown and cheeks dark brown, with *long, broad supercilium to nape*. White spots on tips of tail-feathers conspicuous, *particularly in flight*. Under-parts faintly mottled with pale brown lines. Inconspicuous pale yellow spot on throat visible only when head is raised and seen at close quarters. Juvenile paler, without yellow throat-patch. Very active, often *running* briskly among rocks.

Voice: A characteristic, squeaky '*pey-i*', recalling Goldfinch. Varied chipping notes recall House Sparrow.

Habitat: High rocky mountain slopes, stony ground, ruins, etc., also in dry river-beds and farmlands; seldom among houses though sometimes among trees. Nests in crevices in rocks and trees. Map 335.

SNOWFINCH *Montifringilla nivalis*   Pl. 73
Du – Sneeuwvink   Fr – Niverolle
Ge – Schneefink   Sw – Snöfink

Identification: $7''$. A mountain species. Distinguished from Snow Bunting by *grey head and black throat*, but unlikely to be seen in same localities. Warm chocolate-brown above, creamy-white below. Wings mainly white, with black primaries. Tail mainly white, with black centre, more conspicuous in flight than when perched. Female and juvenile duller, with less white on wings and tail. Bill blackish in spring, yellow in winter and juvenile. Perches upright, with nervous jerking of tail.

Voice: A harsh '*tswik*'. Song, in nuptial flight and when perched, a repeated '*sitticher-sitticher*' and a rapid trill.

Habitat: Bare mountain-tops above 6,000 ft., lower in winter. Visits mountain huts and camps. Nests in rock crevices, walls, under eaves, etc. Map 336.

WAXBILLS: Estrildidae

COMMON WAXBILL *Estrilda astrild*   Pl. 77
Du – Sint Helena-fazantje   Fr – Astrild ondulé
Ge – Wellenastrild   Sw – Helenaastrild

Identification: $3\frac{3}{4}''$. Tiny, sparrow-like. Easily identified by small size and red bill and belly. Dark brown above finely *barred*, as are breast and flanks; *crimson belly*; whitish cheeks; narrow, rounded tail. Adult has *conspicuous red bill* and some red around eye; immature bill is blackish. Usually feeds and flies near ground in twittering flocks. Call-note a short '*tzuk-ut*'. Introduced birds from Africa now feral in Portugal and recorded in Spain. The Black-rumped Waxbill *E. troglodytes* (with blackish tail and rump) is probably also feral there.

FINCHES: Fringillidae

Seed-eating birds, often brightly coloured, with short, strong bills, usually thick
at the base. Nest in trees, bushes, or on ground.

CHAFFINCH   *Fringilla coelebs*   **Pl. 71**
   Du – Vink   Fr – Pinson des arbres
   Ge – Buchfink   Sw – Bofink
Identification: 6″. Commonest finch. Distinguished by *bold double white wing-
bars* and, in flight, by *white outer tail-feathers.* Male pinkish-brown below, with
chestnut mantle, greenish rump, and *slate-blue* crown and nape. Female pale
olive-brown above, lighter below. Flight undulating. Gregarious, with other
finches, except in breeding season; sexes often in separate flocks. Immediately
distinguished from Brambling by *greenish* (not white) rump.
Voice: A loud, repeated '*chwink*', '*wheet*' and '*chwit*'; flight-call a subdued
'*tsip*'. Song, a brief, vigorous cascade of about a dozen notes, terminating in a
flourishing '*choo-ee-o*'; varies widely locally.
Habitat: Hedges, woods, commons, gardens, farmlands. Nests usually fairly
low, in bush or tree. Map 337.

BRAMBLING   *Fringilla montifringilla*   **Pl. 71**
   Du – Keep   Fr – Pinson du nord
   Ge – Bergfink   Sw – Bergfink
Identification: 5¾″. Easily distinguished from Chaffinch by *conspicuous though
narrow white rump* and less white on wings and tail. Male has *bold orange
shoulder-patch* and orange breast; head and mantle in spring are brilliant *black*,
in winter brownish. Female can be confused with female Chaffinch but has
paler, buffer plumage, white rump and dark stripes on crown. Flight more
erratic than Chaffinch. Gregarious with Chaffinches in winter. Bullfinch also
has white though wider rump-patch, but is much heavier bird, with very stubby
bill.
Voice: A metallic '*tsweep*' and '*tchuc*'; latter repeated rapidly as flight-call.
Song, a grating, monotonously repeated Greenfinch-like '*dzweea*', interspersed
with a few very weak chipping notes.
Habitat: Winters in beech woods, and farmlands. Breeds chiefly in birch, but
also in conifers, usually on outskirts of wood. Map 338.

SERIN   *Serinus serinus*   **Pl. 71**
   Du – Europese kanarie   Fr – Serin cini
   Ge – Girlitz   Sw – Gulhämpling
Identification: 4½″. A tiny, streaked, yellowish finch. Distinguished by *stubby
bill*, and *bright yellow rump*. Male has *bright yellow forehead*, supercilium,
throat and breast. Female more streaked, greyer below, browner above;
distinguished from female Siskin by *shorter, stubbier bill, lack of yellow in tail*,
bolder supercilium and heavier streaking below. Juvenile strongly streaked with
brown, lacks yellow on rump. Flight swift and undulating; in nuptial flight rises
vertically and descends in circles. Sociable.
Voice: Twittering flight-call; a rapid '*si-twi-twi-twi*', and a hard, Wren-like
'*chit-chit-chit*'; anxiety-note a liquid '*tsooeet*'. Song, delivered from tree-top.

telegraph wire, or in flight, a rapid, sibilant, almost hissing, jingle, with occasional Canary-like trills.

Habitat: Parks, gardens, vineyards, etc. Nests in trees, vines, small bushes. Map 339.

CITRIL FINCH *Serinus citrinella*   **Pl. 71**
 Du – Citroensijs   Fr – Venturon montagnard
 Ge – Zitronenzeisig   Sw – Citronsiska

Identification: $4\frac{3}{4}''$. Yellowish-green *with greyish nape and sides of neck*; bright yellow under-parts, greenish-yellow rump; blackish wings with greenish-yellow bar. Female duller and faintly streaked. Juvenile greyish-brown with paler under-parts, streaked above and below. Flight dancing. Sociable. Greyish neck and unstreaked under-parts distinguish it from Siskin and Serin. Corsican race *S. c. corsicana* has streaked rusty mantle, paler yellow under-parts and nests down to sea level.

Voice: A plaintive '*tsi-ï*'; also a metallic '*chwick*'. Song, a Siskin-like mixture of creaking notes and musical Goldfinch-like twittering, often during circling flight.

Habitat: Mountains with scattered conifers and open rocky ground; above 5,000 ft. in summer, lower in winter. Nests in conifers. Map 340.

GREENFINCH *Carduelis chloris*   **Pl. 71**
 Du – Groenling   Fr – Verdier
 Ge – Grünling   Sw – Grönfink

Identification: $5\frac{3}{4}''$. Male olive-green, with *yellow-green rump and conspicuous yellow on wings and tail*. Heavy, whitish bill. Pinkish legs. Female duller, greyer, much less yellow. Juvenile browner and streaked. Flight undulating.

Voice: A loud, rapid trill; also a repeated short '*chup*' or '*teu*'. In breeding season a prolonged nasal '*tswe-e-e*'. Song, from tree-tops, or in bat-like flight, a Canary-like twittering, mixed with call-notes.

Habitat: Gardens, shrubberies, farmlands. Nests in hedges, bushes and small trees, particularly evergreens. Map 341.

GOLDFINCH *Carduelis carduelis*   **Pl. 71**
 Du – Putter   Fr – Chardonneret
 Ge – Stieglitz   Sw – Steglits

Identification: $4\frac{3}{4}''$. Sexes similar. *Boldly marked black and yellow wings*; black and white tail; *scarlet face, black and white head*; tawny-brown back merging into whitish rump. Juvenile head and upper-parts greyish-buff, streaked and spotted brown. Flight undulating and dancing. Sociable.

Voice: Unmistakable, liquid, '*switt-witt-witt-witt*' frequently repeated; anxiety note a soft '*ah-ï*'; song, a Canary-like, liquid twitter, incorporating variations on the call-notes.

Habitat: Gardens, orchards, cultivated land. Forages for thistle-seed in wastelands and roadsides during autumn and winter. Nests in trees, usually near tip of branch; occasionally in hedges. Map 342.

SISKIN   *Carduelis spinus*   **Pl. 71**
  Du – Sijs   Fr – Tarin des aulnes
  Ge – Zeisig   Sw – Grönsiska
Identification: 4¾″. Male *yellowish-green*, paler beneath, with *black* crown and chin; yellow rump, wing-bar, sides of tail and stripe behind eye; brown-streaked back and flanks. Female greyer, with less yellow, no black on head, more strongly streaked whitish under-parts. Flight finch-like but very buoyant. Gregarious with redpolls in winter. See also Serin, Citril Finch and Redpoll.
Voice: Almost constant twitter. Call-notes, a high squeaky '*tsy-zi*' and a wheezy '*tsooeet*'. Song, a long, rapid nasal twitter, often terminating with a long Greenfinch-like wheezing note.
Habitat: Coniferous woods, birch and alder thickets and uncut hedges. Nests high in conifers, usually at extremity of branch. Map 343.

LINNET   *Carduelis cannabina*   **Pl. 72**
  Du – Kneu   Fr – Linotte mélodieuse
  Ge – Hänfling   Sw – Hämpling
Identification: 5¼″. Male has chestnut-brown mantle; dark brown wings and forked tail are *edged with white*; head *greyish*; under-parts buff, streaked brownish-black; breast *pinkish*; in breeding season also has *crimson crown and breast*, whitish throat with brown streaks. Female lacks crimson, is more streaked. Flight undulating. Gregarious. In winter distinguished from Twite and Redpoll by streaked chin and throat, prominent white on sides of tail (faint in Twite), and dark bill.
Voice: Usual call '*tsooeet*'; flight-note a rapid twitter; song, a varied, musical twitter, interspersed with pure and nasal notes, delivered from top of bush, sometimes in chorus.
Habitat: Open country with hedges; in winter roams in large flocks over waste ground, farmlands, marshes. Breeds sociably, in gorse, thickets and hedges, occasionally in marram grass and heather. Map 344.

TWITE   *Carduelis flavirostris*   **Pl. 72**
  Du – Frater   Fr – Linotte à bec jaune
  Ge – Berghänfling   Sw – Gulnäbbad hämpling
Identification: 5¼″. Rather Linnet-like in appearance and actions. Dull buff above, streaked black and brown, lighter below. *Throat warm buff.* Male has *dark pinkish rump*, which in female is buff streaked with black. Bill greyish-yellow in summer, light yellow in winter. Distinguished from female and juvenile Linnets by less white in wings and tail, darker upper-parts, almost orange-buff throat and slightly longer tail, and, in winter, also by *yellow* bill; from Redpoll by buffer plumage, lack of black chin, lack of red cap and longer tail.
Voice: A nasal '*chweet*'. Almost constant twitter in flight. Song has curiously hoarse, twanging quality.
Habitat: Breeds sociably on moors and high wastelands. In winter roams in flocks over coastal regions, fields, marshes, etc. Map 345.

REDPOLL *Carduelis flammea* Pl. 72
Du – Barmsijs Fr – Sizerin flammé
Ge – Birkenzeisig Sw – Gråsiska
Identification: 5". A little, streaked, grey-brown finch with a *bright crimson forehead* and a *black chin*. Male also has *pink* flush on breast. Flanks streaked. Flight undulating and buoyant. Sociable. British and Alpine race (Lesser Redpoll, *C. f. cabaret*) is smaller and browner, with more streaked upper-parts and less noticeable wing-bars. Continental race (Mealy Redpoll, *C. f. flammea*) is somewhat larger, with whiter wing-bar and rump and, in winter, paler and greyer plumage. Greenland race (Greater Redpoll, *C. f. rostrata*) is even larger (5½–6") and darker, with larger bill and darker flank-stripes, but usually not safely distinguishable unless in company with smaller redpolls. See also Arctic Redpoll.
Voice: High-pitched, metallic flight-calls: a very rapid sustained twittering '*chuch-uch-uch*', '*tiu-tiu-tiu*', etc. Anxiety-note, a plaintive '*tsooeet*'. Song, a sustained series of brief trills interspersed with flight-calls.
Habitat: Copses, shrubberies, preferably of alder and willow; in northern forests chiefly deciduous; also rocky outcrops above tree-line in mountainous areas and on tundra. Breeds, often sociably, in birch, alder, willow or juniper. Map 346.

ARCTIC REDPOLL *Carduelis hornemanni* Pl. 72
Du – Witstuitbarmsijs Fr – Sizerin blanchâtre
Ge – Polarbirkenzeisig Sw – Snösiska
N. Am – Hoary Redpoll
Identification: 5". Breeding plumage looks '*hoar-frosted*', particularly on head and nape. Rump *unstreaked white* (as in some Mealy Redpolls); this and pale head contrast with grey back to give '*saddle*' *effect*. Wing-bars conspicuous. Under-parts *whiter and less streaked* than other races; male's breast is also much paler pink. Female lacks pink. Both sexes have crimson crown. Habits similar to other redpolls.
Voice: As other redpolls, but notes of flight-twitter slower, more clearly separated.
Habitat: Overlaps with other races, but usually in more open or marshy tundra, nesting in dwarf birch and tussocks of upper latitudes. Map 347.

TWO-BARRED CROSSBILL *Loxia leucoptera* Pl. 72
Du – Witbandkruisbek Fr – Bec-croisé bifascié
Ge – Bindenkreuzschnabel Sw – Bändelkorsnäbb
N. Am – White-winged Crossbill
Identification: 5¾". Smaller than Crossbill. Distinguished even in flight by *bold, double white wing-bars*, which may give Chaffinch-like appearance in poor light. Male plumage more brilliant carmine than Crossbill; female lighter yellow and more streaked. Juvenile has less pronounced wing-bars than adults, otherwise like juvenile Crossbill. See also Pine Grosbeak.
Voice: A liquid '*peet*' and a dry '*chiff-chiff*' (latter corresponding to Crossbill's hard '*chip-chip*'). Song, a succession of loud trills on different pitches.
Habitat: As Crossbill, but prefers larch forests. Breeds rarely N. Finland, N Sweden. Winters Baltic Provinces, sometimes reaching C., NW and W. Europe and British Isles.

CROSSBILL   *Loxia curvirostra*   **Pl. 72**

   Du – Kruisbek   Fr – Bec-croisé des sapins
   Ge – Fichtenkreuzschnabel   Sw – Mindre korsnäbb
   N. Am – Red Crossbill

Identification: 6½". A bird of the conifers. Distinguished by *crossed mandibles, parrot-like actions in feeding and short, forked tail*. Male plumage *brick-red*, brighter on rump, with dark wings and tail. Young male orange-brown. Female olive with yellowish rump and under-parts. Juvenile greenish-grey, strongly streaked below. Gregarious and tame. Heavy head and short tail distinctive in rapid, undulating flight. Irrupts in large numbers in late summer every few years and some Continental birds wander to Britain to breed. Distinguished from Two-barred Crossbill by absence of white on wings. See also Scottish Crossbill, Parrot Crossbill, Pine Grosbeak and Scarlet Rosefinch.

Voice: A loud, emphatic '*chip-chip-chip*'. Song faintly resembles Greenfinch's, but is a more regularly spaced mixture of short trills, creaking, warbling and chipping notes, notably '*ti-chee, ti-chee*'.

Habitat: Coniferous woods, chiefly spruce, but also pine and larch. Dropped, open cones on ground indicate presence. Breeds in conifers. Map 348.

SCOTTISH CROSSBILL   *Loxia scotica*

Identification: 6½". Now regarded as a distinct species. Distinguished from Crossbill by usually (but not always) *much larger bill*; from Parrot Crossbill by slightly smaller size, though bill can be almost as large as Parrot's. Occurs chiefly in pine woods (like Parrot Crossbill), feeding especially on cones of Scots Pine *Pinus sylvestris*. Crossbill prefers spruce (*Picea*); Two-barred prefers larch (*Larix*). Not illustrated.

Voice: Apparently differs slightly from Crossbill, but not yet adequately studied.

Range: Restricted to pine woods in northern half of Scotland. Map 348.

PARROT CROSSBILL   *Loxia pytyopsittacus*   **Pl. 72**

   Du – Grote kruisbek   Fr – Bec-croisé perroquet
   Ge – Kiefernkreuzschnabel   Sw – Större korsnäbb

Identification: 6¾". Slightly larger than Crossbill, but *heavier, more rounded bill* gives more 'top-heavy' appearance. Colouring and parrot-like actions similar, but seldom seen in such large numbers and usually keeps apart from other crossbills. Habitat as Crossbill, but with greater preference for pines. See also Scottish Crossbill.

Voice: Deeper and stronger than Crossbill's, a rounder '*chup-chup-chup*' and distinctive '*tchweng, tchweng*' notes.

Range: Breeds in S. Finland and Scandinavia from 67° southwards sporadically to E. Germany; in winter occurs Denmark, Germany, Austria, occasionally reaching W. (including Britain) and S. Europe.

TRUMPETER FINCH   *Bucanetes githagineus*   **Pl. 65**

   Du – Woestijnvink   Fr – Bouvreuil githagine
   Ge – Wüstengimpel   Sw – Ökentrumpetare

Identification: 5¼". A sparrow-size ground-feeding bird with a stumpy bill. Male is greyish-brown *tinged with rosy-pink* on rump, wings, under-parts and face; in spring bill is *bright coral-red*. Female and winter male duller, with yellowish bills. *Voice very distinctive*. Difficult to observe in typical habitat, crouching close to ground. Has rapid, finch-like flight.

Voice: A remarkable nasal, buzzing, bleating note and a harsh '*chizz*'.

Habitat and Range: Deserts and barren hill country, but often near water sources. Nests in rocky crevices or stone walls. Asiatic and N. African species now breeding SE Spain. Visits Malta; vagrant elsewhere in S., N. and W. Europe (including Britain).

SCARLET ROSEFINCH   *Carpodacus erythrinus*   **Pl. 72**
  Du – Roodmus   Fr – Roselin cramoisi
  Ge – Karmingimpel   Sw – Rosenfink

Identification: 5¾". Male has brilliant *rosy-carmine head, breast and rump*, heavy bill, dark brown wings with two indistinct bars, white belly. Female, first-year male and juvenile rather nondescript: yellowish-brown above, brighter on rump, greyer on head; buff below with fine brown streaks; best distinguished by dumpy shape, bold black eye in large round head, pale double wing-bar and forked tail. Flight undulating. Distinguished from Pine Grosbeak by much smaller size and indistinct wing-bars; from crossbills by longer tail and uncrossed mandibles.

Voice: A quiet, piping '*tiu-eek*'; song, a far-carrying, distinctive '*switi-sweetoo*'

Habitat: In summer, thickets, copses, undergrowth near water. Nests low down, usually in swampy vegetation, locally in dry oak woods. Map 349.

PINE GROSBEAK   *Pinicola enucleator*   **Pl. 72**
  Du – Haakbek   Fr – Dur-bec des sapins
  Ge – Hakengimpel   Sw – Tallbit

Identification: 8". A large, heavy finch with a *longish tail*. Male has *deep rosy-pink head, neck, breast, and rump*; dark wings with *double white bars*; grey belly. In female the pink parts are a striking *greenish golden-brown*. Crown rather flat, bill heavy and Bullfinch-like. Flight very undulating. Usually very tame. Sociable in winter. Two-barred Crossbill and Scarlet Rosefinch are also rosy with wing-bars, but are much smaller (sparrow-size).

Voice: A high, piping '*tee-tee-tew*'. Alarm, a musical '*cheevli-cheevli*'. Song consists of loud, whistling notes, interspersed with a twanging note.

Habitat: Northern mixed and coniferous woods. Usually nests in conifer. Map 350.

BULLFINCH   *Pyrrhula pyrrhula*   **Pl. 72**
  Du – Goudvink   Fr – Bouvreuil pivoine
  Ge – Gimpel   Sw – Domherre

Identification: 5¾". Male, a striking bird with *bright rose-red under-parts conspicuous white rump*, blue-grey upper-parts, *black cap and chin* and *very stubby black bill*. Has black wings and tail, white wing-patch. Female has similar black cap and pattern but is pinkish-brown below, grey-brown above. Flight undulating. Secretive, seldom far from cover. North European race *P. p. pyrrhula* is distinctly larger and brighter than British *P. p. nesa*. See Brambling, which has narrower white rump.

Voice: A soft, piping '*wheeb*'. Song, a very subdued mixture of warbling and creaking notes, such as '*djee-ur-ur*' and '*teek, teek, tioo*'.

Habitat: Plantations, thickets, hedgerows, gardens, orchards. Nests in evergreens, garden bushes, hedges. Map 351.

HAWFINCH *Coccothraustes coccothraustes* **Pl. 71**
Du – Appelvink   Fr – Gros-bec
Ge – Kernbeisser   Sw – Stenknäck

Identification: 7″. *Huge bill*, bull-neck, *short* white-tipped tail, *bold white patches* high on blue-black wings. Tawny head, rich brown back, pale pinkish-brown under-parts, black throat and lores. Bill gun-metal blue in spring, pale horn in winter. Female paler, less rufous on crown. Juvenile is barred with brown and has yellow throat-patch. Flight rapid and usually high, but 'bounding' over short distances. Flight-silhouette (large head, short tail) is unmistakable; overhead, shows *transparent band across primaries*. Walks with upright, waddling gait, and hops powerfully. Often in flocks in winter, feeding on ground in woods. Extremely wary.

Voice: A loud, explosive '*ptik*', or '*ptik . . . ptik-it*', a thin '*tzeeip*', etc. Song, seldom heard, a halting '*teek, teek, tur-whee-whee*', with variations. Usually sings on tree-tops.

Habitat: Chiefly arboreal: mixed woodlands (particularly with beech and hornbeam), parks, orchards. Nests in tree-top, or on low horizontal branch, or against trunk, often in scattered groups. Map 352.

NEW WORLD WARBLERS: Parulidae

Often colourful little vagrants from N. America to Europe. See also Accidentals.

BLACKPOLL WARBLER *Dendroica striata* **Pl. 65**
Identification: 5″. Most likely to be seen in Europe in winter plumage, when general appearance is streaked olive-brown above with greyish crown, pale yellowish below also faintly streaked. Has *two conspicuous white wing-bars*. White under tail-coverts, pale yellowish-brown legs. In breeding plumage male has black cap, white cheeks and black moustachial stripe; white under-parts boldly streaked with black on flanks.

Voice: Has a thin, rather mechanical song of short, buzzy notes on the same pitch, becoming stronger and then diminishing. Calls '*chip*'.

Habitat and Range: Usually in coniferous woodlands, but on migration occurs in deciduous vegetation. Vagrant from N. America to Britain.

BUNTINGS: Emberizidae

Seed-eating birds with short, thick-based bills. Males of most species brightly coloured. Nest in trees, bushes, on ground, or in crevices.

WHITE-THROATED SPARROW *Zonotrichia albicollis* **Pl. 65**
Du – Witkeelgors   Fr – Bruant à gorge blanche
Ge – Weisskehlammer   Sw – Vithalsad sparv

Identification: 6½″. Size of Yellowhammer. Grey-breasted, with clean-cut *white throat-patch*, boldly striped *black and white crown* and broad supercilium which

is yellow before the eye and white behind. Wings and body resemble House
Sparrow. Bill blackish (rather similar White-crowned Sparrow has pale bill –
see Accidentals). Immature has brown and buff head-stripes, less clear-cut
throat-patch. For tan-striped form, see Pl. 65.
Voice: A hard '*chink*' and a slurred '*tseet*'. Song, several clear whistles followed
by three quavering notes.
Habitat and Range: Thickets and low scrub. Vagrant from N. America to W.
(including Britain), N., C. and E. Europe.

LAPLAND BUNTING   *Calcarius lapponicus*   Pl. 73
Du – IJsgors   Fr – Bruant lapon
Ge – Spornammer   Sw – Lappsparv
N. Am – Lapland Longspur

Identification: 6″. Male in spring has *black head, throat, breast and flanks,
conspicuous buffish band from behind eye to white below cheek*, and *bright
chestnut nape*. Upper-parts streaked dark brown; belly whitish, with streaked
flanks; white sides to tail. Female lacks black markings, has striped crown and
whitish throat. In autumn and winter both sexes are more nondescript and
spend most of time *running* on ground; streaked buffish-brown, with narrow
double whitish wing-bars, chestnut on coverts, some dark streaking on flanks,
and varying amount of reddish on nape (in males); often with smudge of streaks
across upper breast. Distinguished from rather similar female Reed Bunting by
stouter form, *shorter tail* showing less white, *pale stripe through crown*, dark
angular mark behind ear-coverts.
Voice: A musical '*teeu*', '*ticky-tick-teu*', etc. Song (in flight) vigorous but
musical, not unlike short extract from Skylark's.
Habitat: Winters in coastal stubble fields, saltings, coastal moors and along
beaches. Breeds in treeless barrens, open tundra and moss-heaths. Map 353.

SNOW BUNTING   *Plectrophenax nivalis*   Pl. 73
Du – Sneeuwgors   Fr – Bruant des neiges
Ge – Schneeammer   Sw – Snösparv

Identification: 6½″. Easily identified by *broad white patches on wings and tail*. In
spring, male has black back, primaries and centre tail-feathers, remainder of
plumage *snow-white*. Female's head grey-brown, with buffish stripe from eye
around ear-coverts, back grey-brown flecked with black. In winter, male's head
is sandy, back browner, under-parts creamy-white with tawny smudges on sides
of breast; female browner, but in flight white wing-patches still conspicuous;
immature has *brown* wings, rufous-buff head and breast-band, creamy-white
under-parts. Flight 'dancing' and usually high. Gregarious; large flocks in flight
resemble drifting snowflakes. See also Snowfinch.
Voice: A loud '*tsweet*', a plaintive '*teup*', and '*teu*' (like Lapland Bunting).
Song, a high, very rapid, but musical '*turi-turi-turi-tetitui*', of almost lark-like
quality; sings on downward glide from circling display-flight and from perch.
Habitat: Winters along sea-shores and open coastal regions, occasionally
inland downs and fields. Nests deep in crevices, in rocky or mountainous
regions. Map 354.

PINE BUNTING   *Emberiza leucocephalos*   **Pl. 74**
  Du – Witkopgors   Fr – Bruant à calotte blanche
  Ge – Fichtenammer   Sw – Tallsparv
Identification: $6\frac{1}{2}''$. Breeding male has unmistakable *chestnut and white head
pattern*; white crown and cheeks edged black, chestnut throat and band through
eye. Chestnut rump. Breast and flanks speckled pale chestnut, with white lower
throat and belly. Much duller in winter. Female is browner, with no white on
head, more like female Yellowhammer but with buffish-white instead of yellow
markings.
Voice: Song resembles short version of Yellowhammer's.
Habitat and Range: Open country with farms and coniferous woods. Vagrant
from Siberia to N., C., W. (including Britain) and S. Europe.

YELLOWHAMMER   *Emberiza citrinella*   **Pl. 74**
  Du – Geelgors   Fr – Bruant jaune
  Ge – Goldammer   Sw – Gulsparv
Identification: $6\frac{1}{2}''$. Male distinguished by *lemon-yellow head and under-parts
and chestnut rump*; streaked chestnut back and streaked flanks. White on outer
tail-feathers conspicuous in flight. Female and juvenile much less yellow, with
more dark markings, particularly on head; distinguished from Cirl by chestnut
rump.
Voice: A metallic '*chip*' and '*twitic*'. Song, a rapid, '*chi-chi-chi-chi-chi . . .
chweee*' usually written 'little-bit-of-bread-and-no-cheese'.
Habitat: Farmlands, roadsides, commons, open country. Breeds on or near
ground at foot of hedge, on ditchside, etc. Map 355.

CIRL BUNTING   *Emberiza cirlus*   **Pl. 74**
  Du – Cirlgors   Fr – Bruant zizi
  Ge – Zaunammer   Sw – Häcksparv
Identification: $6\frac{1}{2}''$. Male has *yellow under-parts with greenish breast-band, black
throat* (latter obscured in winter) and streaked flanks; olive-green head with
dark crown, *yellow stripes above and below eye*, black stripe through eye; back
and sides of breast chestnut; distinguished from Yellowhammer by characteristic head and breast markings. Female and juvenile duller, distinguished
from Yellowhammer by *olive-brown rump*. See also Yellow-breasted and
Ortolan.
Voice: A weak '*sip*', flight-call '*sissi-sissi-sip*'. Song a monotonous, hurried
jingle on one note, recalling Lesser Whitethroat's.
Habitat: Tall hedgerows and trees bordering cultivated land or downs; on
Continent often on bushy and rocky hillsides. Winters in farmlands in mixed
flocks. Nests low down in hedge, trees, sometimes on bank sides. Map 356.

ROCK BUNTING   *Emberiza cia*   **Pl. 74**
  Du – Grijze gors   Fr – Bruant fou
  Ge – Zippammer   Sw – Klippsparv
Identification: $6\frac{1}{4}''$. Distinguished by *ash-grey throat and head, with thin black
stripes* on crown and through and below the eye. Frequently flicks tail open, to
show conspicuous white when feeding on ground. Upper-parts chestnut,
streaked black; rump *unstreaked* chestnut; under-parts *buffish-chestnut*. Female
is duller, browner with breast and flanks slightly streaked. Adult easily

distinguished from all other European buntings by *pale ash-grey throat*. Immature distinguished from young Ortolan and Cretzschmar's by reddish-buff under-parts and chestnut rump.
Voice: Call-note a thin '*seea*'. Song brief and weak, recalls Reed Bunting's: '*zi-zi-zi-zi-zirr*', last note rising.
Habitat: Usually rocky mountainsides, often on trees, occasionally at sea level. Breeds on or near ground. Map 357.

CINEREOUS BUNTING   *Emberiza cineracea*   Pl. 74
Du – Smyrna gors   Fr – Bruant cendré
Ge – Kleinasiatische Ammer   Sw – Gulgrä sparv

Identification: 6½″. A *greyish* bunting with a *dull yellow head* and white flashes on outer tail-feathers. Throat clear yellow. Nape and upper breast ash-grey tinged with yellow; under-parts mainly white. Upper-parts brownish-grey, darkly striped, with coverts and secondaries edged buffish. Bill bluish-horn. Legs flesh-brown. Female duller, with browner, striped head and streaky yellow throat. Immature is darker, with streaked ash-brown under-parts, but throat shows pale sulphur wash; inner secondaries broadly edged buffish-rufous.
Voice: Call-note a short '*kip*'. Brief song has typical bunting character, said to resemble '*zir-zir-zir-zirdli-zi*'.
Habitat and Range: Dry rocky or stony slopes with scanty vegetation up to tree limit. Breeds Greek islands.

ORTOLAN BUNTING   *Emberiza hortulana*   Pl. 74
Du – Ortolaan   Fr – Bruant ortolan
Ge – Ortolan   Sw – Ortolansparv

Identification: 6½″. Distinguished from other buntings by combination of *pinkish-buff under-parts and yellow throat*. Has pale *olive-green head and chest* and *pale yellow throat* with olive moustachial streak. At close quarters narrow yellow eye-ring and pink bill are visible. Upper-parts brown, streaked black. Female is paler, less green, with small dark streaks on chest. Immature browner, streaked on under-parts, but has characteristic *yellow eye-ring and pink bill*. See also Cretzschmar's and Rock Buntings.
Voice: A soft '*tsee-ip*' and '*tsip*' and a piping '*tseu*'. Song slow and variable, usually 6–7 similar clear notes, with final note lower or higher.
Habitat: Open hilly country, often also in lowlands, gardens, scrub. Breeds on or near ground in growing crops or weeds. Map 358.

CRETZSCHMAR'S BUNTING   *Emberiza caesia*   Pl. 74
Du – Bruinkeelortolaan   Fr – Bruant cendrillard
Ge – Grauer Ortolan   Sw – Rostsparv

Identification: 6¼″. Males suggests male Ortolan, but head and breast-band are unmistakable *bright blue-grey* (not olive), throat *rusty* (not yellow). Female distinguished from female Ortolan by *absence of yellow on throat*. Immature doubtfully distinguishable from young Ortolan by buffer appearance; from immature Rock Bunting by pink bill. In autumn both sexes have bright colours partly obscured.
Voice: An insistent '*styip*', less soft than Ortolan's call. Brief song of 3–4 notes on same pitch, the final one emphasized: '*dze-dze-dzree*'; occasionally notes are higher and more musical.

Habitat and Range: Bare rocky hillsides and semi-desert regions with scattered and stunted vegetation. Nests on ground. Summer visitor, breeding commonly in Greece and north to Dalmatia. Vagrant elsewhere in S., E., C., W. (including Britain) and N. Europe.

RUSTIC BUNTING *Emberiza rustica* **Pl. 73**
    Du – Bosgors   Fr – Bruant rustique
    Ge – Waldammer   Sw – Videsparv
Identification: 5¾″. Distinguished from other buntings by pure white throat and under-parts, with large, irregular, *cinnamon breast-band* and a few similar streaks on flanks. Upper-parts chestnut, streaked black. Male has *blackish crown and cheeks* (brownish in winter) with *conspicuous broad white stripe behind eye*. Female has dark brown in place of black on head; faintly suggests big Whinchat. Has nervous habit of raising crest-feathers.
Voice: A repeated, high-pitched '*tsip, tsip, tsip*'. Song rather Dunnock-like, '*seeoo-see-see-sissioo-see-see*'.
Habitat: Thickets near water and mixed woods with rank undergrowth. Breeds in grass or low bushes. Map 359.

LITTLE BUNTING *Emberiza pusilla* **Pl. 74**
    Du – Dwerggors   Fr – Bruant nain
    Ge – Zwergammer   Sw – Dvärgsparv
Identification: 5¼″. Size of Linnet, but rather nondescript except in breeding season when crown and cheeks are *chestnut, boldly outlined with black*. Upper-parts brown, streaked black; under-parts whitish *with fine black streaks*, particularly on upper breast and flanks. Female duller. Distinguished from female Rustic and Reed Buntings by smaller size, dumpy shape, narrower tail, lack of chestnut on wing-coverts and dull chestnut cheeks. Legs pale pinkish (Reed's are always dark brown). In flight looks small and compact, with less prominent tail than Reed Bunting.
Voice: A repeated, Robin-like '*tick*'. Song, a short, melodious jingle recalling Ortolan.
Habitat and Range: Near water in tundra, valleys with undergrowth and marshes. Breeds on ground among willows or dwarf willow scrub. Rare summer visitor, breeding in N. Finland (and eastwards); has bred N. Norway and Sweden. Occasional on passage in most W. European countries (including Britain).

YELLOW-BREASTED BUNTING *Emberiza aureola* **Pl. 74**
    Du – Wilgengors   Fr – Bruant auréole
    Ge – Weidenammer   Sw – Brunhuvad sparv
Identification: 5½″. Male has bright yellow under-parts with *distinctive narrow chestnut breast-band*; Chaffinch-like wing pattern, with broad white shoulder-patch and narrow bar; *black face*, dark chestnut nape and upper-parts; in winter, black and chestnut markings partly obscured, but still distinguishable from other buntings by wing-bars and breast-band. Female also yellow or yellowish below, but lacks breast-band; distinctive head pattern recalls Aquatic Warbler (pale crown-stripe and supercilium separated by dark lines); further distinguished from Cirl and Yellowhammer by paler appearance, unstreaked centre of breast and faint double wing-bars. Both sexes have some white on tail.

Voice: A Robin-like '*tick*' and a soft '*trssit*'. Far-carrying song is melodious, quicker and more liquid than slightly similar Ortolan's.

Habitat and Range: Open country. In summer, chiefly birch and willow scrub near water, but also on steppes. Nests on ground or in small bushes. Breeds in W. Finland. Migrates eastwards, vagrant in C., W. (including Britain) and S. Europe.

REED BUNTING *Emberiza schoeniclus*   Pl. 73
Du – Rietgors   Fr – Bruant des roseaux
Ge – Rohrammer   Sw – Sävsparv

Identification: 6". Male has *black head and throat, with white collar* (this pattern is almost obscured by brown mottling in winter); dark brown upper-parts with black streaks and greyish rump; conspicuous white outer tail-feathers; greyish-white under-parts, flanks streaked black. Female has brown head with pale buff supercilium and *conspicuous black and whitish moustachial streaks*; brownish rump; buff throat and under-parts with black streaks on breast and flanks.

Voice: A loud '*tseek*', a plaintive '*tsiu*', a metallic '*chink*' and (alarm-note) '*chit*'. Song begins slowly, ends hurriedly, '*tseek-tseek-tseek-tississisk*', usually delivered from reed-stem or bush.

Habitat: Reed-beds, sewage-farms, swamps; roams farmlands in winter. Breeds on or near ground in rank vegetation. Map 360.

BLACK-HEADED BUNTING *Emberiza melanocephala*   Pl. 74
Du – Zwartkopgors   Fr – Bruant mélanocéphale
Ge – Kappenammer   Sw – Svarthuvad sparv

Identification: 6½". Male has *unstreaked* yellow under-parts; *black head, with yellow collar*; chestnut back; *no white on tail*. Head brownish in autumn. Female is dull streaked olive-brown above; distinguished from other yellow-breasted buntings by *unstreaked* under-parts; yellow under tail-coverts. But see Red-headed Bunting (Accidentals).

Voice: A soft '*chup*', a short, loud '*zitt*' and a lower-pitched, quieter '*zee*'. Song unusually pleasing for a bunting; 2–5 similar buzzy introductory notes, followed by a brief, quick, rather subdued warble.

Habitat: Open country with scattered woods and undergrowth, olive groves, gardens. Breeds in low vegetation. Map 361.

CORN BUNTING *Miliaria calandra*   Pl. 74
Du – Grauwe gors   Fr – Bruant proyer
Ge – Grauammer   Sw – Kornsparv

Identification: 7". Largest bunting. Heavily built. Brownish, streaked above and below. No white on wings or tail. Distinguished from larks and pipits by larger size, large round head and stubby bill. Sexes similar. Bill and legs yellowish. Flight heavy, often with dangling legs. Perches on posts and telegraph wires. Gregarious. Usually polygynous.

Voice: A short, rasping '*chip*', a harsh, longer '*zeep*'; in autumn '*tip-a-tip*'. Flight-call a loud twitter. Song, a distinctive, rapid, dry jingle, like rattling bunch of keys.

Habitat: Open farmlands, roadsides, wastelands, hedges. Nests in long grass, among thistles, in hedge-bottoms, etc. Map 362.

Accidentals

The following notes give the salient features of species which are of irregular or very local occurrence. Species which have been recorded in Europe more than 20 times are described in the main text. The geographical origin of each species is shown in brackets, followed by the European regions in which it has been officially recorded at least once. In instances where the species is most likely to be seen in Europe in immature or winter plumage, this is briefly described. Alternative names of species are shown in brackets.

PIED-BILLED GREBE *Podilymbus podiceps.* Size of Slavonian, but with *thicker neck, short, stout bill* and *conspicuous white under tail-coverts.* Brownish plumage. In summer has black throat-patch and black ring around whitish bill; in winter lacks throat-patch and bill mark. Immature has striped face. (N. America.) Accidental W. Europe (Britain). See Pl. 15.

WANDERING ALBATROSS *Diomedea exulans.* Largest ocean-bird (11 ft. wing-span). Mainly white, with black wing-tips and a little dark mottling on wing-coverts and tip of tail. Bill pale flesh. Female has darkish patch on crown. Immature mainly brown, with white face and throat; wings blackish above, white below, except for black tips. (Southern oceans.) Accidental W. and S. European waters.

SOUTHERN GIANT PETREL *Macronectes giganteus.* Much the largest of the petrels, with nearly 8 ft. wing-span. Distinguished from the dark albatrosses by stumpier body, shorter wings, fan-shaped tail and very stout, pale bill. Uniform dark grey-brown with pale head and throat. Young birds speckled with white. A white form speckled with brown predominates around Antarctic ice. (Southern oceans.) Accidental W. Europe.

CAPPED PETREL *Pterodroma hasitata.* Size of large Manx Shearwater, resembles Great Shearwater, but distinguished by *whitish nape and forehead* (contrasting with black cap) and more extensive white or greyish on rump. Bill is shorter and thicker than Great Shearwater's. Very rare. (Caribbean.) Accidental W. Europe (including Britain).

BULWER'S PETREL *Bulweria bulwerii.* Noticeably larger than Storm Petrel, a little larger than Leach's. *Entirely sooty-black*, except for grey on chin. Tail wedge-shaped and longer than in most petrels. Feet *pinkish.* (Atlantic islands.) Accidental W. and S. Europe (including Britain).

WHITE-FACED (FRIGATE) PETREL *Pelagodroma marina.* Distinguished from all other small petrels by *entirely white under-surfaces of wings and body.* Upper-parts dark, rump pale grey. White forehead and *stripe over eye; dark crown* and *stripe below eye.* (Atlantic islands.) Accidental W. and C. Europe (including Britain).

MADEIRAN PETREL *Oceanodroma castro*. Distinguishable from Leach's and Storm Petrels by regular horizontal zig-zag flight (without erratic bounding or fluttering). At close range shows browner plumage, *pure white* (not grey-centred) rump and less deeply forked tail. (Atlantic islands.) Accidental W. Europe (including Britain).

MAGNIFICENT FRIGATEBIRD *Fregata magnificens*. Large (7 ft. wing-span), black, piratical sea-bird, with very long, *deeply forked* tail (usually carried in a long point), red throat-patch and a long, slender, hook-tipped bill. Female has white breast. Immature has completely white head and most of under-parts. (Atlantic.) Accidental W. and C. Europe (including Britain).

LEAST BITTERN *Ixobrychus exilis*. Resembles Little Bittern but even smaller, with more rufous on face, hind-neck and wings. White edge to scapulars forms white 'braces', visible perched or flying. (N. America.) Accidental W. Europe.

SCHRENCK'S LITTLE BITTERN *Ixobrychus eurhythmus*. Male distinguished from Little Bittern by *dark chestnut* cheeks, back and wing-bases; greyish-buff (not creamy) wing-coverts and lead-coloured flight-feathers; narrow dark streak down centre of throat and upper breast. Legs green (not yellow). Female and immature rufous-brown, finely speckled with pale buff; under-parts buff with heavy streaking. (E. Asia.) Accidental C. and S. Europe.

GREEN HERON *Butorides virescens*. Near size of Little Bittern. Adults have black crown, chestnut neck, bluish back. Very dark at distance. Immature has heavily streaked under-parts, white spotting on wings. (N. America.) Accidental W. Europe (Britain).

WESTERN REEF HERON *Egretta gularis*. Size and form of Little Egret, with similar yellow toes, a crest and scapular plumes when breeding. Occurs in several colour phases. Western race *E. gularis gularis* is *dark slate-grey with white chin and throat*. Occasional white form very difficult to distinguish from typical white form of Little Egret as both have dark bills and yellow toes, but Reef has slightly thicker brownish (not black) bill and is more usually seen in coastal waters and estuaries. Eastern race *E. g. schistacea* also has white form but with orange-yellow bill. (Africa.) Accidental S. and C. Europe.

BALD IBIS *Geronticus eremita*. Much larger than Glossy Ibis. Black, shaggy plumage, with green, bronze and purple gloss. Head mainly bare and red, with decurved red bill. Legs dark red. (NW Africa, W. Asia.) Accidental S. Europe.

LESSER FLAMINGO *Phoenicopterus minor*. Much smaller and brighter pink than Greater; neck looks proportionately shorter. Bill is *dark carmine* (not pink) with black tip. Beware 'escaped' Chilean race of Greater. (E. Africa.) Accidental S. Europe.

WHITE-FACED TREE DUCK *Dendrocygna viduata*. 19″. A long-legged, erect-standing duck with *very conspicuous white face*, remainder of head and neck black, with white patch on lower throat. Flanks *heavily barred with black and white*. Has loud, clear whistle. Accidental from Africa to S. Europe.

BLACK DUCK *Anas rubripes.* Size and flight-silhouette of Mallard. Dark brown (looks black at distance), with pale cheeks and sides of neck, yellowish bill, purple speculum without white border. In flight *dark body and white wing-linings* are conspicuous. (N. America.) Accidental W. and N. Europe (including Britain).

SPECTACLED EIDER *Somateria fischeri.* Easily distinguished from other eiders by *large, circular, pale eye-patch.* Male has back of head *and forehead* pale green; upper-parts yellowish-white; under-parts blackish. Female closely barred brown and black, with greyish-buff head and neck. (Siberia.) Accidental N. Europe.

BUFFLEHEAD *Bucephala albeola.* A tiny duck. Male at rest looks chiefly white with black back; high-crowned black head, *broadly marked with white from eye around back of crown.* Female brown above, with dusky flanks, a white cheek-spot and white wing-patch. (N. America.) Accidental W. and C. Europe (including Britain).

HOODED MERGANSER *Mergus cucullatus.* Slightly longer than Smew, with typical spike-like saw-bill and slim flight-silhouette, but has generally dark appearance. Male is black and white, with *fan-shaped, white, erectile crest,* outlined with black; breast white, with two black bars in front of wing, brownish flanks. Female much smaller and darker than female Goosander and Red-breasted Merganser, with dark head and neck and *prominent, bushy, buff crest.* (N. America.) Accidental W. and C. Europe (including Britain).

PALLAS'S FISH EAGLE *Haliaeetus leucoryphus.* Dark brown, with whitish throat and sides of head, buffish crown and nape and *a broad white band* on dark tail. Immature all-dark, with pale streaks on head. (Russia, Asia.) Accidental C. and N. Europe.

LAPPET-FACED VULTURE *Torgos tracheliotus.* Size of Black Vulture, with even more massive bill. Distinguished at short range by *naked pink head and throat.* In flight adult shows distinctive narrow whitish bar near front of dark under-side of wing and white thighs and sides of crop. (Africa, W. Asia.) Accidental S. Europe.

DARK CHANTING GOSHAWK *Melierax metabates.* Smaller and longer-legged than Goshawk. Grey, with finely barred under-parts and rump; white-tipped blackish tail. Legs and base of bill are *orange.* In flight broad, pale grey wings with *contrasting black tips* and uniform dark grey upper breast are diagnostic. Immature is brown, with paler barred rump and under-parts. Erect stance and long orange legs noticeable when perched. Has clear whistle and piping notes. (Africa, W. Asia.) Accidental S. Europe.

AMERICAN KESTREL *Falco sparverius.* Resembles Kestrel, but cap and tail of male are *rufous* (not grey), wings blue-grey, face much more strikingly patterned in black and white. Female resembles female Kestrel, except for strong black and white pattern on side of head. (N. America.) Accidental W., C. and S. Europe (including Britain).

SOOTY FALCON *Falco concolor.* Size between Hobby and Eleonora's. Sexes similar but with two colour phases. One almost all black, the other lead-grey with black wing-tips. Black phase closely resembles dark-phase Eleonora's but is slightly smaller, longer-winged and shorter-tailed (not extending beyond closed wings). At close range note two central tail-feathers protrude slightly. Distinguished from male Red-footed by lack of red base to bill and by yellow (not red) legs. Voice like Kestrel's. (Africa, W. Asia.) Accidental S. Europe.

SORA RAIL *Porzana carolina.* Very similar to Spotted Crake, but adult has *black patch* on face and throat. Crown dark rufous with black centre-stripe. Lacks red at base of yellow bill, and the white spots on neck and upper-breast. Immature lacks black face mark. (N. America.) Accidental W. and N. Europe (including Britain).

ALLEN'S GALLINULE *Porphyrula alleni.* Smaller than Moorhen. Plumage black, glossed bronze-green on upper-parts, reddish-blue on neck and under-parts. Bill and legs *dark red*; frontal shield *green*. (Africa.) Accidental S., C., W., and N. Europe (including Britain).

AMERICAN PURPLE GALLINULE *Porphyrula martinica.* Size and shape of Moorhen but with *much longer, yellow legs.* Brilliant bronze above, purple head and under-parts; *all-white* under tail-coverts; red bill tipped yellow, with pale blue frontal shield. Immature like young Moorhen, but with pure white under tail-coverts and no white flank-stripe. (N. America.) Accidental W., N. and C. Europe (including Britain).

AMERICAN COOT *Fulica americana.* Distinguished from Coot and Crested Coot by *divided white patch beneath tail*, which occurs also in immature. Adult has slight reddish bump on upper bill-shield and reddish marks near bill-tip. (N. America.) Accidental W. Europe.

SANDHILL CRANE *Grus canadensis.* Smaller than Crane, without black neck marking. Coloration grey (including prominent drooping 'tail'), often with buff mottling. *Red forehead* and crown, white cheeks. Immature uniform buffish-brown, lacking grey wings of immature Crane. (N. America, Siberia.) Accidental W. Europe (including Britain).

SEMIPALMATED PLOVER *Charadrius semipalmatus.* Difficult to distinguish from Ringed except by *voice.* Is slightly smaller, with more domed crown. Breast-band narrower in centre. Wing-coverts form pale panel against darker mantle. Bill shorter and stouter. Partial webbing between all three toes (some Ringed have webs between middle and outer toes only). Has distinctive call '*che-wee*' and a piping '*chip, chip*'. (N. America.) Accidental W. Europe (Britain).

LESSER SAND PLOVER *Charadrius mongolus.* Distinguishable in winter from Greater Sand Plover only by smaller size, shorter legs and *smaller, less heavy bill*; has similar greyish patches on sides of upper breast; from rather similar Kentish Plover by lack of white collar. In summer often has more extensive buffish-chestnut on breast than Greater. (Asia.) Accidental N. Europe.

CASPIAN PLOVER *Charadrius asiaticus*. Slightly larger than Ringed Plover. Hair-brown above, white below. Has *broad rusty breast-band* narrowly bordered with black below. Face and eye-stripe white. Female has only faint breast-band. Male in winter resembles female. (Asia.) Accidental E., S., C., W. and N. Europe (including Britain).

WESTERN SANDPIPER *Calidris mauri*. Difficult to distinguish in autumn plumage from Semipalmated Sandpiper, but often has some *rusty colour on nape and scapulars* and is more coarsely marked. Bill thicker at base, *longer, often drooping slightly at tip* and carried pointing downwards. Legs black. Less wing-stripe than Dunlin. Call a distinctive '*cheet*'. (N. America.) Accidental W. and C. Europe (including Britain).

RED-NECKED STINT *Calidris ruficollis*. Slightly larger than Little Stint but, like all stints, very difficult to distinguish in winter. In summer has rufous breast and sides of head; lower breast and flanks whitish with dark spots. Short blackish bill. No reliable criteria on which to base distinction from Little Stint in autumn plumage. Calls a thin '*chit-chit*' and a distinctive creaking note. (Asia.) Accidental C. Europe.

LONG-TOED STINT *Calidris subminuta*. Distinguished with difficulty from other stints by *more boldly marked* brown upper-parts and usually greenish-yellow legs. Neck and breast finely streaked buffish-grey. In summer, upper-parts, neck and breast tinged rufous. Bill and leg colours variable. Has high 'towering' flight like Temminck's. Distinctive call a purring '*chrrup*'. Distinguished from rather similar Least Sandpiper (which also has pale legs) by darker outer tail-feathers, bolder back markings and voice. (Asia.) Accidental N. Europe.

STILT SANDPIPER *Micropalama himantopus*. In summer has *strongly barred under-parts*, rusty cheek-patch below white eye-stripe and *long, spindly*, greenish legs, which project well beyond tail in flight. Slender, slightly downcurved bill is longer than in other sandpipers of similar size. No wing-bar. Lower rump white. In winter is paler and greyer, without rusty marking and with little barring, recalling Lesser Yellowlegs (but feeds like Dowitcher). (N. America.) Accidental N., W. and C. Europe (including Britain).

SHORT-BILLED DOWITCHER *Limnodromus griseus*. Closely resembles Long-billed Dowitcher (see Pls. 38, 39), but immature is buffer, with spotted under and lateral tail-coverts; wings just overlap tail and bill is usually shorter. Call a rapid, triple '*kut-kut-kut*'. (N. America.) Accidental W., N. and C. Europe (including Britain).

HUDSONIAN GODWIT *Limosa haemastica*. 14–16″. Distinguished from rather similar Black-tailed by rufous under-parts extending to belly, pale head and neck speckled with black and *blue-grey legs*. In all plumages by *very narrow white wing-bar* and narrow white end to black-banded tail. Under-wings blackish with white central bar. In winter is greyish-backed, with creamy-grey neck and under-parts. Bill can be slightly upturned. (Canadian Arctic.) Accidental W. Europe (Britain).

LITTLE WHIMBREL *Numenius minutus.* A miniature Whimbrel (12″ compared with 16″), with more slender, less curved and shorter bill. Head stripes *buffish* (not black and whitish); rump and tail uniform with back. Wings pale grey-brown and buff below, with dark barring *only in the wing-pits.* Call, a musical titter; alarm, a harsh '*tchew-tchew-tchew*'. (Asia.) Accidental N. Europe.

ESKIMO CURLEW *Numenius borealis.* Resembles small Whimbrel, with shorter, straighter bill and *no white on rump.* Distinguished from rather similar but larger Hudsonian Whimbrel (American race of Whimbrel, which lacks white rump) by *paler*, more buffish under-parts, *cinnamon-buff* under-surfaces of wings. Legs dark greenish. (N. America.) Accidental W. and N. Europe (including Britain). Now nearly extinct.

WANDERING TATTLER *Heteroscelus incanus.* 11″. Medium-size shore-bird of rocky coasts. *Solid dark grey above*, paler grey below, with yellowish legs. In breeding plumage under-parts narrowly barred with black (in winter unbarred). No wing or tail pattern. Bobs like a sandpiper. Calls a clear '*whee-we-we*'. Twittering call resembles Spotted Sandpiper's. (Pacific.) Accidental W. Europe (Britain).

WILLET *Catoptrophorus semipalmatus.* When standing resembles large Greater Yellowlegs, but with *dark blue-grey legs*, thicker neck and stouter bill. In flight shows *striking black and white wing pattern*, with broad white band through centre of wing on upper and lower surfaces. Calls '*pill-will-willet*' or '*kip-kip-kip*'. (N. America.) Accidental W. Europe.

WHITE-EYED GULL *Larus leucophthalmus.* A sooty-backed gull with *very long, black-tipped red bill*, blackish under-wings, black head *and lower throat* contrasting with white collar, white broken eye-ring and *yellow* legs. Dark wings have white trailing edge. Immature lacks whitish nape. Slightly larger than Common Gull but narrower-winged. (Africa.) Accidental S. Europe.

FRANKLIN'S GULL *Larus pipixcan.* Adult recalls Laughing Gull, but is smaller and paler; outer primaries uniquely marked with a black patch *conspicuously bordered by white* except on the leading edge. Immature resembles Laughing, but forehead and under-parts are whiter. (N. America.) Accidental W. and N. Europe (including Britain).

GREY-HEADED GULL *Larus cirrocephalus.* Slightly larger than Black-headed. Easily identified in breeding plumage by *pale grey head*, red-rimmed pale yellow eye and dark under-wings. Bill and legs *red*. Breast sometimes peach-tinted. In winter distinguished from Black-headed by pale grey smudge on cheek (not dark cheek-spot) and by eye colour. Black primaries of adult have white at base (and at tip of first primary), forming a light patch in *centre* of outer wing – not near leading edge as in Black-headed. (Africa.) Accidental S. Europe.

ROYAL TERN *Sterna maxima*. Resembles rather small Caspian, with *less heavy orange bill*; tail longer and more deeply forked; tips of primaries show a little less black; forehead is *white* except at beginning of breeding season; call-note *higher* and less raucous. (N. America and W. Africa.) Accidental S., W. and N. Europe (including Britain).

LESSER CRESTED TERN *Sterna bengalensis*. About size of Sandwich, but with *rich orange-yellow* bill, and more deeply forked tail. Feet black. Crown of adult slightly crested, all-black in summer, streaked with white in winter. (Africa, Asia.) Accidental S., C. and W. Europe.

ALEUTIAN TERN *Sterna aleutica*. About size of Arctic and Bridled. Distinguished from Arctic by shorter tail, clear-cut white forehead extending above the eye, noticeably *darker* grey upper-parts, black bill and feet and more contrasting white rump and tail. From Bridled by lack of pale collar on nape, *paler* grey upper-parts, white rump, tail and vent. Slow, deep wing-beat. Has distinctive, wader-like polysyllabic *whistling call* quite unlike most other terns. (Siberia, Alaska.) Accidental W. Europe (Britain).

FORSTER'S TERN *Sterna forsteri*. Adult in summer distinguished in flight from Common Tern by *silvery* primaries (paler than rest of wing), less white tail, longer legs and longer, more orange bill. First-winter birds have heavy black spot *like an ear-cap* on side of head; bill blackish, feet orange or yellowish. Immature lacks Common's dusky patch on forewing. (N. America.) Accidental W. Europe (including Britain).

BRIDLED TERN *Sterna anaethetus*. Resembles Sooty, but is smaller, with greyer back, a wide whitish collar, and the narrower white forehead-patch extending in a point *behind the eye*. (Caribbean, Africa.) Accidental W. Europe including Britain).

BROWN NODDY *Anous stolidus*. The only *dark brown* tern (except immature Sooty) and the only tern with a full, *rounded* tail though it has a slight notch (Sooty has forked tail). The *whitish crown* on a dark bird gives a reverse, or 'negative' effect, by contrast with other terns having dark caps and pale bodies. (Tropical and subtropical seas.) Accidental C. Europe.

CRESTED AUKLET *Aethia cristatella*. Larger than Little Auk. *Entirely dark, above and below*. Easily distinguished by *short black crest, curving forward*, and tufts of white feathers drooping from behind eye in summer (as in Parakeet Auklet). Bill orange-red with whitish tip. In winter, no orange on bill; crest shorter. (N. Pacific.) Accidental W. Europe.

PARAKEET AUKLET *Cyclorrhynchus psittacula*. Much larger than Little Auk. Distinguished by proportionately larger *orange-red, upturned bill and tufts of elongated white feathers* drooping from behind eye in summer. (N. Pacific.) Accidental N. Europe. See also Crested Auklet.

SPOTTED SANDGROUSE *Pterocles senegallus*. Male almost uniform sandy above and below, with *orange-yellow crown, throat and cheeks* and a pale blue-grey band bordering the crown. Female is *heavily spotted* with black and

218 ACCIDENTALS

has paler yellow throat and cheeks. Both sexes have long 'pin-tails', white wing linings and a *black ventral streak*. (Africa, Asia.) Accidental S. Europe.

CHESTNUT-BELLIED SANDGROUSE *Pterocles exustus*. Very lon 'pin-tails' and *dark chestnut belly and thighs*; blackish axillaries (Spotted ha white). Male sandy-buff above, with fine dark markings, yellowish face pinkish-buff breast, below which a *narrow black band*. Female more closel marked above; breast spotted. (Africa, Asia.) Accidental C. Europe.

RUFOUS TURTLE DOVE *Streptopelia orientalis*. Slightly larger, *darke* and duller than Turtle Dove and *without white on tail*. Upper-parts dar chestnut, more closely speckled than Turtle Dove. Tips of tail-feathers are gre (not white). Under tail-coverts also grey. (Asia.) Accidental S., C., N. and W Europe (including Britain).

BLACK-BILLED CUCKOO *Coccyzus erythrophthalmus*. Closely re sembles Yellow-billed (see Pl. 75), but *lacks rufous on wings*, has *small whit* spots on tail, entirely *black* bill and narrow red eye-ring. (N. America. Accidental W., C. and S. Europe (including Britain).

AFRICAN MARSH OWL *Asio capensis*. Not unlike dark Short-eared, bu under-parts are spotted and vermiculated, not streaked, and wings have *larg pale patch on distal half*; eyes are black. Toes almost bare, feet blackish. Shor ear-tufts. (NW Africa.) Accidental S. Europe.

COMMON NIGHTHAWK *Chordeiles minor*. Smaller, darker and greye than European nightjars and less crepuscular. Has slightly forked tail and *bol white bands* across very long, pointed wings. Flight recalls Kestrel rather than Nightjar. (N. America.) Accidental W. Europe (including Britain).

NEEDLE-TAILED SWIFT *Hirundapus caudacutus*. A large swift with ε very short, squared tail. Blackish, with metallic green gloss on wings, crown anc tail and *greyish patch high on back*. White forehead, throat and *conspicuou horse-shoe mark* on under tail-coverts, continuing on to flanks. Small whit patch on rear of upper wing beside body. (E. Asia.) Accidental E., N. and W Europe (including Britain).

PACIFIC SWIFT *Apus pacificus*. 7½". Larger than common Swift. Re sembles large White-rumped, but with more prominent *white rump-patch* Wings and *deeply forked* tail noticeably long and slender. Throat white. Blac breast and belly narrowly 'scaled' with whitish, but this is visible only at clos range. (Asia.) Accidental W. Europe.

LITTLE SWIFT *Apus affinis*. *Smaller and shorter-winged* than Swift, and ha almost square tail and *broad white rump*. (Africa, Asia.) Accidental S., W. anc N. Europe (including Britain). See also White-rumped, Pl. 75.

WHITE-BREASTED KINGFISHER *Halcyon smyrnensis*. Size betwee Pied and Belted. Head and under-parts chocolate-brown, throat and uppe breast white, wings and tail brilliant blue. Huge red bill. Has loud laughing cry (Middle East, Asia.) Accidental S. Europe.

PIED KINGFISHER *Ceryle rudis.* A large, shaggily crested, *black and white* kingfisher (twice size of Kingfisher), with a broad and a narrow black band across white breast. Female has only one breast-band. Occurs on fresh and salt water. (Africa, Asia.) Accidental S. and C. Europe.

BELTED KINGFISHER *Ceryle alcyon.* Larger than Pied (size of Jackdaw). *Blue-grey* above, white below, with a prominent, ragged crest and a broad grey breast-band; female also has a chestnut band below the grey. (N. America.) Accidental W. and C. Europe (including Britain).

YELLOW-BELLIED SAPSUCKER *Sphyrapicus varius.* Size of Great Spotted Woodpecker. Male has brilliantly patterned red, black and white head, with red on forehead *and throat*, above black breast-patch. Female's throat is white. Long white wing-patch much narrower than Great Spotted's. Back finely barred black and white; rump white; under-parts pale yellowish. Immature barred brownish above and below. (N. America.) Accidental W. Europe (including Britain).

ACADIAN FLYCATCHER *Empidonax virescens.* Size of Spotted. Dull greenish above, paler below with a yellowish wash on the flanks. Distinguished by *conspicuous pale eye-ring* and *two white wing-bars.* Has distinctive sharp call *'spit-chee',* or *'wee-see'* and a thin *'peet'.* (N. America.) Accidental W. Europe.

BAR-TAILED DESERT LARK *Ammomanes cincturus.* Recalls small Desert Lark, but neater, with *round head and small, stubby bill* giving buntinglike appearance; often more rufous, with primaries and tail-feathers variably tipped with black. (N. Africa, Middle East.) Accidental S. Europe.

DESERT LARK *Ammomanes deserti.* Dumpy, with rather flat crown and *longish, yellowish, pointed* bill. Pale grey-brown above, faintly streaked on head; buffish-white below, faintly mottled on throat. In flight rump and primaries show warm buff. (N. Africa, Middle East.) Accidental S. Europe.

HOOPOE LARK *Alaemon alaudipes.* A swift-running, long-tailed desert species, suggesting small Hoopoe in flight. Pale sandy-grey above, with whitish eye-stripe and dark mark through eye. Long, slightly down-curved bill. Long creamy legs. *Two brilliant white bands almost full length of blackish wings.* Under-parts dirty white, strongly spotted on upper breast. (N. Africa, Asia.) Accidental S. Europe.

BIMACULATED LARK *Melanocorypha bimaculata.* Distinguished from Calandra by smaller size, *more brownish* (not white) outer tail-feathers; wings lack white rear edges. *Double* neck-patches are less clear-cut. (Asia.) Accidental N., S. and W. Europe (including Britain).

INDIAN SAND LARK *Calandrella raytal.* Slightly smaller than Short-toed Lark, with *very pale silvery-grey upper-parts* and white throat and upper breast. (Asia.) Accidental S. Europe.

BLYTH'S PIPIT *Anthus godlewskii.* 8″. Very difficult to distinguish from Richard's or Tawny Pipits, having intermediate appearance. About size of Richard's, but with somewhat paler and tawnier plumage nearer to Tawny (perhaps with some orange-buffish on flanks and under tail-coverts). Looks slightly less 'leggy' and less upright in stance than Richard's and has much shorter hind claw. Calls said to be distinctive: a dry, anxious '*dzeerp*' and a harsher '*psheeoo*' recalling Yellow Wagtail, often preceded by a soft '*chup chup*'. (E. Asia.) Accidental W. and N. Europe.

COMMON BULBUL *Pycnonotus barbatus.* Recalls dark, long-tailed thrush, perky and voluble. Earth-brown above, with *rounded, noticeably dark head.* Throat, wings and tail also dark; under-parts paler, with *white under tail-coverts.* (Africa, Asia.) Accidental S. Europe.

BROWN THRASHER *Toxostoma rufum.* Thrush-like, with a long, very mobile tail. Upper-parts chestnut with *two conspicuous white wing-bars*; under-parts white, boldly streaked with blackish spots. Yellow eye contrasts with greyish cheek. Bill rather long and curved. (N. America.) Accidental W. Europe (Britain).

CATBIRD *Dumetella carolinensis.* A slender, long-tailed, dark *slate-grey* bird, with a *black cap* and *chestnut-red* under tail-coverts. About size of Starling, but tail is much longer. Has distinctive mewing call-note. (N. America.) Accidental C. Europe.

SIBERIAN ACCENTOR *Prunella montanella.* Male has *black crown and face*, with *broad ochreous stripe* over eye and around dark cheek. Upper-parts dark red-brown, rump and tail grey-brown. Under-parts warm buff, with streaked flanks. Female duller, with whiter under-parts. (N. Asia.) Accidental N., C. and S. Europe.

SIBERIAN RUBYTHROAT *Luscinia calliope.* Shape of large Robin, with striking head pattern. Breeding male has crimson throat, *conspicuous white supercilium and moustachial stripe* contrasting with dark face. Upper-parts brown, creamy below. Female and winter male have white throats, but retain the striking head pattern. (Asia.) Accidental S. and W. Europe (including Britain).

SIBERIAN BLUE ROBIN *Luscinia cyane.* Robin-like, but with shorter tail and longer, stouter, *pale* legs. Male has *dark blue upper-parts, black face and pure white under-parts.* Female dark olive-brown, mainly white below, with mottled throat. Fairly prominent pale eye-ring. Immature scaly with mottled breast. (Asia.) Accidental W. Europe.

WHITE-THROATED ROBIN *Irania gutturalis.* Size of Nightingale. Male very striking, with *bright rufous breast*, conspicuous narrow white throat-patch and supercilium, black cheeks and sides of throat, *slate-grey upper-parts and black tail.* Has loud, clear song. Cocks and spreads tail when perched. Female nondescript grey-brown with darker wings and tail, buffish under-parts. (Asia.) Accidental N. Europe.

MOUSSIER'S REDSTART *Phoenicurus moussieri.* Short tail and bush-perching habit give impression of cross between Redstart and Stonechat. Male distinguished from other redstarts by *white half-collar and wing-patch.* Upper-parts and head are black; forehead and eye-stripe white; rump, tail and under-parts *orange.* Female is grey-brown above, brownish-orange below, usually lacking white wing-patch. (N. Africa.) Accidental S. Europe.

WHITE-CROWNED BLACK WHEATEAR *Oenanthe leucopyga.* Very like Black Wheatear, though both sexes are usually *blue*-black, usually (but not always) with some white on crown. Rump, under tail-coverts *and ventral region* are always white, as is tail, except for terminal half of centre feathers, which is black. (N. Africa, W. Asia.) Accidental S. and W. Europe (including Britain).

WOOD THRUSH *Hylocichla mustelina.* Resembles small Song Thrush, but easily identified by *rufous head* and rather rufous mantle. Creamy-white breast and flanks strongly marked with *round* black spots. (N. America.) Accidental W. Europe.

HERMIT THRUSH *Catharus guttatus.* Considerably smaller than Song Thrush, which it superficially resembles. Distinguished by *bright rufous rump and tail.* Legs flesh colour. Has distinctive habit of cocking its tail and dropping it slowly. (N. America.) Accidental W. and C. Europe (including Britain).

GREY-CHEEKED THRUSH *Catharus minimus.* Very like Swainson's Thrush, but greyer, less olive, with very pale buffish tinge on upper breast, less distinct buff eye-ring, more diffuse breast-spots. Both lack Song Thrush's orange beneath wings. Identified at close range by *greyish cheeks.* (N. America.) Accidental W. and C. Europe (including Britain).

VEERY *Catharus fuscescens.* Size of Nightingale. Rather thrush-like in shape. Dull, tawny-brown upper-parts, whitish below, with creamy upper breast *indistinctly speckled* with small spots. At a distance spotting is often invisible. Has low '*phew*' call-note. (N. America.) Accidental W. Europe (Britain).

TICKELL'S THRUSH *Turdus unicolor.* Size of Song Thrush. Uniform grey, or grey-brown, above; greyish or buffish across breast, usually (not always) with necklace of sparse streaking on upper breast. (Himalayas.) Accidental C. Europe.

GRAY'S GRASSHOPPER WARBLER *Locustella fasciolata.* Resembles large Savi's Warbler, near size of Great Reed. *Unstreaked* olive-brown above, with greyish cheeks and breast contrasting with white throat. Rufous under tail-coverts. (Asia.) Accidental C. and W. Europe.

PADDYFIELD WARBLER *Acrocephalus agricola.* Resembles very pale Sedge Warbler with whitish under-parts. Difficult to distinguish from Reed, Blyth's Reed and Marsh Warblers, though supercilium slightly more evident and widest *behind* the eye. Usually paler and more rufous above than Reed and Blyth's Reed; more rufous and less olive than Marsh. (S. Russia, Asia.) Accidental E., N., C. and W. Europe (including Britain).

THICK-BILLED WARBLER *Acrocephalus aedon*. Very similar in size, shape and coloration to Great Reed Warbler, but *bill is deeper and shorter*, tail longer in proportion, rump redder, legs blue and *lacks eye-stripe*. In hand rounded first primary is diagnostic. (SE Asia.) Accidental W. Europe (Britain).

TRISTRAM'S WARBLER *Sylvia deserticola*. Male easily confused with Dartford Warbler but is slightly paler with *whitish eye-ring* and *rufous-edged wings*. Distinguished from Subalpine by lack of white moustachial stripe; from Spectacled by dark vinous throat and under-parts. Female much paler resembling female Spectacled. Song recalls Dartford's, but '*chit-it*' call is distinctive. (Africa.) Accidental S. Europe.

MÉNÉTRIES'S WARBLER *Sylvia mystacea*. Closely resembles Sardinian, but has *buffish-orange throat and under-parts* and pale yellow instead of red eye-ring. White division between black cheek and pink throat is conspicuous. Female duller, with less contrasting pattern. Scolding song less varied than Sardinian's. (Middle East.) Accidental S. Europe.

DESERT WARBLER *Sylvia nana*. Very pale, sandy-greyish above, slightly rufous on rump; whitish below, with slightly buffish flanks; tail well rounded, pale *rufous*-brown, with whitish outer feathers. Eyes and legs *pale yellowish*. Spectacled Warbler is much darker, larger, with dark cheeks and dark eyes. (N. Africa, European Russia, Asia.) Accidental S., E., C., W. and N. Europe (including Britain).

BROWN FLYCATCHER *Muscicapa latirostris*. Resembles small female Pied Flycatcher; distinguished by *absence of white wing-patch* and, at close range, by *narrow white eye-ring* and noticeably large eye. Distinguished from Spotted Flycatcher by smaller size and *lack of streaking* on crown and breast. (E. Asia.) Accidental C. and W. Europe.

RED-BREASTED NUTHATCH *Sitta canadensis*. Very like Corsican Nuthatch but rusty below. Has similar black cap, long white stripe from bill above eye to nape and conspicuous black line through eye; whitish throat, but *strong chestnut from breast to vent* (pinkish in female). (N. America.) Accidental W. Europe.

DAURIAN JACKDAW *Corvus dauuricus*. Easily distinguished from Jackdaw by *whitish breast* and broad *whitish collar around throat*. Immature resembles young Jackdaw. (Asia.) Accidental E. Europe.

RED-EYED VIREO *Vireo olivaceus*. Size and shape of Blackcap, but with shorter tail. Adult olive-green above, whitish below, with *blue-grey crown* and conspicuous *black-bordered white supercilium*. Red eyes. Immature has duller head pattern. Call, a nasal '*chway*'. (N. America.) Accidental W. Europe (including Britain).

PALLAS'S ROSEFINCH *Carpodacus roseus*. Larger than Scarlet Rosefinch (of similar form). Male is crimson, browner on back, wings and tail; under-parts crimson, with small white speckles. Female streaked pale brown, slightly rosy on rump. (Asia.) Accidental C. Europe.

EVENING GROSBEAK *Hesperiphona vespertina.* Size and shape of Hawfinch, with massive *whitish* bill. Male dull yellow with dark head, bold yellow eye-stripe and black and white wings. Female silvery-grey and yellowish with black and white wings and tail. (N. America.) Accidental W. Europe (Britain).

BLACK-AND-WHITE WARBLER *Mniotilta varia.* Strongly striped *black and white* on head, body and wings. Female duller, with whiter underparts. Has habit of *tree-creeping.* (N. America.) Accidental W. Europe (Britain).

TENNESSEE WARBLER *Vermivora peregrina.* Slightly smaller and stouter than Willow Warbler. In spring male's head is grey with white supercilium and yellow eye-ring. Bright olive-green upper-parts *brightest on rump.* Under tail-coverts *pure white.* Broad but indistinct wing-bar. Female and winter male have greenish head and yellowish face, breast and flanks (recalling Arctic Warbler except for dark legs), but *green rump and white under tail-coverts* remain conspicuous. (N. America.) Accidental W. Europe (including Britain).

PARULA WARBLER *Parula americana.* Unmistakable *bluish* above, with *yellow* throat and breast and two conspicuous white wing-bars. Male has *dark rusty breast-band.* (N. America.) Accidental W. Europe (including Britain).

YELLOW WARBLER *Dendroica petechia.* Size of Willow Warbler (smaller than Yellow-rumped or Blackpoll). Looks *all yellow* at distance. Adults, particularly male, finely streaked rusty on breast and flanks. *Yellow spots on tail.* Bright tips and edges of wing feathers form two wing-bars. See also Hooded and remember that first-autumn Willow Warblers can look very yellow. (N. America.) Accidental W. Europe (Britain).

BLACK-THROATED GREEN WARBLER *Dendroica virens.* Male has *bright yellow* face framed by black throat and olive-green crown and upperparts; two conspicuous white wing-bars and white under-parts, with black-streaked flanks. Female and autumn birds have much less black on throat and flanks. (N. America.) Accidental C. Europe.

CAPE MAY WARBLER *Dendroica tigrina.* Size of slender Garden Warbler. Dark olive above with *bright yellow under-parts, rump and sides of neck.* Conspicuous black stripes on breast, flanks and belly. Broad white wing-bars. The only warbler combining dark crown, yellow supercilium and *chestnut cheeks.* Winter plumage and female rather nondescript, but distinguishable by yellow patch on side of neck. Call, a high nasal *'swee-swee-swee'.* (N. America.) Accidental W. Europe (Britain).

MAGNOLIA WARBLER *Dendroica magnolia.* $4\frac{3}{4}''$. A black and yellow warbler with *bold white patches on wings and tail.* Grey crown, black cheeks. Yellow rump and under-parts with heavy black flank-stripes. Black tail has striking white side-patches (from below is white with black tip). Prominent double white wing-bars. Immature has greyish-olive head and back and only faint flank-stripes, but black and white tail is conspicuous. (N. America.) Accidental W. Europe (Britain).

YELLOW-RUMPED (MYRTLE) WARBLER *Dendroica coronata.* In all plumages has *bright yellow rump*, yellow on crown and in front of each wing. Male blue-grey above (brownish in winter and female), with bold inverted U on white breast and flanks (partly obscured by streaks in winter). White patches each side of spread tail. (N. America.) Accidental W. Europe (including Britain).

AMERICAN REDSTART *Setophaga ruticilla.* Largely black with *bright orange patches on wings and tail*; belly white. Female olive-brown, white below, with *yellow* patches on wings and tail. Immature resembles female, but the yellow is tinged orange in young males. Tail constantly fanned. (N. America.) Accidental W. Europe (including Britain).

OVENBIRD *Seiurus aurocapillus.* A sparrow-size ground warbler resembling tiny thrush, but *strongly striped* (not spotted) on whitish under-parts. Olive-brown above, with *pale orange crown-stripe* edged with black. Legs pinkish. Song, an emphatic repeated '*tee-cher, tee-cher*', sometimes only the first syllable. (N. America.) Accidental W. Europe (Britain).

NORTHERN WATERTHRUSH *Seiurus noveboracensis.* Resembles plump, sparrow-size thrush with short tail, conspicuous *yellowish supercilium* and heavily streaked yellowish under-parts. Behaviour and habitat recall sandpiper, running along water's edge and 'teetering' constantly. (N. America.) Accidental W. Europe (including Britain).

YELLOWTHROAT *Geothlypis trichas.* Size of Wood Warbler. Male greenish-brown above, with *broad black 'mask' from cheek across forehead* (partly obscured in winter) framed with pale ash-grey; *canary-yellow* throat, with pale buffish breast and flanks and *white belly*. Cocks tail. Female duller, lacks black 'mask', but retains white belly. (N. America.) Accidental W. Europe (Britain).

HOODED WARBLER *Wilsonia citrina.* Larger than Yellow Warbler but also very yellow below, females and immatures suggesting small Melodious. Spring male has yellow face surrounded by conspicuous black 'hood'. Look for *white spots on tail*. (N. America.) Accidental W. Europe (including Britain).

SUMMER TANAGER *Piranga rubra.* Size of Corn Bunting. Adult male unmistakable, *rose-red all over*, with rather large whitish bill. Female yellowish-olive above, deep yellow below. Immature male patched red and green. (N. America.) Accidental W. Europe (Britain).

SCARLET TANAGER *Piranga olivacea.* Size of Crossbill. Breeding male unmistakable *scarlet with black wings and tail*, whitish bill. Female, immature and winter male dull greenish above, yellow below, with dusky brownish-black wings. Female Summer Tanager is deeper yellow, wings not as dusky. (N. America.) Accidental W. Europe (Britain).

RUFOUS-SIDED TOWHEE *Pipilo erythrophalmus.* A large ($7\frac{1}{2}''$) big-tailed American ground-feeder. Male black above and on upper breast, with *white belly and conspicuous rusty flanks*. Large white edges on outer tail-feathers and wing-feathers. Female brown where male is black. Call a loud '*chewink*'. (N. America.) Accidental W. Europe (Britain).

SAVANNAH SPARROW *Passerculus sandvichensis*. A small, heavily streaked open-country American sparrow, with bold whitish crown-stripe and broad yellowish supercilium. Whitish breast and flanks heavily streaked. Legs pink. Distinguished from rather similar Song Sparrow by shorter, *notched* tail and pinker legs. (N. America.) Accidental W. Europe (Britain).

FOX SPARROW *Zonotrichia iliaca*. Much larger than House Sparrow, with *conspicuous chestnut tail* and bunting-like shape. Upper-parts boldly streaked rufous-brown; under-parts creamy; breast and flanks heavily streaked with rufous-brown. (N. America.) Accidental W., C. and S. Europe (including Britain).

SONG SPARROW *Zonotrichia melodia*. Bunting-like. Boldly streaked brown above and below, with *black spot in centre of breast*; heavy streaking extends well down flanks. *Broad buff supercilium*. Slightly rufous on wings. Immature may lack breast-spot. Flits tail open during flight. (N. America.) Accidental W. Europe (Britain).

WHITE-CROWNED SPARROW *Zonotrichia leucophrys*. A bunting-like New World sparrow with distinctively *striped* black and white head. White crown-stripe bordered with black above broad white supercilium and narrow black stripe through eye. Bill pinkish-orange. Upper-parts grey-brown, pale grey below, with white belly. See also White-throated Sparrow (Pl. 65). (N. America.) Accidental W. Europe (including Britain).

SLATE-COLOURED JUNCO *Junco hyemalis*. Smaller than Chaffinch. Uniform dark *slate-grey*, with *conspicuous white lower breast, belly and outer tail-feathers*, and stubby whitish bill. (N. America.) Accidental W., C. and S. Europe (including Britain).

BLACK-FACED BUNTING *Emberiza spodocephala*. Male has dark *olive-grey head*, blacker around bill, and *yellow belly*; wings and tail blackish-brown. Female is browner, without black on face and with yellow throat and breast streaked with brown. (Siberia.) Accidental C. Europe. See Pl. 74.

SIBERIAN MEADOW BUNTING *Emberiza cioides*. Male has bold white supercilium and throat, isolated black moustachial stripes and *dark chestnut crown and cheeks*. Usually has pale chestnut breast-band. Upper-parts like Rock Bunting. Female has similar, though fainter, pattern and streaked crown. (E. Asia.) Accidental S. Europe. See Pl. 74.

YELLOW-BROWED BUNTING *Emberiza chrysophrys*. Black head, with *narrow white crown-stripe and yellow eye-stripe*. Upper-parts brown, streaked blackish; under-parts white, with blackish streaks on breast and flanks. Female duller, more spotted below. (E. Asia.) Accidental C. and W. Europe (including Britain).

CHESTNUT BUNTING *Emberiza rutila*. Male has *chestnut-red* head, upper-parts and breast; under-parts bright yellow, with chestnut flank-stripes. Female olive-brown above, streaked blackish; crown slightly rufous, rump uniform chestnut; under-parts dull yellow; throat white, bordered with chestnut. (E. Asia.) Accidental C. and W. Europe.

PALLAS'S REED BUNTING *Emberiza pallasi*. Resembles small buffish Reed Bunting, but with back boldly striped in pale grey and black and with conspicuously *pale rump*. Breeding male has white nape-collar tinged yellow. Female more nondescript but sometimes with distinctive narrow moustachial stripe sharply angled towards breast. Cocks tail. Calls '*peeseeoo*' and a sparrow-like chirping. (Asia.) Accidental W. Europe (Britain).

RED-HEADED BUNTING *Emberiza bruniceps*. Male has chestnut head and *throat, yellow nape and rump* contrasting with greenish mantle. Female resembles Black-headed, with greener mantle, no yellow on under tail-coverts. Frequent cage-bird – beware 'escapes'. (Asia.) Accidental westward across Europe. See Pl. 74.

ROSE-BREASTED GROSBEAK *Pheucticus ludovicianus*. Size of thrush, with *Hawfinch-like bill*. Male striking black and white above, with *rosy patch on white breast*; in winter under-parts streaked. Female has conspicuous white stripes on head, dull brown above, with dark streaks on back and under-parts. Both sexes have double white wing-bars. (N. America.) Accidental W., N. and S. Europe (including Britain).

INDIGO BUNTING *Passerina cyanea*. Smaller than House Sparrow. Male *rich, deep blue all over*; in winter resembles brown female though retaining some blue on wings and tail. Female featureless, plain brown, paler below with indistinct streaking. (N. America.) Accidental W. Europe.

BOBOLINK *Dolichonyx oryzivorus*. Larger than Skylark. A stout meadow-bird, with *black face and under-parts*; conspicuous white band on 'shoulders' and white rump; *back of head dull yellow*; back strongly striped. Female and immature yellowish-buff, heavily streaked on crown and upper-parts. (N. America.) Accidental W. and N. Europe (including Britain).

YELLOW-HEADED BLACKBIRD *Xanthocephalus xanthocephalus*. Blackbird-size. Male unmistakable, black with *orange-yellow head and breast*, showing conspicuous white wing-patch in flight. Female smaller and browner, with yellow confined to throat, upper breast and around cheek; lower breast streaked with white. Heavy pointed bill. Gregarious, usually seen in marshes. Calls a low '*kruk*' or '*kack*'. (N. America.) Accidental N. Europe.

NORTHERN (BALTIMORE) ORIOLE *Icterus galbula*. Smaller than Golden Oriole. Male vivid *orange with black head, back, wings, and tail*. Bold white wing-bar conspicuous in flight. Female olive above, yellow below, with two white wing-bars. (N. America.) Accidental W. Europe (including Britain).

Index

Vernacular English names are printed in Roman type. Scientific names are in italics. The figures in Roman type refer to the descriptive text pages, those in bold type refer to the colour plates and those in italics refer to the distribution maps. Note that the caption pages opposite the colour plates also indicate the page numbers of the corresponding text matter.

About the Maps

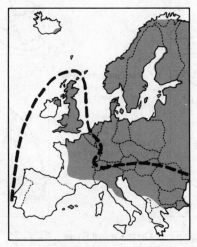

Red area – **Summer**
Dotted line – **Winter**

The red areas represent the bird's **breeding range**. The area below the heavy dotted line, or enclosed by it, is the bird's **winter range**. This does not mean that the bird occurs everywhere within these limits, but locally where its proper habitat is available. Additional information is given in the form of a short caption beside each map. For example, if the bird's winter range is identical with its breeding range, or if the bird entirely leaves the map area, it is so stated, and the dotted line is not used. Thus: 'Resident' (if all the year); 'Partial migrant' (if many but not all individuals leave northern part of range in winter); 'Summer visitor' (if the species winters entirely outside Europe). Areas which may be visited on passage between breeding and winter quarters are not mapped. In the few cases where maps are inappropriate, brief information on range is given in the main text. Further information will be welcomed by the authors, who may be contacted c/o the publishers.

1 Red-throated Diver
Partial migrant. Vagrant
south to Mediterranean
islands

2 Black-throated Diver
Mainly migrant. Vagrant
Faeroes

3 Great Northern Diver
Mainly migrant. Has bred
Scotland. Vagrant C., E.
and S Europe.

4 Little Grebe
Partial migrant. Has bred
Finland. Vagrant Faeroes

5 Great Crested Grebe
Partial migrant. Vagrant
Iceland

6 Red-necked Grebe
Partial migrant. Has bred
Holland, France. Vagrant
Ireland, Iceland, Spain

7 Slavonian Grebe
Partial migrant. Vagrant
C, SE and SW Europe

8 Black-necked Grebe
Partial migrant. Has bred
Ireland, Finland, Italy, etc.
Breeding areas often
changed

9 Fulmar
Partial migrant. Vagrant Finland, C. and S. Europe

10 Cory's Shearwater
Red line marks north limit of nesting. Scarce autumn visitor Atlantic coasts, vagrant C. Europe

11 Manx Shearwater
Partial migrant. Red lines enclose colonies. Ranges widely at sea. Vagrant inland, including C. Europe

12 Storm Petrel
Partial migrant. Lines enclose nesting areas. May breed NW Norway, Aegean. Vagrant inland

13 Leach's Petrel
Summer visitor within red line. Has bred Ireland. Vagrant inland including S. Europe

14 Gannet
Partial migrant. Red line encloses main colonies. Vagrant Baltic, C. Europe, E. Mediterranean

15 Cormorant
Partial migrant. Passage C. Europe

16 Shag
Winter dispersal area includes N. Sea. Vagrant Baltic, inland N. and C. Europe

17 Pygmy Cormorant
Partial migrant. Has bred
Italy. Vagrant N., C. and
W. Europe

18 Dalmatian Pelican
Partial migrant. Vagrant C.
Europe, Italy

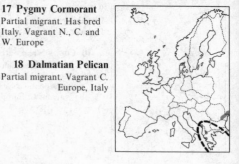

19 Bittern
Partial migrant. Has bred
Greece. Vagrant Iceland

20 Little Bittern
Summer visitor, occasional
winter. Vagrant British
Isles, Iceland, N. Europe

21 Night Heron
Summer visitor. Vagrant
British Isles, N. Europe

22 Squacco Heron
Summer visitor. Has bred
Czechoslovakia. Vagrant
British Isles, C. and N.
Europe

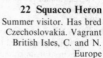

23 Little Egret
Partial migrant. Has bred
Holland, Czechoslovakia.
Vagrant British Isles, C.
and N. Europe

24 Great White Egret
Partial migrant. Has bred
Holland, Switzerland.
Vagrant Britain, W. and
N. Europe.

25 Grey Heron
Partial migrant.

26 Purple Heron
Summer visitor. Vagrant
British Isles, N. Europe

27 Black Stork
Mainly summer visitor.
Has bred France,
Denmark, Sweden.
Vagrant Britain, N. Europe

28 White Stork
Mainly summer visitor.
Vagrant British Isles, N.
Europe

29 Glossy Ibis
Summer visitor. Has bred
Italy, France, Hungary.
Vagrant British Isles, N.
and E. Europe

30 Spoonbill
Mainly summer visitor.
Has bred Denmark,
Portugal, Czechoslovakia.
Vagrant N. and C. Europe

31 Mute Swan
Partial migrant. Vagrant S.
Europe

32 Bewick's Swan
Winter visitor from N.
Russia. Vagrant C. and S.
Europe

33 Whooper Swan
Mainly migrant. Has bred Scotland. Vagrant SW Europe

34 Bean Goose
Migrant. Vagrant Ireland, Iceland, Greece

35 Pink-footed Goose
Migrant. Vagrant E., C., and S. Europe

36 White-fronted Goose
Winter visitor from N. Russia, Greenland. Vagrant SW Europe

37 Lesser White-fronted Goose
Migrant. Vagrant S. and W. Europe (almost annual Britain)

38 Greylag Goose
Partial migrant

39 Barnacle Goose
Winter visitor from high Arctic. Passage Baltic, Iceland. Vagrant S., C. and E. Europe

40 Brent Goose
Winter visitor from high Arctic. Vagrant most Europe south to Mediterranean

41 Ruddy Shelduck
Partial migrant. Vagrant almost all Europe including British Isles and Iceland

42 Shelduck
Partial migrant. Vagrant Iceland, C. Europe

43 Wigeon
Partial migrant. Occasionally breeds Ireland, C., E. and S. Europe

44 Gadwall
Partial migrant. Occasionally breeds Italy, Norway. Vagrant Finland

45 Teal
Partial migrant. Occasionally breeds elsewhere in S. Europe

46 Mallard
Partial migrant

47 Pintail
Mainly migrant. Breeds sporadically south to Mediterranean

48 Garganey
Summer visitor. Has bred Norway, Ireland, Iberia

49 Shoveler
Partial migrant. Has bred
Switzerland

**50 Red-crested
Pochard**
Partial migrant. Has bred
Italy, Greece. Vagrant
British Isles, N. Europe

51 Pochard
Partial migrant. Vagrant
Faeroes

52 Ferruginous Duck
Partial migrant. Has bred
Holland, W. Germany,
Italy

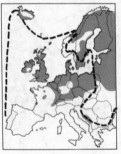

53 Tufted Duck
Partial migrant. Has bred
Hungary

54 Scaup
Mainly migrant. Has bred
Scotland, Denmark.
Vagrant most S. Europe

55 Eider
Partial migrant. Vagrant
C., S. and E. Europe

56 Long-tailed Duck
Mainly migrant. Vagrant
C., S. and E. Europe

57 Common Scoter
Mainly migrant.
Immatures summer N. Sea.
Vagrant C. and SE Europe

58 Velvet Scoter
Migrant. Many moult
Denmark July. Vagrant
Iceland, SE Europe

59 Goldeneye
Mainly migrant. Has bred
Yugoslavia, Switzerland

60 Smew
Migrant. Perhaps annual
Ireland. Vagrant SW
Europe

**61 Red-breasted
Merganser**
Partial migrant. Has bred
Holland

62 Goosander
Partial migrant. Has bred
Ireland, Yugoslavia.
Vagrant SW Europe

63 White-headed Duck
Partial migrant. Erratic
breeding persists elsewhere
in S. Europe. Vagrant C.
Europe

64 Honey Buzzard
Summer visitor. Vagrant
Ireland, Iceland

65 Black Kite
Summer visitor. Has bred
Scandinavia. Vagrant
British Isles

66 Red Kite
Partial migrant. Breeds
Denmark. Vagrant Ireland,
Finland

67 White-tailed Eagle
Mainly resident. Being
reintroduced Scotland. Has
bred Denmark *et al.*
Vagrant W. Europe

68 Lammergeier
Resident, greatly reduced.
Vagrant C. Europe

69 Egyptian Vulture
Mainly migrant but some
midwinter S. Europe.
Vagrant C., N. Europe and
Britain

70 Griffon Vulture
Partial migrant. Few
summer Alps. Vagrant C.,
N. Europe and British Isles

71 Black Vulture
Resident. Extinct Romania
et al. Vagrant C. Europe

72 Short-toed Eagle
Summer visitor. Vagrant
N. Europe

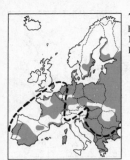

73 Marsh Harrier
Partial migrant. Has bred Norway. Vagrant Ireland, Faeroes

74 Hen Harrier
Partial migrant. Has bred Denmark, Italy. Vagrant Iceland

75 Pallid Harrier
Summer visitor. Has bred Sweden, Germany. Vagrant S., C. and W. Europe including Britian

76 Montagu's Harrier
Summer visitor. Erratic breeder England. Has bred Sweden, Greece, Ireland

77 Goshawk
Mainly resident. Vagrant Ireland

78 Sparrowhawk
Partial migrant. Vagrant Iceland

79 Levant Sparrowhawk
Summer visitor. Has bred Hungary. Vagrant little further north and west

80 Buzzard
Partial migrant

81 Rough-legged Buzzard
Migrant. Vagrant Iceland, Ireland, SW Europe

82 Lesser Spotted Eagle
Migrant. Vagrant N., W. and S. Europe

83 Spotted Eagle
Migrant. Has bred Sweden, Finland. Few may winter France, Holland. Vagrant w. to British Isles, Portugal

84 Imperial Eagle
Partial migrant. Vagrant N., C., W. and S. Europe

85 Golden Eagle
Mainly resident, extending to E. Europe in winter. Has bred Ireland. Vagrant Holland

86 Booted Eagle
Summer visitor. Has wintered S. Europe. Vagrant C. and N. Europe

87 Bonelli's Eagle
Mainly resident. Vagrant C., E. and N. Europe

88 Osprey
Mainly summer visitor. Has bred many countries S. and C. Europe. Vagrant Ireland, Iceland

89 Lesser Kestrel
Mainly summer visitor. Vagrant C., N. and W. Europe including British Isles

90 Kestrel
Partial migrant. Vagrant Iceland

91 Red-footed Falcon
Summer visitor. Has bred N. Europe and west to France. Annual Britain, vagrant Spain, Ireland

92 Merlin
Partial migrant. Vagrant Malta

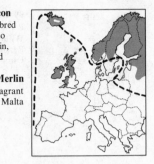

93 Hobby
Summer visitor. Vagrant Ireland, Iceland

94 Lanner
Mainly resident. Vagrant E., C. and SW Europe

95 Saker
Partial migrant. Vagrant C. and N. Europe

96 Gyrfalcon
Mainly resident. Winter vagrant W. (including British Isles), C. and S. Europe

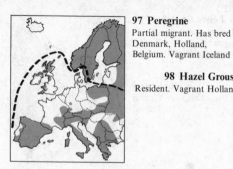

97 Peregrine
Partial migrant. Has bred Denmark, Holland, Belgium. Vagrant Iceland

98 Hazel Grouse
Resident. Vagrant Holland

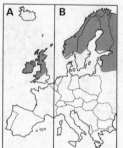

99 Red Grouse (A)
Resident Britain, Ireland
Willow Grouse (B)
Resident continental Europe

100 Ptarmigan
Resident

101 Black Grouse
Resident

102 Capercaillie
Resident. Vagrant Belgium, Denmark

103 Rock Partridge
Resident

104 Red-legged Partridge
Resident

105 Grey Partridge
Resident

106 Quail
Partial migrant. Irregular
or fluctuating most British
Isles, also N. Europe.
Occasional in winter north
to British Isles, Germany

107 Pheasant
Resident

108 Water Rail
Partial migrant

109 Spotted Crake
Mainly summer visitor.
Occasional winter W.
Europe/North Sea.
Vagrant Ireland, Iceland

110 Little Crake
Mainly summer visitor.
Annual Sweden; vagrant
N. and W. Europe incl.
Britain where occasional
winter

111 Baillon's Crake
Mainly summer visitor,
often sporadic. Vagrant n.
to British Isles, Faeroes,
Sweden

112 Corncrake
Summer visitor. Vagrant
Iceland

113 Moorhen
Partial migrant. Vagrant Iceland

114 Coot
Partial migrant. Vagrant Iceland (has bred)

115 Crane
Migrant. Has bred Britain. Some winter NE France. Vagrant Ireland, Iceland

116 Little Bustard
Partial migrant. Vagrant British Isles, C. and N. Europe

117 Great Bustard
Mainly resident, extending range in winter. Vagrant most Europe including Britain

118 Oystercatcher
Partial migrant. Has bred Spain. Vagrant or passage C. Europe

119 Black-winged Stilt
Mainly summer visitor. Irregular breeder to N. Germany. Vagrant British Isles, N. Europe

120 Avocet
Partial migrant. Vagrant Iceland, Finland

121 Stone Curlew
Partial migrant. Formerly bred Holland, Germany. Has wintered England. Vagrant Ireland, Iceland, N. Europe

122 Collared Pratincole
Summer visitor. Vagrant British Isles, C. and N. Europe

123 Little Ringed Plover
Summer visitor. Vagrant Ireland

124 Ringed Plover
Partial migrant. Has bred Spain. Passage S. and E. Europe

125 Kentish Plover
Partial migrant. Has bred England. Vagrant Ireland, S. Baltic

126 Dotterel
Migrant. Vagrant Ireland, Iceland

127 Golden Plover
Partial migrant. Has bred Belgium

128 Grey Plover
Winter visitor from northeast. Immatures summer in winter range. Passage C. Europe. Vagrant Iceland

129 Lapwing
Partial migrant. Breeds Iceland occasionally

130 Knot
Winter visitor. Non-breeders summer coasts W. Europe. Vagrant E. Europe

131 Sanderling
Winter visitor. Non-breeders summer coasts W. Europe. Passage most Europe

132 Little Stint
Migrant. Passage most Europe. Few winter n. to Britain. Vagrant Iceland

133 Temminck's Stint
Migrant. Passage most Europe. Vagrant Ireland, Portugal

134 Purple Sandpiper
Partial migrant. Non-breeders summer s. to England. Vagrant C. and S. Europe

135 Dunlin
Partial migrant. Passage all Europe. Non-breeders summer in winter range. Has bred N. France, Holl.

136 Broad-billed Sandpiper
Summer visitor. Passage Denmark, Italy eastwards. Vagrant W. Europe including British Isles

137 Ruff
Mainly migrant. Has bred
Austria. Vagrant Iceland

138 Jack Snipe
Migrant. Vagrant Iceland

139 Snipe
Partial migrant. Has bred
Yugoslavia

140 Great Snipe
Summer visitor. Passage C.
Europe. Vagrant W.
Europe including British
Isles

141 Woodcock
Partial migrant. Perhaps
annual Iceland

142 Black-tailed Godwit
Mainly migrant. Has bred
Faeroes, Spain, Italy

143 Bar-tailed Godwit
Migrant. Non-breeders
summer coasts Britain, W.
Europe. Vagrant Iceland,
rare inland

144 Whimbrel
Migrant. Non-breeders
summer coasts W. Europe.
Few winter n. to British
Isles, Denmark

145 Curlew
Partial migrant. Has bred
Spain. Non-breeders
summer on coasts s. to
Mediterranean

146 Spotted Redshank
Migrant. Non-breeders
summer s. to
Mediterranean

147 Redshank
Partial migrant

148 Marsh Sandpiper
Summer visitor. Has bred
Finland, wintered Spain.
Vagrant C. Europe w. to
Britain

149 Greenshank
Migrant. Non-breeders
summer s. to
Mediterranean. Has bred
Ireland. Vagrant Iceland

150 Green Sandpiper
Migrant. Has bred
sw. to Britain, Austria, Italy

151 Wood Sandpiper
Summer visitor. Has bred
Iceland. Passage w. to
Ireland. Vagrant Portugal

152 Common Sandpiper
Mainly summer visitor.
Has bred Holland, Greece.
Vagrant Iceland

153 Turnstone
Migrant. Non-breeders summer in winter range. Thin passage or vagrant inland

154 Red-necked Phalarope
Summer visitor. Irregular breeder Ireland. Vagrant or passage England, most Europe

155 Grey Phalarope
Summer visitor. Few autumn (winter) coasts W. Europe; vagrant elsewhere

156 Arctic Skua
Mainly summer visitor. Few winter n. to N. Sea. Thin passage C. Europe, Mediterranean

157 Long-tailed Skua
Summer visitor. Passage Britain, Iceland, perhaps Switzerland; vagrant elsewhere C., E., S. Europe

158 Mediterranean Gull
Partial migrant. Breeds sporadically England, Baltic, most of C. Europe. Vagrant Norway, Ireland

159 Little Gull
Mainly migrant. Has nested Britain, Norway, Germany, Romania. Vagrant Iceland

160 Black-headed Gull
Partial migrant

161 Slender-billed Gull
Partial migrant. Vagrant
Britain, Portugal, C.
Europe

162 Audouin's Gull
Widely scattered in
Mediterranean in winter.
Vagrant Portugal

163 Common Gull
Partial migrant

**164 Lesser Black-
backed Gull**
Partial migrant. Has bred
E. Germany. Some summer
Mediterranean

165 Herring Gull
Partial migrant. Winters
coasts, fewer inland, all
Europe except where
waters freeze

166 Glaucous Gull
Partial migrant. Vagrant
C., S. and E. Europe

**167 Great Black-backed
Gull**
Partial migrant. Immatures
often summer outside
breeding range.

168 Kittiwake
Partial migrant, rarely far
inland. Vagrant SE Europe
north to Baltic

185 Collared Dove
Mainly resident. Has bred
Iceland

186 Turtle Dove
Summer visitor. Irregular
breeder Ireland. Vagrant
N. Europe

187 Cuckoo
Summer visitor. Vagrant
Iceland

188 Barn Owl
Mainly resident. Vagrant
north to Finland

189 Scops Owl
Partial migrant. Vagrant
British Isles, C. and N.
Europe

190 Eagle Owl
Resident. Has bred
Belgium. Vagrant
Denmark, Britain

191 Snowy Owl
Partial migrant. Range
variable. Irregular Scotland
(has bred). Vagrant s. to
France, Yugoslavia

192 Hawk Owl
Partial migrant. Almost
annual Poland. Vagrant s.
to Britain, Yugoslavia

193 Pygmy Owl
Mainly resident. Vagrant Denmark, Holland, Belgium

194 Little Owl
Resident. Vagrant Ireland, Sweden

195 Tawny Owl
Resident

196 Ural Owl
Mainly resident. Vagrant s. to Italy

197 Long-eared Owl
Partial migrant. Farther north in lemming years. Annual Iceland, Faeroes

198 Short-eared Owl
Partial migrant. Has bred Ireland, Italy, Bulgaria

199 Tengmalm's Owl
Partial resident. Has bred Denmark, Belgium. Vagrant Britain, SW Europe

200 Nightjar
Summer visitor. Vagrant Iceland

201 Swift
Summer visitor. Vagrant Iceland

202 Pallid Swift
Summer visitor. Vagrant Britain, C. Europe

203 Alpine Swift
Summer visitor. Vagrant British Isles, C. and N. Europe

204 Kingfisher
Partial migrant. Vagrant Norway

205 Bee-eater
Summer visitor. Has occasionally bred Britain and many countries n. to Sweden. Vagrant Ireland, Finland

206 Roller
Summer visitor. Vagrant n. to British Isles, Iceland, Finland

207 Hoopoe
Mainly summer visitor. Has bred Britain, N. Europe. Annual Ireland, vagrant Iceland

208 Wryneck
Mainly summer visitor. May be extinct England, almost established Scotland. Vagrant Iceland, Ireland

209 Grey-headed Woodpecker
Resident. Vagrant Lapland, Denmark

210 Green Woodpecker
Resident. Vagrant Ireland

211 Black Woodpecker
Mainly resident. Vagrant Denmark

212 Great Spotted Woodpecker
Mainly resident. Vagrant Ireland, Iceland

213 Syrian Woodpecker
Mainly resident

214 Middle Spotted Woodpecker
Mainly resident. Has bred Holland. Vagrant Portugal, Latvia

215 White-backed Woodpecker
Resident

216 Lesser Spotted Woodpecker
Resident

217 Three-toed Woodpecker
Resident

218 Calandra Lark
Mainly resident. Vagrant Britain, C. and N. Europe

219 Short-toed Lark
Summer visitor. Vagrant British Isles, Iceland, C. and N. Europe

220 Crested Lark
Mainly resident. Vagrant England, Finland

221 Woodlark
Partial migrant. Vagrant Ireland (has bred), Scotland

222 Skylark
Partial migrant. Vagrant Iceland; occasionally breeds Faeroes

223 Shore Lark
Mainly migrant. Has bred Scotland. Vagrant many parts of Europe

224 Sand Martin
Summer visitor. Vagrant Faeroes

225 Crag Martin
Partial migrant. May
winter Yugoslavia

226 Swallow
Summer visitor. Has bred
Iceland, Faeroes

**227 Red-rumped
Swallow**
Summer visitor. Vagrant
British Isles, C., E. and N.
Europe

228 House Martin
Summer visitor. Vagrant
Iceland

229 Tawny Pipit
Summer visitor. Has bred
Switzerland. Annual
England, vagrant n. to
Iceland, N. Europe

230 Tree Pipit
Summer visitor. Annual
Ireland, vagrant Iceland

231 Meadow Pipit
Partial migrant

232 Red-throated Pipit
Summer visitor. Passage
Europe w. to Italy.
Vagrant W. Europe
including British Isles

233 Rock Pipit
Partial migrant. Vagrant
Iceland

234 Yellow Wagtail
Summer visitor. Has bred
Ireland. Vagrant Iceland

235 Grey Wagtail
Partial migrant. Vagrant
Iceland, Finland

236 Pied Wagtail
Partial migrant

237 Waxwing
Partial migrant. Extends
most winters beyond limit
shown. Vagrant Iceland,
Ireland, Spain

238 Dipper
Mainly resident

239 Wren
Partial migrant

240 Dunnock
Partial migrant. Vagrant
Iceland

241 Alpine Accentor
Partial migrant. Spreads to
lower levels in winter.
Vagrant n. to Britain, N.
Europe

242 Rufous Bush Robin
Summer visitor. Irregular
S. France, vagrant Italy, E.
and C. Europe, British
Isles

243 Robin
Partial migrant. Annual
Iceland

244 Thrush Nightingale
Summer visitor. Vagrant
w. to Britain, Switzerland,
Italy

245 Nightingale
Summer visitor. Vagrant
Scotland, Ireland, N.
Europe

246 Bluethroat
Summer visitor. Sporadic
breeder Switzerland. Rare
passage Britain (has bred
Scotland); vagrant Ireland,
Iceland

247 Black Redstart
Partial migrant. Has bred
Scotland, Norway. Vagrant
Iceland

248 Redstart
Summer visitor. Vagrant
Iceland

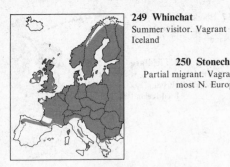

249 Whinchat
Summer visitor. Vagrant
Iceland

250 Stonechat
Partial migrant. Vagrant
most N. Europe

251 Wheatear
Summer visitor

**252 Black-eared
Wheatear**
Summer visitor. Vagrant
British Isles, C. and N.
Europe

253 Black Wheatear
Resident. Vagrant Britain,
C. and SE Europe

254 Rock Thrush
Summer visitor. Vagrant
Britain, N. Europe

255 Blue Rock Thrush
Mainly resident. Vagrant
C. and N. Europe

256 Ring Ouzel
Partial migrant. Has bred
Denmark, Faeroes.
Vagrant Iceland

257 Blackbird
Partial migrant. Has bred
Iceland

258 Fieldfare
Partial migrant. Breeds
irregularly Britain, has
bred Iceland

259 Song Thrush
Partial migrant. Vagrant
Iceland

260 Redwing
Mainly migrant. Has bred
SE England, France,
Czechoslovakia

261 Mistle Thrush
Partial migrant. Vagrant
Iceland

262 Cetti's Warbler
Mainly resident. Has bred
Germany. Vagrant C. and
N. Europe

263 Fan-tailed Warbler
Mainly resident, vulnerable
to hard winters. Vagrant
Britain, Ireland

**264 Grasshopper
Warbler**
Summer visitor. Vagrant
Iceland

265 River Warbler
Summer visitor. Has bred Finland. Annual Sweden. Vagrant Britain

266 Savi's Warbler
Summer visitor. Vagrant Scotland, Ireland, N. Europe

267 Moustached Warbler
Partial resident. Vagrant Britain (has bred), C. Europe

268 Aquatic Warbler
Summer visitor. Has bred w. to France; passage w. to Iberia. Annual Britain; vagrant N. Europe

269 Sedge Warbler
Summer visitor. Vagrant Iceland

270 Marsh Warbler
Summer visitor. Has bred Spain, Norway. Vagrant Scotland, Faeroes

271 Reed Warbler
Summer visitor. Has bred Scotland, Ireland. Vagrant Iceland

272 Great Reed Warbler
Summer visitor. Annual Britain. Vagrant Ireland, Norway

273 Olivaceous Warbler
Summer visitor. Vagrant
British Isles, C. Europe

274 Olive-tree Warbler.
Summer visitor. Vagrant
Italy, Romania

275 Icterine Warbler
Summer visitor. Annual
Britain, Ireland. Vagrant
Faeroes

276 Melodious Warbler
Summer visitor. Annual
Britain, Ireland. Vagrant
C. and N. Europe

277 Dartford Warbler
Mainly resident. Vagrant
Ireland, C. and E. Europe

278 Spectacled Warbler
Mainly summer visitor.
Resident Malta. Vagrant
Britain

279 Subalpine Warbler
Summer visitor. Vagrant
British Isles, C., N. and E.
Europe

280 Sardinian Warbler
Mainly resident. Vagrant
Britain, C., N. and E.
Europe

281 Orphean Warbler
Summer visitor. Vagrant
Britain, C. Europe

282 Barred Warbler
Summer visitor. Rare
passage E. Britain; vagrant
Ireland, Iceland

283 Lesser Whitethroat
Summer visitor. Vagrant
Ireland, Iceland, Spain

284 Whitethroat
Summer visitor. Vagrant
Iceland

285 Garden Warbler
Summer visitor. Vagrant
Iceland

286 Blackcap
Partial migrant. Passage
Faeroes, Iceland

287 Greenish Warbler
Summer visitor. Migrates
east. Has bred Sweden.
Vagrant British Isles, C.
Europe

288 Arctic Warbler
Summer visitor. Migrates
east. Vagrant British Isles,
C. and S. Europe

289 Bonelli's Warbler
Summer visitor. Vagrant British Isles, N. Europe

290 Wood Warbler
Summer visitor. Irregular breeder Ireland. Vagrant Iceland

291 Chiffchaff
Partial migrant. On passage drifts to Iceland

292 Willow Warbler
Summer visitor. On passage drifts to Iceland

293 Goldcrest
Partial migrant. Often Faeroes; vagrant Iceland

294 Firecrest
Partial migrant. May be annual Ireland; vagrant N. Europe

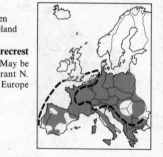

295 Spotted Flycatcher
Summer visitor. Vagrant Iceland

296 Red-breasted Flycatcher
Summer visitor. Rare passage Britain, France, Italy; vagrant w. to Spain, Ireland, Iceland

297 Collared Flycatcher
Summer visitor. Irregular breeder Greece. Vagrant N. and W. Europe including Britain

298 Pied Flycatcher
Summer visitor. Passage Ireland. Vagrant Iceland

299 Bearded Tit
Wanders in winter. Vagrant Scotland, Ireland, N. Europe

300 Long-tailed Tit
Partial migrant

301 Marsh Tit
Mainly resident

302 Sombre Tit
Resident. Vagrant Italy

303 Willow Tit
Mainly resident

304 Siberian Tit
Mainly resident. Vagrant Estonia

305 Crested Tit
Mainly resident

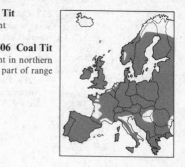

306 Coal Tit
Partial migrant in northern
part of range

307 Blue Tit
Partial migrant in northern
part of range

308 Great Tit
Partial migrant in northern
part of range. Vagrant
Iceland

309 Nuthatch
Resident. Has bred
Finland

310 Rock Nuthatch
Resident

311 Wallcreeper
Partial migrant. Vagrant
Britain, N. Germany,
Malta

312 Treecreeper
Mainly resident

313 Short-toed Treecreeper
Mainly resident. Vagrant England

314 Penduline Tit
Has bred Switzerland, Holland. Wanders in winter, has reached Britain, Finland

315 Golden Oriole
Summer visitor. Has bred Scotland, Norway. Vagrant Ireland, Iceland

316 Red-backed Shrike
Summer visitor. Breeds irregularly Scotland. Vagrant Ireland, Iceland

317 Lesser Grey Shrike
Summer visitor. Vagrant north to British Isles, N. Europe

318 Great Grey Shrike
Partial migrant. Vagrant Ireland, Faeroes

319 Woodchat Shrike
Summer visitor. Vagrant British Isles, N. Europe

320 Jay
Partial migrant in northern part of range

321 Siberian Jay
Mainly resident. Vagrant
C. Europe

322 Magpie
Resident

323 Nutcracker
Mainly resident. Siberian
race occasionally invades
Europe w. to Britain,
Iberia. Irregularly breeds
Denmark

324 Alpine Chough
Resident. Recorded S.
Spain. Vagrant
Czechoslovakia

325 Chough
Resident

326 Jackdaw
Partial migrant. Vagrant
Iceland

327 Rook
Partial migrant. Vagrant
Iceland

328 Carrion Crow
Mainly resident. Vagrant
N. Europe, Poland

329 Hooded Crow
Partial migrant. Vagrant
Iceland, SW Europe

330 Raven
Mainly resident

331 Starling
Partial migrant

332 House Sparrow
Mainly resident. Has bred
Iceland. Line surrounds
range of Italian Sparrow

333 Spanish Sparrow
Mainly resident. Vagrant
Britain, S. France

334 Tree Sparrow
Partial migrant. Has bred
Faeroes; vagrant Iceland

335 Rock Sparrow
Resident. Vagrant Britain,
C. Europe

336 Snowfinch
Resident, rarely to lower
levels in winter. Vagrant C.
Europe, Balearics

337 Chaffinch
Partial migrant. Annual Iceland

338 Brambling
Migrant. Has bred Scotland, more often Holland, Denmark. Annual Iceland

339 Serin
Partial migrant. Has bred England. Vagrant Ireland, Finland

340 Citril Finch
Mainly resident, spreading in winter. Has bred Balearics. Vagrant Britain, C. Europe

341 Greenfinch
Partial migrant. Vagrant Iceland

342 Goldfinch
Partial migrant

343 Siskin
Partial migrant. Has bred Greece. Vagrant Iceland

344 Linnet
Partial migrant. Vagrant Faeroes

345 Twite
Partial migrant. Vagrant S. Europe

346 Redpoll
Partial migrant

347 Arctic Redpoll
Mainly migrant. Vagrant Britain, C. and E. Europe

348 Crossbill
Crossbill part res. (not Scottish Highlands). After irreg. irruptions breeds more widely, incl. Ireland. Vagr. Iceland. **Scottish Crossbill** res., Scottish Highlands

349 Scarlet Rosefinch
Summer visitor. Has bred Britain, NW Europe. Vagrant Iceland, S. Europe

350 Pine Grosbeak
Partial migrant. Vagrant S. and W. Europe including Britain

351 Bullfinch
Mainly resident. Vagrant Iceland

352 Hawfinch
Partial migrant. Balearics in winter. Has bred Norway, Finland. Vagrant Ireland, Faeroes

353 Lapland Bunting
Migrant. Has bred Scotland. Annual passage Ireland. Vagrant Iceland and south to Italy

354 Snow Bunting
Partial migrant. Vagrant most S. European countries

355 Yellowhammer
Partial migrant. Vagrant Iceland, Sicily

356 Cirl Bunting
Mainly resident. Vagrant Ireland, C. Europe

357 Rock Bunting
Mainly resident. Range slightly extended in winter. Vagrant Britain

358 Ortolan Bunting
Summer visitor. Thin passage E. Britain. Vagrant Ireland, Iceland

359 Rustic Bunting
Summer visitor. Vagrant Britain, C. and S. Europe

360 Reed Bunting
Partial migrant. Vagrant Iceland